دَلَآئِلُ الخَيرَاتِ

وَشَوَارِقُ ٱلأَنوَارِ فِي ذِكْرِ الصَّلوَاةِ عَلَى ٱلنَّبِيِّ ٱلمُختَارِ

لِسَيِّدِي أَبِي عَبْدِ اللهِ مُحَمَّدِ بنِ عَبْدِ الرَّحْمَنِ

ابنِ أَبِي بَكْرٍ بنْ سُلَيمَانُ الجَزُولِّي ثُمَّ السِّمْلالِي

ٱلمُتَوَفِّي سَنَةِ ٨٦٩ هـ

Dalā'ilu 'l-Khayrāt

wa Shawāriqu 'l-Anwār fī Dhikri 'ṣ-Ṣalāti ʿalā 'n-Nabīyyi 'l-Mukhtār

The Waymarks to Allāh's Favors and the Advent of Lights Through the Recitation of Prayers Upon the Chosen Prophet

By Our Master Abī ʿAbdillāh Muḥammad bin ʿAbdi 'r-Raḥmān bin Abī Bakrin bin Sulaymān al-Jazūlī as-Simlālī
Who passed to the Divine Mercy in the Year 869 H.

Institute for Spiritual and Cultural Advancement

ISBN: 978-1-930409-96-5

Published and Distributed by:
Institute for Spiritual and Cultural Advancement
17195 Silver Parkway, #201
Fenton, MI 48430 USA
Tel: (888) 278-6624
Fax:(810) 815-0518
Web: http://www.naqshbandi.org

This book is available at International Shopping Network: isn1.net

بسم الله الرحمن الرحيم

إنْ أَنْتَ لازَمتَ الصَّلاةَ عَلَى النَّبي

صَلَّى عَليهِ اللهُ فِي الآيَــاتِ

وَجَعلتَهَا وِرداً عَليـكَ مُؤكَّـدًا

لاحَتْ عَليكَ دَلآئِلُ الخَيرَاتِ

In anta lāzamta aṣ-ṣalāta ʿalā ʾn-Nabī
ṣallā ʿalayhi ʾLlāhu fī ʾl-āyāti
wa jaʿltahā wirdan ʿalayka muʾakkadan
lāḥat ʿalayka Dalāʾilu ʾl-Khayrāt

If you become consistent in praying
upon the Prophet
upon whom Allāh sends His blessings
in the verses of Quran
and if you make praying upon him
your firm daily practice
The Signs of Allāh's Favors
will become evident on you

Contents

Foreword

Bismillāhi 'r-Raḥmāni 'r-Raḥīm wa ṣalla 'Llāhu 'alā Sayyīdinā Muḥammadin wa 'alā ālihi wa ṣaḥbihi wa sallam.

Dear lovers of our Beloved Prophet ﷺ, Sayyīdinā Muḥammad, I am honored and full of joy to be able to preface this great book written purely for the love of the Prophet ﷺ.

Dalā'ilu 'l-Khayrāt has been read for a half a thousand years by Muslims around the world. This is the book of Imām Muḥammad bin Sulayman al-Jazūlī that was read by emperors, kings, caliphs, common people and almost every person that declares *lā ilāha ill 'Llāh muḥammadun Rasūlullāh* for hundreds of years.

The reading of this book as described by Imām Jazūlī, and written in his book will be rewarded tremendously, on the number of the atoms in every crystal, on the number of the drops of rain in every cloud, as the number of waves on every ocean, sea and lake, on the number of the leaves on every tree, on the number of years, months, days, minutes, seconds and moments of every existing thing, on the number of creations which exist. Allāh will reward the reciter of these praises endlessly without stopping until Judgment Day.

> *Prophet Muhammad ﷺ is the source of the light of creation.*
>
> *Prophet Muhammad ﷺ is the light of human beings.*
>
> *Prophet Muhammad ﷺ is the beacon for every seeker,*
>
> *Prophet Muhammad ﷺ is the oasis in every desert,*

Prophet Muhammad ﷺ is the wave in every ocean,

Prophet Muhammad ﷺ is the source of every river,

Prophet Muhammad ﷺ is the heavenly dew on every leaf.

Prophet Muhammad ﷺ is the life in every drop of blood in living creatures,

Prophet Muhammad ﷺ is the motion within every atom.

Prophet Muhammad ﷺ is the source behind stars, constellations and galaxies.

Prophet Muhammad ﷺ is the stars and suns and moons in every sky.

The universes swim in Prophet Muhammad's ﷺ orbit.

Prophet Muhammad ﷺ is known in our traditions and beliefs as the Light from Allah's Light.

Prophet Muhammad ﷺ is our light;

Prophet Muhammad ﷺ is our heart;

Prophet Muhammad ﷺ is our life.

Through our beloved Prophet ﷺ we were guided to know of Allāh, Almighty, the angels, the prophets and messengers, the heavenly books of revelation and the next life. By means of prayers on him, we are saved from disasters, protected from afflictions, relieved of burdens and distress, our loans are paid off, our illnesses are cured, our sadness changed to joy, our anger turned to sweetness, our fields are watered by pouring rain, our livestock are saved, our provisions are increased, our lives are extended, our hearts are comforted and our afterlife is secured.

I recommend everyone to read this book as a cultural practice and as a form of absolutely sincere worship, and for the seekers of this way, as part of their daily spiritual discipline. I am very happy to see this treasured book translated by the Institute for Spiritual and Cultural Advancement which is main headquarters for the Naqshbandi Way in America, as is the new center just established by my son-in-law, Shaykh Hisham Kabbani in the UK known as Centre for Spirituality and Cultural Advancement, in Feltham, and the Center for Spirituality and Cultural Advancement, set up in Melbourne, Australia, as well as a center in Argentina and a center in Chile which they are establishing now, and there are so many hundreds of other centers for spiritual gatherings around the world in which people gather for prayers, recite the Khatm Khawajāgān, recite Mawlid and spend time in worship.

Mawlana Shaykh Muḥammad Nazim al-Haqqani
Lefke, Cyprus
12 Rabīʿa 'l-Awwal 1432, 15 February 2011

Preface

Bismillāhi 'r-Raḥmāni 'r-Raḥīm wa ṣalla 'Llāhu ʿalā Sayyīdinā Muḥammadin wa ʿalā ālihi wa ṣaḥbihi wa sallam.

Alḥamdulillāh, with the support of Mawlana Shaykh Nazim al-Haqqani's prayers we would like to announce to the completion of this book which took three years to put together and prepare. We thank all those who participated in the editing, translating and printing of this book, on behalf of their families and parents, and we have listed the contributors at the back of the book.

This book is of tremendous value for it contains the immense secret of reciting excessive praise of the Prophet ﷺ and invoking blessings and peace on him. For that reason, it is truly the most beloved, renowned and oft-recited book of praise of the Prophet ﷺ throughout the Muslim world, and a sign of its immeasurable beauty, fine prose, immense blessing and perfect suitability for every time and situation.

Imām Jazūlī put this book of invoking blessings on the Prophet ﷺ together after going on a journey where he found himself in great need of water for making ablution. He came upon a well but could not reach its water, as there was no bucket and rope and became very worried. A young girl saw him in this difficulty and came to his aid. She spat into the well and suddenly the water rose to the top of by itself. Amazed at this miracle, Imām Jazūlī asked her, "And how is that possible?" She replied "I was able to do this due to my reciting excessive blessings upon

Prophet Muḥammad ﷺ."[1]

After seeing this *karāmah,* which was due to the girl's excessive praising of the Prophet ﷺ, Imām Jazūlī was inspired to write *Dalā'ilu 'l-Khayrāt.* In it, he compiled litanies invoking peace and blessings upon the Prophet, gathered from many sources from the Sunnah and from inspiration to his heart. It is by far the most popular and universally acclaimed collection of prayers upon the Prophet ﷺ, used throughout the Muslim world and recited individually and in groups, in homes and in mosques, silently and aloud.

His book served as a basis for *al-Ḥizb al-āʿẓam* (The Supreme Daily Recital), composed by Mulla ʿAlī al-Qārī. Included in the *Dalā'ilu 'l-Khayrāt* were many *aḥādīth* describing the value and benefits of reciting praises on the Prophet ﷺ. Despite many of the *aḥādīth* he related being weak or unverified he asked the Prophet ﷺ directly in his spiritual presence, saying, "*Yā Rasūlullāh*! Is that hadith correct?" and getting confirmation the hadith was correct.

Shaykh Muḥammad Hisham Kabbani
Fenton, Michigan
12th Rabīʿa 'l-Awwal 1432, 15 February 2011

---

[1] This story is related in *Dalā'ilu 'l-Khayrāt* (The Waymarks of Benefits), Imām Jazūlī, with Introduction by Shaykh Nuh Ha Mim Keller, Aal al-Bayt Institute, Amman, 2005.

Introduction

Bismillāhi 'r-Raḥmāni 'r-Raḥīm wa ṣalla 'Llāhu ʿalā Sayyīdinā Muḥammadin wa ʿalā ālihi wa ṣaḥbihi wa sallam.

For everyone there is a star. When the Seal of Prophet's star appeared, those who saw it were affected so strongly. His star just appeared through the heavenly sky. It is famous news from scholars of Sīrat an-Nabī, the holy biography of Rasūlullāh ﷺ.

All prophets have stars and it is well-known news from the life of the Seal of Prophets ﷺ, when he was born and giving honor for whole existence, that night a Jewish man was running through the streets of Madinatu 'l-Munawwarah, shouting, "O, Āḥmad's star just appeared!!" That was because he was expected, because his name was written through the New Testament. When Jesus Christ spoke, he said, "O People! My Lord is sending me to you to be *mubashshir* (messenger of glad tidings), giving you happy news that he is going to be the Last Holy One through this life and his name is going to be Āḥmad." That Jewish man was well aware of that; therefore, he was saying, "Āḥmad's star has just appeared!" and he was running about (to announce it).

The biggest grant for whole Mankind living on this planet is the understanding that Prophet ﷺ is the representative for the Lord of Heavens.

O People! Try to understand something about that one that had been blessed by his Creator from the beginning of Creation and when Creation began, no one knows. It is *azalīyyun*, no beginning and *abadīyyun*, no ending also.

That night is the holiest night through the year because he who was born this night is the holiest of creation. Therefore, the Lord was saying, "I created everything for your honor O my beloved one." Therefore, we must be happy! I am asking for the Lord of Heavens to make one wave of illumination to reach our hearts and to shake our hearts, to move them. That one wave should be enough to become like those who are drunk in the ecstasy of that taste. Try to reach an understanding of Sayyīdinā Muḥammad's greatness. As much as you are understanding, your level is going to be raised higher and higher. And however high a level you reach, yet it remains impossible to reach *Ḥaqīqatu 'l-Muḥammadīyyah,* the Muḥammadan Reality. We may only approach the circles of lights and illumination around his holy existence; and you can never reach *al-Ḥaqīqatu'l-Muḥammadīyyah,* "Grant him, O our Lord, more honor and nobility, joy and light."

If you are speaking from now up to the end of this world about the honor of Allāh's most honored one, no one can bring a limit to his honor! If Allāh ﷻ is honoring someone, no one can know the beginning of that honoring, and they can certainly never knows its end.

The secret of the reality of the phrase *Lā ilāha illā Hū,* there is no God except He, was dressing Sayyīdinā Muḥammad ﷺ taking him from Nāsūt (the human realm) and dressing him from Lāhūt (the Divine Realm). The night of his coming into this creation is such a great night, it is impossible for anyone to understand what takes place in the Divine Presence on this night. The entire heavens were decorated with such lights that night, that no one can imagine. That night, such greatness adorned the heavens and the angels, that to imagine it is beyond our grasp.

May Allāh give us a good understanding, for the honor of His most honored one Sayyīdinā Muḥammad ﷺ. The Lord of Heavens never gives from Himself to any of His servants directly. Rather that grant is first given to the Seal of Prophets ﷺ and from him, *'alā qadar marātibihim,* according to their (others) stations and positions and levels, it is coming to them. And it is not the same for everyone.

The Seal of Prophets ﷺ, is the most beloved, the most honored, the most glorified of all Creation. If he were not in existence, nothing else would be in existence! Therefore, the Lord of Heavens was saying, "O My most blessed one and beloved one; the most glorified one in existence! For your honor alone I created everything." And no one knows when that dialogue happened between Allāh Almighty and His most beloved one, Sayyīdinā Muḥammad ﷺ.

The Seal of Prophets ﷺ is taking his knowledge and understanding from Allāh Almighty, and Allāh Almighty is always giving him more and higher understandings that no one else is ever reaching. Even the other four of the great prophets, Sayyīdinā Ibrāhīm ﷺ, Sayyīdinā Mūsā ﷺ, Sayyīdinā 'Īsā ﷺ, Sayyīdinā Nūḥ ﷺ, cannot understand at the level and understanding of the Seal of Prophets ﷺ.

The station of Ḥabībullāh, Allāh's Beloved's level of understanding is always higher. Therefore no one can try to reach to his knowledge if he is not giving an understanding to you. Millions of books have been written through the centuries by *'ulamā* taking knowledge from those endless Knowledge Oceans of the Prophet ﷺ and his knowledge is from the Holy Qur'an. The knowledge of the Holy Qur'an belongs to the Lord of Heavens and it is only a very small drop besides Divine Knowledge. If instead 114 surahs, if was going to be 200, this earth could not carry it. Further even the entire existence could not carry it! Therefore, the Prophet ﷺ, the most beloved one, whose heart was most full among all Creation, was keeping it. He was giving, endlessly giving. Whole libraries of books you can write from him and it will never finish; that is a well which will never dry up, for Sayyīdinā Muḥammad ﷺ is Allāh Almighty's most precious, most beloved servant, who is His true deputy, and whose reality is to be Allāh Almighty's representative through the entire Creation.

Ya Muhammad canım arzular seni,
bütün hayatınızı o en sevgili en, anlı olana verin.
Rabbinin ilahi huzurunda, ereflene verin.
Yaa Muhammad canım arzular seni.
Dost Muhammad canım pek sever seni.

O Muhammad, my soul desires you,
give all of your life to this One Who is the glorious.
In the presence of your Lord, give it with honor.
O Muhammad, my soul loves you.
O Friend Muhammad, my soul desires you so much!

Mawlana Shaykh Muḥammad Nazim al-Haqqani
Lefke, Cyprus
12 Rabīʿa 'l-Awwal 1431, 24 February 2010

Dalā'ilu 'l-Khayrāt

Publisher's Notes

This book is specifically designed for readers relatively familiar with Islamic and Sufi terms. Qur'ānic quotes are centered, highlighted in bold and italics and footnoted, citing chapter name, number and verse.

Universally Recognized Symbols

Muslims around the world typically offer praise upon speaking, hearing, or reading the name "*Allāh*" and any of the Islamic names of God. Muslims also offer salutation and/or invoke blessing upon speaking, hearing or reading the names of Prophet Muḥammad, other prophets, his family, his companions, and saints. We have applied the following international standards, using Arabic calligraphy and lettering:

ﷺ *ṣall-Allāhu ʿalayhi wa sallam* (God's blessings and greetings of peace be upon him) following the names of the Prophet ﷺ.

عليه السلام *ʿalayhi 's-salām* (peace be upon him) following the names of other prophets, angels, and Khiḍr.

عليها السلام *ʿalayhā 's-salām* (peace be upon her) following the name of Mary, Mother of Jesus.

رضي الله عنها/رضي الله عنه *raḍīy-Allāhu ʿanhu/ʿanhā* (may God be pleased with him/her) following the name of a male or female companion of the Prophet ﷺ.

ق *qaddas-Allāhu sirrah* (may God exalt his secret) following the name of a saint.

Transliteration

Transliteration is provided to facilitate correct pronunciation and is based on the following system:

Symbol	Trans-literation	Symbol	Trans-literation	Vowels: Long	
ء	ʼ	ط	ṭ	آى	ā
ب	b	ظ	ẓ	و	ū
ت	t	ع	ʻ	ي	ī
ث	th	غ	gh	Short	
ج	j	ف	f	◌َ	a
ح	ḥ	ق	q	◌ُ	u
خ	kh	ك	k	◌ِ	i
د	d	ل	l		
ذ	dh	م	m		
ر	r	ن	n		
ز	z	ه	h		
س	s	و	w		
ش	sh	ي	y		
ص	ṣ	ة	ah; at		
ض	ḍ	ال	al-/'l-		

مُقَدِّمَة دَلَآئِلِ الخَيْرَاتِ

Muqaddimat Dalā'ilu 'l-Khayrāt

Introduction to the Waymarks to Allāh's Favors

بِسْمِ اللهِ الرَّحمَنِ الرَّحِيمِ وَ صَلَّى اللهُ عَلَى سَيِّدِنَا مُحَمَّدٍ وَعَلَى آلِهِ وَ صَحْبِهِ وَ سَلَّمَ

قَالَ الشَّيخُ الإِمَامِ الوَلِيُّ ٱلكَبيرُ القُطبُ ٱلشَّهيرُ سُلْطَانُ المُقَرَّبينَ وَقُطبُ دَائِرَةِ ٱلْمُحَقِّقِينَ

Bismillāhi 'r-Raḥmāni 'r-Raḥīm wa ṣalla 'Llāhu ʿalā Sayyīdinā Muḥammadin wa ʿalā ālihi wa ṣaḥbihi wa sallam.

Qāl ash-shaykh al-īmāmu 'l-walīyyu 'l-kabīru 'l-quṭbu 'sh-shahīru sulṭānu 'l-muqarrabīna wa quṭbu dā'irati 'l-muḥaqqiqīna,

In the Name of Allāh, The Compassionate, The Most Merciful and Allāh's prayers upon our master Muḥammad and upon his family and companions,

My master the Shaykh, the Imām, the great saint, the famous pole, the Sultan of those near to the Divine Presence, the Pole of the Circle of Those Who Ascertained the Truth, ➢

وَسَيِّدُ العَارِفِينَ، صَاحِبُ الكَرَامَاتِ الظَّاهِرَةِ، وَالْأَسرَارِ البَاهِرَةِ، سَيِّدِي أَبُو عَبدِالله بْنُ سُلَيْمَانَ الجَزُولِيُّ رَضِيَ اللهُ عَنْهُ:

wa sayyidu 'l-'ārifīna, ṣāḥibu 'l-karāmāṭi 'ẓ-ẓāhirati wa 'l-asrāri 'l-bāhirati, sayyīdī Abū 'Abdillāh ibnu Sulaymāna 'l-Jazūlīyyu raḍīy-Allāḥu 'anhu:

and the master of the knowers, the owner of great miracles and astonishing secrets, Abū 'Abd Allāh ibnu Sulaymān 'l-Jazūlī may Allāh be pleased with him, said: ➢

الحَمدُ لله الَّذِي هَدَانَا لِلإِسْلامِ وَالإِيمَانِ، والصَّلَاةُ وَالسَّلَامُ عَلَى سَيِّدِنَا مُحَمَّدٍ الَّذِي اسْتَنْقَذَنَا بِهِ مِنْ عِبَادَةِ الْأَوثَانِ وَالْأَصنامِ، وَعَلَى آلِهِ وَأَصْحَابِهِ النُّجَبَاءِ البَرَرَةِ الكِرَامِ وَبَعدُ هَذَا، فَالغَرَضُ فِي هَذَا الكِتَابِ ذِكرُ الصَّلَاةِ عَلَى النَّبِيِّ ﷺ وَفَضَائِلِهَا

Alḥamdulillāhi 'Lladhī hadānā li 'l-Islāmi wa 'l-īmāni, wa 'ṣ-ṣalātu wa 's-salāmu 'alā sayyīdinā Muḥammadini 'Lladhī 'stanqadhanā bihi min 'ibādi 'l-awthāni wa 'l-aṣnāmi, wa 'alā ālihi wa aṣḥābihi 'n-nujabā'i 'l-bararati 'l-kirāmi wa ba'ḍu hadhā, fa 'l-gharaḍu fī hadhā 'l-kitābi dhikru 'ṣ-ṣalāti 'alā 'n-nabī ﷺ wa faḍā'ilihā

Praise be to Allāh who guided us to Islam and to faith, and blessings and peace upon our master Muḥammad—by whose means Allāh saved us from worshipping graven images and idols—and upon his pure, virtuous and honored companions. The purpose of this book is to recall the different manners of invoking blessings on Prophet Muḥammad ﷺ, and a recollection of the benefits of such prayers. ➢

نَذكُرُهَا مَحذُوفَةَ الْأَسَانِيدِ لِيَسْهُلَ حِفظُهَا عَلَى القَارِئِ، وَهِيَ مِنْ أَهَمِّ المُهِمَّاتِ لِمَنْ يُرِيدُ القُرْبَ مِنْ رَبِّ الْأَرْبَابِ،

nadhkuruhā maḥdhūfata 'l-asānīd li-yas-hula ḥifẓuhā ʿalā 'l-qārī, wa ḥīya min ahammi 'l-muhimmāti liman yurīdu 'l-qurba min rabbi 'l-arbāb.

I did so without mentioning the chains of narrators, in order to make their memorization easy for the reader. Reciting these prayers is one of the most important duties for those seeking nearness to the Lord of Lords. ➢

وَسَمَّيتُهُ بِكِتَابِ **دَلَائِلِ الخَيرَاتِ وَشَوَارِقِ الْأَنوَارِ فِي ذِكْرِ الصَّلاةِ عَلَى النَّبِيِّ المُختَارِ** ابْتِغَاءً لِمَرضَاةِ اللهِ تَعَالَى وَمَحَبَّةً فِي رَسُولِهِ الْكَرِيمِ سَيِّدِنَا مُحَمَّدٍ ﷺ ، وَاللهُ المَسؤولُ أَنْ يَجعَلَنَا لِسُنَّتِهِ مِنَ التَّابِعِينَ، وَلِذَاتِهِ الكَامِلَةِ مِنَ المُحِبِّينَ،

Wa sammaytuhu bi-kitābi ***Dalā'ili 'l-Khayrāti wa shawāriqi 'l-anwār fī dhikri 'ṣ-ṣalāti ʿalā 'n-nabīyyi 'l-mukhtāri*** *'btighā'in li-marḍātillāhi taʿalā wa maḥabbatan fī rasūlihi 'l-karīmi sayyīdinā Muḥammadin ﷺ, w 'Allāḥu 'l-mas'ūlu an yajʿalnā li-sunnatihi min at-tābiʿīna wa li-dhātihi 'l-kāmilati mina 'l-muḥibbīna*

I named this volume *"The Waymarks to Allāh's Favors, and the Advent of Lights through the Recitation of Prayers upon the Chosen Prophet"* seeking through it Allāh's pleasure, and the love of his honored Prophet our master Muḥammad ﷺ. And it is in Allāh's Hands, to make us to follow his Way (*sunnah*), and to love His perfect person. ➢

فَإِنَّهُ عَلَى ذَلِكَ قَدِيرٌ لَا إِلَهَ غَيْرُهُ وَلاَ خَيْرَ إِلَّا خَيْرُهُ وَهُوَ نِعْمَ المَولَى وَنِعْمَ ٱلنَّصِيرُ ولا حَولَ وَلا قُوَّةَ إِلا بِاللهِ العَلِيِّ العَظِيمِ ❁

fa-innahu ʿalā dhalika qadīrun lā ilāha ghayruhu wa lā khayra illā khayruhu wa huwa niʿama 'l-mawlā wa niʿama 'n-naṣīru wa lā ḥawla wa lā quwwata illā bi'Llāhi 'l-ʿAlīyyi 'l-ʿAẓīm. •

He is able to do that, no God is there but He, and there are no goodnesses except His. He is The Best of Guardians and The Best of Supporters; and there is no will or power except with Allāh, The Most High, The Most Great. ❁

فَصلٌ في فَضْلِ الصَّلاةِ عَلَى النَّبِيِّ صَلَّى اللهُ عَليهِ وَسَلَّمَ

Faṣlun fī Faḍli 'ṣ-Ṣalāti 'alā 'n-Nabī ﷺ

Regarding the Virtue of Invoking Blessing upon the Prophet ﷺ

قَالَ اللهُ عَزَّ وَجَلَّ إِنَّ اللهَ وَمَلآئِكَتَهُ يُصَلُّونَ عَلَى ٱلنَّبِيِّ يَا أَيُّهَا الَّذِينَ آمَنُوا
صَلُّوا عَلَيهِ وَسَلِّمُوا تَسلِيماً ۞

Qāl Allāhu ﷻ*: "inna 'Llāha wa malā'ikatahu yuṣallūna 'alā 'n-Nabīyy yā ayyuhā 'Lladhīna āmanū ṣallū 'alayhi wa sallimū taslīma"*

Allāh ﷻ, said: *"Allāh and His angels invoke blessings on the Prophet. O you who believe! Invoke blessings on him and salute him with a worthy salutation."* (Quran 33:56)

'Abd al-Majīd ash-Sharnūbi wrote:

> The meaning of invoking blessings (*ṣalli 'alā*) here is "show affection for", and Allāh the Most High shows His affection for His Prophet through His Mercy combined with His Exaltation of the Prophet ﷺ. And the angels show affection by seeking Allāh's forgiveness [for the Nation of the Prophet] and by invoking for them, as do the believers."[2] ➤

[2] 'Abd al-Majīd ash-Sharnūbi al-Azharī's *Commentary on the Dalā'ilu 'l-Khayrāt*.

(١) وَيُرْوَى أَنَّ النَّبِيُّ ﷺ جَاءَ ذَاتَ يَوْمٍ وَالبُشْرَى تُرَى فِي وَجْهِهِ فَقَالَ إِنَّهُ جَاءَنِي جِبْرِيلُ عليه السلام ، فَقَالَ أَمَا تَرْضَىٰ يَا مُحَمَّدُ أَنْ لَا يُصَلِّي عَلَيكَ أَحَدٌ مِنْ أُمَّتِكَ إِلَّا صَلَّيتُ عَلَيهِ عَشْراً وَلا يُسَلِّمَ عَلَيكَ أَحَدٌ مِنْ أُمَّتِكَ إِلَّا سَلَّمتُ عَلَيهِ عَشْراً ❋

(1) Wa yurwā anna 'n-Nabīyyu ﷺ jā'a dhāta yawmin wa 'l-bushrā turā fī wajhihi fa-qāla innahu jā'anī Jibrīla عليه السلام, fa-qāla amā tarḍā yā Muḥammadu an lā yuṣalli ʿalayka aḥadun min ummatika illā ṣallaytu ʿalayhi ʿashran, wa lā yusallima ʿalayka āḥadun min ummatika illā sallamtu ʿalayhi ʿashran •

(1) It is related that the Messenger of Allāh ﷺ came out one day and joy could be seen in his face. He said, "Jibrīl عليه السلام, came to me and said, 'Are you not pleased, O Muḥammad, that none of your community invokes blessings on you but that I bless him ten times, and none of your community prays for peace on you, but that I pray it for him ten times.'"[3] ❋

(٢) وَقَالَ ﷺ إِنَّ أَوْلَى ٱلنَّاسِ بِيْ أَكثَرُهُمْ عَلَيَّ صَلَاةً ❋

(2) Wa qāla ﷺ inna awlā 'n-nāsi bī aktharuhum ʿalayya ṣalātan •

(2) The Prophet ﷺ said, "The people most deserving of me are those who invoke the most blessings on me."[4] ❋

---

[3] Narrated by Ibn Abī Shaybah, Āḥmad, ʿAbd bin Ḥumayd and Tirmidhī with slightly different wording than found in the *Dalā'il*.

[4] Āḥmad, at-Tirmidhī and Ibn Ḥibbān said it had a good chain (*ḥasan*).

(٣) وَقَالَ ﷺ مَنْ صَلَّى عَلَيَّ صَلَّتْ عَلَيهِ المَلَآئِكَةُ مَا دَامَ يُصَلِّيْ عَلَيَّ فَلْيُقَلِّلْ عِنْدَ ذَلِكَ اَوْ لِيُكَثِّرْ ❋

(3) Wa qāla ﷺ, man ṣalla ʿalayyā ṣallat ʿalayhi 'l-malā'ikatu mā dāma yuṣalli ʿalayya, fal-yuqallal ʿinda dhalika aw li-yukaththar •

(3) The Prophet ﷺ said, "If someone invokes blessings on me, the angels bless him as long as he continues to invoke blessings on me, so let him reduce that or increase it."[5] ❋

(٤) وَقَالَ ﷺ بِحَسْبِ ٱلْمَرءِ مِنَ البُخْلِ أَنْ أُذْكَرَ عِنْدَهُ وَلا يُصَلِّي عَلَيَّ ❋

(4) Wa qāla ﷺ bi-ḥasbi 'l-marʿi mina 'l-bukhli an udhkara ʿindahu wa lā yuṣallī ʿalayya.•

(4) The Prophet ﷺ said, "It is sufficient miserliness in a man that when I am mentioned in his presence, he does not invoke blessings on me."[6] ❋

(٥) وَقَالَ ﷺ أَكْثِرُوا الصَّلاَةَ عَلَيَّ يَوْمَ الجُمُعَةِ ❋

(5) Wa qāla ﷺ akthirū 'ṣ-ṣalāta ʿalayya yawma 'l-Jumuʿati •

(5) The Prophet ﷺ said, "Invoke blessings on me a lot every Friday."[7] ❋

---

[5] Imām Āḥmad reported it in his *Musnad.*

[6] reported in *Kanz al-ʿUmmāl.*

[7] Bukhārī. Shāfiʿī's*Musnad* adds, "for surely it is presented to me."

(٦) وَقَالَ ﷺ مَنْ صَلَّى عَلَيَّ مِنْ أُمَّتِي مَرَّةً وَاحِدَةً كُتِبَتْ لَهُ عَشْرُ حَسَنَاتٍ وَمُحِيَتْ عَنْهُ عَشْرُ سَيِّئَاتٍ ❋

(6) Wa qāla ﷺ man ṣalla ʿalayya min ummatī marratan wāḥidatan kutibat lahu ʿashru ḥasanātin wa muḥīyat ʿanhu ʿashru sayyīʿātin •

(6) He ﷺ said, "If anyone of my community invokes one blessing on me, ten good actions are written for him and ten bad actions are erased."[8] ❋

(٧) وَقَالَ ﷺ مَن قَالَ حِينَ يَسمَعُ الْأَذَانَ وَالإِقَامَةَ اللَّهُمَّ رَبَّ هَذِهِ الدَّعْوَةِ النَّافِعَةِ وَالصَّلاةِ القَائِمَةِ آتِ مُحَمَّداً الوَسِيلَةَ وَالفَضِيلَةَ وَابْعَثْهُ مَقَاماً مَحْمُودًا الَّذِي وَعَدْتَهُ حَلَّتْ لَهُ شَفَاعَتِي يَوْمَ الْقِيَامَةِ ❋

(7) Wa qāla ﷺ man qāla ḥīna yasmaʿu 'l-adhāna wa 'l-'iqāmata 'Llāhumma rabba hādhihi 'd-daʿwati 'n-nāfiʿati wa 'ṣ-ṣalāti 'l-qā'imati āti Muḥammadan 'l-wasīlata wa 'l-faḍīlata wa 'bʿath-hu maqāman maḥmūdan alladhī waʿadtahu ḥallat lahu shafāʿatī yawma 'l-qīyāmah •

(7) The Prophet ﷺ said, "My intercession will be available on the Day of Rising to anyone who says, after hearing the *adhān*, 'O Allāh! Lord of this perfect call and established prayer, give Muḥammad *al-wasīlah* (the Station of Intercession) and superiority and raise him up to the Praiseworthy Station which You promised him.'"[9] ❋

---

[8] Reported by an-Nisāʾī.

[9] *Saḥīḥ Bukhārī.*

(٨) وَقَالَ ﷺ مَنْ صَلَّى عَلَيَّ فِي كِتَابٍ لَمْ تَزَلِ الْمَلَآئِكَةُ تُصَلِّي عَلَيهِ مَا دَامَ اِسمِي فِي ذَلِكَ الكِتَابِ ❋

(8) Wa qāla ﷺ man ṣalla ʿalayya fī kitābin lam tazali 'l-malā'ikatu tuṣṣalīya ʿalayhi mā dāma ismī fī dhalika 'l-kitābi •

(8) The Prophet ﷺ said, "If someone blesses me in a book, the angels do not cease to bless him as long as my name is in that book."[10] ❋

(٩) وَقَالَ أَبُو سُلَيْمَانَ الدَّرَانِيُّ مَنْ أَرَادَ أَنْ يَسأَلَ اللهَ حَاجَتَهُ فَلْيُكْثِرْ مِنَ الصَّلَاةِ عَلَى النَّبِيِّ ثُمَّ يَسأَلِ اللهَ حَاجَتَهُ وَلْيَخْتُمْ بِالصَّلَاةِ عَلَى النَّبِيِّ ﷺ، فَإِنَّ اللهَ يَقْبَلُ الصَّلَاتَينِ وَهُوَ أَكرَمُ أَنْ يَدَعَ مَا بَينَهُمَا ❋

(9) Wa qāla Abū Sulaymāna 'd-Dārānīyyu man arāda an yas'ala 'Llāha ḥājatahu fal-yukthir mina 'ṣ-ṣalāti ʿalā 'n-Nabīyyu thumma yas'ali 'Llāha ḥājatahu wa 'l-yakhtum bi 'ṣ-ṣalāti ʿalā 'n-Nabīyyi ﷺ fa-inna 'Llāha yaqbalu 'ṣ-ṣalātayni wa hūwa akramu an yadaʿa mā baynahumā •

(9) Abū Sulaymān ad-Darānī said, "If someone wants to ask Allāh for a need, he should begin with prayers on the Prophet may Allāh bless him and grant him peace, then ask Allāh for his need, and then seal it with prayers on the Prophet, may Allāh bless him and grant him peace. Allāh will accept the two prayers and is too generous to omit what is between the two." ❋

---

[10] Aṭ-Ṭabarānī in his *Awṣaṭ*, Imām al-Qurṭubī in his *tafsīr*, *Jāmiʿ*.

(١٠) وَرُوِيَ عَنْهُ ﷺ أَنَّهُ قَالَ مَنْ صَلَّى عَلَيَّ يَوْمَ الْجُمُعَةِ مِائَةَ مَرَّةٍ غُفِرَتْ لَهُ خَطِيئَتُهُ ثَمَانِينَ سَنَةً ❁

(10) Wa ruwīya ʿanhu ﷺ annahu qāla man ṣalla ʿalayya yawma 'l-Jumʿati mi'ata marratin ghufirat lahu khaṭī'atuhu thamānīna sanah •

(10) It is related that The Prophet ﷺ said, "If someone invokes blessings on me 100 times on Friday, he will be forgiven the mistakes of 80 years."[11] ❁

(١١) وَعَنْ أَبِي هُرَيْرَةَ ﵁ أَنَّ رَسُولَ اللهِ ﷺ قَالَ لِلْمُصَلِّي عَلَيَّ نُورٌ عَلَى الْصِرَاطِ وَمَنْ كَانَ عَلَى الْصِرَاطِ مِنْ أَهْلِ النُّورِ لَمْ يَكُنْ مِنْ أَهْلِ النَّارِ ❁

(11) Wa ʿan Abī Hurayrata ﵁ anna Rasūlallāh ﷺ qāla li 'l-muṣallīya ʿalayya nūrun ʿalā 'ṣ-ṣirāṭi wa man kāna ʿalā 'ṣ-ṣirāṭi min āhli 'n-nūri lam yakun min āhli 'n-nār. •

(11) Abū Hurayra ﵁ reported that the Messenger of Allāh ﷺ said, "The one who sends blessings on me has a light on the Bridge (over Hell, aṣ-Ṣirāt), and whoever is among the people of light on the Bridge is not one of the people of the Fire."[12] ❁

---

[11] Related by ad-Dāraqutnī and Ibn Nuʿmān with the wording "blesses me 80 times." He graded it *ḥasan* (good).
[12] No *sanad* found.

(١٢) وَقَالَ ﷺ مَنْ نَسِيَ الصَّلاةَ عَلَيَّ فَقَدْ أَخْطَأَ طَرِيقَ الْجَنَّةِ وَإِنَّمَا أَرَادَ بِالنِّسيَانِ التَّرْكَ وَإِذَا كَانَ التَّارِكُ يُخْطِئُ طَرِيقَ الْجَنَّةِ كَانَ الْمُصَلِّي عَلَيهِ سَالِكًا إِلَى الْجَنَّةِ ❋

(12) Wa qāla ﷺ man nasīya 'ṣ-ṣalāta 'alayya faqad akhṭā' ṭarīqa 'l-jannati wa innamā arāda bi-n-nisyāni at-tarka wa idhā kāna 't-tāriku yukhṭi'u ṭarīqa 'l-jannati kāna 'l-muṣalli 'alayhi sālikan ilā 'l-jannah. •

(12) The Prophet ﷺ said, "Whoever forgets to pray invoke blessings on me has missed the Path of the Garden." "Forgetting" means omission. As the omitter misses the Path of the Garden, the one invoking blessings on him is traveling the way to the Garden.[13] ❋

(١٣) وَفِي رِوَايَةِ عَبدِ الرَّحمَنِ بْنِ عَوفٍ قَالَ: قَالَ رَسُولُ اللهِ ﷺ جَاءَنِي جِبْرِيلُ عليه السلام فَقَالَ يَا مُحَمَّدُ لَا يُصَلِّي عَلَيكَ أَحَدٌ مِنْ أُمَّتِكَ إِلَّا صَلَّى عَلَيهِ سَبعُونَ أَلْفَ مَلَكٍ وَمَنْ صَلَّتْ عَلَيهِ الْمَلَائِكَةُ كَانَ مِنْ أَهْلِ الْجَنَّةِ ❋

(13) Wa fī riwāyati 'Abdi 'r-Raḥmāni 'bni 'Awfin qāl: Qāla Rasūlullāhi ﷺ jā'anī Jibrīlu عليه السلام fa-qāla yā Muḥammad lā yuṣalli 'alayka āḥadun min ummatika illā ṣalla 'alayhi sab'ūna alfa malakin wa man ṣallat 'alayhi 'l-malā'ikatu kāna min āhli 'l-jannah •

(13) In 'Abdu 'r-Raḥmān ibn 'Awf's رضي الله عنه narration he said the Prophet of Allāh ﷺ said, "Jibrīl عليه السلام came to me, and said, 'O Muḥammad! No one invokes blessings on you but that 70,000 angels bless him, and the one who is prayed upon by the angels is from the people of the Garden.'"[14]

---

[13] Ibn Mājah, Bayhaqī, aṭ-Ṭabarānī.

[14] Reported by an-Nisā'ī, Ibn Ḥibbān.

(١٤) وَقَالَ ﷺ أَكْثَرُكُم عَلَيَّ صَلَاةً أَكْثَرُكُمْ أَزْوَاجاً فِي الْجَنَّةِ ❁

(14) Wa qāla ﷺ aktharukum ʿalayya ṣalātan aktharukum azwājan fī ʾl-jannah. •

(14) The Prophet ﷺ said, "Those of you who do the most prayers on me will have the most spouses in Paradise."[15] ❁

(١٥) وَرُوِيَ عَنْهُ ﷺ أَنَّهُ قَالَ مَنْ صَلَّى عَلَيَّ صَلَاةً تَعْظِيمًا لِحَقِّي خَلَقَ اللهُ عَزَّ وَجَلَّ مِن ذَلِكَ الْقَوْلِ مَلَكًا لَهُ جَنَاحٌ بِالْمَشْرِقِ وَالآخَرُ بِالْمَغْرِبِ وَرِجْلاهُ مَقْرُونَتَانِ فِي الأَرْضِ السَّابِعَةِ السُّفْلَى وَعُنُقُهُ مُلْتَوِيَةٌ تَحْتَ الْعَرْشِ، يَقُولُ اللهُ عَزَّ وَجَلَّ لَهُ صَلِّ عَلَى عَبْدِي كَمَا صَلَّى عَلَى نَبِيِّ، فَهُوَ يُصَلِّي عَلَيهِ إِلَى يَوْمِ الْقِيَامَةِ ❁

(15) Wa ruwīya ʿanhu ﷺ annahu qāla man ṣalla ʿalayya ṣalātan taʿẓīman li-ḥaqqī khalaqa ʾLlāhu ﷻ min dhālika ʾl-qawli malakan lahu janāḥun bi ʾl-mashriqi wa ʾl-ākharu bi ʾl-maghrib wa rijlāhu maqrūnatāni fī ʾl-arḍi ʾs-sābiʿati ʾs-suflā wa ʿunuquhu multawīyatun taḥta ʾl-ʿarshi, yaqūlu ʾLlāhu ﷻ lahu ṣalli ʿalā ʿabdī kamā ṣalla ʿalā ʾn-Nabīyyī, fa-hūwa yuṣalli ʿalayhi ilā yawmi ʾl-qīyāmah. •

(15) It is related that the Prophet ﷺ said, "When someone invokes blessings upon me magnifying me according to my right, Allāh creates from that word an angel with one wing in the east and one wing in the west with his feet resting in the lowest of the earth, and his neck bowed under the Throne. Allāh says to him, 'Invoke blessing on My slave as he invoked blessings on My Prophet' and he will continue to invoke blessings on him until the Day of Resurrection."[16] ❁

---

[15] It has no confirmed basis in hadith.

[16] It has no confirmed basis in hadith.

(١٦) وَرُوِيَ عَنْهُ ﷺ أَنَّهُ قَالَ لَيَرِدَنَّ عَلَى ٱلْحَوضِ يَوْمَ ٱلْقِيَامَةِ اَقوَامٌ لا أَعْرِفُهُم إِلَّا بِكَثْرَةِ ٱلصَّلاةِ عَلَيَّ ❁

(16) Wa ruwīya 'anhu ﷺ annahu qāla la-yaridanna 'alā 'l-ḥawḍi yawma 'l-qīyāmati aqwāmun lā ā'rifuhum illā bi-kathrati 'ṣ-ṣalāti 'alayya. •

(16) It is related the Prophet ﷺ said, "People will come to the Pond on the Day of Resurrection whom I will recognise only by their invoking blessings on me a lot."[17] ❁

(١٧) وَرُوِيَ عَنْهُ ﷺ أَنَّهُ قَالَ مَنْ صَلَّى عَلَيَّ مَرَّةً وَاحِدَةً صَلَّى اللهُ عَلَيهِ عَشْرَ مَرَّاتٍ، وَمَنْ صَلَّى عَلَيَّ عَشْرَ مَرَّاتٍ صَلَّى اللهُ عَلَيهِ مِائَةَ مَرَّةٍ، وَمَنْ صَلَّى عَلَيَّ مِائَةَ مَرَّةٍ صَلَّى اللهُ عَلَيهِ أَلْفَ مَرَّةٍ،

(17) Wa ruwīya 'anhu ﷺ annahu qāla man ṣalla 'alayya marratan wāḥidatan ṣalla 'Llāhu 'alayhi 'ashra marrātin, wa man ṣalla 'alayya 'ashra marrātin ṣalla 'Llāhu 'alayhi mi'ata marratin wa man ṣalla 'alayya mi'ata marratin ṣalla 'Llāhu 'alayhi alfa marratin,

(17) It is related that he Prophet ﷺ said, "If someone invokes blessings on me once, Allāh blesses him ten times; and if someone invokes blessings on me ten times, Allāh blesses him one hundred times; and if someone invokes blessings on me one hundred times, Allāh blesses him one thousand times; ➤

[17] Related in Qāḍī Iyād's a*sh-Shifā* and Imam Suyūṭī with no *sanad.*

وَمَنْ صَلَّى عَلَيَّ أَلْفَ مَرَّةٍ حَرَّمَ اللهُ جَسَدَهُ عَلَى ٱلنَّارِ وَثَبَّتَهُ بِالقَوْلِ الثَّابِتِ فِي ٱلْحَيَاةِ الدُّنْيَا وَفِي الآخِرَةِ عِنْدَ ٱلْمَسْأَلَةِ وَأَدْخَلَهُ الْجَنَّةَ وَجَاءَتْ صَلَوَاتُهُ عَلَيَّ نُورٌ لَهُ يَوْمَ ٱلْقِيَامَةِ عَلَى ٱلصِّرَاطِ مَسِيرَةَ خَمْسَمِائَةِ عَامٍ، وَأَعْطَاهُ اللهُ بِكُلِّ صَلاةٍ صَلَّاهَا عَلَيَّ قَصْرًا فِي الْجَنَّةِ قَلَّ ذَلِكَ أَوْ كَثُرَ ❋

wa man ṣalla ʿalayya alfa marratin ḥarrama 'Llāhu jasadahu ʿalā 'n-nāri wa thabbatahu bi 'l-qawli 'th-thābiti fī 'l-ḥayāti 'd-dunyā wa fī 'l-ākhirati ʿinda 'l-mas'alati wa adkhalahu 'l-jannata wa jā'at ṣalawātuhu ʿalayya nūrun lahu yawma 'l-qīyāmati ʿalā 'ṣ-ṣirāṭi masīrata khamsa mā'ati ʿāmin, wa āʿṭāhu 'Llāhu bi-kulli ṣalātin ṣallāhā ʿalayya qasran fī 'l-jannati qalla dhalika aw kathur. •

and whoever invokes blessings on me one hundred times, Allāh will forbid his body from the Fire, strengthen him with a firm word in the life of this world and in the Next during the questioning, and He will admit him to the Garden. His prayers on me will come to him as a light on the Day of Resurrection on the Bridge (Ṣirāṭ), visible at a distance of 500 years, and Allāh will give him a castle in the Garden for every invocation of blessings he did for me, whether a little or a lot."[18] ❋

---

[18] No established *sanad* (chain).

(١٨) وَقَالَ ٱلنَّبِيُّ ﷺ مَا مِنْ عَبدٍ صَلَّى عَلَيَّ إِلَّا خَرَجَتِ ٱلْصَلَاةُ مُسرِعَةً مِنْ فِيهِ فَلا يَبْقَى بَرٌّ وَلا بَحرٌ وَلا شَرْقٌ وَلا غَرْبٌ إِلَّا وَتَمُرُّ بِهِ وَتَقُولُ أَنا صَلَاةُ فُلانِ بْنِ فُلانٍ صَلَّى عَلَى مُحَمَّدٍ ٱلْمُختَارِ خَيْرِ خَلْقِ الله ، فَلا يَبقَى شَيءٌ إِلَّا وَصَلَّى عَلَيهِ وَيُخلَقُ مِنْ تِلكَ ٱلْصَّلَاةِ طَائِرٌ لَهُ سَبعُونَ أَلْفَ جَناحٍ، فِي كُلِّ جَناحٍ سَبعُونَ أَلْفَ رِيشَةٍ، فِي كُلِّ رِيشَةٍ سَبعُونَ أَلْفَ رَأسٍ، فِي كُلِّ رَأسٍ سَبعُونَ أَلْفَ وَجْهٍ،

(18) Wa ruwīya ʿanhu ﷺ mā min ʿabdin ṣalla ʿalayya illā kharajati 'ṣ-ṣalātu musriʿatan min fīhi fa-lā yabqā barrun wa lā baḥrun wa lā sharqun wa lā gharbun illā wa tamurru bihi wa taqūlu anā ṣalātu fulāni 'bni fulānin ṣalla ʿalā Muḥammadini 'l-Mukhtāri khayri khalqi 'Llāhi, falā yabqā shay'un illā wa ṣalla ʿalayhi wa yukhlaqu min tilka 'ṣ-ṣalāti ṭā'irun lahu sabʿūna alfa janāḥin, fī kulli janāḥin sabʿūna alfa rīshatin, fī kulli rīshatin sabʿūna alfa rāsin, fī kulli rāsin sabʿūna alfa wajhin,

(18) The Prophet ﷺ said, "Not one of Allāh's servants invokes blessings on me but that the prayer issues quickly from his mouth, and there is no piece of land nor sea nor east nor west but that it passes by them and says, 'I am the blessing of so-and-so, which he invoked for Muḥammad, the Chosen, the best of Allāh's creation,' and there is nothing which does not invoke blessings on him. From that prayer, a bird is created for him with 70,000 wings, and on each wing are 70,000 feathers, and each feather has 70,000 faces, ➢

فِي كُلِّ وَجْهٍ سَبعُونَ أَلْفَ فَمٍ، فِي كُلِّ فَمٍ سَبعُونَ أَلْفَ لِسَانٍ، كُلُّ لِسَانٍ يُسَبِّحُ اللهَ تَعَالَى بِسَبعِينَ أَلْفَ لُغَةٍ، وَيَكتُبُ اللهُ لَهُ ثَوَابَ ذَلِكَ كُلِّهِ ❁

fī kulli wajhin sabʿūna alfa famin fī kulli famin sabʿūna alfa lisānin, kullu lisānin yusabbiḥu 'Llāha taʿālā bi-sabʿīna alfa lughatin, wa yaktubu 'Llāhu lahu thawāba dhalika kullih •

and each face has 70,000 mouths, and every mouth has 70,000 tongues, and every tongue glorifies Allāh the Exalted in 70,000 languages, and Allāh writes the reward of all of that for him."[19] ❁

(١٩) وَعَنْ عَلِيِّ بْنِ أَبِي طَالِبٍ ﷺ قَالَ: قَالَ رَسُولُ اللهِ ﷺ مَنْ صَلَّى عَلَيَّ يَوْمَ الْجُمُعَةِ مِائَةَ مَرَّةٍ جَاءَ يَوْمَ الْقِيَامَةِ وَمَعَهُ نُورٌ لَوْ قُسِمَ ذَلِكَ النُّورُ بَينَ الخَلْقِ كُلِّهِمْ لَوَسِعَهُمْ ❁

(19) Wa ʿan ʿAlīyyi 'bni Abī Ṭālibin ﷺ: Qāla Rasūlullāhi ﷺ man ṣalla ʿālayya yawma 'l-Jumuʿati mi'ata marratin jā'a yawma 'l-qīyāmati wa maʿahu nūrun law qusima dhālika 'n-nūru bayna 'l-khalqi kullihim la-wasiʿahum •

(19) It is related from ʿAlī ibn Abī Ṭālib ﷺ, that the Messenger of Allāh ﷺ said, "If someone asks for blessing on me 100 times on Friday, he will come on the Day of Resurrection with a light, which, were that light to be divided among all of creation, it would suffice them."[20] ❁

---

[19] No established *sanad* (chain).

[20] Abū Nuʿaym in his *Ḥilyah*.

(٢٠) ذُكِرَ فِي بَعضِ ٱلأَخْبَارِ مَكتُوبٌ عَلَى سَاقِ ٱلعَرْشِ: مَنِ ٱشْتَاقَ إِلَيَّ رَحِمتُهُ وَمَن سَأَلَنِي أَعطَيتُهُ وَمَنْ تَقَرَّبَ إِلَيَّ بِالصَّلاَةِ عَلَى مُحَمَّدٍ غَفَرتُ لَهُ ذُنُوبَهُ وَلَوْ كَانَت مِثلَ زَبَدِ ٱلْبَحرِ ❋

(20) Dhukira fī ba'ḍi 'l-'akhbāri maktūbun 'alā sāqi 'l-'Arshi: Man ishtāqa ilayya raḥimtuhu wa man sa'alanī ā'ṭaytuhu wa man taqarraba ilayya bi 'ṣ-ṣalāti 'alā Muḥammadin ghafartu lahu dhunūbahu wa law kānat mithla zabadi 'l-baḥr. •

(20) It is mentioned in some traditions that on the leg of the Throne is inscribed, "If someone yearns for Me, I show mercy to him. If someone asks of Me, I give him. If someone draws near to Me by prayers on Muḥammad, I forgive him his sins, even if they were like the foam on the sea." ❋

(٢١) وَرُوِيَ عَنْ بَعضِ ٱلصَّحَابَةِ رِضوَانُ الله عَلَيهِمْ أَجْمَعِينَ أَنَّهُ قَالَ: مَا مِن مَجْلِسٍ يُصَلَّى فِيهِ عَلَى مُحَمَّدٍ ﷺ إِلَّا قَامَتْ مِنهُ رَائِحَةٌ طَيِّبَةٌ

(21) Wa ruwīya 'an ba'ḍi 'ṣ-ṣaḥābati riḍwānu 'Llāhi 'alayhim ajma'īna annahu qāla: Mā min majlisin yuṣalla fīhi 'alā Muḥammadin ﷺ illā qāmat minhu rā'iḥatun ṭayyibatun

(21) It is related that one of the Companions, may Allāh be pleased with them all, said, "There is no gathering in which blessings are invoked on our master Muḥammad ﷺ except that a pleasant scent spreads from it ➢

حَتَّى تَبلُغَ عَنَانَ ٱلسَّمَاءِ فَتَقُولُ ٱلمَلَآئِكَةُ هَذَا مَجلِسٌ صُلِّيَ فِيهِ عَلَى مُحَمَّدٍ ﷺ ❋

ḥattā tablugha ʿanāna 's-samā'i fa-taqūlu 'l-malā'ikatu hadhā majlisun ṣullīya fīhi ʿalā Muḥammadin ﷺ •

until it reaches the clouds of the sky and the angels say, 'This is a gathering in which blessings were invoked on Muḥammad ﷺ.''' ❋

(٢٢) ذُكِرَ فِي بَعضِ الأَخبَارِ أَنَّ ٱلعَبدَ ٱلمُؤمِنَ أَوِ الأَمَةَ ٱلمُؤمِنَةَ إِذَا بَدَأَ بِالصَّلَوَاةِ عَلَى مُحَمَّدٍ ﷺ فُتِحَت لَهُ أَبوابُ ٱلسَّمَاءِ وَٱلسُّرَادِقَاتُ حَتَّى إِلَى العَرْشِ فَلا يَبقَى مَلَكٌ فِي ٱلسَّمَواتِ إِلَّا صَلَّى عَلَى مُحَمَّدٍ وَيَستَغفِرُونَ لِذَلِكَ ٱلعَبدِ أَوِ الأَمَةِ مَا شَاءَ اللهُ ❋

(22) Dhukira fī baʿḍi 'l-akhbāri anna 'l-ʿabda 'l-mu'mina awi 'l-'amata 'l-mu'minata idhā bada'ā bi 'ṣ-ṣalāti ʿalā Muḥammadin ﷺ *futiḥat lahu abwābu 's-samā'i wa 's-surādiqātu ḥattā ilā 'l-ʿArshi fa-lā yabqā malakun fī 's-samāwāti illā ṣalla ʿalā Muḥammadin wa yastaghfirūna li-dhālika 'l-ʿabdi awi 'l-'amati mā shā' Allāh* •

(22) It is mentioned in some traditions that when a believing servant of Allāh, male or female, begins invoking prayers on Muḥammad ﷺ the doors of heaven are opened to him as well as its pavilions as far as the Throne. Not an angel remains in the heavens who does not invoke blessings on our master Muḥammad ﷺ and seek forgiveness for that servant, male or female, as Allāh wills. ❋

(23) وَقَالَ ﷺ مَنْ عَسُرَتْ عَلَيهِ حَاجَةٌ فَلْيُكْثِرْ بِالصَّلَاةِ عَلَيَّ فَإِنَّهَا تَكْشِفُ الْهُمُومَ وَالغُمُومَ وَالكُرُوبَ وَتُكْثِرُ الْأَرْزَاقَ وَتَقضِي الْحَوَائِجَ ❁

(23) Wa qāla ﷺ man ʿasurat ʿalayhi ḥājatun fal-yukthir bi 'ṣ-ṣalāti ʿalayya fa-innahā takshifu 'l-humūma wa 'l-ghumūma wa 'l-kurūba wa tukthiru 'l-arzāq wa taqḍi 'l-ḥawā'ij •

(23) The Prophet ﷺ said, "If someone has a pressing need, he should increase invoking blessings on me, for it removes cares, griefs and sorrows, and it increases provision and fulfills needs."[21] ❁

(٢٤) وَعَنْ بَعضِ الْصَّالِحِينَ أَنَّهُ قَالَ كَانَ لِي جَارٌ نَسَّاخٌ فَمَاتَ فَرَأَيتُهُ فِي الْمَنَامِ فَقُلتُ لَهُ، مَا فَعَلَ اللهُ بِكَ؟ فَقَالَ غَفَرَ لِي، فَقُلتُ فَبِمَ ذَلِكَ؟

Wa ʿan baʿḍi 'ṣ-ṣāliḥīna annahu qāla kāna lī jārun nassākhun fa-māta fa-ra'aytuhu fī 'l-manāmi fa-qultu lahu, mā faʿalā 'Llāhu bika? Fa-qāla ghafara lī, fa-qultu fa-bima dhalika?

(24) It is related that one of the righteous said, "I had a neighbour who was a scribe. He died, and I saw him in a dream and I asked him, 'What has Allāh done with you?' He replied, 'He has forgiven me.' I asked, 'For what reason?' ➢

---

[21] No established *sanad* (chain).

فَقَالَ كُنْتُ إِذَا كَتَبْتُ اِسْمَ مُحَمَّدٍ ﷺ فِي كِتَابٍ صَلَّيتُ عَلَيهِ فَأَعْطَانِي رَبِّي مَا لا عَينٌ رَأَتْ وَلا أُذُنٌ سَمِعَتْ وَلا خَطَرَ عَلَى قَلْبِ بَشَرٍ ❁

Fa-qāla kuntu idhā katabtu isma Muḥammadin ﷺ fī kitābin ṣallaytu ʿalayhi fa āʿṭānī rabbī mā lā ʿaynun rāʾat wa lā udhunun samiʿat wa lā khaṭara ʿalā qalbi basharin •

He said, 'When I used to write the name of Muḥammad ﷺ in a book, I invoked blessings on him, so my Lord has given me what no eye has seen nor ear has heard nor has occurred to a mortal heart.'" ❁

(٢٥) وَعنْ أَنسٍ رَضِيَ اللهُ عَنْهُ أَنَّهُ قَالَ: قَالَ رَسُولُ اللهِ صَلَّى اللهُ عَلَيهِ وسَلَّمَ، لا يُؤْمِنُ أَحَدُكُم حَتَّى أَكُونَ أَحَبَّ إِلَيْهِ مِنْ نَفْسِهِ وَمَالِهِ وَوَلَدِهِ وَوَالِدِهِ وَالنَّاسِ أَجْمَعِينَ ❁

(25) Wa ʿan Anasin ﷺ *annahu qāla: Qāla Rasūlullāhi* ﷺ *lā yuʾminu āḥadukum ḥattā akūna aḥabba ilayhi min nafsihi wa mālihi wa waladihi wa wālidihi wa 'n-nāsi ajmaʿīna* •

(25) It is reported from Anas ﷺ that the Messenger of Allāh ﷺ said, "None of you believes until I am more beloved to him than himself and what he possesses and his son and father and mankind altogether."[22] ❁

---

[22] Bukhārī and Muslim.

(٢٦) وَفِي حَدِيثِ عُمَرَ بْنِ الْخَطَّابِ ﵁ أَنْتَ أَحَبُّ إِلَيَّ يَا رَسُولَ اللهِ مِنْ كُلِّ شَيْءٍ إِلَّا نَفسِي الَّتِي بَيْنَ جَنْبَيَّ، فَقَالَ عَلَيهِ الصَّلَاةُ وَالسَّلَامُ لا تَكُونُ مُؤْمِنًا حَتَّى أَكُونَ أَحَبَّ إِلَيكَ مِنْ نَفْسِكَ، فَقَالَ عُمَرُ وَالَّذِي أَنزَلَ عَلَيكَ الْكِتَابَ لَأَنْتَ أَحَبُّ إِلَيَّ مِنْ نَفسِي الَّتِي بَيْنَ جَنْبَيَّ، فَقَالَ رَسُولُ اللهِ صَلَّى اللهُ عَلَيهِ وَسَلَّمَ الآنَ يَا عُمَرُ تَمَّ إِيمَانُكَ ❁

(26) Wa fī ḥadīthi 'Umara 'bni 'l-Khaṭṭābi ﵁ anta aḥabbu ilayya yā Rasūlallāhi min kulli shayin illā nafsīya 'l-latī bayna janbayya, fa-qāla 'alayhi 'ṣ-ṣalatu wa 's-salām lā takūnu mu'minan ḥattā akūna aḥabba ilayka min nafsika, fa-qāla 'Umar wa 'Lladhī anzala 'alayka 'l-kitāba la-anta aḥabbu ilayya min nafsīya 'l-latī bayna janbayya, fa-qāla Rasūlullāhi ﷺ al-ān yā 'Umaru tamma īmānuka •

(26) 'Umar ﵁ said, "O Messenger of Allāh, you are more beloved to me than everything except myself which is between my two sides." He, ﷺ, said, "You will not be a believer until I am more beloved to you than yourself" whereupon 'Umar said, "By He who revealed the Book to you, you are more beloved to me than myself." So, the Messenger of Allāh ﷺ said, "Now, 'Umar, your faith is complete."[23] ❁

[23] Bukhārī.

(٢٧) وَقِيلَ لِرَسُولِ ٱللهِ ﷺ مَتَى أَكُونُ مُؤمِناً، وَفِي لَفظٍ آخَرَ مُؤمِنًا صَادِقًا، قَالَ إِذَا أَحْبَبْتَ اللهَ، فَقِيلَ وَمَتَىٰ أُحِبُّ اللهَ، قَالَ إِذَا أَحْبَبْتَ رَسُولَهُ، فَقِيلَ وَمَتَى أُحِبُّ رَسُولَهُ، قَالَ إِذَا اتَّبَعْتَ طَرِيقَتَهُ وَاسْتَعْمَلتَ سُنَّتَهُ وَأَحْبَبْتَ بِحُبِّهِ وَأَبغَضْتَ بِبُغْضِهِ وَوَالَيتَ بِوِلَايَتِهِ وَعَادَيتَ بِعَدَاوَتِهِ، وَيَتَفَاوَتُ ٱلنَّاسُ فِي الإِيمَانِ عَلَى قَدْرِ تَفَاوُتِهِم فِي مَحَبَّتِي،

(27) Wa qīla li-Rasūlillāhi ﷺ matā akūnu mu'minan, wa fī lafẓin ākhar mu'minan ṣādiqan, qāla idhā aḥbabta 'Llāha, fa-qīla wa matā uḥibbu 'Llāha, qāla idhā aḥbabta Rasūlahu, fa-qīla wa matā uḥibbu Rasūlahu, qāla idhā 't-tabaʿta ṭarīqatahu wa 'staʿmalta sunnatahu wa aḥbabta bi-ḥubbihi wa abghaḍta bi-bughḍihi wa wālayta bi-wilāyatihi wa ʿādawta bi-ʿadāwatihi, wa yatafāwatu 'n-nāsu fī 'l-īmāni ʿalā qadri tafāwutihim fī maḥabbatī,

(27) It was asked, "And when will I love Allāh?" He replied, "When you love His Messenger." It was said, "And when will I love His Messenger?" He said, "When you follow his Path, apply his Sunnah, love with his love and hate with his hate, and befriend those he befriends and oppose those enemies he opposed. People differ in faith according to the difference in their love of me, The Messenger of Allāh ﷺ was asked, "When will I be a believer?" (or in another variant, "a sincere believer") He answered, "When you love Allāh." ➤

وَيَتَفَاوَتُونَ فِي الكُفْرِ عَلَى قَدْرِ تَفَاوُتِهِم فِي بُغْضِي، أَلا لا إِيْمَانَ لِمَنْ لا مَحَبَّةَ لَهُ، أَلا لا إِيْمَانَ لِمَن لا مَحَبَّةَ لَهُ، أَلا لا إِيْمَانَ لِمَن لا مَحَبَّةَ لَهُ ❁

wa yatafāwatūna fī ʼl-kufri ʻalā qadri tafāwutihim fī bughḍī, alā lā īmāna liman lā maḥabbata lahu, alā lā īmāna liman lā maḥabbata lahu, alā lā īmāna liman lā maḥabbata lah. •

and they differ in unbelief in accordance to their hatred for me. Verily he has no faith who has no love for me? Verily he has no faith who has no love for me? Verily he has no faith who has no love for me?"[24] ❁

(٢٨) وَقِيلَ لِرَسُولِ اللهِ ﷺ نَرَىٰ مُؤْمِنًا يَخْشَعُ وَمُؤْمِنًا لا يَخْشَعُ، مَا السَّبَبُ فِي ذَلِكَ ؟ فَقَالَ مَنْ وَجَدَ لِإِيمَانِهِ حَلاوَةً خَشَعَ، وَمَنْ لَمْ يَجِدْهَا لَمْ يَخْشَعْ، فَقِيلَ بِمَا تُوجَدُ أَوْ بِمَ تُنَالُ وَتُكْتَسَبُ؟

(28) Wa qīla li-Rasūlillāhi ﷺ narā muʼminan yakh-shaʻu wa muʼminan lā yakhshaʻu, mā ʼs-sababu fī dhalika? Fa-qāla man wajad li-īmānihi ḥalāwatan khashaʻa, wa man lam yajidhā lam yakhshaʻ fa-qīla bimā tūjad aw bimā tunālu wa tuktasab,

(28) It was said to the Messenger of Allāh ﷺ "We see believers who are humble and believers who are not humble. What is the cause of that?" He replied, "The one who experiences sweetness in his faith is humble, and the one does not experience it is not humble." It was asked, "By what is it found, or obtained and earned?" ➤

[24] No established *sanad* (chain).

قَالَ بِصِدْقِ الْحُبِّ فِي اللهِ فَقِيلَ وَبِمَ يُوجَدُ حُبُّ اللهِ أَوْ بِمَ يُكْتَسَبُ؟ فَقَالَ بِحُبِّ رَسُولِهِ فَالْتَمِسُوا رِضَاءَ اللهِ وَرِضَاءَ رَسُولِهِ فِي حُبِّهِمَا ❁

fa-qāla bi-ṣidqi 'l-ḥubbi fī 'Llāhi, fa-qīla wa bimā yūjad ḥubbu 'Llāhi aw bimā yuktasab? Fa-qāla bi-ḥubbi Rasūlihi faltamisū riḍā'a 'Llāhi wa riḍā'a Rasūlihi fī ḥubbihimā. •

He answered, "By sincere love for Allāh." It was asked, "And by what is love of Allāh found or by what is it earned?" He said, "By love of His Messenger. So seek the pleasure of Allāh and the pleasure of His Messenger through loving them."[25] ❁

(٢٩) وَقِيلَ لِرَسُولِ اللهِ ﷺ مَنْ آلُ مُحَمَّدٍ الَّذِينَ أُمِرْنَا بِحُبِّهِم وَإِكْرَامِهِمْ وَالبُرُورِ بِهِم، فَقَالَ أَهْلُ الصَّفَاءِ وَالوَفَاءِ مَنْ آمَنَ بِي وَأَخلَصَ، قِيلَ وَمَا عَلامَاتُهُمْ

(29) Wa qīla li-Rasūlillāhi ﷺ man ālu Muḥammadini 'Lladhīna umirnā bi-ḥubbihim wa ikrāmihim wa 'l-burūri bihim, fa-qāla āhlu 'ṣ-ṣafā'i wa 'l-wafā'i man āman bī wa akhlaṣa, qīla wa mā ʿalāmātuhum?

(29) The Messenger of Allāh ﷺ was asked, "Who are the Family of Muḥammad whom we are commanded to love, honour and show reverence to?" He replied, "The people of purity and fidelity who believes in me and are sincere." He was asked, "What are their signs?" ➤

[25] No established *sanad* (chain).

فَقَالَ إِيثَارُ مَحَبَّتِي عَلَىٰ كُلِّ مَحْبُوبٍ وَانْشِغَالُ الْبَاطِنِ بِذِكْرِي بَعْدَ ذِكْرِ اللهِ، وَفِي أُخْرَى عَلَامَتُهُمْ إِدْمَانُ ذِكْرِي وَالْإِكْثَارُ مِنَ الصَّلَاةِ عَلَيَّ ❁

Fa-qāla īthāru maḥabbatī ʿalā kulli maḥbūbin wa inshighālu 'l-bāṭinu bi-dhikrī baʿda dhikrillāhi, wa fī ukhrā ʿalāmātuhum idmānu dhikrī wa 'l-'ikthāru mina 'ṣ-ṣalātu ʿalayya •

He answered, "Preferring love of me above every other beloved and being occupied inwardly remembering me after remembering Allāh." In a variant wording: "Their sign is constantly remembering me and frequently invoking blessings on me."[26] ❁

(٣٠) وَقِيلَ لِرَسُولِ اللهِ ﷺ مَنِ الْقَوِيُّ فِي الْإِيمَانِ بِكَ؟ فَقَالَ مَنْ آمَنَ بِي وَلَمْ يَرَنِي فَإِنَّهُ مُؤْمِنٌ بِي عَلَى شَوْقٍ مِنْهُ وَصِدْقٍ فِي مَحَبَّتِي، وَعَلَامَةُ ذَلِكَ مِنْهُ أَنَّهُ يَوَدُّ رُؤْيَتِي بِجَمِيعِ مَا يَمْلِكُ

(30) Wa qīla li-Rasūlillāhi ﷺ mani 'l-qawīyyu fī 'l-īmāni bika? Fa-qāla man āmana bī wa lam yaranī fa-innahu mu'minun ʿalā shawqin minhu wa ṣidqin fī maḥabbatī wa ʿalāmatu dhalika minhu annahu yawaddu ru'yatī bi-jamīʿi mā yamliku

(30) The Messenger of Allāh ﷺ was asked, "Who is the one strongest in faith in you?" He answered, "The one who did not see me and yet believed in me with yearning for me and sincere love for me. The sign of that is that he would wish to give all he possesses to see me. ➢

[26] No established *sanad* (chain).

وَفِي أُخْرَى مِلْءُ ٱلأَرْضِ ذَهَبًا، ذَلِكَ ٱلْمُؤمِنُ بِي حَقًا وَالْمُخلِصُ فِي مَحَبَّتِي صِدْقًا ❋

wa fī ukhrā mil'u 'l-arḍi dhahaban, dhalika 'l-mu'minu bī ḥaqqan wa 'l-mukhliṣu fī maḥabbatī ṣidqan. •

(Another variant has: "all the gold in the earth") Such is the one who truly believes in me and is sincere in true love for me."[27] ❋

(٣١) وَقِيلَ لِرَسُولِ الله ﷺ أَرَأَيتَ صَلاةَ ٱلْمُصَلِّينَ عَلَيكَ مِمَّنْ غَابَ عَنْكَ وَمَنْ يَأتِي بَعْدَكَ، مَا حَالُهُمَا عِنْدَكَ؟ فَقَالَ أَسْمَعُ صَلاةَ أَهْلِ مَحَبَّتِي وَأَعْرِفُهُمْ وَتُعْرَضُ عَلَيَّ صَلاةُ غَيْرِهِمْ عَرْضًا ❋

(31) Wa qīla li-Rasūlillāhi ﷺ ara'ayta ṣalāta 'l-muṣallīna ʿalayka mimmān ghāba ʿanka wa man yā'tī baʿdaka, mā ḥāluhumā ʿindaka? Fa-qāla asmaʿu ṣalāta āhli maḥabbatī wa āʿrifuhum wa tuʿraḍu ʿalayya ṣalātu ghayrihim ʿarḍan. •

(31) It was said to the Messenger of Allāh ﷺ "What do you think is the state of those who invoke blessings on you who are not with you or who will come after you?" He said, "I hear the prayers of the people of my love and I know them. The prayers of other than them are presented to me." [28] ❋

---

[27] No established *sanad* (chain).

[28] No established *sanad* (chain).

صِفَةُ الرَّوْضَةِ النبوِيَةِ الشَّرِيفَةِ

Ṣiffatu 'r-Rawḍati 'n-Nabawīyati 'sh-Sharīfah

Description of the Holy Garden of Paradise of the Prophet ﷺ

بِسْمِ اللهِ الرَّحْمَـنِ الرَّحِيم

اللَّهُمَّ صَلِّ عَلَى سَيِّدِنَا مُحَمَّدٍ وَعَلَى آلِ سَيِّدِنَا مُحَمَّد

Bismillāhi 'r-Raḥmāni 'r-Raḥīm. Allāhumma ṣalli ʿalā Sayyīdinā Muḥammadin wa ʿalā āli Sayyīdinā Muḥammad.

In the Name of Allāh, all-Merciful, The Mercy-Giving. O Allāh exalt our master Muḥammad and the family of our master Muḥammad. ➢

هَذِهِ صِفَةُ الرَّوْضةِ المُبَارَكَةِ الَّتِي دُفِنَ فِيْهَا ٱلرَّسُوْلُ ﷺ وَصَاحِبَاهُ أَبُو بَكْرٍ وَعُمَرُ ﵄: هَكَذَا ذَكَرَهُ عُروَةُ بْنُ الزُّبَيْرِ ﵁

Hadhihi ṣiffatu 'r-rawḍati 'l-mubārakati 'Llatī dufina fīhā 'r-Rasūl ﷺ wa ṣāḥibāhu Abū Bakr wa ʿUmar ﵄. Hakadhā dhakarahu ʿUrwatu 'bnu 'z-Zubayr.

This is the description of the blessed Garden of Paradise (Rawḍah) in which the Prophet of Allah ﷺ is buried and his two companions, Abū Bakr and ʿUmar ﵄ That is how ʿUrwah ibn az-Zubayr ﵁ recalled it. ➢

قَالَ: دُفِنَ رَسُوْلُ اللهِ ﷺ فِي ٱلسَّهْوَةِ، وَدُفِنَ أَبُو بَكرٍ ﷺ خلف رَسُولِ اللهِ ﷺ وَدُفِنَ عُمَرُ بْنُ الخَطَّابِ ﷺ عِنْدَ رِجلَيْ أَبِي بَكرٍ، وَبَقِيَتِ ٱلسَّهوَةُ ٱلشَّرْقِيَّةُ فَارِغَةً فِيهَا مَوضِعُ قَبرٍ يُقَالُ وَاللهُ أَعلَمُ أَنَّ عِيسَى بْنَ مَرِيَمَ ﷺ يُدْفَنُ فِيهِ، وَكَذَلِكَ جَاءَ فِي الخَبَرِ عَنْ رَسُولِ اللهِ ﷺ. ❋

qāla: dufina Rasūlullāhi fī 's-sahwati wa dufina Abū Bakrin khalf Rasūlullāhi wa dufina ʿUmaru 'bnu 'l-Khaṭṭāb ʿinda rijlay Abī Bakrin, wa baqīyati 's-sahwatu 'sh-sharqīyyatu fārighatun fīhā mawḍiʿu qabrin yuqālu w'Allāḥu āʿlamu anna ʿĪsā ibni Maryama yudfanu fīhi, wa kadhalika jā'a fī 'l-khabri ʿan Rasūlullāhi ﷺ •

He said: "The Prophet of Allah, ﷺ was buried in the alcove. Abū Bakr ﷺ was buried behind the Messenger of Allah, ﷺ, and ʿUmar ibn al-Khaṭṭāb ﷺ was buried at the feet of Abū Bakr. The eastern niche remained with an empty place for a grave and it is said, and Allah knows best, that ʿIsā ibn Maryam ﷺ will be buried there. That is how it is reported from the Prophet of Allah ﷺ." ❋

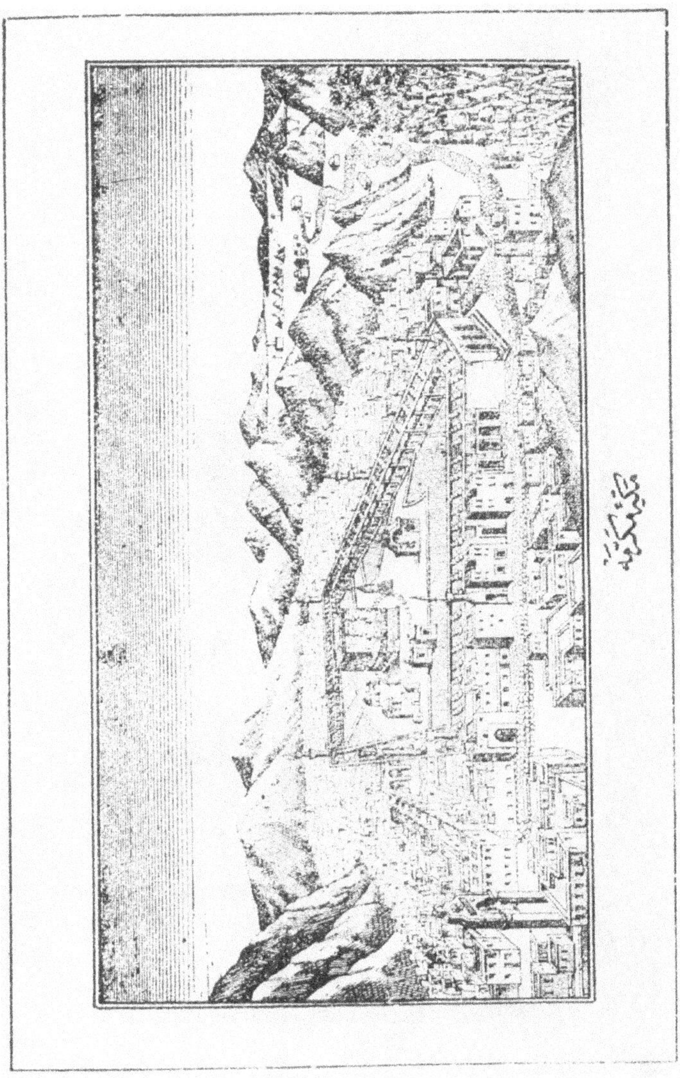

Madīnatu 'l-Munawwarah

قَالَتْ عَائِشَةُ ﵂: رَأَيْتُ ثَلاثَةَ أَقمَارٍ سُقُوطاً فِي حُجْرَتِي فَقَصَصْتُ رُؤْيَايَ عَلَى أَبِي بَكْرٍ فَقَالَ لِي: يَا عَائِشَةُ لَيُدْفَنَنَّ فِي بَيْتِكِ ثَلاثَةٌ هُم خَيرُ أَهْلِ الْأَرْضِ، فَلَمَّا تُوُفِّيَ رَسُولُ اللهِ ﷺ وَدُفِنَ فِي بَيتِي قَالَ لِي أَبُو بَكرٍ: هَذَا وَاحِدٌ مِن أَقْمَارِكِ وَهُوَ خَيرُهُمْ صَلَّى اللهُ عَلَيهِ وَسَلَّمَ كَثِيراً، وَعَلَى آلِهِ أَجْمَعِينَ صَلَاةً دَائِمَةً تَامَّةً إِلَى يَوْمِ الدِّينِ وَالحَمْدُ للهِ رَبِّ الْعَالَمِينَ ❋

Wa qālat ʿA'ishatu ﵂: ra'āitu thalāthata aqmārin suqūṭan fī ḥujratī fa-qaṣaṣtu rū'yāya ʿalā Abī Bakrin fa-qāla lī: yā ʿA'ishah! La-yudfananna fī baytiki thalāthatun hum khayru āhli 'l-arḍ. Fa lammā tuwufiyya rasūlullāhi ﷺ wa dufina fī baytī qāla lī Abū Bakrin: hadhā wāḥidun min aqmāriki wa huwa khayruhum ṣalla 'Llāhu ʿalayhi wa sallama kathīra, wa ʿalā ālihi ajmaʿīna ṣalātan dā'imatan tāmatan ilā yawmi 'd-dīn w 'alḥamdulillāhi rabbi 'l-ʿālamīn. •

ʿĀ'isha ﵂ said, "I dreamt that three moons setting in my room. I told Abū Bakr about my dream and he said to me, ''Ā'isha, three persons will be buried in your home, they are the best of the people of the earth.' When the Prophet of Allāh ﷺ died and was buried in my room, Abū Bakr said to me, 'This is one of your moons, and he is the best of them.'" May Allāh exalt him and grant him great peace and upon his entire family, an ongoing exaltation, complete, up to the Day of Judgment, and all praise is to Allāh Lord of the Worlds. ❋

كَيفية بَدْءِ دَلَآئِلُ الخَيرَاتِ

Kayfīyyat Bad'i Dalā'ilu 'l-Khayrāt

Method of Beginning Reading *Dalā'ilu 'l-Khayrāt*

(to be read before starting the recitation of the *Dalā'il*)

(١) أَوَّلاً الإستِغْفَارُ "استَغفِرُ اللهَ العَظِيمَ" (ثَلاثاً)، وَ"حَسبِيَ اللهُ وَنِعمَ الوَكِيلُ" (ثَلاثاً) ❋

(1) Astaghfiru 'Llāha 'l-ʿAẓīma (3x), wa ḥasbuna 'Llāhu wa niʿma 'l-wakīl (3x) •

(1) I seek forgiveness from Allāh the Great (3x), and Allāh is Sufficient for us and He is the Best of Protectors. ❋

(٢) ثانياً تُصَلِّي عَلَى النَبِي ﷺ (ثَلاثاً) ❋

(2) Allāhumma ṣalli ʿalā Sayyīdinā Muḥammadin wa ʿalā āli Sayyīdinā Muḥammadin (3x) •

(2) Then you say: O Allāh send blessings upon our master Muḥammad and upon the family of our master Muḥammad. ❋

(٣) ثُمَّ تَقْرَأُ سُورَةُ **الفَاتِحَة** (ثَلاثاً): مَرَّةً لِرِضَاءِ اللهِ تَعَالَى، وَمَرَّةً لِرُوحِ سَيِّدِنَا مُحَمَّدٍ ﷺ، وَمَرَّةً لِرُوحِ سَيِّدِيْ أَبِي عَبْدِاللهِ مُحَمَّدِ بْنِ سُلَيْمَانَ الجَزُّولِي رَحِمَةُ اللهِ عَلَيهِ ❋

(3) Then read Sūratu 'l-Fātiḥah (3x): once with the intention of pleasing Allāh Almighty; once with the intention of presenting it as a gift to the soul of our master Muḥammad ﷺ and once for the soul of our master Muḥammad ibn Sulaymān al-Jazūlī, on him be Allāh's Mercy. ❋

بِسْمِ اللهِ الرَّحْمَـنِ الرَّحِيمِ ،الْحَمْدُ للهِّ رَبِّ الْعَالَمِينَ، الرَّحْمَـنِ الرَّحِيمِ، مَـالِكِ يَوْمِ الدِّينِ، إِيَّاكَ نَعْبُدُ وإِيَّاكَ نَسْتَعِينُ، اهدِنَـــا الصِّرَاطَ المُستَقِيمَ، صِرَاطَ الَّذِينَ أَنعَمتَ عَلَيهِمْ غَيرِ المَغضُوبِ عَلَيهِمْ وَلاَ الضَّالِّينَ

Bismi'Llāhi 'r-Raḥmāni 'r-Raḥīm. Alḥamdu lillāhi Rabbi 'l-ʿālamīn ar-Raḥmāni 'r-Raḥīmi Māliki yawmi 'd-dīni iyyāka naʿbudu wa 'iyyāka nastaʿīnu ihdina 'ṣ-ṣirāṭa 'l-mustaqīma sirāṭa 'Lladhīna anʿamta ʿalayhim ghayri 'l-maghḍūbi ʿalayhim wa lā 'ḍ-ḍāllīn•

In the name of Allāh, The Beneficent, The Merciful all Praise is for Allāh the Lord and Cherisher of the worlds, The Beneficent, the Merciful, Master of the Day of Judgment, we worship You alone and seek Your help alone, guide us to the straight path, the path of those whom Thou hast favored, not of those who earn Thine anger nor of those who go astray ❋

(٤) ثم : بِسْمِ اللهِ الرَّحْمَنِ الرَّحِيمِ، قُلْ هُوَ اللهُ أَحَدٌ، اللهُ الصَّمَدُ، لَمْ يَلِدْ وَلَمْ يُولَدْ، وَلَمْ يَكُنْ لَهُ كُفُوًا أَحَدٌ (ثلاثا) ❋

(4) Sūratu 'l-'Ikhlāṣ (3x): Bismi 'Llāhi 'r-Raḥmāni 'r-Raḥīm. Qul hūwa 'Llāhu Aḥad Allāhu 'ṣ-Ṣamad lam yalid wa lam yūlad wa lam yakūn lahū kufūwan āḥad •

(4) Then recite the "Chapter of Sincerity" (3x): In the name of Allāh, The Beneficent, The Merciful. Say: He is Allāh, The One. Allāh the eternally besought of all! He begets not nor was He begotten and there is none comparable unto Him. ❋

(٥) ثُمَّ الْمُعَوِّذَتَيْنِ (مَرَّة) بِالبَسمَلَةِ: بِسْمِ اللهِ الرَّحْمَنِ الرَّحِيمِ ، قُلْ أَعُوذُ بِرَبِّ الْفَلَقِ ، مِنْ شَرِّ مَا خَلَقَ، وَمِنْ شَرِّ غَاسِقٍ إِذَا وَقَبَ ، وَمِنْ شَرِّ النَّفَّاثَاتِ فِي الْعُقَدِ ، وَمِنْ شَرِّ حَاسِدٍ إِذَا حَسَدَ ❋

Bismillāhi 'r-Raḥmāni 'r-Raḥīm. Qul āʻūdhu bi-rabbi 'l-falaqi min shārri mā khalaq wa min sharri ghāsiqin idhā waqab wa min sharri 'n-naffāthāti fī 'l-ʻuqad wa min sharri ḥāsidin idhā ḥasad •

(5) Then you recite "al-Muʻawwidhatayn" (the two *Qul āʻūdhu sūras*) one time each with Basmalah:

In the name of Allāh, The Beneficent, The Merciful Say: I seek refuge in the Lord of daybreak, from the evil of what He created, and from the evil of darkness when it prevails, and from the evil of women who blow into the knots [witchcraft], and from the evil of the envier when he envies. ➢

بِسْمِ اللهِ الرَّحْمَنِ الرَّحِيمِ ،قُلْ أَعُوذُ بِرَبِّ النَّاسِ ،مَلِكِ النَّاسِ ،إِلَهِ النَّاسِ ،مِنْ شَرِّ الْوَسْوَاسِ الْخَنَّاسِ ،الَّذِي يُوَسْوِسُ فِي صُدُورِ النَّاسِ ،مِنَ الْجِنَّةِ وَ النَّاسِ

Bismi 'Llāhi 'r-Raḥmāni 'r-Raḥīm. Qul āʿūdhu bi-Rabbī 'n-nās Maliki 'n-nās ilāhi 'n-nās min sharri 'l-waswāsi 'l-khannāsi 'Lladhī yuwaswisu fī ṣudūri 'n-nāsi mina 'l-jinnati wa 'n-nās •

In the name of Allāh, the Beneficent, the Merciful. Say: "I seek refuge in the Lord of mankind, King of mankind, God of mankind, from the evil of the sneeking whisperer who whispers in the hearts of mankind, from the Jinn and mankind. ❋

دُعَاء بَدْءِ دَلَآئِلِ الخَيْرَاتِ

Du'ā' Bad'i Dalāi'li 'l-Khayrāt

Supplication before Beginning Recitation of the *Dalā'il.*

بِسْمِ اللهِ الرَّحْمَنِ الرَّحِيمِ اِلَهِي بِجَاهِ نَبِيِّكَ سَيِّدِنَا مُحَمَّدٍ صَلَّى اللهُ تَعَالَى عَلَيهِ وَسَلَّمَ عِنْدَكَ، وَمَكَانَتِهِ لَدَيكَ، وَمَحَبَّتِكَ لَهُ وَمَحَبَّتِهِ لَكَ، وَبِالسِّرِّ الَّذِي بَيْنَكَ وَبَيْنَهُ، أَسْأَلُكَ أَنْ تُصَلِّيَ وَتُسَلِّمَ عَلَيهِ وَعَلَىْ آلِهِ وَصَحْبِهِ، وَضَاعِفِ اللَّهُمَّ مَحَبَّتِي فِيهِ وَعَرِّفْنِي بِحَقِّهِ وَرُتَبِهِ،

Bismi 'Llāhi 'r-Raḥmāni 'r-Raḥīm. Ilāḥī bi-jāhi Nabīyyika wa ḥabībika Sayyīdinā Muḥammadin ﷺ 'indaka, wa makānatahu ladayka, wa maḥabbataka lahu wa maḥabbatihi laka, wa bi-s-sirri 'Lladhī baynak wa baynahu, as-'aluka an tuṣallīya wa tusallima 'alayhi wa 'alā ālihi wa ṣaḥbihi, wa ḍā'ifi 'Llāhuma maḥabbatī fīhi wa 'arrifnī bi-ḥaqqihi wa rutabihi

In the name of Allāh, All-Merciful, The Mercy-Giving. O Allāh for the sake of the high honor you hold for Your Prophet, our master Muḥammad ﷺ, and his station with You, and Your love for him and his love for You and the secret between You and him, I ask you to bless him and send peace on him, his family and his companions. O Allāh exponentially increase my love for him, show me his rank and what is rightfully his ➢

وَوَفِّقْنِي لِاتِّبَاعِهِ وَالْقِيَامِ بِأَدَبِهِ وَسُنَّتِهِ، وَاجْمَعْنِي عَلَيهِ وَمَتِّعْنِي بِرُؤيَتِهِ وَأَسْعِدْنِي بِمُكَالَمَتِهِ، وَارْفَعْ عَنِّيَ الْعَوَائِقَ وَالعَلائِقَ وَالوَسَائِطَ وَالحِجَابَ، وَشَنِّفْ سَمْعِيَ مَعَهُ بِلَذِيذِ الخِطَابِ، وَهَيِّئْنِي لِلْتَلَقِّي مِنهُ وَأَهِّلْنِي بِخِدْمَتِهِ، وَاجْعَلْ صَلَاتِي عَلَيهِ نُوراً نَيِّرًا كَامِلاً مُكَمَّلاً طَاهِراً مُطَهَّراً مَاحِياً كُلَّ ظُلْمَةٍ وَشَكٍّ وَكُفْرٍ وَزُورٍ وَوِزْرٍ، وَاجْعَلَهَا سَبَبًا لِلْتَّمْحِيصِ وَمَرَقاً

wa waffiqnī li itbā-ʿihi wa 'l-qīyāmi bi-adabihi wa sunnatihi.wa 'jmaʿnī ʿalayhi wa mattiʿnī bi-rūʿyatihi wa asʿidnī bi-mukālamatihi, wa 'rfaʿ ʿannī al-ʿawā'iqa wa 'l-ʿalā'iqa wa 'l-wasā'iṭa wa 'l-ḥijāb, wa shannif samʿīy maʿahu bi-ladhīdhi 'l-khiṭāb, wa hayyi'nī li 't-talaqīya minhu wa ahhilnīya bi-khidmatihi, wa 'jʿal ṣalātī ʿalayhi nūran nayyiran kāmilan mukammilan ṭāhiran muṭāhharan māḥīyyan kulla ẓulmin wa ẓulmatin wa shakkin wa shirkin wa kufrin wa zūrin wa wizrin, wa 'j ʿalhā sababan li 't-tamḥīṣi wa maraqan

and grant me success in following him and establishing his excellent manners and his way. O Allāh, gather me with him, let me delight in seeing him, and grant me the joy of hearing his words. O Allāh, remove all the obstacles, intermediaries and veils between myself and him, and honor my hearing with the sound of his speech. O Allāh prepare me for receiving from him, make me fit for his service, and turn my praise of him into a shining, perfect, perfected, pure and purifying light, erasing by it, every darkness, all doubt, disbelief, falsehood and affliction, and make my praise of him a cause for clemency, ➢

حَتَّى أَنالَ بِهَا مَقَامَ الإِخْلاصِ وَالتَّخْصِيصِ، حَتَّىٰ لَا يَبْقَىٰ فِيَّ رَبَّانِيَّةٌ لِغَيرِكَ،
وَحَتَّى أَصْلُحَ لِحَضْرَتِكَ وَأَكُونَ مِنْ أَهْلِ خُصُوصِيَّتِكَ، مُسْتَمْسِكًا بِأَدَبِهِ
صَلَّى اللهُ تَعَالَىٰ عَلَيهِ وَسَلَّمَ مُسْتَمِدًّا مِنْ حَضْرَتِهِ العَالِيَةِ فِي كُلِّ وَقتٍ وَحِينٍ ❋

ḥattā anāla bihā maqāmi 'l-'ikhlāṣi wa 't-takhṣīṣi ḥattā lā yabqā fiyya rabbānīyyatan li-ghayrika wa ḥattā aṣluḥa li-ḥaḍratika wa akūna min āhli khuṣūṣīyyatika, mustamsikan bi-adabihi wa sunnatihi ṣalla 'Llāhu ta'alā 'alayhi wa sallama, mustamiddan min ḥaḍratihi 'l-'ālīyati fī kulli waqtin wa ḥīn. •

and a cause for me to attain the Station of Sincerity and Honor, until no lordship but Yours remains in me, and so that I become fit for Your Presence and I become amongst Your select ones, while holding tight to his excellent manners—may Allāh send peace and blessings on him—and receiving from his high presence at every time and proper moment.

يَا اللهُ ﷻ ❋ يَا نُورُ ﷻ ❋ يَا حَقُّ ﷻ ❋ يَا مُبِينُ ﷻ ❋ (ثَلاثًا)

Yā Allāh ﷻ, *Yā Nūr* ﷻ, *Yā Ḥaqq* ﷻ, *Yā Mubīn* ﷻ, *(3x)* •

O Allāh, O Light, O Truth, O Clarifier. (3x) ❋

دُعَاءُ ٱلنِّيَّةِ

Du'āu 'n-Nīyyah

Supplication of the Intention

بِسمِ اللهِ الرَّحمَنِ الرَّحِيمِ الحَمْدُ لله رَبِّ العَالَمِينَ، حَسبِيَ اللهُ وَنِعْمَ ٱلْوَكِيلُ وَلا حَولَ وَلا قُوَّةَ إِلَّا بِاللهِ العَلِيِّ العَظِيمِ، اللَّهُمَّ إِنِّي أَبْرَأُ مِنْ حَولِي وَقُوَّتِي إِلَى حَولِكَ وَقُوَّتِكَ، اللَّهُمَّ إِنِّي أَتَقَرَّبُ إِلَيكَ بِالصَّلاةِ عَلَى سَيِّدِنَا مُحَمَّدٍ

Bismi 'Llāhi 'r-Raḥmāni 'r-Raḥīm al-ḥamdu lillāhi Rabbi 'l-'ālamīn, ḥasbīya 'Llāhu wa ni'mā 'l-wakīlu wa lā ḥawla wa lā quwwata illā bi 'Llāhi 'l-'Alīyyi 'l-'Aẓīm, Allāhumma innī abrā'u min ḥawlī wa quwwatī ilā ḥawlika wa quwwatik, allāhumma innī ataqarrabu ilayka bi 'ṣ-ṣalāti 'alā Sayyīdinā Muḥammadin

In the name of Allāh, All-Merciful, The Mercy-Giving. Praise be to Allāh, Lord of the Worlds. Allāh is sufficient for me, and He is the best of Protectors. There is no help or power save with Allāh The High, The Mighty. O Allāh, I rid myself of reliance upon my own help and power in order to rely only upon Your Help and Your Power, O Allāh. O Allāh! I seek closeness to You through praising our master Muḥammad, ➤

عَبْدِكَ وَنَبِيِّكَ وَرَسُولِكَ سَيِّدِ الْمُرْسَلِينَ صَلَّى اللهُ تَعَالَى وَسَلَّمَ عَلَيْهِ وَعَلَيْهِمْ أَجْمَعِينَ امْتِثَالاً لِأَمْرِكَ وَتَصْدِيقاً لَهُ وَمَحَبَّةً فِيهِ وَشَوْقاً إِلَيْهِ وَتَعْظِيماً لِقَدْرِهِ وَلِكَوْنِهِ صَلَّى اللهُ عَلَيْهِ وَسَلَّمَ أَهْلاً لِذَلِكَ فَتَقَبَّلْهَا مِنِّي بِفَضْلِكَ وَاجْعَلْنِي مِنْ عِبَادِكَ الصَّالِحِينَ وَوَفِّقْنِي لِقِرَاءَتِهَا عَلَى الدَّوَامِ بِجَاهِهِ عِنْدَكَ، وَصَلَّى اللهُ عَلَى سَيِّدِنَا مُحَمَّدٍ وَآلِهِ وَصَحْبِهِ أَجْمَعِينَ ❁

ʿabdika wa nabīyyika wa rasūlika sayyidi 'l-mursalīna ṣalla 'Llāhu taʿalā ʿalayhi wa ālihi wa sallam wa ʿalayhim ajmaʿīna imtithālan li amrika wa taṣdīqan lahu wa maḥabbatan fīhi wa shawqan ilayhi wa taʿẓīman li-qadrihi wa li-kawnihi ﷺ *āhlan li-dhālika fataqabbalhā minnī bi-faḍlika wa 'jʿalnī min ʿibādika 'ṣ-ṣalīḥīna wa waffiqnī li-qirā'atihā ʿalā 'd-dawāmi bi-jāhihi ʿindaka, wa ṣalla 'Llāhu ʿalā Sayyīdinā Muḥammadin wa ālihi wa ṣāḥbihi ajmaʿīn* •

Your Servant, Your Prophet, Your Messenger and the Master of All the Messengers peace and blessings upon them all. I do so by obeying your order, by confirming the truthfulness of Your Prophet, due to my love and yearning for him, extolling the greatness of his rank and because he is deserving of this. Accept this from me through Your Favours and Your Grace, and make the veil of forgetfulness drop from my heart and make me one of Your righteous slaves, and may the blessings and peace of Allāh be upon our master Muḥammad and his Family and Companions. ❁

الْأَسَمَاءُ الْحُسْنَى

Asmā'u 'Llāhi 'l-Ḥusnā

Allāh's Beautiful Names

ثُمَّ تَقْرَأ بِسمِ اللهِ الرَّحْمَنِ الرَّحِيمِ "وَللهِ الْأَسَمَاءُ الْحُسْنَى فَادْعُوهُ بِهَا":

هُوَ اللهُ الَّذِي لا إِلَهَ إِلَّا هُوَ ﷻ (١) الرَّحْمَنُ ﷻ (٢) الرَّحِيمُ ﷻ

(٣) المَلِكُ ﷻ (٤) القُدوسُ ﷻ (٥) السَّلامُ ﷻ (٦) المُؤْمِنُ ﷻ

(٧) المُهَيمِنُ ﷻ (٨) العَزيزُ ﷻ (٩) الجَبَّارُ ﷻ (١٠) المُتَكَبِّرُ ﷻ

(١١) الخَالِقُ ﷻ (١٢) البَارِئُ ﷻ (١٣) المُصَوِّرُ ﷻ (١٤) الغَفَّارُ ﷻ

Bismi 'Llāhi 'r-Raḥmāni 'r-Raḥīm, Wa li 'Llāhi 'l-'asmā'u 'l-ḥusnā fa 'd-d'ūhu bihā: Hūwa 'Llāhu 'Lladhī lā ilāha illā Hūwa ﷻ *(1) 'r-Raḥmānu* ﷻ *(2) 'r-Raḥīmu* ﷻ *(3) 'l-Maliku* ﷻ *(4) 'l-Quddusu* ﷻ *(5) as-Salāmu* ﷻ *(6) 'l-Mu'minu* ﷻ *(7) Al-Muhayminu* ﷻ *(8) 'l-'Azīzu* ﷻ *(9) 'l-Jabbāru* ﷻ *(10) 'l-Mutakabbiru* ﷻ *(11) 'l-Khāliqu* ﷻ *(12) 'l-Bāri'u* ﷻ *(13) 'l-Muṣawwiru* ﷻ *(14) 'l-Ghaffāru* ﷻ

"For to Allāh belong the Beautiful Names, so call upon Him by means of them." He is Allāh the One besides whom there in no other god ﷻ (1) The All-Merciful ﷻ (2) The Mercy-Giving ﷻ (3) The King ﷻ (4) The Holy ﷻ (5) The Saviour ﷻ (6) The Guardian of Faith ﷻ (7) The Protector ﷻ (8) The Mighty ﷻ (9) The Compeller ﷻ (10) The Victorious ﷻ (11) The Creator ﷻ (12) The Inventor ﷻ (13) The Designer ﷻ (14) The Forgiver ﷻ ➤

(١٥) القَهَّارُ ﷻ (١٦) الوَهَّابُ ﷻ (١٧) الرَّزَّاقُ ﷻ
(١٨) الفَتَّاحُ ﷻ (١٩) العَليمُ ﷻ (٢٠) القَابِضُ ﷻ (٢١) البَاسِطُ ﷻ
(٢٢) الخَافِضُ ﷻ (٢٣) الرَّافِعُ ﷻ (٢٤) المُعِزُّ ﷻ
(٢٥) المُذِلُّ ﷻ (٢٦) السَّمِيعُ ﷻ (٢٧) البَصِيرُ ﷻ
(٢٨) الحَكَمُ ﷻ (٢٩) العَدْلُ ﷻ (٣٠) اللَّطِيفُ ﷻ
(٣١) الخَبِيرُ ﷻ (٣٢) الحَلِيمُ ﷻ (٣٣) العَظِيمُ ﷻ
(٣٤) الغَفُورُ ﷻ (٣٥) الشَّكُورُ ﷻ (٣٦) العَلِيُّ ﷻ

(15) 'l-Qahhāru ﷻ *(16) 'l-Wahhābu* ﷻ *(17) 'r-Razzāqu* ﷻ *(18) Al-Fattāḥu* ﷻ *(19) 'l-ʿAlīmu* ﷻ *(20) 'l-Qābiḍu* ﷻ *(21) 'l-Bāsiṭu* ﷻ *(22) 'l-Khāfiḍu* ﷻ *(23) 'r-Rāfiʿu* ﷻ *(24) 'l-Muʿizzu* ﷻ *(25) 'l-Mudhillu* ﷻ *(26) 's-Samīʿu* ﷻ *(27) 'l-Baṣīru* ﷻ *(28) 'l-Ḥakamu* ﷻ *(29) 'l-ʿAdlu* ﷻ *(30) 'l-Laṭīfu* ﷻ *(31) 'l-Khabīru* ﷻ *(32) 'l-Ḥalīmu* ﷻ *(33) 'l-ʿAẓīmu* ﷻ *(34) 'l-Ghafūru* ﷻ *(35) 'sh-Shakūru* ﷻ *(36) 'l-ʿAlīyyu* ﷻ

(15) The Subduer ﷻ (16) The Bestower ﷻ (17) The Provider ﷻ (18) The Opener ﷻ (19) The Knower ﷻ (20) The Straitener ﷻ (21) The Expander ﷻ (22) The Abaser ﷻ (23) The Exalter ﷻ (24) The Honourer ﷻ (25) The Dishonourer ﷻ (26) The All-Hearing ﷻ (27) The All-Seeing ﷻ (28) The Judge ﷻ (29) The Just ﷻ (30) The Subtle ﷻ (31) The Aware ﷻ (32) The Forbearer ﷻ (33) The Magnificent ﷻ (34) The All-Forgiving ﷻ (35) The Benefactor ﷻ (36) The High ﷻ ➤

(٣٧) الكَبِيرُ ﷻ (٣٨) الحَفِيظُ ﷻ (٣٩) المُقِيتُ ﷻ
(٤٠) الحَسِيبُ ﷻ (٤١) الجَلِيلُ ﷻ (٤٢) الكَرِيمُ ﷻ
(٤٣) الرَّقِيبُ ﷻ (٤٤) المُجِيبُ ﷻ (٤٥) الوَاسِعُ ﷻ
(٤٦) الحَكِيمُ ﷻ (٤٧) الوَدُودُ ﷻ (٤٨) المَجِيدُ ﷻ
(٤٩) البَاعِثُ ﷻ (٥٠) الشَّهِيدُ ﷻ (٥١) الحَقُّ ﷻ (٥٢) الوَكِيلُ ﷻ
(٥٣) القَوِيُّ ﷻ (٥٤) المَتِينُ ﷻ (٥٥) الوَلِيُّ ﷻ (٥٦) الحَمِيدُ ﷻ
(٥٧) المُحْصِي ﷻ (٥٨) المُبدِئُ ﷻ (٥٩) المُعِيدُ ﷻ

(37) 'l-Kabīru ﷻ (38) 'l-Ḥafīẓu ﷻ (39) 'l-Muqītu ﷻ (40) 'l-Ḥasību ﷻ (41) 'l-Jalīlu ﷻ (42) 'l-Karīmu ﷻ (43) 'r-Raqību ﷻ (44) 'l-Mujību ﷻ (45) 'l-Wāsi'u ﷻ (46) 'l-Ḥakīmu ﷻ (47) 'l-Wadūdu ﷻ (48) 'l-Majīdu ﷻ (49) Al-Bā'ithu ﷻ (50) 'sh-Shahīdu ﷻ (51) 'l-Ḥaqqu ﷻ (52) 'l-Wakīlu ﷻ (53) 'l-Qawīyyu ﷻ (54) 'l-Matīnu ﷻ (55) 'l-Walīyu ﷻ (56) 'l-Ḥamīdu ﷻ (57) 'l-Muḥsī ﷻ (58) 'l-Mubdīu ﷻ (59) 'l-Mu'īdu ﷻ

(37) The Greatest ﷻ (38) The Preserver ﷻ (39) The Nourisher ﷻ (40) The Reckoner ﷻ (41) The Glorious ﷻ (42) The Generous ﷻ (43) The Observer ﷻ (44) The Responsive ﷻ (45) The All-Embracing ﷻ (46) The Wise ﷻ (47) The Loving ﷻ (48) The Majestic ﷻ (49) The Resurrector ﷻ (50) The Witness ﷻ (51) The Truth ﷻ (52) The Provident ﷻ (53) The Strong ﷻ (54) The Firm ﷻ (55) The Protecting Friend ﷻ (56) The Praiseworthy ﷻ (57) The Reckoner ﷻ (58) The Originator ﷻ (59) The Renewer ﷻ ➤

(٦٠) المُحْيِيُ ﷻ (٦١) المُمِيتُ ﷻ (٦٢) الحَيُّ ﷻ (٦٣) القَيُّومُ ﷻ
(٦٤) الوَاجِدُ ﷻ (٦٥) المَاجِدُ ﷻ (٦٦) الوَاحِدُ ﷻ (٦٧) الأَحَدُ ﷻ
(٦٨) الصَمَدُ ﷻ (٦٩) القَادِرُ ﷻ (٧٠) المُقتَدِرُ ﷻ (٧١) المُقَدِّمُ ﷻ
(٧٢) المُؤَخِّرُ ﷻ (٧٣) الأَوَّلُ ﷻ (٧٤) الآخِرُ ﷻ (٧٥) الظَّاهِرُ ﷻ
(٧٦) البَاطِنُ ﷻ (٧٧) الوَالِي ﷻ (٧٨) المُتَعَالِي ﷻ (٧٩) البَرُّ ﷻ
(٨٠) التَوَّابُ ﷻ (٨١) المُنْتَقِمُ ﷻ (٨٢) العفو ﷻ (٨٣) الرَؤُوفُ ﷻ

(60) 'l-Muḥyī ﷻ (61) 'l-Mumītu ﷻ (62) 'l-Ḥayyu ﷻ (63) 'l-Qayyūmu ﷻ (64)'l-Wājidu ﷻ (65) 'l-Mājidu ﷻ (66) 'l-Wāḥidu ﷻ (67) 'l-'Aḥadu ﷻ (68) 'ṣ-Ṣamadu ﷻ (69) 'l-Qādiru ﷻ (70) 'l-Muqtadiru ﷻ (71) 'l-Muqaddimu ﷻ (72) 'l-Muakhkhiru ﷻ (73) 'l-Āwwalu ﷻ (74) 'l-Ākhiru ﷻ (75) 'ẓ-Ẓāhiru ﷻ (76) 'l-Bāṭinu ﷻ (77) 'l-Wāli ﷻ (78) 'l-Muta'āli ﷻ (79) 'l-Barru ﷻ (80) 't-Tawwābu ﷻ (81) Al-Muntaqimu ﷻ (82) 'l-'Afūwwu ﷻ (83) 'r-Ra'ūfu ﷻ

(60) The Giver of Life ﷻ (61) The Giver of Death ﷻ (62) The Living ﷻ (63) The Self-Existing ﷻ (64) The Finder ﷻ (65) The Most Glorious ﷻ (66) The Unique ﷻ (67) The One ﷻ (68) The Eternal ﷻ (69) The Able ﷻ (70) The All-Powerful ﷻ (71) The Expediter ﷻ (72) The Delayer ﷻ (73) The First ﷻ (74) The Last ﷻ (75) The Manifest ﷻ (76) The Hidden ﷻ (77) The Governor ﷻ (78) The Supreme ﷻ (79) The Good ﷻ (80) The Acceptor of Repentance ﷻ (81) The Avenger ﷻ (82) The Pardoner ﷻ (83) The Gentle ﷻ ➢

(٨٤) مَالِكُ المُلْكِ ﷻ (٨٥) ذُو الجَلالِ وَالإِكرَامِ ﷻ (٨٦) المُقْسِطُ ﷻ
(٨٧) الجَامِعُ ﷻ (٨٨) الغَنِيُّ ﷻ (٨٩) المُغْنِيْ ﷻ (٩٠) المَانِعُ ﷻ
(٩١) الضَّارُّ ﷻ (٩٢) النَّافِعُ ﷻ (٩٣) النُّورُ ﷻ (٩٤) الهَادِي ﷻ
(٩٥) البَدِيعُ ﷻ (٩٦) البَاقِي ﷻ (٩٧) الوَارِثُ ﷻ (٩٨) الرَّشِيدُ ﷻ
(٩٩) الصَّبُورُ ﷻ الَّذِيْ لَمْ يَلِدْ وَلَمْ يُولَدْ وَلَمْ يَكُنْ لَهُ كُفُوًا أَحَدٌ لَيسَ كَمِثْلِهِ
شَيءٌ وَهُوَ السَّمِيعُ البَصِيرُ ❁

(84) Māliku 'l-mulki ﷻ (85) Dhu 'l-Jalāli wa 'l-'Ikrām ﷻ (86) 'l-Muqsiṭu ﷻ (87) 'l-Jāmi'u ﷻ (88) 'l-Ghanīyyu ﷻ (89) 'l-Mughnī ﷻ (90) 'l-Māni'u ﷻ (91) 'ḍ-Ḍārru ﷻ (92) 'n-Nāfi'u ﷻ (93) 'n-Nūru ﷻ (94) 'l-Hādi ﷻ (95) 'l-Badī'u ﷻ (96) 'l-Bāqī ﷻ (97) 'l-Wārithu ﷻ (98) 'r-Rashīdu ﷻ (99) 'ṣ-Ṣabūru ﷻ 'Lladhī lam yalid wa lam yūlad wa lam yakūn lahū kufūwan āḥad laysa ka-mithlihi shayun wa Hūwa 's-Samī'u 'l-Baṣīru •

(84) The Eternal Sovereign ﷻ (85) The Lord of Glory and Nobility ﷻ (86) The Equitable ﷻ (87) The Gatherer ﷻ (88) The Self-Sufficient ﷻ (89) The Enricher ﷻ (90) The Preventer of Harm ﷻ (91) The Afflicter ﷻ (92) The Creator of Good ﷻ (93) The Light ﷻ (94) The Guider ﷻ (95) The Originator ﷻ (96) The Everlasting ﷻ (97) The Inheritor ﷻ (98) The Guide ﷻ (99) The Patient ﷻThe One Who neither beget nor is begotten and And there is none like unto Him. There is nothing which resembles Him, and He is the All-Knowing, All-Seeing. ❁

ثُمَّ يُقرَأ هَذَا ٱلدُّعَاء:

Thumma yuqrā' hādhā 'd-du'ā'

Then recite this supplication:

اَللَّهُمَّ جَدِّدْ وَجَرِّدْ فِي هَذَا الوَقتِ وَفِي هَذِهِ السَّاعَةِ مِنْ صَلَوَاتِكَ التَّامَّاتِ وَتَحِيَّاتِكَ الزَّاكِيَاتِ وَرِضْوَانِكَ ٱلاَكبَرِ الاَتَمَّ ٱلأَدْوَمِ عَلَى أَكْمَلِ عَبدٍ ذَلِكَ فِي هَذَا ٱلعَالَمِ ٱلَّذِي أَقَمْتَهُ لَكَ ظِلاًّ وَجَعَلْتَهُ لِحَوَائِجِ خَلْقِكَ قِبلَةً وَمَحَلاًّ وَٱصْطَفَيْتَهُ لِنَفْسِكَ وَأَقَمْتَهُ بِحُجَّتِكَ وَأَظهَرْتَهُ بِصُورَتِكَ

Allāhumma jaddid wa jarrid fī hadhā 'l-waqti wa fī hādhihi 's-sā'ati min ṣalawātika 't-tāmāti wa taḥiyyātika 'z-zākiyāti wa riḍwānika 'l-akbaru 'l-atammu 'l-adwamu 'alā akmali 'abdin dhālika fī hādhā 'l-'ālami 'Lladhī aqamtahu laka ẓillan wa ja'altahu li-ḥawā'iji khalqika qiblatan wa maḥallan wa 'ṣṭafaytahu li-nafsika wa aqamtahu bi-ḥujjatika wa aẓhartahu bi-ṣūratika

O Allāh in this time and in this hour renew and single out from amongst Your perfect blessings, purifiying greetings and the greatest of Your complete and perfect pleasure, and send them upon the most perfect one amongst Your servants in this world, the one whom You have established as a shadow for Yourself, and You made him a point of direction and destination for fulfilling the needs of Your Creation. You have chosen him for Yourself, established him with Your proof, manifested him after Your image, ➤

وَاخْتَرْتَهُ مُستَوىً لِتَجَلِّيكَ وَمَنْزِلاً لِتَنفِيذِ أَوَامِرِكَ وَنَوَاهِيكَ فِي أَرْضِكَ وَسَمَوَاتِكَ وَوَاسِطَةً بَينَكَ وَبَينَ مُكَوِّنَاتِكَ وَبَلِّغْ سَلامَ عَبدِكَ هَذَا إِلَيْهِ (تذكر اسمك) فَعَلَيهِ مِنكَ الآنَ مِنْ عَبدِكَ أَشرَفُ التَحِيَّاتِ وَأَزْكَى التَّسلِيمَاتِ، اَللَّهُمَّ ذَكِّرْهُ بِي لِيَذْكُرَنِي عِنْدَكَ بِمَا أَنْتَ أَعْلَمُ أَنَّهُ نَافِعٌ لِي عَاجِلاً وَآجِلاً عَلَى قَدرِ مَعرِفَتِهِ بِكَ وَمَنزِلَتِهِ لَدَيْكَ

wa 'khtartahu mustawan li-tajallīka wa manzilan li-tanfīdhi awāmirika wa nawāhīka fī arḍika wa samāwatika wa wāsiṭatan baynaka wa bayna mukawwinātika wa balligh salām ʿabdika hādhā (your name) ilayhi fa-ʿalayhi mink al-āna min ʿabdika ashrafa 't-taḥiyyatī wa azkā 't-taslīmatī. Allāhumma dhakkirhu bī li-yadhkuranī ʿindaka bimā anta aʿlamu annahu nāfiʿun lī ʿājillan wa ājillan ʿalā qadri maʿrifatihi bika wa manzilatihi ladayka,

chose him fit for Your manifestation and the place for applying Your orders and prohibitions in your earth and heavens, and an intermediary between You and Your Creation. O Allāh! Deliver the greetings of this servant of Your's (your name ------) to him and upon him now from You and Your servant, the most honorable of salutations and the purest of greetings. O Allāh! Remind him of me so that he will remember me in Your presence regarding things which You know to be beneficial for me in this world and in the next, according to Your Knowledge of himself and his rank with You, ➢

لا عَلَى قَدْرِ عِلْمِيَ وَمُنْتَهَى فَهْمِي إِنَّكَ بِكُلِّ فَضْلٍ جَدِيرٌ وَعَلَى مَا تَشَاءُ قَدِيرٌ، اَللَّهُمَّ اجْعَلْنِي فِي قَلْبِ الْإِنْسَانِ الْكَامِلِ وَحَبِّبْهُ فِيَّ وَصَلَّى اللهُ عَلَى سَيِّدِنَا مُحَمَّدٍ وَعَلَى آلِهِ وَصَحْبِهِ عَدَدَ ذَرَّاتِ الْوُجُودِ وَعَدَدَ مَعلُومَاتِ اللهِ اللَّهُمَّ وَفِّقْنِي لِقِرَاءَتِهَا عَلَى الدَّوَامِ آمِينْ يَا رَبَّ الْعَالَمِينَ ❋

lā ʿalā qadri ʿilmīya wa muntahā fahmī, innaka bi-kulli faḍlin jadīrun wa ʿalā mā tashāʾu qadīrun. Allāhumma ʾjʿalnī fī qalbi ʾl-ʾinsāni ʾl-kāmili wa ḥabbibhu fiyya wa ṣalla ʾLlāhu ʿalā Sayyīdinā Muḥammadin wa ʿalā ālihi wa ṣaḥbihi ʿadada dharrati ʾl-wujūdi wa ʿadada maʿlūmāti ʿLlāhi. Allāhumma waffiqnī li-qirāʾatihā ʿalā ʾd-dawāmi, āmīn yā Rabba ʾl-ʿālamīn. •

and not according to the measure of my knowledge and the limits of my understanding. You are able to grant any favour and able to do as You choose, O Allāh! Place me in the heart of the perfect man, and make him to love me. And Allāh's blessings upon our master Muḥammad, his family and companions according to the number of atoms in existence and according to the knowledge of Allāh. O Allāh grant me to continuously recite it (the *Dalāʾil*). Amen, O Lord of All the Worlds. ❋

ثم تقرأ أسماءَ النَّبيِّ ﷺ

Asmā'u 'n-Nabī ﷺ

Then recite the Holy Names of Prophet Muḥammad ﷺ.

The one reciting these holy names must recite *ṣall-Allāhu 'alayhi wa sallam* (abbreviated ﷺ) after each name.

اللَّهُمَّ صَلِّ وسَلِّم وَبَارِكْ عَلَى مَنْ أَشْرَفُ أَسْمَائِهِ: (١) سَيِّدُنَا مُحَمَّدٌ ﷺ، (٢) سَيِّدُنَا أَحْمَد ﷺ، (٣) سَيِّدُنَا حَامِدٌ ﷺ، (٤) سَيِّدُنَا مَحْمُودٌ ﷺ، (٥) سَيِّدُنَا أَحِيدٌ ﷺ، (٦) سَيِّدُنَا وَحِيدٌ ﷺ، (٧) سَيِّدُنَا مَاحٍ ﷺ، (٨) سَيِّدُنَا حاشِرٌ ﷺ، (٩) سَيِّدُنَا عَاقِبٌ ﷺ، (١٠) سَيِّدُنَا طَهَ ﷺ،

Allāhumma ṣalli wa sallim wa bārik 'alā man ashrafa asmā'ihi (1) Sayyīdunā Muḥammadun ﷺ (2) Sayyīdunā Āḥmadu ﷺ (3) Sayyīdunā Ḥāmidun ﷺ (4) Sayyīdunā Maḥmūdun ﷺ (5) Sayyīdunā Aḥīdun ﷺ (6) Sayyīdunā Wāḥīdun ﷺ (7) Sayyīdunā Māḥin ﷺ (8) Sayyīdunā Ḥāshirun ﷺ (9) Sayyīdunā 'Aqibun ﷺ (10) Sayyīdunā Ṭāhā ﷺ

O Allāh, bless, exalt and grant peace to the one whom amongst his most honorable names are: (1) Our master the Praised One ﷺ (2) Our master the Most Praised ﷺ (3) Our master the Praiser ﷺ (4) Our master the Most Highly-Praised ﷺ (5) Our master Aḥīd (the Prophet's name in the Torah) ﷺ (6) Our master the Unique ﷺ (7) Our master the Effacer ﷺ (8) Our master the Gatherer ﷺ (9) Our master the Last in Succession ﷺ (10) Our master Ṭāḥā ﷺ ➤

(١١) سَيِّدُنَا يَسٓ ﷺ ، (١٢) سَيِّدُنَا طَاهِرٌ ﷺ ، (١٣) سَيِّدُنَا مُطَهَّرٌ ﷺ ،
(١٤) سَيِّدُنَا طَيِّبٌ ﷺ ، (١٥) سَيِّدُنَا سَيِّدٌ ، (١٦) سَيِّدُنَا رَسُولٌ ﷺ ،
(١٧) سَيِّدُنَا نبيٌّ ﷺ ، (١٨) سَيِّدُنَا رَسُولُ الرَّحْمَةِ ﷺ ، (١٩) سَيِّدُنَا قَيِّمٌ ﷺ ،
(٢٠) سَيِّدُنَا جَامِعٌ ﷺ ، (٢١) سَيِّدُنَا مُقْتَفٍ ﷺ ، (٢٢) سَيِّدُنَا مُقَفِّي ﷺ ،
(٢٣) سَيِّدُنَا رَسُولُ المَلَاحِمِ ﷺ ، (٢٤) سَيِّدُنَا رَسُولُ الرَّاحَةِ ﷺ ،
(٢٥) سَيِّدُنَا كَامِلٌ ﷺ ،

(11) Sayyīdunā Yāsīn ﷺ (12) Sayyīdunā Ṭāhirun ﷺ (13) Sayyīdunā Muṭṭāharun ﷺ (14) Sayyīdunā Ṭayyibun ﷺ (15) Sayyīdunā Sayyidun ﷺ (16) Sayyīdunā Rasūlun ﷺ (17) Sayyīdunā Nabīyyun ﷺ (18) Sayyīdunā Rasūlu 'r-raḥmati ﷺ (19) Sayyīdunā Qayyimun ﷺ (20) Sayyīdunā Jāmiʿun ﷺ (21) Sayyīdunā Muqtafin ﷺ (22) Sayyīdunā Muqaffī ﷺ (23) Sayyīdunā Rasūlu 'l-malāhimi ﷺ (24) Sayyīdunā Rasūlu 'r-Rāḥatun ﷺ (25) Sayyīdunā Kāmilun ﷺ

(11) Our master YaSīn ﷺ (12) Our master the Pure ﷺ (13) Our master the Purifier ﷺ (14) Our master the Good ﷺ (15) Our master the Master ﷺ (16) Our master the Messenger ﷺ (17) Our master the Prophet ﷺ (18) Our master the Messenger of Mercy ﷺ (19) Our master the Straight One ﷺ (20) Our master the Gatherer ﷺ (21) Our master the Selected One ﷺ (22) Our master the Best Example ﷺ (23) Our master the Messenger of Fierce Battles ﷺ (24) Our master the Messenger of Comfort ﷺ (25) Our master the Perfect One ﷺ ➢

(٢٦) سَيِّدُنَا إِكلِيلٌ ﷺ ، (٢٧) سَيِّدُنَا مُـدَّثِّرٌ ﷺ ، (٢٨) سَيِّدُنَا مُـزَّمِّلٌ ﷺ ،
(٢٩) سَيِّدُنَا عَبدُ اللهِ ﷺ ، (٣٠) سَيِّدُنَا حَبِيبُ اللهِ ﷺ ،
(٣١) سَيِّدُنَا صَفِيُّ اللهِ ﷺ ، (٣٢) سَيِّدُنَا نَجِيُّ اللهِ ﷺ ،
(٣٣) سَيِّدُنَا كَلِيمُ اللهِ ﷺ ، (٣٤) سَيِّدُنَا خَاتَمُ الْأَنْبِيَاءِ ﷺ ،
(٣٥) سَيِّدُنَا خَاتَمُ الرُّسُلِ ﷺ ، (٣٦) سَيِّدُنَا مُحْيِي ﷺ ، (٣٧) سَيِّدُنَا مُنْجٍ ﷺ ،
(٣٨) سَيِّدُنَا مُذَكِّرٌ ﷺ ،

(26) Sayyīdunā Iklīlun ﷺ (27) Sayyīdunā Mudaththirun ﷺ (28) Sayyīdunā Muzammilun ﷺ (29) Sayyīdunā ʿAbdullāhi ﷺ (30) Sayyīdunā Ḥabībillāhi ﷺ (31) Sayyīdunā Ṣafiyyullāhi ﷺ (32) Sayyīdunā Najīyyullāhi ﷺ (33) Sayyīdunā Kalīmullāhi ﷺ (34) Sayyīdunā Khātimu 'l-Anbīyā'i ﷺ (35) Sayyīdunā Khātimu 'r-rusuli ﷺ (36) Sayyīdunā Muḥīyy ﷺ (37) Sayyīdunā Munjin ﷺ (38) Sayyīdunā Mudhakkirun ﷺ

(26) Our master the Crown ﷺ (27) Our master the Covered One ﷺ (28) Our master the One Wrapped Up ﷺ (29) Our master the Slave of Allāh ﷺ (30) Our master the Beloved of Allāh ﷺ (31) Our master the Intimate of Allāh ﷺ (32) Our master the Confidant of Allāh ﷺ (33) Our master the Speaker with Allāh ﷺ (34) Our master Seal of the Prophets ﷺ (35) Our master the Seal of the Messengers ﷺ (36) Our master the Reviver ﷺ (37) Our master the Rescuer ﷺ (38) Our master the Reminder ﷺ ➤

(٣٩) سَيِّدُنَا نَاصِرٌ ﷺ ، (٤٠) سَيِّدُنَا مَنْصُورٌ ﷺ ، (٤١) سَيِّدُنَا نَبِيُّ الرَّحْمَةِ ﷺ ،

(٤٢)سَيِّدُنَا نَبِيُّ التَّوبَةِ ﷺ ، (٤٣) سَيِّدُنَا حَرِيصٌ عَلَيكُم ﷺ ،

(٤٤) سَيِّدُنَا مَعلُومٌ ﷺ ، (٤٥) سَيِّدُنَا شَهِيرٌ ﷺ ، (٤٦) سَيِّدُنَا شَاهِدٌ ﷺ ،

(٤٧) سَيِّدُنَا شَهِيدٌ ﷺ ، (٤٨) سَيِّدُنَا مَشهُودٌ ﷺ ، (٤٩) سَيِّدُنَا بَشِيرٌ ﷺ ،

(٥٠) سَيِّدُنَا مُبَشِّرٌ ﷺ ،(٥١) سَيِّدُنَا نَذِيرٌ ﷺ ،

(39) Sayyīdunā Nāṣirun ﷺ (40) Sayyīdunā Manṣūrun ﷺ (41) Sayyīdunā Nabīyyu 'r-raḥmati ﷺ (42) Sayyīdunā Nabīyyu 't-tawbati ﷺ (43) Sayyīdunā Ḥarīsun 'alaykum ﷺ (44) Sayyīdunā Ma'lūmun ﷺ (45) Sayyīdunā Shahīrun ﷺ (46) Sayyīdunā Shāhidun ﷺ (47) Sayyīdunā Shahīdun ﷺ (48) Sayyīdunā Mash-hūdun ﷺ (49) Sayyīdunā Bashīrun ﷺ (50) Sayyīdunā Mubashshirun ﷺ (51) Sayyīdunā Nadhīrun ﷺ

(39) Our master the Helper ﷺ (40) Our master Victorious One ﷺ (41) Our master Prophet of Mercy ﷺ (42) Our master Prophet of Repentance ﷺ (43) Our master Watchful over you ﷺ (44) Our master the Known One ﷺ (45) Our master the Famous ﷺ (46) Our master the Witnesser ﷺ (47) Our master the Witness ﷺ (48) Our master the Attestor ﷺ (49) Our master the Glad-tidings ﷺ (50) Our master the Spreader of Good News ﷺ (51) Our master the Warner ﷺ ➤

(٥٢) سَيِّدُنَا مُنْذِرٌ ﷺ ، (٥٣) سَيِّدُنَا نُورٌ ﷺ ، (٥٤) سَيِّدُنَا سِراجٌ ﷺ ، (٥٥) سَيِّدُنَا مِصْبَاحٌ ﷺ ، (٥٦) سَيِّدُنَا هُدًى ﷺ ، (٥٧) سَيِّدُنَا مَهْدِيٌّ (٥٨) سَيِّدُنَا مُنِيرٌ ﷺ ، (٥٩) سَيِّدُنَا دَاعٍ ﷺ ، (٦٠) سَيِّدُنَا مَدْعُوٌّ ﷺ ، (٦١) سَيِّدُنَا مُجِيبٌ ﷺ ، (٦٢) سَيِّدُنَا مُجَابٌ ﷺ ، (٦٣) سَيِّدُنَا حَفِيٌّ ﷺ ، (٦٤) سَيِّدُنَا عَفُوٌّ ﷺ ، (٦٥) سَيِّدُنَا وَلِيٌّ ﷺ ، (٦٦) سَيِّدُنَا حَقٌّ ﷺ ،

(52) Sayyīdunā Mundhirun ﷺ (53) Sayyīdunā Nūrun ﷺ (54) Sayyīdunā Sirājun ﷺ (55) Sayyīdunā Misbāḥun ﷺ (56) Sayyīdunā Hudan ﷺ (57) Sayyīdunā Mahdīyyun ﷺ (58) Sayyīdunā Munīrun ﷺ (59) Sayyīdunā Daʿin ﷺ (60) Sayyīdunā Madʿūwwun ﷺ (61) Sayyīdunā Mujībun ﷺ (62) Sayyīdunā Mujābun ﷺ (63) Sayyīdunā Ḥafīyyu ﷺ (64) Sayyīdunā ʿAfūwwun ﷺ (65) Sayyīdunā Walīyyun ﷺ (66) Sayyīdunā Ḥaqqun ﷺ

(52) Our master the Admonisher ﷺ (53) Our master the Light ﷺ (54) Our master the Lamp ﷺ (55) Our master the Lantern ﷺ (56) Our master the Guidance ﷺ (57) Our master the Rightly-Guided ﷺ (58) Our master the Illumined One ﷺ (59) Our master the Caller ﷺ (60) Our master the Called One ﷺ (61) Our master the Responsive ﷺ (62) Our master the One Responded to ﷺ (64) Our master the Overlooker of sins ﷺ (65) Our master the Friend ﷺ (66) Our master the Truth ﷺ ➤

(٦٧) سَيِّدُنَا قَوِيٌّ ﷺ ، (٦٨) سَيِّدُنَا أَمِينٌ ﷺ ، (٦٩) سَيِّدُنَا مَأْمُونٌ ﷺ ،

(٧٠) سَيِّدُنَا كَرِيمٌ ﷺ ، (٧١) سَيِّدُنَا مُكَرَّمٌ ﷺ ، (٧٢) سَيِّدُنَا مَكِينٌ ﷺ ،

(٧٣) سَيِّدُنَا مَتِينٌ ﷺ ، (٧٤) سَيِّدُنَا مُبِينٌ ﷺ ، (٧٥) سَيِّدُنَا مُؤَمَّلٌ ﷺ ،

(٧٦) سَيِّدُنَا وَصولٌ ﷺ ، (٧٧) سَيِّدُنَا ذُو قُوَّةٍ ﷺ ، (٧٨) سَيِّدُنَا ذُو حُرمَةٍ ﷺ ،

(٧٩) سَيِّدُنَا ذُو مَكَانَةٍ ﷺ ، (٨٠) سَيِّدُنَا ذُو عِزٍّ ﷺ ،

(67) Sayyīdunā Qawīyyun ﷺ (68) Sayyīdunā Amīnun ﷺ (69) Sayyīdunā Mā'mūnun ﷺ (70) Sayyīdunā Karīmun ﷺ (71) Sayyīdunā Mukarramun ﷺ (72) Sayyīdunā Makīnun ﷺ (73) Sayyīdunā Matīnun ﷺ (74) Sayyīdunā Mubīnun ﷺ (75) Sayyīdunā Mūmmalun ﷺ (76) Sayyīdunā Waṣūlun ﷺ (77) Sayyīdunā Dhū-quwwatin ﷺ (78) Sayyīdunā Dhū-Ḥurmatin ﷺ (79) Sayyīdunā Dhū-Makānatin ﷺ (80) Sayyīdunā Dhū-ʿIzzin ﷺ

(67) Our master the Powerful ﷺ (68) Our master the Trustworthy ﷺ (69) Our master the Trusted ﷺ (70) Our master the Generous ﷺ (71) Our master the Honored ﷺ (72) Our master the Firm ﷺ (73) Our master the Steadfast ﷺ (74) Our master the Evident ﷺ (75) Our master the One Hoped for ﷺ (76) Our master the Connection ﷺ (77) Our master the Possessor of Power ﷺ (78) Our master the Possessor of Honor ﷺ (79) Our master the Possessor of Firmness ﷺ (80) Our master the Possessor of Might ﷺ ➢

(٨١) سَيِّدُنَا ذُو فَضْلٍ ﷺ ، (٨٢) سَيِّدُنَا مُطَاعٌ ﷺ ، (٨٣) سَيِّدُنَا مُطِيعٌ ﷺ ،
(٨٤) سَيِّدُنَا قَدَمُ صِدْقٍ ﷺ ، (٨٥) سَيِّدُنَا رَحْمَةٌ ﷺ ،
(٨٦) سَيِّدُنَا بُشْرَى ﷺ ، (٨٧) سَيِّدُنَا غَوْثٌ ﷺ ، (٨٨) سَيِّدُنَا غَيْثٌ ﷺ ،
(٨٩) سَيِّدُنَا غِيَاثٌ ﷺ ، (٩٠) سَيِّدُنَا نِعْمَةُ اللهِ ﷺ ، (٩١) سَيِّدُنَا هَدِيَّةُ اللهِ ﷺ ،
(٩٢) سَيِّدُنَا عُرْوَةٌ وُثْقَى ﷺ ، (٩٣) سَيِّدُنَا صِرَاطُ اللهِ ﷺ ،

(81) Sayyīdunā Dhū-faḍlin ﷺ (82) Sayyīdunā Muṭāʿun ﷺ (83) Sayyīdunā Muṭīʿun ﷺ (84) Sayyīdunā Qadamu Sidqin ﷺ (85) Sayyīdunā Raḥmatun ﷺ (86) Sayyīdunā Bushrā ﷺ (87) Sayyīdunā Ghawthun ﷺ (88) Sayyīdunā Ghaythun ﷺ (89) Sayyīdunā Ghīyāthun ﷺ (90) Sayyīdunā Niʿmatullāhi ﷺ (91) Sayyīdunā Hadīyyatullāhi ﷺ (92) Sayyīdunā ʿUrwatun Wuthqā ﷺ (93) Sayyīdunā Sirāṭullāhi ﷺ

(81) Our master the Possessor of Grace ﷺ (82) Our master the One Obeyed ﷺ (83) Our master the Obedient ﷺ (84) Our master the Firm Foothold ﷺ (85) Our master Mercy ﷺ (86) Our master the Good News ﷺ (87) Our master the Redeemer ﷺ (88) Our master the Rain ﷺ (89) Our master the Rescuer ﷺ (90) Our master the Favor of Allāh ﷺ (91) Our master the Gift of Allāh ﷺ (92) Our master the Trusty Handhold ﷺ (93) Our master the Path of Allāh ﷺ ➢

(٩٤) سَيِّدُنَا صِرَاطٌ مُسْتَقِيمٌ ﷺ ، (٩٥) سَيِّدُنَا ذِكْرُ اللهِ ﷺ ،

(٩٦) سَيِّدُنَا سَيْفُ اللهِ ﷺ ، (٩٧) سَيِّدُنَا حِزْبُ اللهِ ﷺ ،

(٩٨) سَيِّدُنَا النَّجْمُ الثَّاقِبُ ﷺ ، (٩٩) سَيِّدُنَا مُصْطَفَى ﷺ ،

(١٠٠) سَيِّدُنَا مُجْتَبَى ﷺ ، (١٠١) سَيِّدُنَا مُنْتَقَى ﷺ ،(١٠٢) سَيِّدُنَا أُمِّيٌّ ﷺ ،

(١٠٣) سَيِّدُنَا مُخْتَارٌ ﷺ ، (١٠٤) سَيِّدُنَا أَجِيرٌ ﷺ ، (١٠٥) سَيِّدُنَا جَبَّارٌ ﷺ ،

(١٠٦) سَيِّدُنَا أَبُو الْقَاسِمِ ﷺ ،

(94) Sayyīdunā Sirāṭun Mustaqīmun ﷺ *(95) Sayyīdunā Dhikrullāhi* ﷺ *(96) Sayyīdunā Sayfullāhi* ﷺ *(97) Sayyīdunā Ḥizbullāhi* ﷺ *(98) Sayyīdunā an-Najmu 'th-Tḥāqibu* ﷺ *(99) Sayyīdunā Musṭafā* ﷺ *(100) Sayyīdunā Mujtabā* ﷺ *(101) Sayyīdunā Muntaqā* ﷺ *(102) Sayyīdunā Ummīyyun* ﷺ *(103) Sayyīdunā Mukhtārun* ﷺ *(104) Sayyīdunā Ajīrun* ﷺ *(105) Sayyīdunā Jabbārun* ﷺ *(106) Sayyīdunā Abū 'l-Qāsimi* ﷺ

(94) Our master the Straight Path ﷺ (95) Our master the Remembrance of Allāh ﷺ (96) Our master the Sword of Allāh ﷺ (97) Our master Party of Allāh ﷺ (98) Our master the Piercing Star ﷺ (99) Our master the Chosen One ﷺ (100) Our master the Singled-out One (101) Our master the Selected One ﷺ (102) Our master the Unlettered ﷺ (103) Our master the Chosen ﷺ (104) Our master Allāh's Worker ﷺ (105) Our master the Compelling One ﷺ (106) Our master Father of Qāsim ﷺ ➤

(١٠٧) سَيِّدُنَا أَبُو الطَّاهِرِ ﷺ ، (١٠٨) سَيِّدُنَا أَبُو الطَّيِّبِ ﷺ ،

(١٠٩) سَيِّدُنَا أَبُو إِبْرَاهِيمَ ﷺ ، (١١٠) سَيِّدُنَا مُشَفَّعٌ ﷺ ،

(١١١) سَيِّدُنَا شَفِيعٌ ﷺ ، (١١٢) سَيِّدُنَا صَالِحٌ ﷺ ،

(١١٣) سَيِّدُنَا مُصْلِحٌ ﷺ ، (١١٤) سَيِّدُنَا مُهَيْمِنٌ ﷺ ،

(١١٥) سَيِّدُنَا صَادِقٌ ﷺ ، (١١٦) سَيِّدُنَا مُصَدَّقٌ ﷺ ،

(١١٧) ، سَيِّدُنَا صِدْقٌ ﷺ ، (١١٨) سَيِّدُنَا سَيِّدُ الْمُرْسَلِينَ ﷺ ،

(107) Sayyidunā Abū 'ṭ-Ṭāhiri ﷺ *(108) Sayyidunā Abū 'ṭ-Ṭayyibi* ﷺ *(109) Sayyidunā Abū Ibrāhīma* ﷺ *(110) Sayyidunā Mushaffa'un* ﷺ *(111) Sayyidunā Shafī'un* ﷺ *(112) Sayyidunā Ṣāliḥun* ﷺ *(113) Sayyidunā Muṣliḥun* ﷺ *(114) Sayyidunā Muhayminun* ﷺ *(115) Sayyidunā Ṣādiqun* ﷺ *(116) Sayyidunā Muṣaddaqun* ﷺ *(117) Sayyidunā Ṣidqun* ﷺ *(118) Sayyidunā Sayyidu 'l-Mursalīna* ﷺ

(107) Our master Father of Ṭāhir ﷺ (108) Our master Father of Ṭayyib ﷺ (109) Our master Father of Abraham ﷺ (110) Our master the One Whose Intercession is Accepted ﷺ (111) Our master the Intercessor ﷺ (112) Our master the Righteous ﷺ (113) Our master the Conciliator ﷺ (114) Our master the Guardian ﷺ (115) Our master the Truthful ﷺ (116) Our master the Confirmer ﷺ (117) Our master Sincerity ﷺ (118) Our master the Master of Messengers ﷺ ➢

(١١٩) سَيِّدُنَا إِمَامُ الْمُتَّقِينَ ﷺ ، (١٢٠) سَيِّدُنَا قَائِدُ الغُرِّ الْمُحَجَّلِينَ ﷺ ، (١٢١) سَيِّدُنَا خَلِيلُ الرَّحْمَنِ ﷺ ، (١٢٢) سَيِّدُنَا بَرٌّ ﷺ ، (١٢٣) سَيِّدُنَا مَبَرٌّ ﷺ ، (١٢٤) سَيِّدُنَا وَجِيهٌ ﷺ ، (١٢٥) سَيِّدُنَا نَصِيحٌ ﷺ ، (١٢٦) سَيِّدُنَا نَاصِحٌ ﷺ ،(١٢٧) سَيِّدُنَا وَكِيلٌ ﷺ ، (١٢٨) سَيِّدُنَا مُتوكِلٌّ ﷺ ، (١٢٩) سَيِّدُنَا كَفِيلٌ ﷺ ، (١٣٠) سَيِّدُنَا شَفِيقٌ ﷺ ، (١٣١) سَيِّدُنَا مُقِيمُ السُّنَّةِ ﷺ ،

(119) Sayyīdunā Imāmu 'l-Muttaqīna ﷺ (120) Sayyīdunā Qā'idu 'l-ghurri 'l-Muḥajjalīna ﷺ (121) Sayyīdunā Khalīlu 'r-Raḥmāni ﷺ (122) Sayyīdunā Barrun ﷺ (123) Sayyīdunā Mabarrun ﷺ (124) Sayyīdunā Wajīhun ﷺ (125) Sayyīdunā Naṣīḥun ﷺ (126) Sayyīdunā Nāṣiḥun ﷺ (127) Sayyīdunā Wakīlun ﷺ (128) Sayyīdunā Mutawakkilun ﷺ (129) Sayyīdunā Kafīlun ﷺ (130) Sayyīdunā Shafīqun ﷺ (131) Sayyīdunā Muqīmu 's-Sunnati ﷺ

(119) Our master Leader of the God-Fearing ﷺ (120) Our master Guide of the Bright Shining Ones ﷺ (121) Our master Friend of the Merciful ﷺ (122) Our master the Pious ﷺ (123) Our master the Venerated ﷺ (124) Our master the Eminent ﷺ (125) Our master the Advisor ﷺ (126) Our master the Counselor ﷺ (127) Our master the Advocate ﷺ (128) Our master Reliant on Allāh ﷺ (129) Our master the Guarantor ﷺ (130) Our master the Benevolent ﷺ (131) Our master Establisher of the Way ﷺ ➤

(١٣٢) سَيِّدُنَا مُقَدَّسٌ ﷺ ، (١٣٣) سَيِّدُنَا رُوحُ الْقُدُسِ ﷺ ،

(١٣٤) سَيِّدُنَا رُوحُ الحَقِّ ﷺ ، (١٣٥) سَيِّدُنَا رُوحُ القِسطِ ﷺ ،

(١٣٦) سَيِّدُنَا كَافٍ ﷺ ، (١٣٧) سَيِّدُنَا مُكتفٍ ﷺ ،

(١٣٨) سَيِّدُنَا بَالِغٌ ﷺ ، (١٣٩) سَيِّدُنَا مُبَلِّغٌ ﷺ ، (١٤٠) سَيِّدُنَا شَافٍ ﷺ ،

(١٤١) سَيِّدُنَا وَاصِلٌ ﷺ ، (١٤٢) سَيِّدُنَا مَوصُولٌ ﷺ ،

(١٤٣) سَيِّدُنَا سَابِقٌ ﷺ ،(١٤٤) سَيِّدُنَا سَائِقٌ ﷺ ،

(132) Sayyīdunā Muqaddansu ﷺ (133) Sayyīdunā Rūḥu 'l-Qudusi ﷺ (134) Sayyīdunā Rūḥu 'l-Ḥaqqi ﷺ (135) Sayyīdunā Rūḥu 'l-Qisṭi ﷺ (136) Sayyīdunā Kāfin ﷺ (137) Sayyīdunā Muktafin ﷺ (138) Sayyīdunā Bālighun ﷺ (139) Sayyīdunā Muballighun ﷺ (140) Sayyīdunā Shāfin ﷺ (141) Sayyīdunā Wāṣilun ﷺ (142) Sayyīdunā Mawṣūlun ﷺ (143) Sayyīdunā Sābiqun ﷺ (144) Sayyīdunā Sā'iqun ﷺ

(132) Our master the Sacred ﷺ (133) Our master the Holy Spirit ﷺ (134) Our master the Spirit of Truth ﷺ (135) Our master the Spirit of Justice ﷺ (136) Our master the Qualified ﷺ (137) Our master the Broad-Shouldered One ﷺ (138) Our master the Proclaimer ﷺ (139) Our master the Informer ﷺ (140) Our master the Healing ﷺ (141) Our master the Inseparable Friend ﷺ (142) Our master the One Connected to Allāh ﷺ (143) Our master the Foremost ﷺ (144) Our master the Driver ﷺ ➤

(١٤٥) سَيِّدُنَا هَادٍ ﷺ ، (١٤٦) سَيِّدُنَا مُهدٍ ﷺ ، (١٤٧) سَيِّدُنَا مُقَدَّمٌ ﷺ ،

(١٤٨) سَيِّدُنَا عَزِيزٌ ﷺ ، (١٤٩) سَيِّدُنَا فَاضِلٌ ﷺ ،

(١٥٠) سَيِّدُنَا مُفَضَّلٌ ﷺ ، (١٥١) سَيِّدُنَا فَاتِحٌ ﷺ ، (١٥٢) سَيِّدُنَا مِفْتَاحٌ ﷺ ،

(١٥٣) سَيِّدُنَا مِفْتَاحُ الرَّحْمَةِ ﷺ ، (١٥٤) سَيِّدُنَا مِفْتَاحُ الْجَنَّةِ ﷺ ،

(١٥٥) سَيِّدُنَا عَلَمُ الإِيمَانِ ﷺ ، (١٥٦) سَيِّدُنَا عَلَمُ الْيَقِينِ ﷺ ،

(١٥٧) سَيِّدُنَا دَلِيلُ الْخَيْرَاتِ ﷺ ،

(145) Sayyīdunā Hādin ﷺ (146) Sayyīdunā Muhtadin ﷺ (147) Sayyīdunā Muqaddamun ﷺ (148) Sayyīdunā ʿAzīzun ﷺ (149) Sayyīdunā Fāḍilun ﷺ (150) Sayyīdunā Mufaḍḍalun ﷺ (151) Sayyīdunā Fātiḥun ﷺ (152) Sayyīdunā Miftāḥun ﷺ (153) Sayyīdunā Miftāḥu 'r-Raḥmah ﷺ (154) Sayyīdunā Miftāḥu 'l-Jannah ﷺ (155) Sayyīdunā ʿAlamu 'l-Īmāni ﷺ (156) Sayyīdunā ʿAlamu 'l-Yaqīni ﷺ (157) Sayyīdunā Dalīlu 'l-Khayrāti ﷺ

(145) Our master the Guide ﷺ (146) Our master the Guided ﷺ (147) Our master the Overseer ﷺ (148) Our master the Mighty ﷺ (149) Our master the Outstanding ﷺ (150) Our master the Favoured ﷺ (151) Our master the Opener ﷺ (152) Our master the Key ﷺ (153) Our master Key to Mercy ﷺ (154) Our master Key to the Garden ﷺ (155) Our master Teacher of the Faith ﷺ (156) Our master the Teacher of Certainty ﷺ (157) Our master Guide to Good Things ﷺ ➢

(١٥٨) سَيِّدُنَا مُصَحِّحُ الحَسَناتِ ﷺ ، (١٥٩) سَيِّدُنَا مُقِيلُ الْعَثَراتِ ﷺ ،

(١٦٠) سَيِّدُنَا صَفُوحٌ عنِ الزَّلَّاتِ ﷺ ، (١٦١) سَيِّدُنَا صَاحِبُ الشَّفَاعَةِ ﷺ ،

(١٦٢) سَيِّدُنَا صَاحِبُ المَقَامِ ﷺ ، (١٦٣) سَيِّدُنَا صَاحِبُ القَدَمِ ﷺ ،

(١٦٤) سَيِّدُنَا مَخْصُوصٌ بِالعِزِّ ﷺ ، (١٦٥) سَيِّدُنَا مَخْصُوصٌ بِالمَجْدِ ﷺ ،

(١٦٦) سَيِّدُنَا مَخْصُوصٌ بِالشَّرَفِ ﷺ ،(١٦٧) سَيِّدُنَا صَاحِبُ الوَسِيْلَةِ ﷺ ،

(158) Sayyidunā Musaḥḥihu 'l-Ḥasanāti ﷺ (159) Sayyidunā Muqīlu 'l-ʿAtharāti ﷺ (160) Sayyidunā Ṣafūḥun ʿani 'z-Zallāti ﷺ (161) Sayyidunā Ṣāḥibu 'l-Shafāʿati ﷺ (162) Sayyidunā Ṣāḥibu 'l-Maqāmi ﷺ (163) Sayyidunā Ṣāḥibu 'l-qadami ﷺ (164) Sayyidunā Makhṣūṣun bi 'l-ʿIzzi ﷺ (165) Sayyidunā Makhṣūṣun bi 'l-Majdi ﷺ (166) Sayyidunā Makhṣūṣun bi 'sh-Sharafi ﷺ (167) Sayyidunā Ṣāḥibu 'l-Wasīlati ﷺ

(158) Our master the Verifier of Good Deeds ﷺ (159) Our master the Remover of Obstacles ﷺ (160) Our master the Pardoner of Sins ﷺ (161) Our master the Possessor of Intercession ﷺ (162) Our master the Possessor of the Honored Station ﷺ (163) Our master the Owner of the Footprint ﷺ (164) Our master Distinguished with Might ﷺ (165) Distinguished with Glory ﷺ (166) Our master Distinguished with Nobility ﷺ (167) Our master the Possessor of the Closest Access ﷺ ➤

(١٦٨) سَيِّدُنَا صَاحِبُ السَّيْفِ ﷺ ، (١٦٩) سَيِّدُنَا صَاحِبُ الفَضِيلَةِ ﷺ ،

(١٧٠) سَيِّدُنَا صَاحِبُ الإِزَارِ ﷺ ، (١٧١) سَيِّدُنَا صَاحِبُ الْحُجَّةِ ﷺ ،

(١٧٢) سَيِّدُنَا صَاحِبُ السُّلْطَانِ ﷺ ، (١٧٣) سَيِّدُنَا صَاحِبُ الرِّدَاءِ ﷺ ،

(١٧٤) سَيِّدُنَا صَاحِبُ الدَّرَجَةِ الرَّفِيعَةِ ﷺ ، (١٧٥) سَيِّدُنَا صَاحِبُ التَّاجِ ﷺ ،

(١٧٦) سَيِّدُنَا صَاحِبُ المِغْفَرِ ﷺ ، (١٧٧) سَيِّدُنَا صَاحِبُ اللِّوَاءِ ﷺ ،

(١٧٨) سَيِّدُنَا صَاحِبُ المِعْرَاجِ ﷺ،

(168) Sayyīdunā Ṣāḥibu 's-Sayfi ﷺ (169) Sayyīdunā Ṣāḥibu 'l-Faḍīlata ﷺ (170) Sayyīdunā Ṣāḥibu 'l-Izāri ﷺ (171) Sayyīdunā Ṣāḥibu 'l-Ḥujjati ﷺ (172) Sayyīdunā Ṣāḥibu 's-Sulṭāni ﷺ (173) Sayyīdunā Ṣāḥibu 'r-Ridā'i ﷺ (174) Sayyīdunā Ṣāḥibu' d-Darajati 'r-Rafiʿati ﷺ (175) Sayyīdunā Ṣāḥibu' t-Tāji ﷺ (176) Sayyīdunā Ṣāḥibu 'l-Mighfari ﷺ (177) Sayyīdunā Ṣāḥibu 'l-Liwā'i ﷺ (178) Sayyīdunā Ṣāḥibu 'l-Miʿrāji ﷺ

(168) Our master the Owner of the Sword ﷺ (169) the Possessor of Pre-Eminence ﷺ (170) Our master the Owner of the Waist-Wrap ﷺ (171) Our master the Possessor of Proof ﷺ (172) Possessor of Authority ﷺ (173) Our master the Owner of the Robe ﷺ (174) Our master Possessor of the Lofty Rank ﷺ (175) Our master the Possessor of the Crown ﷺ (176) Our master the Possessor of Forgiveness ﷺ (177) Our master the Possessor of the Flag ﷺ (178) Our master the Owner of the Night Journey ﷺ ➢

(١٧٩) سَيِّدُنَا صَاحِبُ الْقَضِيبِ ﷺ ، (١٨٠) صَاحِبُ الْبُرَاقِ ﷺ ،
(١٨١) سَيِّدُنَا صَاحِبُ الْخَاتَمِ ﷺ ، (١٨٢) سَيِّدُنَا صَاحِبُ الْعَلَامَةِ ﷺ ،
(١٨٣) سَيِّدُنَا صَاحِبُ الْبُرْهَانِ ﷺ ، (١٨٤) سَيِّدُنَا صَاحِبُ الْبَيَانِ ﷺ ،
(١٨٥) سَيِّدُنَا فَصِيحُ اللِّسَانِ ﷺ ، (١٨٦) سَيِّدُنَا مُطَهَّرُ الْجَنَانِ ﷺ ،
(١٨٧) سَيِّدُنَا رَؤُوفٌ ﷺ ، (١٨٨) سَيِّدُنَا رَحِيمٌ ﷺ ، (١٨٩) سَيِّدُنَا أُذُنُ خَيْرٍ ﷺ ،
(١٩٠) سَيِّدُنَا صَحِيحُ الإِسْلَامِ ﷺ ،

(179) Sayyīdunā Ṣāḥibu 'l-Qaḍībi ﷺ (180) Sayyīdunā Ṣāḥibu 'l-Burāqi ﷺ (181) Sayyīdunā Ṣāḥibu 'l-Khātami ﷺ (182) Sayyīdunā Ṣāḥibu 'l-'Alāmati ﷺ (183) Sayyīdunā Ṣāḥibu 'l-Burhāni ﷺ (184) Sayyīdunā Ṣāḥibu 'l-Bayāni ﷺ (185) Sayyīdunā Faṣīḥu 'l-Lisāni ﷺ (186) Sayyīdunā Muṭṭaharu 'l-Janāni ﷺ (187) Sayyīdunā Ra'ūfun ﷺ (188) Sayyīdunā Raḥīm ﷺ (189) Sayyīdunā Udhunu Khayrin ﷺ (190) Sayyīdunā Ṣaḥīḥu 'l-'Islāmi ﷺ

(179) Our master Possessor of the Staff ﷺ (180) Our master Owner of Burāq ﷺ (181) Our master Owner of the Ring ﷺ (182) Our master Owner of the Sign ﷺ (183) Our master Possessor of the Evidence ﷺ (184) Our master Possessor of Evident Proof ﷺ (185) Our master the Good Communicator ﷺ (186) Our master Purifier of Souls ﷺ (187) Our master the Kind ﷺ (188) Our master the Mercy-Giving (189) Our master the Good Listener ﷺ (190) Our master Perfect Islām ﷺ ➤

(١٩١) سَيِّدُنَا سَيِّدُ الكَوْنَيْنِ ﷺ ،(١٩٢) سَيِّدُنَا عَيْنُ النَعِيمِ ﷺ ،
(١٩٣) سَيِّدُنَا عَيْنُ الغُرِّ ﷺ ، (١٩٤) سَيِّدُنَا سَعْدُ الله ﷺ ،
(١٩٥) سَيِّدُنَا سَعْدُ الخَلْقِ ﷺ ، (١٩٦) سَيِّدُنَا خَطِيبُ الأُمَمِ ﷺ ،
(١٩٧) سَيِّدُنَا عَلَمُ الْهُدَى ﷺ ، (١٩٨) سَيِّدُنَا كَاشِفُ الكُرَبِ ﷺ ،
(١٩٩) سَيِّدُنَا رَافِعُ الرُتَبِ ﷺ ،(٢٠٠) سَيِّدُنَا عِزُّ العَرَبِ ﷺ ،
(٢٠١) سَيِّدُنَا صَاحِبُ الفَرَجِ صَلَّى الله عَلَيهِ وَعَلَى آلِهِ

(191) Sayyīdunā Sayyidu 'l-Kawnayni ﷺ (192) Sayyīdunā 'Aynu 'n-Na'īmi ﷺ (193) Sayyīdunā 'Aynu 'l-Ghurri ﷺ (194) Sayyīdunā Sa'dullāhi ﷺ (195) Sayyīdunā Sa'du 'l-Khalqi ﷺ (196) Sayyīdunā Khaṭību 'l-'Umami ﷺ (197) Sayyīdunā 'Alamu 'l-Hudā ﷺ (198) Sayyīdunā Kāshifu 'l-Kurabi ﷺ (199) Sayyīdunā Rāfi'u 'r-Rutabi ﷺ (200) Sayyīdunā 'Izzu 'l-'Arabi ﷺ (201) Sayyīdunā Ṣāḥibu 'l-Faraji ﷺ ṣalla 'Llāhu 'alayhi wa 'alā ālihi •

(191) Our master Master of the Two Universes ﷺ (192) Our master the Spring of Bliss ﷺ (193) Our master the Spring of Beauty ﷺ (194) Our master the Joy of Allāh ﷺ (195) Our master Joy of the Creator ﷺ (196) Our master Preacher to Nations ﷺ (197) Our master Teacher of Guidance ﷺ (198) Our master Remover of Worries ﷺ (199) Our master Raiser of Ranks ﷺ (200) Our master Might of the Arab ﷺ (201) Our master Owner of Relief. ❋

اللَّهُمَّ يَا رَبِّ بِجَاهِ نَبِيِّكَ الْمُصْطَفَى وَرَسُولِكَ الْمُرْتَضَى طَهِّر قُلُوبَنَا مِنْ كُلِّ وَصْفٍ يُبَاعِدُنَا عَنْ مُشَاهَدَتِكَ وَمَحَبَّتِكَ وَأَمِتْنَا عَلَى السُّنَّةِ وَالْجَمَاعَةِ وَالشَّوْقِ إِلَى لِقَائِكَ يَا ذَا الْجَلَالِ وَالْإِكْرَامِ وَ صَلَّى اللهُ عَلَى سَيِّدِنَا مُحَمَّدٍ خَاتَمِ النَّبِيِّينَ وَإِمَامِ الْمُرْسَلِينَ وَعَلَى آلِهِ وَصَحْبِهِ أَجْمَعِينَ وَسَلَامٌ عَلَى الْمُرْسَلِينَ وَالْحَمْدُ لله رَبِّ الْعَالَمِينَ ❋

Allāhumma yā rabbī bi-jāhi Nabīyyika 'l-Musṭafā wa Rasūlika 'l-Murtaḍā ṭahhir qulūbanā min kulli waṣfin yubā'idunā 'an mushā-hadatika wa maḥabbatika wa amitnā 'alā 's-sunnati wa 'l-jamā'ati wa 'sh-shawqi ilā liqā'ika yā Dhal-Jalāli wa 'l-Ikrām wa ṣalla 'Llāhu 'alā Sayyīdunā Muḥammadin khātam an-nabīyyīna wa īmām al-mursalīna wa 'alā ālihi wa ṣāḥbihi ajmā'īna wa salāmun 'alā 'l-mursalīn wa 'l-ḥamdulillāhi Rabbi 'l-'ālamīn. •

O Allāh, O Lord, for the honor of Your Prophet, the Chosen One, and Your Messenger, the one with whom You are well-pleased, purify our hearts from every characteristic which distances us from witnessing Your Presence and Your Love, and let us pass away while following his way and his community, longing to meet You, O Owner of Majesty and Nobility and blessing and abundant peace of Allāh be upon our master Muḥammad, the Seal of the prophets and Leader of the messengers and on his family and his companions and praise be to Allāh Lord of the Worlds! ❋

الحِزْبُ الْأَوَّلُ فِي يَوْمِ الإِثْنَيْنِ

Monday

Al-Ḥizbu 'l-Āwwalu fī Yawmi 'l-Ithnayn

First Chapter on Monday

فَصلٌ فِي كَيْفِيَّةِ الصَّلَاةِ عَلَى النَّبِيِّ ﷺ وَهُوَ يُقْرَأُ بَعْدَ خَتْمِ الحِزْبِ الثَّامِنِ فِي يَوْمِهِ:

Faṣlun fī kayfīyyati 'ṣ-ṣalāti ʿalā 'n-nabīyyi ﷺ wa hūwa yuqrāu bʿada khatmi 'l-ḥizbi 'th-thāmini fī yawmih.

This chapter explains the method of invoking blessings upon the Prophet ﷺ, to be read after completing the eighth chapter on Monday. ➤

(١) بِسْمِ اللهِ الرَّحْمَٰنِ الرَّحِيمِ صَلَّى اللهُ عَلَى سَيِّدِنَا وَمَوْلَانَا مُحَمَّدٍ وَعَلَى آلِهِ وَصَحْبِهِ وَسَلَّمَ ❋

(1) Bismillāhi 'r-Raḥmāni 'r-Raḥīm ṣalla 'Llāhu ʿalā Sayyīdinā wa mawlānā Muḥammadin wa ʿalā ālihi wa ṣaḥbihi wa sallam •

(1) In the name of Allāh, All-Merciful, The Mercy-Giving, Allāh's blessings and peace be upon our master Muḥammad and his family and companions. ❋

(٢) اللَّهُمَّ صَلِّ عَلَى سَيِّدِنَا مُحَمَّدٍ وَأَزْوَاجِهِ وَذُرِيَّتِهِ كَمَا صَلَّيْتَ عَلَى سَيِّدِنَا إِبْرَاهِيمَ وَبَارِكْ عَلَى سَيِّدِنَا مُحَمَّدٍ وَأَزْوَاجِهِ وَذُرِيَّتِهِ كَمَا بَارَكْتَ عَلَى آلِ سَيِّدِنَا إِبْرَاهِيمَ إِنَّكَ حَمِيدٌ مَجِيدٌ ❋

(2) Allāhumma ṣalli ʿalā Sayyīdinā Muḥammadin wa azwājihi wa dhurrīyyatihi kamā ṣallayta ʿalā Sayyīdinā Ibrāhīma wa bārik ʿalā Sayyīdinā wa mawlānā Muḥammadin wa azwājihi wa dhurrīyyatihi kamā bārakta ʿalā āli Sayyīdinā Ibrāhīma innaka Ḥamīdun Majīd. •

(2) O Allāh, exalt our master Muḥammad and his wives and his descendants just as You exalted our master Abraham. O Allāh, bless our master Muḥammad and his wives and his descendants just as You blessed our master Abraham, in all the worlds for You are The Praiseworthy, The Glorious! ❋

(٣) اللَّهُمَّ صَلِّ عَلَى سَيِّدِنَا مُحَمَّدٍ وَعَلَى آلِهِ كَمَا صَلَّيْتَ عَلَى سَيِّدِنَا إِبْرَاهِيمَ

(3) Allāhumma ṣalli ʿalā Sayyīdinā Muḥammadin wa ʿalā ālihi kamā ṣallayta ʿalā Sayyīdinā Ibrāḥima,

(3) O Allāh, exalt our master Muḥammad and his family just as You exalted our master Abraham

وَبَارِكْ عَلَى سَيِّدِنَا مُحَمَّدٍ وَعَلَى آلِ سَيِّدِنَا مُحَمَّدٍ

wa bārik ʿalā Sayyīdinā Muḥammadin wa ʿalā āli Sayyīdinā Muḥammadin

and bless our master Muḥammad and the family of our master Muḥammad ➢

كَمَا بَارَكْتَ عَلَى آلِ سَيِّدِنَا إِبْرَاهِيمَ فِي العَالَمِينَ إِنَّكَ حَمِيدٌ مَجِيدٌ ❋

kamā bārakta 'alā āli Sayyīdinā Ibrāhīma fī 'l-'ālamīna innaka Ḥamīdun Majīd •

just as You blessed Abraham and the family of Abraham in all the worlds for You are The Praiseworthy, The Glorious. ❋

(٤) اللَّهُمَّ صَلِّ عَلَى سَيِّدِنَا مُحَمَّدٍ وَآلِ سَيِّدِنَا مُحَمَّدٍ كَمَا صَلَّيْتَ عَلَى سَيِّدِنَا إِبْرَاهِيمَ، وَبَارِكْ عَلَى سَيِّدِنَا مُحَمَّدٍ وَآلِ سَيِّدِنَا مُحَمَّدٍ كَمَا بَارَكْتَ عَلَى سَيِّدِنَا إِبْرَاهِيمَ، إِنَّكَ حَمِيدٌ مَجِيدٌ ❋

(4) Allāhumma ṣalli 'alā Sayyīdinā Muḥammadin wa āli Sayyīdinā Muḥammadin kamā ṣallayta 'alā Sayyīdinā Ibrāhīma wa bārik 'alā Sayyīdinā Muḥammadin wa āli Sayyīdinā Muḥammadin kamā bārakta 'alā Sayyīdinā Ibrāhīma innaka Ḥamīdun Majīd •

(4) O Allāh, exalt our master Muḥammad and the family of our master Muḥammad just as You exalted our master Abraham and bless our master Muḥammad and the family of Muḥammad just as You blessed our master Abraham for You are The Praiseworthy, The Glorious! ❋

(٥) اللَّهُمَّ صَلِّ عَلَى سَيِّدِنَا مُحَمَّدٍ النَّبِيِّ الأُمِّيِّ وَعَلَى آلِ سَيِّدِنَا مُحَمَّدٍ ❋

(5) Allāhumma ṣalli 'alā Sayyīdinā Muḥammadini 'n-Nabīyyi 'l-'Ummīyyi wa 'alā āli Sayyīdinā Muḥammadin •

(5) O Allāh, exalt our master, the unlettered Prophet and the family of our master Muḥammad! ❋

(٦) اللَّهُمَّ صَلِّ عَلَى سَيِّدِنَا مُحَمَّدٍ عَبْدِكَ وَرَسُولِكَ ❁

(6) Allāhumma ṣalli ʿalā Sayyīdinā Muḥammadin ʿabdika wa rasūlik •

(6) O Allāh bless your servant and Messenger Muḥammad ﷺ! ❁

(٧) اللَّهُمَّ صَلِّ عَلَى سَيِّدِنَا مُحَمَّدٍ وَعَلَى آلِ سَيِّدِنَا مُحَمَّدٍ كَمَا صَلَّيْتَ عَلَى سَيِّدِنَا إِبْرَاهِيمَ وَعَلَى آلِ سَيِّدِنَا إِبْرَاهِيمَ إِنَّكَ حَمِيدٌ اللَّهُمَّ بَارِكْ عَلَى سَيِّدِنَا مُحَمَّدٍ وَعَلَى آلِ سَيِّدِنَا مُحَمَّدٍ كَمَا بَارَكْتَ عَلَى سَيِّدِنَا إِبْرَاهِيمَ وَعَلَى آلِ سَيِّدِنَا إِبْرَاهِيمَ إِنَّكَ حَمِيدٌ مَجِيدٌ

(7) Allāhumma ṣalli ʿalā Sayyīdinā Muḥammadin wa ʿalā āli Sayyīdinā Muḥammadin kamā ṣallayta ʿalā Sayyīdinā Ibrāhīma wa ʿalā āli Sayyīdinā Ibrāhīma innaka Ḥamīdun Majīd Allāhumma bārik ʿalā Sayyīdinā Muḥammadin wa ʿalā āli Sayyīdinā Muḥammadin kamā bārakta ʿalā Sayyīdinā Ibrāhīma wa ʿalā āli Sayyīdinā Ibrāhīma innaka Ḥamīdun Majīd.

(7) O Allāh exalt our master Muḥammad and the family of our master Muḥammad just as You exalted our master Abraham and the family of our master Abraham for You are The Praiseworthy, The Mighty! O Allāh bless our master Muḥammad and the family of our master Muḥammad just as You blessed our master Abraham and the family of Abraham for You is The Praiseworthy, The Mighty! ➤

اللَّهُمَّ وَتَرَحَّمْ عَلَى سَيِّدِنَا مُحَمَّدٍ وَعَلَى آلِ سَيِّدِنَا مُحَمَّدٍ كَمَا تَرَحَّمْتَ عَلَى سَيِّدِنَا إِبْرَاهِيمَ وَعَلَى آلِ سَيِّدِنَا إِبْرَاهِيمَ إِنَّكَ حَمِيدٌ مَجِيدٌ

Allāhumma wa taraḥḥam 'alā Sayyīdinā Muḥammadin wa 'alā āli Sayyīdinā Muḥammadin kamā taraḥḥamta 'alā Sayyīdinā Ibrāhīma wa 'alā āli Sayyīdinā Ibrāḥima innaka Ḥamīdun Majīd.

O Allāh, be merciful to our master Muḥammad and the family of our master Muḥammad just as You were the merciful to our master Abraham and the family of Abraham for You are The Praiseworthy, The Mighty! ➢

اللَّهُمَّ وَتَحَنَّنْ عَلَى سَيِّدِنَا مُحَمَّدٍ وَعَلَى آلِ سَيِّدِنَا مُحَمَّدٍ كَمَا تَحَنَّنْتَ عَلَى سَيِّدِنَا إِبْرَاهِيمَ وَعَلَى آلِ سَيِّدِنَا إِبْرَاهِيمَ إِنَّكَ حَمِيدٌ مَجِيدٌ اللَّهُمَّ وَسَلِّمْ عَلَى سَيِّدِنَا مُحَمَّدٍ وَعَلَى آلِ سَيِّدِنَا مُحَمَّدٍ

Allāhumma wa taḥḥannan 'alā Sayyīdinā Muḥammadin wa 'alā āli Sayyīdinā Muḥammadin kamā taḥḥannanta 'alā Sayyīdinā Ibrāhīma wa 'alā āli Sayyīdinā Ibrāhīma innaka Ḥamīdun Majīd Allāhumma wa sallim 'alā Sayyīdinā Muḥammadin wa 'alā ali Sayyīdinā Muḥammadin

O Allāh, be kind to our master Muḥammad and the family of our master Muḥammad as You were kind to our master Abraham and the family of our master Abraham, for You are The Praiseworthy, The Mighty! O Allāh, grant peace of our master Muḥammad and the family of our master Muḥammad ➢

كَمَا سَلَّمتَ عَلَى سَيِّدِنَا إِبْرَاهِيمَ وَعَلَى آلِ سَيِّدِنَا إِبْرَاهِيمَ إِنَّكَ حَمِيدٌ مَجِيدٌ ❋

kamā sallamta ʿalā Sayyīdinā Ibrāhīma wa ʿalā āli Sayyīdinā Ibrāhīma, innaka Ḥamīdun Majīd •

just as You granted peace to our master Abraham and the families of our master Abraham for You are The Praiseworthy, The Mighty! ❋

(٨) اللَّهُمَّ صَلِّ عَلَى سَيِّدِنَا مُحَمَّدٍ وَعَلَى آلِ سَيِّدِنَا مُحَمَّدٍ وَارْحَمْ سَيِّدَنَا مُحَمَّدً وَآلَ سَيِّدِنَا مُحَمَّدٍ وَبَارِكْ عَلَى سَيِّدِنَا مُحَمَّدٍ وَعَلَى آلِ سَيِّدِنَا مُحَمَّدٍ كَمَا صَلَّيْتَ وَرَحِمتَ وَبَارَكْتَ عَلَى سَيِّدِنَا إِبْرَاهِيمَ وَعَلَى آلِ سَيِّدِنَا إِبْرَاهِيمَ فِي الْعَالَمِينَ إِنَّكَ حَمِيدٌ مَجِيدٌ ❋

(8) Allāhumma ṣalli ʿalā Sayyīdinā Muḥammadin wa ʿalā āli Sayyīdinā Muḥammadin wa 'rḥam sayyidanā Muḥammadan wa āla Sayyīdinā Muḥammadin wa bārik ʿalā Sayyīdinā Muḥammadin wa ʿalā āli Sayyīdinā Muḥammadin kamā ṣallayta wa raḥimta wa bārakta ʿalā Sayyīdinā Ibrāhīma wa ʿalā āli Sayyīdinā Ibrāhīma fī 'l-ʿālamīna innaka Ḥamīdun Majīd •

(8) O Allāh, exalt our master Muḥammad and the family of our master Muḥammad, and be merciful to our master Muḥammad and the family of our master Muḥammad, and bless our master Muḥammad and the family of our master Muḥammad just as You exalted, and were merciful to, and blessed our master Abraham and the family of our master Abraham, In the worlds for You are The Praiseworthy, The Mighty! ❋

(٩) اللَّهُمَّ صَلِّ عَلَى سَيِّدِنَا مُحَمَّدٍ النَّبِيِّ وَأَزْوَاجِهِ أُمَّهَاتِ الْمُؤْمِنِينَ وَذُرِّيَّتِهِ وَأَهْلِ بَيْتِهِ كَمَا صَلَّيْتَ عَلَى سَيِّدِنَا إِبْرَاهِيمَ إِنَّكَ حَمِيدٌ مَجِيدٌ ❋

(9) Allāhumma ṣalli ʿalā Sayyīdinā Muḥammadin 'n-Nabīyyi wa azwājihi ummahāṭi 'l-mu'minīna wa dhurrīyyatihi wa āhli baytihi kamā ṣallayta ʿalā Sayyīdinā Ibrāhīma innaka Ḥamīdun Majīd •

(9) O Allāh, exalt our master Muḥammad, the Prophet, and his wives, the Mothers of the Believers, and his descendants and the People of his House just as You exalted our master Abraham for You are The Praiseworthy, The Mighty! ❋

(١٠) اللَّهُمَّ بَارِكْ عَلَى سَيِّدِنَا مُحَمَّدٍ وَعَلَى آلِ سَيِّدِنَا مُحَمَّدٍ كَمَا بَارَكْتَ عَلَى سَيِّدِنَا إِبْرَاهِيمَ إِنَّكَ حَمِيدٌ مَجِيدٌ ❋

(10) Allāhumma bārik ʿalā Sayyīdinā Muḥammadin wa ʿalā āli Sayyīdinā Muḥammadin kamā bārakta ʿalā Sayyīdinā Ibrāhīma innaka Ḥamīdun Majīd •

(10) O Allāh, bless our master Muḥammad and the family of our master Muḥammad just as You blessed our master Abraham for You are The Praiseworthy, The Mighty! ❋

(١١) اللَّهُمَّ دَاحِيَ الْمَدْحُوَّاتِ وَبارِئَ المَسمُوكَاتِ وَجَبَّارَ الْقُلُوبِ عَلَى فِطْرَتِهَا

(11) Allāhumma dāḥī 'l-madḥūwwāti wa bārī al-masmūkāti wa jabbāra 'l-qulūbi ʿalā fiṭratihā

(11) O Allāh, the Leveler of the Plains, the Maker of the Firmament, and the Molder of Hearts ➢

شَقِيِّهَا وَسَعِيدِهَا اِجْعَلْ شَرَائِفَ صَلَوَاتِكَ وَنَوَامِيَ بَرَكَاتِكَ وَرَأْفَةَ تَحَنُّنِكَ عَلَى سَيِّدِنَا مُحَمَّدٍ

shaqīyyihā wa saʿīdihā ijʿal sharāʾifa ṣalawātika wa nawāmīya barakātika wa rāfata taḥannunika ʿalā Sayyīdinā Muḥammadin

into the good and the bad, grant Your noblest blessings, most fruitful favors, and most loving kindness to our master Muḥammad, ➢

عَبْدِكَ وَرَسُولِكَ الفَاتِحِ لِمَا أُغْلِقَ وَالخَاتِمِ لِمَا سَبَقَ وَالْمُعْلِنِ الحَقَّ بِالحَقِّ وَالدَامِغِ لِجَيشَاتِ الْأَبَاطِيلِ

ʿabdika wa rasūlika 'l-fātiḥi limā ughliqa wa 'l-khātimi limā sabaqa wa 'l-muʿlini 'l-ḥaqqa bi 'l-ḥaqqi wa 'd-dāmighi li-jayshāti 'l-abāṭīli

Your slave and Your Messenger, the Opener of what was locked and the Seal of what came before, the Announcer of Truth with Truth, and the Refuter of the forces of falsehood! ➢

كَمَا حُمِّلَ فَاضْطَلَعَ بِأَمْرِكَ بِطَاعَتِكَ مُسْتَوْفِزًا فِي مَرْضَاتِكَ وَاعِيًا لِوَحْيِكَ حَافِظًا لِعَهْدِكَ

kamā ḥummīla faḍ-ṭalaʿa bi amrika bi ṭāʿatika mustawfizan fī marḍātika wāʿīyan li-waḥyīka ḥāfiẓan li-ʿahdika

He took upon himself the responsibility of Your order in obedience to You, speedily seeking Your Pleasure, earnestly heeding Your Revelation, keeping Your promise, ➢

مَاضِيًا عَلَى نَفَاذِ أَمْرِكَ حَتَّى أَوْرَى قَبَسًا لِقَابِسٍ آلَاءُ اللهِ تَصِلُ بِأَهْلِهِ أَسْبَابَهُ

māḍīyan ʿalā nafādhi amrika ḥattā awrā qabasan li-qābisin ālā'u 'Llāhi taṣilu bi āhlihi asbābahu

carrying out and executing Your command, so that, by kindling a burning brand for the seeker, his family gains access through him to the blessings of Allāh! ➢

بِهِ هُدِيَتِ الْقُلُوبُ بَعْدَ خَوْضَاتِ الْفِتَنِ وَالْإِثْمِ وَأَبْهَجَ مُوضِحَاتِ الْأَعْلَامِ وَنَائِرَاتِ الْأَحْكَامِ وَمُنِيرَاتِ الإِسْلَامِ

bihi hudyati 'l-qulūbu baʿda khawḍāti 'l-fitani wa 'l-ithmi wa abhaja mawḍiḥāti 'l-āʿalāmi wa nā'irati 'l-aḥkāmi wa munīrāti 'l-Islāmi

Hearts were guided through him after having entered into discord and sin, and he gladdened with evident signs with enlightening laws and illuminating Islām! ➢

فَهُوَ أَمِينُكَ الْمَأْمُونُ وَخَازِنُ عِلْمِكَ الْمَخْزُونِ وشَهِيدُكَ يَوْمَ الدِّينِ وَبَعِيثُكَ نِعْمَةً وَرَسُولُكَ بِالْحَقِّ رَحْمَةً ❋

fa-hūwa amīnuka 'l-ma'mūnu wa khāzinu ʿilmiki 'l-makhzūni wa shahīdūka yawma 'd-dīni wa baʿīthuka niʿmatan wa rasūluka bi 'l-ḥaqqi raḥmatan •

And he is Your Trustworthy One and Safe Custodian of Your Secret knowledge, your witness on the Day of Judgment and Your Envoy, a Favour for us, and Your Messenger, in truth, a Mercy of us! ❋

(١٢) اللَّهُمَّ اِفْسَحْ لَهُ فِي عَدَنِكَ وَاجْزِهِ مُضَاعَفَاتِ الْخَيْرِ مِنْ فَضْلِكَ مُهَنَّئَاتٍ لَهُ غَيرَ مُكَدَّرَاتٍ مِنْ فَوْزِ ثَوَابِكَ الْمَحْلُولِ وَجَزِيلِ عَطَائِكَ الْمَعْلُولِ

(12) Allāhumma ifsaḥ lahu fī ʿadanika wa 'jzihi muḍāʿafāti 'l-khayri min faḍlika muhanna'ātin lahu ghayra mukaddarātin min fawzi thawābika 'l-māḥlūli wa jazīli ʿatā'ika 'l-maʿlūli.

(12) O Allāh, widen for him his place in Your Garden of Eden and reward him doubly with the goodness of Your Favor granting him untarnished felicitations from the victory of Your reward, which is plentiful and fitting, and from Your Lofty Gift. ➢

اللَّهُمَّ أَعْلِ عَلَى بِنَاءِ النَّاسِ بِنَاءَهُ وَأَكْرِمْ مَثْوَاهُ لَدَيكَ وَنُزُلَهُ وَأَتْمِمْ لَهُ نُورَهُ وَاجْزِهِ مِنْ اِبْتِعَاثِكَ لَهُ مَقبُولَ ٱلشَّهَادَةِ وَمَرضِيَّ ٱلْمَقَالَةِ ذَا مَنْطِقٍ عَدلٍ وَخُطَّةٍ فَصْلٍ وَبُرْهَانٍ عَظِيمٍ ❋

Allāhumma āʿlin ʿalā binā'i 'n-nāsi binā'ahu wa 'krim mathwāhu ladayka wa nuzulahu wa 'tmim lahu nūrahu wa 'jzihi min ibtiʿāthika lahu maqbūla 'sh-shahādati wa marḍīyya 'l-maqālati dha manṭiqin ʿadlin wa khuṭṭatin faṣlin wa burhānin ʿaẓīmin •

O Allāh, raise that which he built up over all that mankind has built up and ennoble his place and his sojourn with You, and complete for him His light and reward him with Your approval so that his testimony is accepted and his word is pleasing to You making him the one whose utterance is just and whose course is distinct and whose argument is mighty! ❋

(١٣) إِنَّ اللهَ وَمَلائِكَتَهُ يُصَلُّونَ عَلَى النَّبِيِّ يَا أَيُّهَا الَّذِينَ آمَنُوا صَلُّوا عَلَيْهِ وَسَلِّمُوا تَسْلِيماً لَبَّيْكَ اللَّهُمَّ رَبِّي وَسَعْدَيْكَ صَلَوَاتُ اللهِ الْبَرِّ الرَّحِيمِ وَالْمَلَائِكَةِ الْمُقَرَّبِينَ وَالنَّبِيِّينَ وَالصِّدِّيقِينَ وَالشُّهَدَاءِ وَالصَّالِحِينَ

(13) inna 'Llāha wa malā'ikatahu yuṣallūna 'alā 'n-nabī yā ayyuha 'Lladhīna āmanū ṣallū 'alayhi wa ṣallimū taslīma. Labbayka ' l-lāhumma rabbī wa sa'dayka ṣalawātu 'Llāhi 'l-Barri 'r-Raḥīmi wa 'l-malā'ikati 'l-muqarrabīna wa 'n-nabīyyīnā wa 'ṣ-ṣiddīqīna wa 'sh-shuhadā'i wa 'ṣ-ṣāliḥīna

(13) Verily, Allāh and his angels exalt the Prophet! you, who believe, ask (Allāh) to exalt him and grant him abundant peace! I am here, O Allāh, at Your service and at Your Command! The blessing of Allāh ﷻ, the Good, the Merciful, and of His closest angels, and of the Prophets and of the sincere ones, and of the martyrs and of the good ones ➤

وَمَا سَبَّحَ لَكَ مِنْ شَيْءٍ يَا رَبَّ الْعَالَمِينَ عَلَى سَيِّدِنَا مُحَمَّدِ بْنِ عَبْدِ اللهِ خَاتَمِ النَّبِيِّينَ وَسَيِّدِ الْمُرْسَلِينَ وَإِمَامِ الْمُتَّقِينَ وَرَسُولِ رَبِّ الْعَالَمِينَ الشَّاهِدِ الْبَشِيرِ

wa mā sabbaḥa laka min shay'in yā rabba 'l-'ālamīna 'alā Sayyīdinā Muḥammadin ibn 'abdi 'Llāhi khātami 'n-Nabīyyīnā wa sayyidi 'l-mursalīna wa imāmi 'l-muttaqīna wa rasūli rabbi 'l-'ālamīna 'sh-shāhidi 'l-bashīri

and of whatever else exists which glorifies You, Lord of the worlds, are for our master Muḥammad ﷺ, son of 'Abdullāh the Seal of the Prophets and the master of Messengers, the Leader of the Pious and the Messenger of the Lord of the Worlds, the Witness, the Bringer of Good Tidings, ➤

الدَّاعِي إِلَيْكَ بِإِذْنِكَ السِّرَاجِ الْمُنِيرِ ﷺ ❋

ad-dāʿī ilayka bi-idhnika 's-sirāji 'l-munīri ﷺ •

the Caller to You by Your leave, the Lamp, the Illumined One, upon him be peace! ❋

(١٤) اللَّهُمَّ اِجْعَلْ صَلَوَاتِكَ وَبَرَكَاتِكَ وَرَحْمَتَكَ عَلَى سَيِّدِ الْمُرْسَلِينَ وإِمَامِ الْمُتَّقِينَ وَخَاتَمِ النَّبِيِّينَ مُحَمَّدٍ عَبْدِكَ وَرَسُولِكَ إِمَامِ الْخَيْرِ وَقَائِدِ الْخَيْرِ وَرَسُولِ الرَّحْمَةِ،

(14) Allāhumma 'ijʿal ṣalawātika wa barakātika wa raḥmataka ʿalā sayyidi 'l-mursalīna wa imāmi 'l-muttaqīna wa khātamu 'n-nabīyyīna Sayyīdinā Muḥammadin ʿabdika wa rasūlika imāmi 'l-khayri wa qā'idi 'l-khayri wa Rasūli 'r-raḥmah.

(14) O Allāh grant Your Praise,Your Blessings and Your Mercy to the Master of the Messengers and the Leader of the pious ones and the Seal of the Prophets, our master Muḥammad, Your servant and Your Messenger, the Pioneer of Goodness and the Guide to Goodness and the Messenger of Mercy! ➢

اللَّهُمَّ ابْعَثْهُ مَقَامًا مَحْمُوداً يَغْبِطُهُ فِيهِ الْأَوَّلُونَ وَالآخِرُونَ

Allāhumma 'bʿath-hu maqāman maḥmūdan yaghbiṭuhu fīhi 'l-āwwalūna wa 'l-'ākhirūn.

O Allāh send him to the Most-Praised Station, the envy of the first to come and those who came last! ➢

اللَّهُمَّ صَلِّ عَلَى سَيِّدِنَا مُحَمَّدٍ وَعَلَى آلِ سَيِّدِنَا مُحَمَّدٍ كَمَا صَلَّيْتَ عَلَى سَيِّدِنَا إِبْرَاهِيمَ إِنَّكَ حَمِيدٌ مَجِيدٌ

Allāhumma ṣalli ʿalā Sayyīdinā Muḥammadin wa ʿalā āli Sayyīdinā Muḥammadin kamā ṣallayta ʿalā Sayyīdinā Ibrāhīma innaka Ḥamīdun Majīd.

O Allāh'exalt our master Muḥammad and the family of our master Muḥammad as You exalted our master Abraham for You are The Praiseworthy, The Mighty! ➢

اللَّهُمَّ بَارِكْ عَلَى سَيِّدِنَا مُحَمَّدٍ وَعَلَى آلِ سَيِّدِنَا مُحَمَّدٍ كَمَا بَارَكْتَ عَلَى سَيِّدِنَا إِبْرَاهِيمَ إِنَّكَ حَمِيدٌ مَجِيدٌ ❋

Allāhumma bārik ʿalā Sayyīdinā Muḥammadin wa ʿalā āli Sayyīdinā Muḥammadin kamā bārakta ʿalā Sayyīdinā Ibrāhīma innaka Ḥamīdun Majīd •

O Allāh bless our master Muḥammad and the family of our master Muḥammad Just as You blessed our master Abraham for You are The Praiseworthy, The Mighty! ❋

(١٥) اللَّهُمَّ صَلِّ عَلَى سَيِّدِنَا مُحَمَّدٍ وَعَلَى آلِهِ وَأَصْحَابِهِ وَأَوْلَادِهِ وَأَزْوَاجِهِ

(15) Allāhumma ṣalli ʿalā Sayyīdinā Muḥammadin wa ʿalā ālihi wa aṣḥābihi wa awlādihi wa azwājihi

(15) O Allāh, exalt our master Muḥammad, his family, his companions, his children, his wives, ➢

وَذُرِيَّتِهِ وَأَهْلِ بَيْتِهِ وَأَصْهَارِهِ وَأَنْصَارِهِ وَأَشْيَاعِهِ وَمُحِبِّيهِ وَأُمَّتِهِ وَعَلَينَا مَعَهُم

أَجْمَعِينَ يَا ارْحَمْ الرَّاحِمِينَ ❁

wa dhurrīyyatihi wa āhli baytihi wa aṣ-hārihi wa anṣārihi wa ashyā'ihi wa muḥibbīhi wa ummatihi wa 'alaynā ma'ahum ajma'īna yā arḥama 'r-rāḥimīn •

his descendants, the People of his House, his relations by marriage, his Helpers (the Anṣār), his adherents, his lovers, his nation and all of us along with them, O Allāh Most Merciful of the Merciful! ❁

(١٦) اللَّهُمَّ صَلِّ عَلَى سَيِّدِنَا مُحَمَّدٍ عَدَدَ مَنْ صَلَّى عَلَيهِ وعَدَدَ مَنْ لَمْ يُصَلِّ

عَلَيهِ وَصَلِّ عَلَى سَيِّدِنَا مُحَمَّدٍ كَمَا أَمَرتَنَا بِالصَّلاةِ عَلَيهِ وَصَلِّ عَلَى سَيِّدِنَا مُحَمَّدٍ

كَمَا يُحِبُّ أَنْ يُصَلَّى عَلَيْهِ ❁

(16) Allāhumma ṣalli 'alā Sayyīdinā Muḥammadin 'adada man ṣalla 'alayhi wa ṣalli 'alā Sayyīdinā Muḥammadin 'adada man lam yuṣalli 'alayhi wa ṣalli 'alā Sayyīdinā Muḥammadin kamā amartanā bi 'ṣ-ṣalāti 'alayhi wa ṣalli 'alayhi kamā yuḥibbu an-yuṣalla 'alayh •

(16) O Allāh, exalt our master Muḥammad as many times as those who have sought his exaltation and exalt our master Muḥammad as many times as those who have not sought his exaltation! And exalt Sayyidina Muhammad as we have been ordered to ask You to exalt him and exalt him just as he would like to be exalted! ❁

(١٧) اللَّهُمَّ صَلِّ عَلَى سَيِّدِنَا مُحَمَّدٍ وَعَلَى آلِ سَيِّدِنَا مُحَمَّدٍ كَمَا أَمَرْتَنَا أَنْ نُصَلِّيَ عَلَيْهِ اللَّهُمَّ صَلِّ عَلَى سَيِّدِنَا مُحَمَّدٍ وَعَلَى آلِ سَيِّدِنَا مُحَمَّدٍ كَمَا هُوَ أَهْلُهُ اللَّهُمَّ صَلِّ عَلَى سَيِّدِنَا مُحَمَّدٍ وَعَلَى آلِ سَيِّدِنَا مُحَمَّدٍ كَمَا تُحِبُّ وَتَرْضَاهُ لَهُ ❁

(17) Allāhumma ṣalli ʿalā Sayyīdinā Muḥammadin wa ʿalā āli Sayyīdinā Muḥammadin kamā amartanā an nuṣallīya ʿalayhi. Allāhumma ṣalli ʿalā Sayyīdinā Muḥammadin wa ʿalā āli Sayyīdinā Muḥammadin kamā hūwa āhluh. Allāhumma ṣalli ʿalā Sayyīdinā Muḥammadin wa ʿalā āli Sayyīdinā Muḥammadin kamā tuḥibbu wa tarḍāhu lah •

(17) O Allāh, exalt our master Muḥammad and the family of our master Muḥammad as we have been ordered to ask for blessings upon him! O Allāh, bless our master Muḥammad and the family of Master Muḥammad as he deserves! O Allāh, bless our master Muḥammad and the family of master Muḥammad just as You like and in the way (O Allāh) with which You pleased. ❁

(١٨) اللَّهُمَّ يَا رَبَّ سَيِّدِنَا مُحَمَّدٍ وَآلِ سَيِّدِنَا مُحَمَّدٍ صَلِّ عَلَى سَيِّدِنَا مُحَمَّدٍ وَآلِ سَيِّدِنَا مُحَمَّدٍ وَأَعْطِ سَيِّدَنَا مُحَمَّدًا الدَّرَجَةَ وَالوَسِيلَةَ فِي الجَنَّةِ ❁

(18) Allāhumma yā rabba Sayyīdinā Muḥammadin wa āli Sayyīdinā Muḥammadin ṣalli ʿalā Sayyīdinā Muḥammadin wa āli Sayyīdinā Muḥammadin wa āʿṭi Sayyīdanā Muḥammadani 'd-darajata wa 'l-wasīlata fī 'l-jannah •

(18) O Allāh Lord of our master Muḥammad and the family of our master Muḥammad, exalt our master Muḥammad and the family of our master Muḥammad and grant to master Muḥammad the rank of the Closest Access in the Garden! ❁

(١٩) اللَّهُمَّ يا رَبَّ سَيِّدِنا مُحَمَّدٍ و آلِ سَيِّدِنا مُحَمَّدٍ اِجْزِ سَيِّدَنا مُحَمَّداً صَلَّى اللهُ عَلَيهِ وسَلَّمَ مَا هُوَ أَهْلُهُ ❁

(19) Allāhumma yā rabba Sayyīdinā Muḥammadin wa āli Sayyīdinā Muḥammadin ijzi sayyīdinā Muḥammadan ﷺ *mā hūwa āhluh •*

(19) O Allāh! Lord of our master Muḥammad and the family of our master Muḥammad, reward our master Muḥammad, may Allāh ﷻ bless him and give him peace, just as he deserves! ❁

(٢٠) اللَّهُمَّ صَلِّ عَلَى سَيِّدِنا مُحَمَّدٍ وَعَلَى آلِ سَيِّدِنا مُحَمَّدٍ وَعَلَى أَهْلِ بَيْتِهِ ❁

(20) Allāhumma ṣalli ʿalā Sayyīdinā Muḥammadin wa ʿalā āli Sayyīdinā Muḥammadin wa ʿalā āhli baytih •

(20) O Allāh, exalt our master Muḥammad and the family of our master Muḥammad and the People of his house! ❁

(٢١) اللَّهُمَّ صَلِّ عَلَى سَيِّدِنا مُحَمَّدٍ و عَلَى آلِ سَيِّدِنا مُحَمَّدٍ حَتَّى لَا يَبْقَى مِنَ الصَّلَاةِ شَيْءٌ

(21) Allāhumma ṣalli ʿalā Sayyīdinā Muḥammadin wa ʿalā āli Sayyīdinā Muḥammadin ḥattā lā yabqā mina 'ṣ-ṣalāti shay'un

(21) O Allāh, exalt our master Muḥammad and the family of our master Muḥammad until not a single drop of exaltation remains! ➢

وارْحَمْ سَيِّدِنَا مُحَمَّداً وَآلِ سَيِّدِنَا مُحَمَّدٍ حَتَّى لَا يَبْقَى مِنَ الرَّحْمَةِ شَيْءٌ وَبَارِكْ عَلَى سَيِّدِنَا مُحَمَّدٍ وَعَلَى آلِ سَيِّدِنَا مُحَمَّدٍ حَتَّى لَا يَبْقَى مِنَ البَرَكَةِ شَيْءٌ

wa ʾrḥam Sayyīdinā Muḥammadan wa āli Sayyīdinā Muḥammadin ḥattā lā yabqā mina ʾr-raḥmati shayʾun wa bārik ʿalā Sayyīdinā Muḥammadin wa ʿalā āli Sayyīdinā Muḥammadin ḥattā lā yabqā mina ʾl-barakati shayʾun

O Allāh, have Mercy on our master Muḥammad and the family of our master Muḥammad until there remains not a single drop of mercy, and bless our master Muḥammad and the family of our master Muḥammad until there remains not a single drop of blessings, ➢

وَسَلِّمْ عَلَى سَيِّدِنَا مُحَمَّدٍ وَعَلَى آلِ سَيِّدِنَا مُحَمَّدٍ حَتَّى لَا يَبقَى مِنَ السَّلَامِ شَيْءٌ ❋

wa sallim ʿalā Sayyīdinā Muḥammadin wa ʿalā āli Sayyīdinā Muḥammadin ḥattā lā yabqā mina ʾs-salāmi shayʾun •

and grant peace to our master Muḥammad and the family of our master Muḥammad until there remains not a single drop of peace! ❋

(٢٢) اللَّهُمَّ صَلِّ عَلَى سَيِّدِنَا مُحَمَّدٍ فِي الأَوَّلِينَ

(22) Allāhumma ṣalli ʿalā Sayyīdinā Muḥammadin fī ʾl-awwalīn

(22) O Allāh bless our master Muḥammad among the First! ➢

وَصَلِّ عَلَى سَيِّدِنَا مُحَمَّدٍ فِي الْآخِرِينَ وَصَلِّ عَلَى سَيِّدِنَا مُحَمَّدٍ فِي النَّبِيِّينَ وَصَلِّ عَلَى سَيِّدِنَا مُحَمَّدٍ فِي الْمُرْسَلِينَ وَصَلِّ عَلَى سَيِّدِنَا مُحَمَّدٍ فِي الْمَلَإِ الْأَعْلَى إِلَى يَوْمِ الدِّينِ ❋

wa ṣalli ʿalā Sayyīdinā Muḥammadin fī 'l-ākhirīn wa ṣalli ʿalā Sayyīdinā Muḥammadin fī 'n-nabīyyīna wa ṣalli ʿalā Sayyīdinā Muḥammadin fī 'l-mursalīna wa ṣalli ʿalā Sayyīdinā Muḥammadin fī 'l-malā'i 'l-āʿlā ilā yawmi 'd-dīn •

O Allāh, bless our master Muḥammad among the last! O Allāh, bless our master Muḥammad among the Prophets among the Messengers! O Allāh, bless our master Muḥammad in the Heavenly Assembly until the day of Resurrection! ❋

(٢٣) اللَّهُمَّ أَعْطِ سَيِّدَنَا مُحَمَّداً الْوَسِيلَةَ وَالْفَضِيلَةَ وَالشَّرَفَ وَالدَّرَجَةَ الرَّفِيعَةَ ❋

(23) Allāhumma āʿṭi sayyīdanā Muḥammadan al-wasīlata wa 'l-faḍīlata wa 'sh-sharafa wa 'd-darajata 'r-rafīʿāta •

(23) O Allāh, grant our master Muḥammad the position of the Closest Access, the Pre-eminence and the noblest and the greatest rank! ❋

(٢٤) اللَّهُمَّ إِنِّي آمَنْتُ بِمُحَمَّدٍ وَلَمْ أَرَهُ فَلَا تَحْرِمْنِي فِي الْجِنَانِ رُؤْيَتَهُ

(24) Allāhumma innī āmantu bi-Muḥammadin wa lam arahu falā taḥrimnī fī 'l-jināni ru'yatahu

(24) O Allāh, I have believed in our master Muḥammad ﷺ and I have not seen him so do not deprive my heart of a vision of him ➢

وَارْزُقْنِي صُحْبَتَهُ وَتَوَفَّنِي عَلَى مِلَّتِهِ وَاسْقِنِي مِنْ حَوْضِهِ مَشْرَباً رَوِيّاً سَائِغاً هَنِيئاً لَا نَظْمَأُ بَعْدَهُ أَبَداً إِنَّكَ عَلَى كُلِّ شَيْءٍ قَدِيرٌ ❋

wa 'rzuqnī ṣuḥbatahu wa tawaffanī 'alā millatihi wa 'sqinī min ḥawdihi mashraban rawīyyan sā'ighan hanīyyan lā naẓmā'u ba'dahu abadan innaka 'alā kulli shayyin qadīr •

and provide me with his companionship and have me die on his way and lead me to drink from his Pond plentifully, blissfully, heartily, a drink after which we will never feel thirst, for You have Power over all things! ❋

(٢٥) اللَّهُمَّ أَبْلِغْ رُوحَ سَيِّدِنَا مُحَمَّدٍ مِنِّي تَحِيَّةً وَسَلَامًا ❋

(25) Allāhumma abligh rūḥa Sayyīdinā Muḥammadin minnī taḥīyyatan wa salāma •

(25) O Allāh'send to the soul of our master Muḥammad my greetings and my salutations! ❋

(٢٦) اللَّهُمَّ وَكَمَا آمَنْتُ بِهِ وَلَمْ أَرَهُ فَلَا تَحْرِمْنِي فِي الْجِنَانِ رُؤْيَتَهُ ❋

(26) Allāhumma wa kamā āmantu bihi wa lam arahu falā taḥrimnī fī 'l-jināni ru'yatah •

(26) O Allāh, just as I have believed in our master Muḥammad ﷺ without seeing him, so do not deprive my heart of a vision of him! ❋

(٢٧) اللَّهُمَّ تَقَبَّلْ شَفَاعَةَ سَيِّدِنَا مُحَمَّدٍ الْكُبْرَى وَارْفَعْ دَرَجَتَهُ الْعُلْيَا وَآتِهِ سُؤْلَهُ فِي الْآخِرَةِ وَالْأُوْلَى كَمَا آتَيْتَ سَيِّدَنَا إِبْرَاهِيمَ وَ سَيِّدَنَا مُوسَى ❋

(27) Allāhumma taqabbal shafā'ata Sayyīdinā Muḥammadini 'l-kubrā, wa 'rfa' darajatahu 'l-'ulyā, wa 'ātihi su'lahu fī 'l-'ākhirati wa 'l-'ūla kamā ātayta Sayyīdanā Ibrāhīma wa Sayyīdanā Mūsā •

(27) O Allāh, accept the great intercession of our master Muḥammad, raise his rank high and give him that which he asks for in the Hereafter and in this present life, just as You gave to our master Abraham and our master Moses. ❋

(٢٨) اللَّهُمَّ صَلِّ عَلَى سَيِّدِنَا مُحَمَّدٍ و عَلَى آلِ سَيِّدِنَا مُحَمَّدٍ كَمَا صَلَّيْتَ عَلَى سَيِّدِنَا إِبْرَاهِيمَ وَعَلَى آلِ سَيِّدِنَا إِبْرَاهِيمَ وَبَارِكْ عَلَى سَيِّدِنَا مُحَمَّدٍ وَعَلَى آلِ سَيِّدِنَا مُحَمَّدٍ كَمَا بَارَكْتَ عَلَى سَيِّدِنَا إِبْرَاهِيمَ و عَلَى آلِ سَيِّدِنَا إِبْرَاهِيمَ إِنَّكَ حَمِيدٌ مَجِيدٌ ❋

(28) Allāhumma ṣalli 'alā Sayyīdinā Muḥammadin wa 'alā āli Sayyīdinā Muḥammadin kamā ṣallayta 'alā Sayyīdinā Ibrāhīma wa 'alā āli Sayyīdinā Ibrāhīma, wa bārik 'alā Sayyīdinā Muḥammadin wa 'alā āli Sayyīdinā Muḥammadin kamā bārakta 'alā Sayyīdinā Ibrāhīma wa 'alā āli Sayyīdinā Ibrāhīma, innaka Ḥamīdun Majīd •

(28) O Allāh, bless our master Muḥammad and the family of our master Muḥammad just as You blessed our master Abraham and the family of Abraham, and exalt our master Muḥammad and the family of master Muḥammad just as You exalted our master Abraham and the family of our master Abraham, for You are The Praiseworthy, The Mighty! ❋

(٢٩) اللَّهُمَّ صَلِّ وسَلِّم وَبَارِكْ عَلَى سَيِّدِنَا مُحَمَّدٍ نَبِيِّكَ وَرَسُولِكَ وسَيِّدِنَا إِبْرَاهِيمَ خَلِيلِكَ وَصَفِيِّكَ وَسَيِّدِنَا مُوسَى كَلِيمِكَ ونَجِيِّكَ وسَيِّدِنَا عِيسَى رُوحِكَ وَكَلِمَتِكَ

(29) Allāhumma ṣalli wa sallim wa bārik 'alā Sayyīdinā Muḥammadin nabīyyika wa rasūlik wa Sayyīdinā Ibrāhīma khalīlika wa ṣafīyyika wa Sayyīdinā Mūsā kalīmika wa najīyyik wa Sayyīdinā 'Īsā rūḥika wa kalimatika

(29) O Allāh (O Allāh), bless, exalt and grant peace to our master Muḥammad, Your Prophet, Your Messenger! And also our master Abraham, Your Friend and Your Pure One and our master Moses, Your Interlocuter and Intimate Friend and also our master Jesus, Your Spirit and Your Word, ➢

وَعَلَى جَمِيعِ مَلَآئِكَتِكَ وَرُسُلِكَ وَأَنْبِيَائِكَ وَخِيرَتِكَ مِنْ خَلْقِكَ وَأَصْفِيَائِكَ وَخَاصَّتِكَ وَأَولِيَائِكَ مِنْ أَهْلِ أَرْضِكَ وَسَمَائِكَ ❋

wa 'alā jamī'i malā-'ikatika wa rusulika wa anbīyā'ika wa khīyratika min khalqika wa aṣfīyā'ika wa khāṣṣatika wa awlīyā'ika min āhli arḍika wa samā'ika •

and on Your angels, Your messengers and Your prophets, on the righteous ones from Your Creation, on Your pure servants, on Your elect ones and on Your saints from the folk of Your Earth and Your Heaven! ❋

(٣٠) وَصَلَّى اللهُ عَلَى سَيِّدِنَا مُحَمَّدٍ عَدَدَ خَلْقِهِ وَرِضَا نَفْسِهِ وَزِنَةَ عَرْشِهِ وَمِدَادَ كَلِمَاتِهِ وَكَمَا هُوَ أَهْلُهُ وَكُلَّمَا ذَكَرَهُ الذَّاكِرُونَ وَغَفَلَ عَنْ ذِكْرِهِ الغَافِلُونَ وَعَلَى أَهْلِ بَيْتِهِ وَعِتْرَتِهِ الطَّاهِرِينَ وَسَلَّمْ تَسْلِيمًا ❁

(30) Wa ṣalla 'Llāhu ʿalā Sayyīdinā Muḥammadin ʿadada khalqihi wa riḍā'a nafsihi wa zinata ʿarshihi wa midāda kalimātihi wa kamā hūwa āhluhu, wa kullamā dhakarahu 'dh-dhākirūna wa ghafala ʿan dhikrihi 'l-ghāfilūna wa ʿalā āhli baytihi wa ʿitratihi 'ṭ-ṭāhirīna wa sallama taslīma •

(30) And Allāh's blessings on our master Muḥammad on the number of His Creation, to the extent of His Pleasure,in the decoration of His Throne, in the ink of His Words, to the measure that He deserves, and whenever those who remember him do so and whenever those who neglect to remember him do so, and on the People of His House and his pure perfumed descendants, on whom be peace, over and over again! ❁

(٣١) اللَّهُمَّ صَلِّ عَلَى سَيِّدِنَا مُحَمَّدٍ وَعَلَى أَزْوَاجِهِ وَذُرِّيَّتِهِ وَعَلَى جَمِيعِ النَّبِيِّينَ وَالْمُرْسَلِينَ وَ الْمَلَآئِكَةِ وَالْمُقَرَّبِينَ وَجَمِيعِ عِبَادِ اللهِ الصَّالِحِينَ

(31) Allāhumma ṣalli ʿalā Sayyīdinā Muḥammadin wa ʿalā azwājihi wa dhurrīyatihi wa ʿalā jamīʿi 'n-nabīyyīnā wa 'l-mursalīna wa 'l-malā'ikati 'l-muqarrabīna wa jamīʿi ʿibādi 'Llāhi 'ṣ-ṣāliḥīna,

(31) O Allāh, bless our master Muḥammad and his wives and progeny and all the prophets and messengers and closest angels and all the righteous servants of Allāh ➢

عَدَدَ مَا أَمْطَرتِ السَّمَاءُ مُنْذُ بَنَيْتَهَا وَصَلِّ عَلَى سَيِّدِنَا مُحَمَّدٍ عَدَدَ مَا أَنبَتَتِ الْأَرْضُ مُنْذُ دَحَوْتَهَا وَصَلِّ عَلَى سَيِّدِنَا مُحَمَّدٍ عَدَدَ النُّجُومِ فِي السَّمَاءِ فَإِنَّكَ أَحْصَيتَهَا

ʿadada mā amṭarati 's-samā'u mundhu banaytahā wa ṣalli ʿalā Sayyīdinā Muḥammadin ʿadada mā anbatati 'l-arḍu mundhu daḥawtahā wa ṣalli ʿalā Sayyīdinā Muḥammadin ʿadada 'n-nujūmi fī 's-samā'i fa innaka aḥṣaytahā

on the amount of all rain that has showered from the sky since it was formed and bless our master Muḥammad on the number of all plants the earth has produced since it was spread out and bless our master Muḥammad on the number of the stars in the sky for You Alone are able to tally them! ➤

وَصَلِّ عَلَى سَيِّدِنا مُحَمَّدٍ عَدَدَ مَا تَنَفَّسَتِ الأَروَاحُ مُنْذُ خَلَقتَهَا وَصَلِّ عَلَى سَيِّدِنا مُحَمَّدٍ عَدَدَ مَا خَلَقْتَ وَمَا تَخْلُقُ ومَا أَحَاطَ بِهِ عِلْمُكَ وَأَضْعَافَ ذَلِكَ ❋

wa ṣalli ʿalā Sayyīdinā Muḥammadin ʿadada mā tanaffasati 'l-'arwāḥu mundhu khalaqtahā wa ṣalli ʿalā Sayyīdinā Muḥammadin ʿadada mā khalaqta wa mā takhluqu wa mā aḥāṭa bihi ʿilmuka wa aḍʿafa dhālika •

And bless our master Muḥammad on every breath of every soul from the moment You created themand bless our master Muḥammad in everything You have already created and in what You will create and in whatever is encompassed by Your Knowledge and then double all of that! ❋

(٣٢) اللَّهُمَّ صَلِّ عَلَيهِ عَدَدَ خَلْقِكَ وَرِضَا نَفْسِكَ وَزِنَةَ عَرْشِكَ وَمِدَادَ كَلِمَاتِكَ وَمَبْلَغَ عِلْمِكَ وَآيَاتِكَ ❋

(32) Allāhumma ṣalli ʿalayhi ʿadada khalqika wa riḍā'a nafsika wa zinata ʿarshika wa midāda kalimātika wa mablagha ʿilmika wa āyātika •

(32) O Allāh, exalt him on the number of Your Creation and as much as it pleases Yourself, as the decoration of Your Throne, as the ink of Your Words and to the extent of Your Knowledge and Signs! ❋

(٣٣) اللَّهُمَّ صَلِّ عَلَيهِ صَلَاةً تَفُوقُ وَتَفضُلُ صَلاةَ الْمُصَلِّينَ عَلَيهِ مِنَ الْخَلْقِ أَجْمَعِينَ كَفَضْلِكَ عَلَى جَمِيعِ خَلْقِكَ ❋

(33) Allāhumma ṣalli ʿalayhi ṣalātan tafūqu wa tafḍulu ṣalāta 'l-muṣallīna ʿalayhi mina 'l-khalqi ajmaʿīna ka-faḍlika ʿalā jamīʿi khalqika •

(33) O Allāh, exalt him, with blessings excellent, and more gracious, with exaltation equal to all the requests for blessing ever uttered by the whole of creation just as the whole of creation enjoys Your Favour in like measure! ❋

(٣٤) اللَّهُمَّ صَلِّ عَلَيهِ صَلَاةً دَائِمَةً مُستَمِرَّةَ الدَّوَامِ عَلَى مَرِّ اللَّيَالِي وَالْأَيَّامِ

(34) Allāhumma ṣalli ʿalayhi ṣalātan dā'imatan mustamirrata 'd-dawāmi ʿalā marri 'l-layāli wa 'l-ayyāmi

(34) O Allāh, exalt him, with eternal and permanent exaltation, for as long as the duration of all future nights and days, never ending and perpetual, ➢

مُتَّصِلَةَ الدَّوَامِ لَا اِنْقِضَاءَ لَهَا وَلَا اِنْصِرَامَ عَلَى مَرِّ اللَّيَالِي وَ الْأَيَّامِ عَدَدَ كُلِّ وَابِلٍ وَطَلٍّ ❋

muttaṣilata 'd-dawāmi lā inqiḍā'a lahā wa lā inṣirama ʿalā marri 'l-lāyāli wa 'l-ayyāmi ʿadada kulli wābilin wa ṭallin •

with blessings equal to the duration of all the days and nights which have already passed, with blessings as copious as the rain contained in every downpour and in every shower which has ever fallen! ❋

(٣٥) اللَّهُمَّ صَلِّ عَلَى سَيِّدِنَا مُحَمَّدٍ نَبِيِّكَ وَسَيِّدِنَا اِبْرَاهِيمَ خَلِيلِكَ وَعَلَى جَمِيعِ أَنْبِيَائِكَ وَأَصفِيائِكَ مِنْ أَهْلِ أَرْضِكَ وَسَمَائِكَ عَدَدَ خَلْقِكَ وَرِضَا نَفْسِكَ وَزِنَةَ عَرْشِكَ وَمِدَادَ كَلِمَاتِكَ وَمُنْتَهَى عِلْمِكَ وَزِنَةَ جَمِيعِ مَخْلُوقَاتِكَ

(35) Allāhumma ṣalli ʿalā Sayyīdinā Muḥammadin nabīyyika, wa Sayyīdinā Ibrāhīma khalīlika wa ʿalā jamīʿi anbīyā'ika wa aṣfiyā'ika min āhli arḍika wa samā'ika ʿadada khalqika wa riḍā'a nafsika wa zinata ʿarshika wa midāda kalimātika wa muntahā ʿilmika wa zinata jamīʿi makhluqātika

(35) O Allāh, exalt our master Muḥammad Your Prophet, and our master Abraham, Your Friend, and all the prophets and pure ones of the folk of Your earth and Your Heaven, in all of Your Creation, to the limit of Your pleasure, as the decoration of Your Throne, as the ink of Your Words, to the extent of Your Knowledge and the Adornments of Your created beings ➢

صَلَاةً مُكَرَّرَةً أَبَداً عَدَدَ مَا اَحْصَى عِلْمُكَ وَمِلْءَ مَا أَحْصَى عِلْمُكَ وَأَضْعَافَ مَا أَحْصَى عِلْمُكَ صَلَاةً تَزِيدُ وَتَفُوقُ وَتَفْضُلُ صَلَاةَ الْمُصَلِّينَ عَلَيهِ مِنَ الْخَلْقِ أَجْمَعِينَ كَفَضْلِكَ عَلَى جَمِيعِ خَلْقِكَ ❋

ṣalātan mukarraratan abadan ʿadada mā aḥṣā ʿilmuka wa mil'ā mā aḥsā ʿilmuka wa aḍʿāfa mā aḥṣā ʿilmuka ṣalātan tazīdu wa tafūqu wa tafḍulu ṣalāta 'l-muṣallīna ʿalayhim mina 'l-khalqi ajmaʿīna ka-faḍlika ʿalā jamīʿi khalqika •

With blessings repeated eternally as much as Your Knowledge and to the depth of Your Knowledge and then double this! With blessings, abundant, excellent and gracious equal to all the requests for blessings ever uttered by all of creation just as the whole of creation enjoys Your Favour in like measure! ❋

ثُمَّ تَدْعُو بِهَذَا الدُّعَاءِ فَإِنَّهُ مَرجُوُّ الْإِجَابَةِ إِنْ شَاءَ اللهُ تَعَالَى بَعْدَ الصَّلاَةِ عَلَى النَّبِيِّ ﷺ:

Thumma tadʿū bi-hadha 'd-duʿāi fa-innahu marjū'u 'l-ijābati inshā-Allāhu taʿalā bʿad aṣ-ṣalāta ʿalā 'n-nabī ﷺ.

Then make the following supplication, for it is believed to facilitate Allāh's response; after invoking blessings upon the Prophet ﷺ (*Allāhumma ṣalli ʿalā Sayyīdinā Muḥammad*) followed by the following prayer: ➤

(٣٦) اللَّهُمَّ اجْعَلْنِي مِمَّنْ لَزِمَ مِلَّةَ نَبِيِّكَ سَيِّدِنَا مُحَمَّدٍ ﷺ وَعَظَّمَ حُرْمَتَهُ وَأَعَزَّ كَلِمَتَهُ وَحَفِظَ عَهْدَهُ وَذِمَّتَهُ وَنَصَرَ حِزْبَهُ وَدَعْوَتَهُ وَكَثَّرَ تَابِعِيهِ وَفِرْقَتَهُ وَوَافَى زُمْرَتَهُ وَلَمْ يُخَالِفْ سَبِيلَهُ وَسُنَّتَهُ ❁

(36) Allāhumma 'j'alnī mimmān lazima millata Nabīyyika Sayyīdinā Muḥammadin ﷺ wa 'aẓama ḥurmatahu wa a'azza kalimātahu wa ḥafiẓa 'ahdahu wa dhimmatahu wa naṣara ḥizbahu wa da'watahu wa kathara tābi'īhi wa firqatahu wa wafā zumratahu wa lam yukhālif sabīlahu wa sunnatahu •

(36) O Allāh, grant me to be from among those who stick close to the way of Your Prophet, our master Muḥammad, ﷺ! Strengthen his holiness, empower his words, protect his promise and security, and give victory to his party and calling and increase those who pledge him and his company allegiance and grant that we may die in his company and do not allow us to stray from his path and way! ❁

(٣٧) اللَّهُمَّ إِنِّي أَسْأَلُكَ الإِسْتِمْسَاكَ بِسُنَّتِهِ وَأَعُوذُ بِكَ مِنَ الإِنْحِرَافِ عَمَّا جَاءَ بِهِ ❁

(37) Allāhumma innī as'aluka 'l-istimsāka bi-sunnatihi wa ā'ūdhū bika mina 'l-inḥirāfi 'ammā jā'a bihi •

(37) O Allāh, I ask You for loyalty to his way and seek refuge in You from all distortion of what he brought! ❁

(٣٨) اللَّهُمَّ إِنِّي أَسْأَلُكَ مِنْ خَيْرِ مَا سَأَلَكَ مِنْهُ سَيِّدُنَا مُحَمَّدٌ نَبِيُّكَ وَرَسُولُكَ ﷺ وَأَعُوذُ بِكَ مِنْ شَرِّ مَا اسْتَعَاذَكَ مِنْهُ سَيِّدُنَا مُحَمَّدٌ نَبِيُّكَ وَرَسُولُكَ ﷺ ❋

(38) Allāhumma innī as'aluka min khayri mā sa'alaka minhu sayyīdunā Muḥammadun Nabīyyuka wa rasūluka ﷺ *wa āʿūdhū bika min sharri mā 'staʿadhaka minhu sayyīdunā Muḥammadun nabīyyuka wa rasūluka* ﷺ •

(38) O Allāh, I ask You the good that our master Muḥammad, Your Prophet and Your Messenger asked of You, and I seek refuge in You from the evil of which our master Muḥammad, Your Prophet and Your Messenger sought refuge in You, ﷺ. ❋

(٣٩) اللَّهُمَّ اَعْصِمْنِي مِنْ شَرِّ الفِتَنِ وَعَافِنِي مِنْ جَمِيعِ الْمِحَنِ وَأَصْلِحْ مِنِّي مَا ظَهَرَ وَمَا بَطَنَ وَنَقِّ قَلْبِي مِنَ الحِقْدِ وَالحَسَدِ وَلاَ تَجْعَلْ عَلَيَّ تِبَاعَةً لِأَحَدٍ ❋

(39) Allāhumā āʿṣimnī min sharri 'l-fitani wa ʿāfinī min jamīʿi 'l-miḥani wa aṣliḥ minnī mā ẓahara wa mā baṭana wa naqqi qalbī mina 'l-ḥiqdi wa 'l-ḥasadi wa lā tajʿal ʿalayya tibāʿatan li-aḥad •

(39) O Allāh, protect me from the evil of discord and absolve me from all tests and purify me from within and cleanse my heart from hatred and envy and do not allow any one to oppress me! ❋

(٤٠) اللَّهُمَّ إِنِّي أَسْأَلُكَ الْأَخْذَ بِأَحْسَنِ مَا تَعْلَمُ وَالتَّرْكَ لِسَيِّءِ مَا تَعْلَمُ وَأَسْأَلُكَ التَّكَفُّلَ بِالرِّزْقِ وَالزُّهْدَ فِي الكَفَافِ وَالْمَخْرَجَ بِالبَيَانِ مِنْ كُلِّ شُبْهَةٍ وَالفَلَجَ بِالصَّوَابِ فِي كُلِّ حُجَّةٍ وَالعَدْلَ فِي الغَضَبِ وَالرِّضَا

(40) Allāhumma innī as'aluka 'l-akhdha bi-aḥsani mā ta'lamu wa 't-tarka li-sayy'i mā ta'lamu wa as'aluka 't-takaffula bi-'r-rizqi wa 'z-zuhda fī 'l-kafāfi wa 'l-makhraja bi 'l-bayāni min kulli shubhatin wa 'l-falaja bi 'ṣ-ṣawābi fī kulli ḥujjatin wa 'l-'adlu fī 'l-ghaḍabi wa 'r-riḍā

(40) O Allāh, I ask Youfor the best of what You know and to let me leave the worst of that You know and I ask You to surety in my provision, for austerity in subsistence, a clear way out from every uncertainty, a proper stance in every argument, and fairness, whether in anger or pleasure, ➤

وَالتَّسلِيمَ لِمَا يَجْرِي بِهِ القَضَاءُ وَالاِقتِصَادَ فِي الفَقْرِ وَالْغِنَى وَالتَوَاضُعَ فِي القَوْلِ وَالفِعْلِ وَالصِّدْقِ فِي الجِدِّ وَالْهَزْلِ ❋

wa 't-taslīma limā yajrī bihi 'l-qaḍā wa 'l-iqtiṣāda fī 'l-faqri wa 'l-ghinā wa 't-tawāḍu'i fī 'l-qawli wa 'l-fi'ali wa 'ṣ-ṣidqi fī 'l-jaddi wa 'l-hazli •

acceptance of whatever fate ordains, economy in poverty and wealth, humility in my words and actions and sincerity in both solemnity and jest! ❋

(٤١) اللَّهُمَّ إِنَّ لِي ذُنُوباً فِيمَا بَينِي وَبَيْنِكَ وَذُنُوباً فِيمَا بَيْنِي وَبَيْنَ خَلْقِكَ اللَّهُمَّ مَا كَانَ لَكَ مِنْهَا فَاغْفِرْهُ وَمَا كَانَ مِنْهَا لِخَلْقِكَ فَتَحَمَّلْهُ عَنِّي وَاغْنِنِي بِفَضْلِكَ إِنَّكَ وَاسِعُ المَغْفِرَةِ ❋

(41) Allāhumma inna lī dhunūban fīmā baynī wa baynaka wa dhunūban fīmā baynī wa bayna khalqik. Allāhumma mā kāna laka minhā fa'ghfirhu wa mā kāna minhā li-khalqika fa-taḥammalhu ʿannī w 'aghninī bi-faḍlika innaka wāsiʿu 'l-maghfirah •

(41) O Allāh, indeed I have commited sins against Your Rights over me and I have commited sins against Your Creation! O Allāh, whatever relates to You, forgive, and whatever relates to Your Creation them for me and enrich me with Your Favours, for You are vast in forgiveness! ❋

(٤٢) اللَّهُمَّ نَوِّرَ بِالعِلْمِ قَلْبِي وَاسْتَعْمِلْ بِطَاعَتِكَ بَدَنِي وَخَلِّصْ مِنَ الفِتَنِ سِرِّي وَاشْغَلَ بِالإِعْتِبَارِ فِكْرِي

(42) Allāhumma nawwir bi 'l-ʿilmi qalbī, wa 'staʿmil bi-ṭāʿatika badanī wa khalliṣ mina 'l-fitani sirrī wa 'shghil bi 'l-'iʿtibāri fikrī

(42) O Allāh, enlighten the knowledge of my heart and render my body obedient to You and purify me from inner discord and occupy my mind with reflection ➤

وَقِنِي شَرَّ وَسَاوِسِ الشَّيطَانِ وَأَجِرْنِي مِنْهُ يَا رَحْمَنُ حَتَّى لَا يَكُونَ لَهُ عَلَيَّ سُلْطَان ❊

wa qinī sharra wasāwisi 'sh-shayṭāni wa ajirnī minhu yā raḥmānu ḥattā lā yakūna lahu 'alayya sulṭān •

and protect me from the whisperings of Satan and save me from him, O Most Compassionate, until he no longer holds any power over me! ❊

الثُّلاثَاء

Tuesday

الْحِزْبُ الثَّانِي فِي يَوْمِ الثُّلاثَاء

Al-Ḥizbu 'th-Thānī fī Yawmi 'th-Thulāthā'

Second Chapter to be Read on Tuesday

(١) اللهُمَّ إِنِّي أَسْأَلُكَ مِنْ خَيْرِ مَا تَعْلَمُ وَأَعُوذُ بِكَ مِنْ شَرِّ مَا تَعْلَمُ وَأَسْتَغْفِرُكَ مِنْ كُلِّ مَا تَعلَمُ إِنَّكَ تَعلَمُ وَلَا نَعْلَمُ وَأَنتَ عَلَّامُ الغُيُوبِ ❋

(1) Allāhumma innī as'aluka min khayri mā taʿlamu wa āʿūdhū bika min sharri mā taʿlamu wa astaghfiruka min kulli mā taʿlamu innaka taʿlamu wa lā naʿlamu wa anta ʿallāmu 'l-ghuyūb •

(1) O Allāh , I ask You from the good of that which You know, and I seek refuge in You from the evil of that which You know, and I seek Your forgiveness for everything You know, for You indeed know and we know not and indeed You are Knower of the Unseen! ❋

(٢) اللَّهُمَّ ارْحَمْنِي مِنْ زَمَانِي هَذَا وَإِحْدَاقِ الْفِتَنِ وَتَطَاوُلِ أَهْلِ الْجُرْأَةِ عَلَيَّ وَاسْتِضْعَافِهِمْ إِيَّايَ ❋

(2) Allāhumma 'rḥamnī min zamānī hādhā wa iḥdāqi 'l-fitani wa taṭawuli āhli 'l-jur'āti ʿalayya wa 'stiḍʿāfihim iyyāy •

(2) O Allāh have mercy on me from this era in which I live, from being encompassed by tribulation, from the oppression of the insolent and from my weakness before them ❋

(٣) اللَّهُمَّ اجْعَلْنِي مِنْكَ فِي عِيَاذٍ مَنِيعٍ وَحِرْزٍ حَصِينٍ مِنْ جَمِيعِ خَلْقِكَ حَتَّى تُبَلِّغَنِي أَجَلِي مُعَافًى ❋

(3) Allāhumma 'jʿalnī minka fī ʿiyadhin manīʿin wa ḥirzin ḥaṣīnin min jamīʿi khalqika ḥattā tuballighanī ajalī muʿafā •

(3) O Allāh, make from You for me an unassailable refuge, and an impenetrable fortress from all Your Creation until You cause me to reach to a virtuous end! ❋

(٤) اللَّهُمَّ صَلِّ عَلَى سَيِّدِنَا مُحَمَّدٍ وَعَلَى آلِ سَيِّدِنَا مُحَمَّدٍ عَدَدَ مَنْ صَلَّى عَلَيهِ

(4) Allāhumma ṣalli ʿalā Sayyīdinā Muḥammadin wa ʿalā āli Sayyīdinā Muḥammadin ʿadada man ṣalla ʿalayhi

(4) Allāh, bless our master Muḥammad and the family of our master Muḥammad as many times as those who have asked for blessings upon him! ➢

وَصَلِّ عَلَى سَيِّدِنَا مُحَمَّدٍ وَعَلَى آلِ سَيِّدِنَا مُحَمَّدٍ عَدَدَ مَنْ لَمْ يُصَلِّ عَلَيْهِ وَصَلِّ عَلَى سَيِّدِنَا مُحَمَّدٍ وَعَلَى آلِ سَيِّدِنَا مُحَمَّدٍ كَمَا تَنْبَغِي الصَّلَاةُ عَلَيْهِ

wa ṣalli ʿalā Sayyīdinā Muḥammadin wa ʿalā āli Sayyīdinā Muḥammadin ʿadada man lam yuṣalli ʿalayhi wa ṣalli ʿalā Sayyīdinā Muḥammadin wa ʿalā āli Sayyīdinā Muḥammadin kamā tambaghī 'ṣ-ṣalātu ʿalayhi

O Allāh, exalt our master Muḥammad and the family of our master Muḥammad on the number of those who have not asked for blessings upon him and exalt our master Muḥammad and the family of our master Muḥammad with as much praise as befits him ➢

وَصَلِّ عَلَى سَيِّدِنَا مُحَمَّدٍ وَعَلَى آلِ سَيِّدِنَا مُحَمَّدٍ كَمَا تَجِبُ الصَّلَاةُ عَلَيْهِ وَصَلِّ عَلَى سَيِّدِنَا مُحَمَّدٍ وَعَلَى آلِ سَيِّدِنَا مُحَمَّدٍ كَمَا أَمَرتَ أَنْ يُصَلَّى عَلَيْهِ

wa ṣalli ʿalā Sayyīdinā Muḥammadin wa ʿalā āli Sayyīdinā Muḥammadin kamā tajibu 'ṣ-ṣalātu ʿalayhi wa ṣalli ʿalā Sayyīdinā Muḥammadin wa ʿalā āli Sayyīdinā Muḥammadin kamā amarta an yuṣalla ʿalayhi

and exalt our master Muḥammad and the family of our master Muḥammad with as much praise as is his due and exalt our master Muḥammad and the family of our master Muḥammad as much as You have ordered creation to praise him! ➢

وَصَلِّ عَلَى سَيِّدِنَا مُحَمَّدٍ وَعَلَى آلِ سَيِّدِنَا مُحَمَّدٍ الَّذِي نُورُهُ مِنْ نُورِ الْأَنْوَارِ وَأَشْرَقَ بِشُعَاعِ سِرِّهِ الْأَسْرَارُ اللَّهُمَّ صَلِّ عَلَى سَيِّدِنَا مُحَمَّدٍ وَعَلَى آلِ سَيِّدِنَا مُحَمَّدٍ وَعَلَى أَهْلِ بَيْتِهِ الْأَبْرَارِ أَجْمَعِينَ ❋

wa ṣalli ʿalā Sayyīdinā Muḥammadini 'Lladhī nūruhu min nūri 'l-anwāri wa ashraqa bi-shuʿā'i sirrihi 'l-asrār. Allāhumma ṣalli ʿalā Sayyīdinā Muḥammadin wa ʿalā āli Sayyīdinā Muḥammadin wa ʿalā āhli baytihi 'l-abrāri ajmaʿīn •

And exalt our master Muḥammad and the family of our master Muḥammad whose light is from the light of lights, and who by the secret of his shining ray illuminated all secrets! O Allāh, bless our master Muḥammad and the family of our master Muḥammad and all the chosen people of his House! ❋

(٥) اللَّهُمَّ صَلِّ عَلَى سَيِّدِنَا مُحَمَّدٍ وَعَلَى آلِهِ بَحْرِ أَنْوَارِكَ وَمَعْدِنِ أَسْرَارِكَ وَلِسَانِ حُجَّتِكَ وَعَرُوسِ مَمْلَكَتِكَ وَإِمَامِ حَضْرَتِكَ

(5) Allāhumma ṣalli ʿalā Sayyīdinā Muḥammadin wa ʿalā ālihi baḥri anwārika wa maʿdini asrārika, wa lisāni ḥujjatika wa ʿarūsi mamlakatika wa imāmi ḥaḍratika

(5) O Allāh, exalt our master Muḥammad and his family, the Sea of Your lights, the Mine of Your Secrets, the Tongue of Your Proof, the Bridegroom of Your Kingdom and Leader of Your Divine Presence ➢

وَخَاتِمِ أَنْبِيَائِكَ صَلَاةً تَدُومُ بِدَوامِكَ وَتَبْقَى بِبَقَائِكَ صَلَاةً تُرْضِيكَ وَتُرْضِيهِ وَتَرضَى بِهاَ عَنّا يَا ارْحَمْ الرَّاحِمِينَ ❋

wa khātimi anbīyā'ika ṣalātan tadūmu bi-dawāmika wa tabqā bi-baqā'ika ṣalātan turḍīka wa turḍīhi wa tarḍā bihā 'annā yā arḥama 'r-rāḥimīn •

and the Seal of Your Prophets, with praise enduring as long as You last and remaining as long as You remain, praise which pleases You, which pleases him and which makes You pleased with us, O Most Merciful of Those Who Show Mercy ❋

(٦) اللَّهُمَّ رَبَّ الحِلِّ وَالحَرَامِ ورَبَّ الْمَشْعَرِ الحَرَامِ وَرَبَّ البَيتِ الحَرَامِ وَرَبَّ الرُّكْنِ وَالمَقَامِ أَبْلِغْ لِسَيِّدِنَا وَمَوْلَانَا مُحَمَّدٍ مِنَّا السَّلَامَ ❋

(6) Allāhumma rabba 'l-ḥilli wa 'l-ḥarāmi wa rabba 'l-mash'ari 'l-ḥarāmi wa rabba 'l-bayti 'l-ḥarāmi wa rabba 'r-rukni wa 'l-maqāmi abligh li-Sayyīdinā wa mawlānā Muḥammadin minna 's-salām •

(6) O Allāh! Lord of the Permissible and the Forbidden, Lord of the Sacred Monuments, Lord of the Sacred House and Lord of the Corner and the Station of Abraham, send peace from us to our master and guardian Muḥammad! ❋

(٧) اللَّهُمَّ صَلِّ عَلَى سَيِّدِنَا وَمَوْلَانَا مُحَمَّدٍ سَيِّدِ الأَوَّلِينَ وَالآخِرِينَ

(7) Allāhumma ṣalli 'alā Sayyīdinā wa mawlānā Muḥammadin sayyidi 'l-awwalīna wa 'l-ākhirīn.

(7) O Allāh exalt our master and guardian Muḥammad the master of the firsts and the lasts! ➢

اللَّهُمَّ صَلِّ عَلَى سَيِّدِنَا وَمَوْلَانَا مُحَمَّدٍ فِي كُلِّ وَقْتٍ وَحِينٍ اللَّهُمَّ صَلِّ عَلَى سَيِّدِنَا وَمَوْلَانَا مُحَمَّدٍ فِي الْمَلَإِ الْأَعْلَى إِلَى يَوْمِ الدِّينِ اللَّهُمَّ صَلِّ عَلَى سَيِّدِنَا وَمَوْلَانَا مُحَمَّدٍ حَتَّى تَرِثَ الْأَرْضَ وَمَنْ عَلَيْهَا وَأَنْتَ خَيْرُ الْوَارِثِينَ ❋

Allāhumma ṣalli ʿalā Sayyīdinā wa mawlānā Muḥammadin fī kulli waqtin wa ḥīn. Allāhumma ṣalli ʿalā Sayyīdinā wa mawlānā Muḥammadin fī 'l-mala'i 'l-'āʿlā ilā yawmi 'd-dīn. Allāhumma ṣalli ʿalā Sayyīdinā wa mawlānā Muḥammadin ḥattā taritha 'l-arḍa wa man ʿalayhā wa anta khayru 'l-wārithīn •

O Allāh exalt our master and guardian Muḥammad at every moment and every instant! O Allāh, exalt our master and our guardian Muḥammad in the Heavenly Assembly until the Day of Judgment! O Allāh, bless our master and our guardian Muḥammad until the earth bequeaths itself and whoever is on it and You are The Best of Inheritors! ❋

(٨) اللَّهُمَّ صَلِّ عَلَى سَيِّدِنَا مُحَمَّدٍ النَّبِيِّ الْأُمِّي وَعَلَى آلِ سَيِّدِنَا مُحَمَّدٍ كَمَا صَلَّيْتَ عَلَى سَيِّدِنَا إِبْرَاهِيمَ إِنَّكَ حَمِيدٌ مَجِيدٌ

(8) Allāhumma ṣalli ʿalā Sayyīdinā Muḥammadini 'n-nabīyyi 'l-ummīyyi wa ʿalā āli Sayyīdinā Muḥammadin kamā ṣallayta ʿalā Sayyīdinā Ibrāhīma innaka Ḥamīdun Majīd

(8) O Allāh, exalt our lord and master Muḥammad, the Unlettered Prophet, and the family of Muḥammad just as You exalted our master Abraham, for You are The Praiseworthy, The Mighty! ➤

وَبَارِكْ عَلَى سَيِّدِنَا مُحَمَّدٍ النَّبِيِّ الْأُمِّي كَمَا بَارَكْتَ عَلَى سَيِّدِنَا إِبرَاهِيمَ إِنَّكَ حَمِيدٌ مَجِيدٌ ❋

wa bārik ʿalā Sayyīdinā Muḥammadini 'n-nabīyyi 'l-ummīyyi kamā bārakta ʿalā Sayyīdinā Ibrāhīma innaka Ḥamīdun Majīd •

And bless our master Muḥammad, the Unlettered Prophet, and the family of Muḥammad just as You blessed our master Abraham for You are The Praiseworthy, The Mighty! ❋

(٩) اللَّهُمَّ صَلِّ عَلَى سَيِّدِنَا مُحَمَّدٍ وَعَلَى آلِ سَيِّدِنَا مُحَمَّدٍ عَدَدَ مَا أَحَاطَ بِهِ عِلْمُكَ وَجَرَى بِهِ قَلَمُكَ وَسَبَقَتْ بِهِ مَشِيئَتُكَ وَصَلَّتْ عَلَيهِ مَلَآئِكَتُكَ صَلَاةً دَائِمَةً بِدَوَامِكَ

(9) Allāhumma ṣalli ʿalā Sayyīdinā Muḥammadin wa ʿalā āli Sayyīdinā Muḥammadin ʿadada mā aḥaṭa bihi ʿilmuka wa jarā bihi qalamuka wa sabaqat bihi mashī'atuka wa ṣallat ʿalayhi malā'ikatuka ṣalātan dā'imatan bi-dawāmika

(9) O Allāh, exalt our master Muḥammad and the family of our master Muḥammad as much as Your Knowledge has encompassed, in everything that Your Pen writes and in all that Your Will preordains, and as often as Your angels have praised him, with eternal blessings, lasting as long as You last, ➢

بَاقِيَةً بِفَضْلِكَ وَإِحسَانِكَ إِلَى أَبَدِ الْأَبَدِ أَبَداً لَا نِهَايَةَ لِأَبدِيَّتِهِ وَلَا فَنَاءَ لِدَيْمُومِيَّتِهِ ❋

bāqīyyatan bi-faḍlika wa iḥsānika ilā abadi 'l-abadi abadan lā nihāyata li-abdīyyatihi wa lā fanā'a li-daymūmīyyatihi •

subsisting by Your Grace and Your Generosity, until the end of eternity, never-ending, with no beginning to them, and no end to them, forever and ever! ❋

(١٠) اللَّهُمَّ صَلِّ عَلَى سَيِّدِنَا مُحَمَّدٍ وَعَلَى آلِ سَيِّدِنَا مُحَمَّدٍ عَدَدَ مَا أَحَاطَ بِهِ عِلْمُكَ وَأَحْصَاهُ كِتَابُكَ وَشَهِدَتْ بِهِ مَلَآئِكَتُكَ وَارْضَ عَنْ أَصْحَابِهِ وَارْحَمْ أُمَّتَهُ إِنَّكَ حَمِيدٌ مَجِيدٌ ❋

(10) Allāhumma ṣalli ʿalā Sayyīdinā Muḥammadin wa ʿalā āli Sayyīdinā Muḥammadin ʿadada mā aḥāṭa bihi ʿilmuka wa aḥṣāhu kitābuka wa shahidat bihi malā'ikatuka wa 'rḍā ʿan aṣḥābihi wa 'rḥam ummatahu innaka Ḥamīdun Majīd •

(10) O Allāh, exalt our master Muḥammad and the family of our master Muḥammad as much Your Knowledge encompasses, and as much as the knowledge contained in Your Book and as much Your angels witnessed, and be pleased with his Companions and be merciful on his nation for You are The Praiseworthy, The Mighty! ❋

(11) اللَّهُمَّ صَلِّ عَلَى سَيِّدِنَا مُحَمَّدٍ وَعَلَى آلِ سَيِّدِنَا مُحَمَّدٍ وَعَلَى جَمِيعِ أَصْحَابِ سَيِّدِنَا مُحَمَّدٍ ❁

(11) Allāhumma ṣalli 'alā Sayyīdinā Muḥammadin wa 'alā āli Sayyīdinā Muḥammadin wa 'alā jamī'i aṣ-ḥābi Sayyīdinā Muḥammadin •

(11) O Allāh, exalt our master Muḥammad and the family of our master Muḥammad, and all the companions of our master Muḥammad! ❁

(١٢) اللَّهُمَّ صَلِّ عَلَى سَيِّدِنَا مُحَمَّدٍ وَعَلَى آلِ سَيِّدِنَا مُحَمَّدٍ كَمَا صَلَّيْتَ عَلَى سَيِّدِنَا إِبْرَاهِيمَ وَبَارِكْ عَلَى سَيِّدِنَا مُحَمَّدٍ وَعَلَى آل سَيِّدِنَا مُحَمَّدٍ كَمَا بَارَكْتَ عَلَى سَيِّدِنَا إِبْرَاهِيمَ وَعَلَى آلِ سَيِّدِنَا إِبْرَاهِيمَ فِي العَالَمِينَ إِنَّكَ حَمِيدٌ مَجِيدٌ ❁

(12) Allāhumma ṣalli 'alā Sayyīdinā Muḥammadin wa 'alā āli Sayyīdinā Muḥammadin kamā ṣallayta 'alā Sayyīdinā Ibrāhīma wa bāriki' Llāhumma 'alā Sayyīdinā Muḥammadin wa 'alā āli Sayyīdinā Muḥammadin kamā bārakta 'alā Sayyīdinā Ibrāhīma wa 'alā āli Sayyīdinā Ibrāhīma fī 'l-'Ālamīna innaka Ḥamīdun Majīd •

(12) O Allāh, exalt our master Muḥammad and the family of our master Muḥammad Just as You have exalted our master Abraham, and bless our master Muḥammad and the family of our master Muḥammad just as You have blessed our master Abraham. In all the worlds You are The Praiseworthy, The Mighty! ❁

(١٣) اللَّهُمَّ صَلِّ عَلَى سَيِّدِنَا وَمَوْلَانَا مُحَمَّدٍ عَدَدَ مَا أَحَاطَ بِهِ عِلْمُكَ اللَّهُمَّ صَلِّ عَلَى سَيِّدِنَا وَمَوْلَانَا مُحَمَّدٍ عَدَدَ مَا أَحْصَاهُ كِتَابُكَ اللَّهُمَّ صَلِّ عَلَى سَيِّدِنَا وَمَوْلَانَا مُحَمَّدٍ عَدَدَ مَا نَفذَتْ بِهِ قُدرَتُكَ اللَّهُمَّ صَلِّ عَلَى سَيِّدِنَا وَمَوْلَانَا مُحَمَّدٍ عَدَدَ مَا خَصَّصَتْهُ إِرَادَتُكَ

(13) Allāhumma ṣalli ʿalā Sayyīdinā wa mawlānā Muḥammadin ʿadada mā aḥāṭa bihi ʿilmuka Allāhumma ṣalli ʿalā Sayyīdinā wa mawlānā Muḥammadin ʿadada mā aḥṣāhu kitābuk Allāhumma ṣalli ʿalā Sayyīdinā wa mawlānā Muḥammadin ʿadada mā nafadhat bihi qudratuk Allāhumma ṣalli ʿalā Sayyīdinā wa mawlānā Muḥammadin ʿadada mā khaṣṣaṣat-hu irādatuk

(13) O Allāh, exalt our master and guardian Muḥammad to the extent of that emcompassed by Your Knowledge! O Allāh exalt our master and guardian Muḥammad as much as is specified by Your Book! O Allāh exalt our master and guardian Muḥammad on the number of things subject to Your Power! O Allāh, exalt our master and guardian Muḥammad on the number of things chosen by Your Will! ➢

اللَّهُمَّ صَلِّ عَلَى سَيِّدِنَا و مَوْلَانَا مُحَمَّدٍ عَدَدَ مَا تَوَجَّهَ إِلَيْهِ أَمْرُكَ وَنَهْيُكَ

Allāhumma ṣalli ʿalā Sayyīdinā wa mawlānā Muḥammadin ʿadada mā tawajjaha ilayhi amruka wa nahīyuk

O Allāh exalt our master Muḥammad on the number of things to which You directed Your order and prohibition! ➢

اللَّهُمَّ صَلِّ عَلَى سَيِّدِنَا وَمَوْلَانَا مُحَمَّدٍ عَدَدَ مَا وَسِعَهُ سَمْعُكَ اللَّهُمَّ صَلِّ عَلَى سَيِّدِنَا وَمَوْلَانَا مُحَمَّدٍ عَدَدَ مَا أَحَاطَ بِهِ بَصَرُكَ ❋

Allāhumma ṣalli 'alā Sayyīdinā wa mawlānā Muḥammadin 'adada mā wasi'ahu sam'uk Allāhumma ṣalli 'alā Sayyīdinā wa mawlānā Muḥammadin 'adada mā aḥāṭa bihi baṣaruk •

O Allāh exalt our master and guardian Muḥammad on the number of things within Your Hearing! O Allāh exalt our master and guardian Muḥammad in whatever is encompassed by Your Vision! ❋

(١٤) اللَّهُمَّ صَلِّ عَلَى سَيِّدِنَا وَمَوْلَانَا مُحَمَّدٍ عَدَدَ مَا ذَكَرَهُ الذَّاكِرُونَ اللَّهُمَّ صَلِّ عَلَى سَيِّدِنَا وَمَوْلَانَا مُحَمَّدٍ عَدَدَ مَا غَفَلَ عَنْ ذِكْرِهِ الْغَافِلُونَ ❋

(14) Allāhumma ṣalli 'alā Sayyīdinā wa mawlānā Muḥammadin 'adada mā dhakarahu 'dh-dhākirūn Allāhumma ṣalli 'alā Sayyīdinā Muḥammadin 'adada mā ghafala 'an dhikrihi 'l-ghāfilūn •

(14) O Allāh exalt our master and guardian Muḥammad as much as those who remember him do so! O Allāh exalt our master Muḥammad as many times as those who neglect to remember him do so! ❋

(١٥) اللَّهُمَّ صَلِّ عَلَى سَيِّدِنَا وَمَوْلَانَا مُحَمَّدٍ عَدَدَ قَطْرِ الْأَمْطَارِ

(15) Allāhumma ṣalli 'alā Sayyīdinā wa mawlānā Muḥammadin 'adada qaṭri 'l-amṭār

(15) O Allāh, bless our master and guardian Muḥammad on the number of the drops of rain! ➢

اللَّهُمَّ صَلِّ عَلَى سَيِّدِنَا وَمَوْلَانَا مُحَمَّدٍ عَدَدَ دَوابِّ الْقِفَارِ اللَّهُمَّ صَلِّ عَلَى سَيِّدِنَا وَمَوْلَانَا مُحَمَّدٍ عَدَدَ دَوابِّ الْبِحَارِ اللَّهُمَّ صَلِّ عَلَى سَيِّدِنَا وَمَوْلَانَا مُحَمَّدٍ عَدَدَ مِيَاهِ البِحَارِ اللَّهُمَّ صَلِّ عَلَى سَيِّدِنَا وَمَوْلَانَا مُحَمَّدٍ عَدَدَ مَا أَظْلَمَ عَلَيهِ اللَّيلُ وَأَضَاءَ عَلَيهِ النَّهَارُ ❁

Allāhumma ṣalli ʿalā Sayyīdinā wa mawlānā Muḥammadin ʿadada awrāqi 'l-ashjār Allāhumma ṣalli ʿalā Sayyīdinā wa mawlānā Muhammmadin ʿadada dawābbi 'l-qifār Allāhumma ṣalli ʿalā Sayyīdinā wa mawlānā Muḥammadin ʿadada dawābbi 'l-bihār Allāhumma ṣalli ʿalā Sayyīdinā wa mawlānā Muḥammadin ʿadada mīyāhi 'l-bihār Allāhumma ṣalli ʿalā Sayyīdinā wa mawlānā Muḥammadin ʿadada mā aẓlama ʿalayhi 'l-laylu wa aḍā'a ʿalayhi 'n-nahār •

O Allāh, exalt our master and guardian Muḥammad on the number of leaves on the trees! O Allāh, exalt our master and guardian Muḥammad on the number of the beasts of the desert! O Allāh, exalt our master and guardian Muḥammad on the number of creatures in the sea! O Allāh, exalt our master and guardian Muḥammad, as much as the water in the sea! O Allāh, exalt our master and guardian Muḥammad on the number of things covered by the darkness of the night and illuminated by the light of the day! ❁

(١٦) اللَّهُمَّ صَلِّ عَلَى سَيِّدِنَا وَمَوْلَانَا مُحَمَّدٍ بِالْغُدُوِّ وَالْآصَالِ اللَّهُمَّ صَلِّ عَلَى سَيِّدِنَا وَمَوْلَانَا مُحَمَّدٍ عَدَدَ الرِمَالِ اللَّهُمَّ صَلِّ عَلَى سَيِّدِنَا وَمَوْلَانَا مُحَمَّدٍ عَدَدَ النِّسَاءِ وَالرِّجَالِ ❋

(16) Allāhumma ṣalli ʿalā Sayyīdinā wa mawlānā Muḥammadin bi 'l-ghudūwwi wa 'l-āṣāl Allāhumma ṣalli ʿalā Sayyīdinā wa mawlānā Muḥammadin ʿadada 'r-rimāl Allāhumma ṣalli ʿalā Sayyīdinā wa mawlānā Muḥammadin ʿadada 'n-nisā'i wa 'r-rijāl •

(16) O Allāh, exalt our master and guardian Muḥammad in the morning and in the evening! O Allāh exalt our master and guardian Muḥammad on the number of the grains of sand! O Allāh, exalt our master and guardian Muḥammad on the number of men and women! ❋

(١٧) اللَّهُمَّ صَلِّ عَلَى سَيِّدِنَا وَمَوْلَانَا مُحَمَّدٍ رِضَا نَفْسِكَ اللَّهُمَّ صَلِّ عَلَى سَيِّدِنَا وَمَوْلَانَا مُحَمَّدٍ مِدَادَ كَلِمَاتِكَ

(17) Allāhumma ṣalli ʿalā Sayyīdinā wa mawlānā Muḥammadin riḍā nafsika Allāhumma ṣalli ʿalā Sayyīdinā wa mawlānā Muḥammadin midāda kalimātika

(17) O Allāh, exalt our master and guardian Muḥammad as as is pleasing to You! O Allāh, bless our master and guardian Muḥammad to the extent of Your Words! ➢

اللَّهُمَّ صَلِّ عَلَى سَيِّدِنَا وَمَوْلَانَا مُحَمَّدٍ مِلْءَ سَمَاوَاتِكَ وَأَرْضِكَ اللَّهُمَّ صَلِّ عَلَى سَيِّدِنَا وَمَوْلَانَا مُحَمَّدٍ زِنَةَ عَرْشِكَ ❊

Allāhumma ṣalli ʿalā Sayyīdinā wa mawlānā Muḥammadin mila' samāwātika wa arḍik Allāhumma ṣalli ʿalā Sayyīdinā wa mawlānā Muḥammadin zinata ʿarshika •

O Allāh, exalt our master and guardian Muḥammad to the fullness of Your heavens and Your earth! O Allāh, exalt our master and guardian Muḥammad as the ornamentation of Your Throne! ❊

(١٨) اللَّهُمَّ صَلِّ عَلَى سَيِّدِنَا وَمَوْلَانَا مُحَمَّدٍ عَدَدَ مَخْلُوقَاتِكَ اللَّهُمَّ صَلِّ عَلَى سَيِّدِنَا وَمَوْلَانَا مُحَمَّدٍ أَفْضَلَ صَلَوَاتِكَ ❊

(18) Allāhumma ṣalli ʿalā Sayyīdinā wa mawlānā Muḥammadin ʿadada makhlūqātika Allāhumma ṣalli ʿalā Sayyīdinā wa mawlānā Muḥammadin afḍala ṣalawātika •

(18) O Allāh, exalt our master and helper Muḥammad on the number of created beings! O Allāh, praise our master and guardian Muḥammad with Your best praises ❊

(١٩) اللَّهُمَّ صَلِّ عَلَى نَبِيِّ الرَّحْمَةِ اللَّهُمَّ صَلِّ عَلَى شَفِيعِ الْأُمَّةِ

(19) Allāhumma ṣalli ʿalā nabīyyi 'r-raḥmah Allāhumma ṣalli ʿalā shafīʿi 'l-ummati

(19) O Allāh, exalt the Prophet of Mercy! O Allāh, exalt the Intercessor of the Nation! ➢

اللَّهُمَّ صَلِّ عَلَى كَاشِفِ الْغُمَّةِ اللَّهُمَّ صَلِّ عَلَى مُجْلِي الظُّلْمَةِ اللَّهُمَّ صَلِّ عَلَى مُوْلِي النِّعْمَةِ اللَّهُمَّ صَلِّ عَلَى مُؤْتِي الرَّحْمَةِ ❋

Allāhumma ṣalli ʿalā kashifi 'l-ghummati Allāhumma ṣalli ʿalā mujlī 'ẓ-ẓulmati Allāhumma ṣalli ʿalā muwli 'n-niʿmati, Allāhumma ṣalli ʿalā mū'tī 'r-raḥmati •

O Allāh, exalt the Remover of Grief! O Allāh, exalt the Clarifier of Darkness! O Allāh, exalt the Guardian of Favors! O Allāh exalt the Grantor of Mercy! ❋

(٢٠) اللَّهُمَّ صَلِّ عَلَى صَاحِبِ الْحَوْضِ الْمَوْرُودِ اللَّهُمَّ صَلِّ عَلَى صَاحِبِ الْمَقَامِ الْمَحْمُودِ اللَّهُمَّ صَلِّ عَلَى صَاحِبِ اللِّوَاءِ الْمَعْقُودِ اللَّهُمَّ صَلِّ عَلَى صَاحِبِ الْمَكَانِ الْمَشْهُودِ اللَّهُمَّ صَلِّ عَلَى الْمَوْصُوفِ بِالْكَرَمِ وَالْجُودِ

(20) Allāhumma ṣalli ʿalā ṣāḥibi 'l-ḥawḍi 'l-mawrūdi Allāhumma ṣalli ʿalā ṣāḥibi 'l-maqāmi 'l-maḥmūdi Allāhumma ṣalli ʿalā ṣāḥibi 'l-liwā'i 'l-maʿqūdi Allāhumma ṣalli ʿalā ṣāḥib 'l-makāni 'l-mash-hūdi Allāhumma ṣalli ʿalā 'l-mawṣūfi bi-'l-karami wa 'l-jūdi

(20) O Allāh, exalt the Owner of the Much-frequented Pool! O Allāh, bless the Owner of the Most Praised Station! O Allāh, exalt the Owner of the Raised Banner! O Allāh, exalt the Owner of the Witnessed Site! O Allāh, exalt the One characterized by bobility and generosity! ➢

اللَّهُمَّ صَلِّ عَلَى مَنْ هُوَ فِي السَّمَاءِ سَيِّدُنَا مَحْمُودٌ وَفِي الأَرْضِ سَيِّدُنَا مُحَمَّدٌ ❋

Allāhumma ṣalli ʿalā man hūwa fī 's-samā'i Sayyīdunā Maḥmūdun wa fī 'l-arḍi sayyidunā Muḥammadun •

O Allāh, exalt the one called Maḥmūd in Heaven and Muḥammad on the earth! ❋

(٢١) اللَّهُمَّ صَلِّ عَلَى صَاحِبِ الشَّامَةِ اللَّهُمَّ صَلِّ عَلَى صَاحِبِ العَلَامَةِ اللَّهُمَّ صَلِّ عَلَى المَوْصُوفِ بِالْكَرَامَةِ اللَّهُمَّ صَلِّ عَلَى المَخْصُوصِ بِالزَّعَامَةِ اللَّهُمَّ صَلِّ عَلَى مَنْ كَانَ تُظِلُّهُ الغَمَامَةِ اللَّهُمَّ صَلِّ عَلَى مَنْ كَانَ يَرَى مَنْ خَلْفَهُ كَمَا يَرَى مَنْ أَمَامَهُ اللَّهُمَّ صَلِّ عَلَى الشَّفِيعِ المُشَفَّعِ يَوْمَ الْقِيَامَةِ ❋

(21) Allāhumma ṣalli ʿalā ṣāḥibi 'sh-shāmati Allāhumma ṣalli ʿalā ṣāḥibi 'l-ʿalamati Allāhumma ṣalli ʿalā 'l-mawṣūfi bi 'l-karamāti Allāhumma ṣalli ʿalā 'l-makhṣūṣi bi 'z-zaʿāmati Allāhumma ṣalli ʿalā man kāna tuẓilluhu 'l-ghamāmati Allāhumma ṣalli ʿalā man kāna yarā man khalfahu kamā yarā man amāmahu Allāhumma ṣalli ʿalā 'sh-shafīʿi 'l-mushaffaʿi yawma 'l-qīyāmah •

(21) O Allāh, exalt the Possessor of the Mole! O Allāh, exalt the Possessor of the Distinguishing Mark! O Allāh, exalt the One ascribed with miracles! O Allāh, exalt the One possessing special leadership! O Allāh, exalt the One Shaded by Clouds! O Allāh, exalt the One who sees equally behind as in front! O Allāh, exalt the One whose intercession is accepted on the Day of Resurrection! ❋

(٢٢) اللَّهُمَّ صَلِّ عَلَى صَاحِبِ الضَّرَاعَةِ اللَّهُمَّ صَلِّ عَلَى صَاحِبِ الشَّفَاعَةِ اللَّهُمَّ صَلِّ عَلَى صَاحِبِ الوَسِيلَةِ اللَّهُمَّ صَلِّ عَلَى صَاحِبِ الْفَضِيلَةِ اللَّهُمَّ صَلِّ عَلَى صَاحِبِ الدَّرَجَةِ الرَّفِيعَةِ ❋

(22) Allāhumma ṣalli ʿalā ṣāḥibi 'ḍ-ḍarāʿati Allāhumma ṣalli ʿalā ṣāḥibi 'sh-shafāʿatī Allāhumma ṣalli ʿalā ṣāḥibi 'l-wasīlati Allāhumma ṣalli ʿalā ṣāḥibi 'l-faḍīlati Allāhumma ṣalli ʿalā ṣāḥibi 'd-darajati 'r-rafīʿah •

(22) O Allāh, exalt the Possessor of the Fervent Plea! O Allāh, exalt the Possessor of Intercession! O Allāh, exalt the Possessor of the Station of the Means to Allāh! O Allāh, exalt the Possessor of Pre-eminence! O Allāh, exalt the Possessor of the Lofty Rank! ❋

(٢٣) اللَّهُمَّ صَلِّ عَلَى صَاحِبِ الْهِرَاوَةِ اللَّهُمَّ صَلِّ عَلَى صَاحِبِ النَّعْلَيْنِ اللَّهُمَّ صَلِّ عَلَى صَاحِبِ الْحُجَّةِ اللَّهُمَّ صَلِّ عَلَى صَاحِبِ الْبُرْهَانِ اللَّهُمَّ صَلِّ عَلَى صَاحِبِ السُّلْطَانِ ❋

(23) Allāhumma ṣalli ʿalā ṣāḥibi 'l-hirāwati Allāhumma ṣalli ʿalā ṣāḥibi 'n-naʿlayn Allāhumma ṣalli ʿalā ṣāḥibi 'l-ḥujjati Allāhumma ṣalli ʿalā ṣāḥibi 'l-burhāni Allāhumma ṣalli ʿalā ṣāḥibi 's-sulṭān •

(23) O Allāh, exalt the Owner of the Stalwart Staff! O Allāh, exalt the Owner of the Sandals! O Allāh, exalt the Possessor of Proof! O Allāh, exalt the Possessor of Sound Evidence! O Allāh, exalt the Possessor of Authority! ❋

(٢٥) اللَّهُمَّ صَلِّ عَلَى صَاحِبِ التَّاجِ اللَّهُمَّ صَلِّ عَلَى صَاحِبِ المِعْرَاجِ ❋

(25) Allāhumma ṣalli ʿalā Ṣāḥibi 't-tāji, Allāhumma ṣalli ʿalā Ṣāḥibi 'l-miʿrāji •

(25) O Allāh, exalt the Owner of the Crown! O Allāh, exalt the Master of the Night Journey! ❋

(٢٦) اللَّهُمَّ صَلِّ عَلَى صَاحِبِ القَضِيبِ اللَّهُمَّ صَلِّ عَلَى رَاكِبِ النَّجِيبِ اللَّهُمَّ صَلِّ عَلَى رَاكِبِ البُرَاقِ اللَّهُمَّ صَلِّ عَلَى مُخْتَرِقِ السَّبعِ الطِّبَاقِ ❋

(26) Allāhumma ṣalli ʿalā Ṣāḥibi 'l-qaḍībi Allāhumma ṣalli ʿalā rākibi 'n-najībi Allāhumma ṣalli ʿalā rākibi 'l-burāqi Allāhumma ṣalli ʿalā mukhtariqi 's-sabʿi 'ṭ-ṭibāq •

(26) O Allāh, exalt the Owner of the Scepter! O Allāh, exalt the Camel Rider! O Allāh, exalt the Rider of the Burāq! O Allāh, exalt the One Who Traversed the Seven Heavens! ❋

(٢٨) اللَّهُمَّ صَلِّ عَلَى الشَّفِيعِ فِي جَمِيعِ الْأَنَامِ اللَّهُمَّ صَلِّ عَلَى مَنْ سَبَّحَ فِي كَفِّهِ الطَّعَامُ ❋

(28) Allāhumma ṣalli ʿalā 'sh-shafīʿi fī jamīʿi 'l-anāmi Allāhumma ṣalli ʿalā man sabbaḥa fī kaffihi 'ṭ-ṭʿām •

(28) O Allāh, exalt the Intercessor of All Creatures! O Allāh, exalt the One in whose hands food glorified Allāh ❋

(٢٩) اللَّهُمَّ صَلِّ عَلَى مَنْ بَكَى إِلَيْهِ الْجِذْعُ وَحَنَّ لِفِرَاقِهِ اللَّهُمَّ صَلِّ عَلَى مَنْ تَوَسَّلَ بِهِ طَيْرُ الْفَلَاةِ اللَّهُمَّ صَلِّ عَلَى مَنْ سَبَّحَتْ فِي كَفِّهِ الْحَصَاةُ ❋

(29) Allāhumma ṣalli ʿalā man bakā ilayhi 'l-jidhʿu wa ḥanna li-firāqihi Allāhumma ṣalli ʿalā man tawassala bihi ṭayru 'l-falāt Allāhumma ṣalli ʿalā man sabbaḥāṭ fī kaffihi 'l-ḥaṣāt •

(29) O Allāh, exalt the One for whom a palm trunk wept and sighed at separation from him! O Allāh, exalt the One whose mediation was sought by birds of the desert! O Allāh, exalt the One who held in his hand stones which Glorified You. ❋

(٣٠) اللَّهُمَّ صَلِّ عَلَى مَنْ تَشَفَّعَ إِلَيْهِ الظَّبْيُ بِأَفْصَحِ كَلامٍ اللَّهُمَّ صَلِّ عَلَى مَنْ كَلَّمَهُ الضَّبُّ فِي مَجْلِسِهِ مَعَ أَصْحَابِهِ الْأَعْلَامِ ❋

(30) Allāhumma ṣalli ʿalā man tashaffaʿa ilayhi 'ẓ-ẓabīyu bi afsaḥi kalāmin Allāhumma ṣalli ʿalā man kallamahu 'ḍ-ḍabbu fī majlisihi maʿ aṣḥābihi 'l-āʿlām •

(30) O Allāh, exalt the One whose intercession the gazelles sought with most eloquent human speech! O Allāh, exalt the One to whom a lizard spoke in an open gathering of the most-learned Companions! ❋

(٣١) اللَّهُمَّ صَلِّ عَلَى الْبَشِيرِ النَّذِيرِ اللَّهُمَّ صَلِّ عَلَى السِّرَاجِ الْمُنِيرِ اللَّهُمَّ صَلِّ عَلَى مَنْ شَكَا إِلَيْهِ الْبَعِيرُ اللَّهُمَّ صَلِّ عَلَى مَنْ تَفَجَّرَ مِنْ بَيْنِ أَصَابِعِهِ الْمَاءُ النَّمِيرُ ❁

(31) Allāhumma ṣalli ʿalā 'l-bashīri 'n-nadhīri Allāhumma ṣalli ʿalā 's-siraji 'l-munīri Allāhumma ṣalli ʿalā man shakā ilayhi 'l-baʿīru Allāhumā ṣalli ʿalā man tafajjara min bayni aṣābiʿihi 'l-mā'u 'n-namīru •

(31) O Allāh, exalt the Bearer of Glad Tidings and the Warner! O Allāh, exalt the Brilliant Lamp! O Allāh, exalt the One to whom a camel complained! O Allāh, exalt the One for whom sparkling water burst forth from his fingertips for his companions to drink! ❁

(٣٢) اللَّهُمَّ صَلِّ عَلَى الطَّاهِرِ الْمُطَهَّرِ اللَّهُمَّ صَلِّ عَلَى نُورِ الْأَنْوَارِ اللَّهُمَّ صَلِّ عَلَى مَنِ انْشَقَّ لَهُ الْقَمَرُ ❁

(32) Allāhumma ṣalli ʿalā 'ṭ-ṭāhiri 'l-muṭṭahhar Allāhumma ṣalli ʿalā nūri 'l-anwāri Allāhumma ṣalli ʿalā man inshaqqa lahu 'l-qamar •

(32) O Allāh, exalt the Pure One, the Purifier! O Allāh, exalt the Light of Lights! O Allāh, exalt the One for whom the moon was split in two! ❁

(٣٣) اللَّهُمَّ صَلِّ عَلَى الطَّيِّبِ الْمُطَيَّبِ اللَّهُمَّ صَلِّ عَلَى الرَّسُولِ الْمُقَرَّبِ ❁

(33) Allāhumma Ṣalli ʿalā 'ṭ-ṭayyibi 'l-muṭṭayyabi, Allāhumma ṣalli ʿalā 'r-rasūli 'l-muqarrabi •

(33) Exalt the One who was good and did good! O Allāh, exalt the Messenger Close to Allāh! ❁

(٣٤) اللَّهُمَّ صَلِّ عَلَى الفَجْرِ السَّاطِعِ اللَّهُمَّ صَلِّ عَلَى النَّجْمِ الثَّاقِبِ اللَّهُمَّ صَلِّ عَلَى العُرْوَةِ الوُثْقَى ❋

(34) Allāhumma ṣalli ʿalā 'l-fajri 's-sāṭiʿi Allāhumma ṣalli ʿalā 'n-najmi 'th-thāqibi Allāhumma ṣalli ʿalā 'l-ʿurwati 'l-wuthqā •

(34) O Allāh, exalt the Breaking Dawn! O Allāh, exalt the Piercing Star! O Allāh, exalt the Firm Handhold! ❋

(٣٥) اللَّهُمَّ صَلِّ عَلَى نَذِيرِ أَهْلِ الأَرْضِ اللَّهُمَّ صَلِّ عَلَى الشَّفِيعِ يَوْمَ العَرْضِ اللَّهُمَّ صَلِّ عَلَى السَّاقِي لِلنَّاسِ مِنَ الحَوْضِ اللَّهُمَّ صَلِّ عَلَى صَاحِبِ لِوَاءِ الحَمْدِ اللَّهُمَّ صَلِّ عَلَى المُشَمِّرِ عَنْ سَاعِدِ الجِدِّ اللَّهُمَّ صَلِّ عَلَى المُستَعمِلِ فِي مَرضَاتِكَ غَايَةَ الجُهدِ ❋

(35) Allāhumma ṣalli ʿalā nadhīri āhli 'l-arḍi Allāhumma ṣalli ʿalā 'sh-shafīʿi yawma al-ʿarḍi Allāhumma ṣalli ʿalā 's-sāqi li 'n-nāsi mina 'l-ḥawḍi Allāhumma ṣalli ʿalā ṣāḥibi liwā'i 'l-ḥamdi Allāhumma ṣalli ʿalā 'l-mushammiri ʿan sāʿidi 'l-jiddi Allāhumma ṣalli ʿalā 'l-mustaʿmili fī marḍātika ghāyata 'l-juhd •

(35) O Allāh, exalt the Warner of the inhabitants of the earth! O Allāh, exalt the Intercessor on the Day of Petition! O Allāh, exalt the One who will give people to drink from the Pool! O Allāh, exalt the Owner of the Flag of Praise! O Allāh, exalt the One who was ever ready for Your service! O Allāh, exalt the One who strived to his utmost to please you ❋

(٣٦) اللَّهُمَّ صَلِّ عَلَى النَّبِيِّ الْخَاتَمِ اللَّهُمَّ صَلِّ عَلَى الرَّسُولِ الْخَاتَمِ اللَّهُمَّ صَلِّ عَلَى الْمُصْطَفَى الْقَائِمِ اللَّهُمَّ صَلِّ عَلَى رَسُولِكَ أَبِي الْقَاسِمِ ❋

(36) Allāhumma ṣalli ʿalā 'n-nabīyyi 'l-khātami Allāhumma ṣalli ʿalā 'r-rasūli 'l-khātami Allāhumma ṣalli ʿalā 'l-Muṣṭafā 'l-qā'imi Allāhumma ṣalli ʿalā Rasūlika Abi 'l-Qāsim •

(36) O Allāh, exalt the Seal of Prophets! O Allāh, exalt the Seal of Messengers! O Allāh, exalt the Upright Chosen One! O Allāh, exalt Your Messenger, the Father of Qāsim! ❋

(٣٧) اللَّهُمَّ صَلِّ عَلَى صَاحِبِ الآيَاتِ اللَّهُمَّ صَلِّ عَلَى صَاحِبِ الدِلَالَاتِ اللَّهُمَّ صَلِّ عَلَى صَاحِبِ الإِشَارَاتِ اللَّهُمَّ صَلِّ عَلَى صَاحِبِ الْكَرَامَاتِ اللَّهُمَّ صَلِّ عَلَى صَاحِبِ الْعَلَامَاتِ

(37) Allāhumma ṣalli ʿalā ṣāḥibi 'l-āyāt Allāhumma ṣalli ʿalā ṣāḥibi 'd-dilālāti Allāhumma ṣalli ʿalā ṣāḥibi 'l-ishārāti Allāhumma ṣalli ʿalā ṣāḥibi 'l-karāmati Allāhumma ṣalli ʿalā ṣāḥibi 'l-ʿalāmāti

(37) O Allāh, exalt the Possessor of Signs! O Allāh, exalt the Possessor of Portents! O Allāh, exalt the Possessor of Indications! O Allāh, exalt the Possessor of Miracles! O Allāh, exalt the Possessor of Clear Signs! ➢

اللَّهُمَّ صَلِّ عَلَى صَاحِبِ البَيِّنَاتِ اللَّهُمَّ صَلِّ عَلَى صَاحِبِ الْمُعْجِزَاتِ اللَّهُمَّ صَلِّ عَلَى صَاحِبِ خَوَارِقِ الْعَادَاتِ ❋

Allāhumma ṣalli ʿalā ṣāḥibi 'l-bayyināti Allāhumma ṣalli ʿalā ṣāḥibi 'l-muʿjizāt Allāhumma ṣalli ʿalā Ṣāḥibi khawāriqi 'l-ʿādāt •

O Allāh, exalt the Possessor of Proofs! O Allāh, exalt the Possessor of Marvels! O Allāh, exalt the Possessor of Wondrous Events ❋

(٣٨) اللَّهُمَّ صَلِّ عَلَى مَنْ سَلَّمَتْ عَلَيْهِ الْأَحْجَارُ اللَّهُمَّ صَلِّ عَلَى مَنْ سَجَدَتْ بَيْنَ يَدَيْهِ الْأَشْجَارُ اللَّهُمَّ صَلِّ عَلَى مَنْ تَفَتَّقَتْ مِنْ نُورِهِ الْأَزْهَارُ اللَّهُمَّ صَلِّ عَلَى مَنْ طَابَتْ بِبَرَكَتِهِ الثِّمَارُ

(38) Allāhumma ṣalli ʿalā man sallamat ʿalayhi 'l-aḥjāru Allāhumma ṣalli ʿalā man sajadat bayna yadayhi 'l-ashjāru Allāhumma ṣalli ʿalā man tafattaqat min nūrihi 'l-azhāru Allāhumma ṣalli ʿalā man ṭābat bi-barkatihi 'th-thimār

(38) O Allāh, exalt the One greeted by stones! O Allāh, exalt the One before whom trees prostrated! O Allāh, exalt the One from whose light roses bloomed! O Allāh, exalt the One by whose blessings fruits ripened! ➢

اللَّهُمَّ صَلِّ عَلَى مَنِ اخْضَرَّتْ مِنْ بَقِيَّةِ وَضُوئِهِ الْأَشْجَارُ اللَّهُمَّ صَلِّ عَلَى مَنْ فَاضَتْ مِنْ نُورِهِ جَمِيعُ الْأَنْوَارِ اللَّهُمَّ صَلِّ عَلَى مَنْ بِالصَّلاةِ عَلَيهِ تُحَطُّ الْأَوْزَارُ اللَّهُمَّ صَلِّ عَلَى مَنْ بِالصَّلَاةِ عَلَيهِ تُنَالُ مَنَازِلُ الْأَبْرَارُ اللَّهُمَّ صَلِّ عَلَى مَنْ بِالصَّلَاةِ عَلَيهِ يُرْحَمُ الْكِبَارُ والصِّغَارُ اللَّهُمَّ صَلِّ عَلَى مَنْ بِالصَّلاةِ عَلَيهِ نَتَنَعَّمُ فِي هَذِهِ الدَّارِ وَفِي تِلْكَ الدَّارِ ❋

Allāhumma ṣalli ʿalā man ikhḍarrat min baqīyyati waḍū'ihi 'l-ashjār Allāhumma ṣalli ʿalā man fāḍat min nūrihi jamiʿu 'l-anwār Allāhumma ṣalli ʿalā man bi 'ṣ-ṣalāti ʿalayhi tuḥaṭṭu 'l-awzār Allāhumma ṣalli ʿalā man bi 'ṣ-ṣalāti ʿalayhi tunālu manāzilu 'l-abrār Allāhumma ṣalli ʿalā man bi 'ṣ-ṣalāti ʿalayhi yurḥamu 'l-kibāru wa 'ṣ-ṣighāru Allāhumma ṣalli ʿalā man bi 'ṣ-ṣalāti ʿalayhi natanaʿʿamu fī hadhihi 'd-dāri wa fī tilka 'd-dār •

O Allāh, exalt the One who from whose leftover ablution water trees became green! O Allāh, exalt the One from whose light all other lights sprang forth! O Allāh, exalt the One by whose praise burdens are lightened. O Allāh exalt the one by whose praise the stations of the pious are reached! O Allāh, exalt the One for whose praise Allāh will grant mercy to the old and the young! O Allāh exalt the One by whose praise we will be granted enjoyment in this world and the next! ❋

(٣٩) اللَّهُمَّ صَلِّ عَلَى مَنْ بِالصَّلَاةِ عَلَيهِ تُنَالُ رَحْمَةُ العَزِيزِ الغَفَّارِ اللَّهُمَّ صَلِّ عَلَى المَنْصُورِ المُؤَيَّدِ اللَّهُمَّ صَلِّ عَلَى المُخْتَارِ المُمَجَّدِ اللَّهُمَّ صَلِّ عَلَى سَيِّدِنَا وَمَوْلَانَا مُحَمَّدٍ ❋

(39) Allāhumma ṣalli ʿalā man bi 'ṣ-ṣalāti ʿalayhi tunālu raḥmatu 'l-ʿazīzi 'l-ghaffār Allāhumma ṣalli ʿalā 'l-Manṣūri 'l-Mu'ayyad Allāhumma ṣalli ʿalā 'l-Mukhtāri 'l-Mumajjad Allāhumma ṣalli ʿalā Sayyīdinā wa mawlānā Muḥammad •

(39) O Allāh praise the One by whose praise the mercy and forgiveness of Allāh is attained! O Allāh, exalt the Victorious and Supported One! O Allāh, exalt the Chosen and Exalted One! O Allāh, exalt our master and guardian Muḥammad! ❋

(٤٠) اللَّهُمَّ صَلِّ عَلَى مَنْ كَانَ إِذَا مَشَى فِي البَرِّ الْأَقْفَرِ تَعَلَّقَتِ الْوُحُوشُ بِأَذْيَالِهِ اللَّهُمَّ صَلِّ عَلَيهِ وَعَلَى آلِهِ وَصَحْبِهِ وَسَلِّمْ تَسْلِيمًا كَثِيراً وَالحَمْدُ للهِ رَبِّ العَالَمِينَ❋

(40) Allāhumma ṣalli ʿalā man kāna idhā mashā fī 'l-barri 'l-aqfari taʿallaqati 'l-wuḥūshu bi adhyālihi Allāhumma ṣalli ʿalayhi wa ʿalā ālihi wa ṣaḥbihi wa sallim taslīman kathīran wa 'l-ḥamdu li 'Llāhi rabbi 'l-ʿālamīn •

(40) O Allāh exalt the One who when he walked in the desert wild creatures would cling to the hem of his cloak! O Allāh exalt and grant abundant peace to him and his Family and Companions, and praise be to Allāh, Lord of all the worlds! ❋

ابْتِدَاءُ الرُّبْعِ الثَّانِي

Ibtidā'u 'r-Rub'i 'th-Thānī

Beginning of the Second Quarter

(٤١) الْحَمْدُ لله عَلَى حِلْمِهِ بَعْدَ عِلْمِهِ وَعَلَى عَفْوِهِ بَعْدَ قُدْرَتِهِ *

(41) Alḥamdu li 'Llāhi 'alā ḥilmihi ba'da 'ilmihi wa 'alā 'afwihi ba'da qudratihi •

(41) Praise be to Allāh ﷻ for His forbearance in spite of His knowledge (of our sins), and for His clemency in spite of His power! *

(٤٢) اللَّهُمَّ إِنِّي أَعُوذُ بِكَ مِنَ الْفَقْرِ إِلاَّ إِلَيْكَ وَمِنَ الذُّلِّ إِلَّا لَكَ وَمِنَ الْخَوفِ إِلاَّ مِنْكَ وَأَعُوذُ بِكَ أَنْ أَقُولَ زُوراً أَوْ أَغْشَى فُجُوراً أَوْ أَكُونَ بِكَ مَغْرُوراً

(42) Allāhumma innī ā'ūdhu bika mina 'l-faqri illā ilayka, wa mina 'dh-dhulli illā laka wa mina 'l-khawfi illā minka wa ā'ūdhu bika an aqūla zūran aw aghshā fujūran aw akūna bika maghrūran

(42) O Allāh, I seek refuge in You from being poor to other than You and from all humility except humility to You, and from all fear except fear of You and I seek refuge in You from making false statements! Or From being dishonest and immoral! Or what I become proudly arrogant in front of You! ➢

وَأَعُوذُ بِكَ مِنْ شَمَاتَةِ الْأَعْدَاءِ وَعُضَالِ الدَّاءِ وَخَيبَةِ الرَّجَاءِ وَزَوَالِ النِّعْمَةِ وَفُجَاءَةِ النِّقْمَةِ ❋

wa āʿūdhu bika min shamātati 'l-aʿdā'i wa ʿuḍāli 'd-dā'i wa khaybati 'r-rajā'i wa zawāli 'n-niʿmati wa fujā'ati 'n-niqmah •

And I seek refuge in You from the happiness of my enemies at my expense, from disease, malady and despair, and from the waning of favours and from sudden catastrophies! ❋

(٤٣) اللَّهُمَّ صَلِّ عَلَى سَيِّدِنَا مُحَمَّدٍ وسَلِّم عَلَيهِ واْجزِهِ عَنْا مَا هُوَ أَهْلُهُ حَبِيبُكَ (ثلاثاً)❋

(43) Allāhumma ṣalli ʿalā Sayyīdinā Muḥammadin wa sallim ʿalayhi wa 'jzihi ʿannā mā hūwa āhluhu ḥabībuka (3x) •

(43) O Allāh exalt our master Muḥammad and grant him peace and reward him on our behalf as much as he deserves, and he is Your Beloved! (3x) ❋

(٤٤) اللَّهُمَّ صَلِّ عَلَى سَيِّدِنَا إِبْرَاهِيمَ وسَلِّمْ عَلَيهِ واجْزِهِ عَنْا مَا هُوَ أَهْلُهُ خَلِيلُكَ (ثلاثاً) ❋

(44) Allāhumma ṣalli ʿalā Sayyīdinā Ibrāhīma wa sallim ʿalayhi wa 'jzihi ʿannā mā hūwa āhluhu khalīluka (3x) •

(44) O Allāh exalt our master Abraham and grant him peace and reward him on our behalf as much as he deserves, and he is Your Friend! (3x) ❋

(٤٥) اللَّهُمَّ صَلِّ عَلَى سَيِّدِنَا مُحَمَّدٍ وَعَلَى آلِ سَيِّدِنَا مُحَمَّدٍ كَمَا صَلَّيْتَ وَرَحِمتَ وَبَارَكْتَ عَلَى سَيِّدِنَا إِبْرَاهِيمَ فِي العَالَمِينَ إِنَّكَ حَمِيدٌ مَجِيدٌ عَدَدَ خَلْقِكَ وَرِضَا نَفْسِكَ وَزِنَةَ عَرْشِكَ وَمِدَادَ كَلِمَاتِكَ ❋

(45) Allāhumma ṣalli ʿalā Sayyīdinā Muḥammadin wa ʿalā āli Sayyīdinā Muḥammadin kamā ṣallayta wa raḥimta wa bārakta ʿalā Sayyīdinā Ibrāhīma fī 'l-ʿālamīna innaka Ḥamīdun Majīdʿadada khalqika wa riḍā nafsika wa zinata ʿarshika wa midāda kalimātik •

(45) O Allāh, exalt our master Muḥammad and the family of our master Muḥammad just as You exalted and granted mercy to our master Abraham, in all the worlds, You are The Praiseworthy ,The Mighty, on the number of Your Creations, to the extent of Your Pleasure, as the decorations of Your Throne and in the ink of Your Words! ❋

(٤٦) اللَّهُمَّ صَلِّ عَلَى سَيِّدِنَا مُحَمَّدٍ عَدَدَ مَنْ صَلَّى عَلَيهِ اللَّهُمَّ صَلِّ عَلَى سَيِّدِنَا مُحَمَّدٍ عَدَدَ مَنْ لَمْ يُصَلِّ عَلَيه

(46) Allāhumma ṣalli ʿalā Sayyīdinā Muḥammadin ʿadada man ṣalla ʿalayhi Allāhumma ṣalli ʿalā Sayyīdinā Muḥammadin ʿadada man lam yuṣalli ʿalayhi

(46) O Allāh, exalt our master Muḥammad on the numher of those who have sent praises upon him! O Allāh, exalt our master Muḥammad on the number of those who have not praised him! ➢

اللَّهُمَّ صَلِّ عَلَى سَيِّدِنَا مُحَمَّدٍ عَدَدَ مَا صُلِّيَ عَلَيهِ اللَّهُمَّ صَلِّ عَلَى سَيِّدِنَا مُحَمَّدٍ أَضْعَافَ مَا صُلِّيَ عَلَيهِ اللَّهُمَّ صَلِّ عَلَى سَيِّدِنَا مُحَمَّدٍ كَمَا هُوَ أَهْلُهُ اللَّهُمَّ صَلِّ عَلَى سَيِّدِنَا مُحَمَّدٍ كَمَا تُحِبُّ وَتَرْضَى لَهُ ❁

Allāhumma ṣalli 'alā Sayyīdinā Muḥammadin 'adada mā ṣullīya 'alayhi Allāhumma ṣalli 'alā Sayyīdinā Muḥammadin aḍ'āfa mā ṣullīya 'alayhi Allāhumma ṣalli 'alā Sayyīdinā Muḥammadin kamā hūwa āhluhu Allāhumma ṣalli 'alā Sayyīdinā Muḥammadin kamā tuḥibbu wa tarḍā lahu •

O Allāh, exalt our master Muḥammad on the number of praises which have been sent upon him! O Allāh, exalt our master Muḥammad manifold times on the number of praises which have been sent upon him! O Allāh, exalt our master Muḥammad just as he deserves! O Allāh, exalt our master Muḥammad according to what you love and according to that which pleases You. ❁

يَوْمُ الأَرْبِعَاءِ

Wednesday

الْحِزْبُ الثَّالِثُ فِي يَوْمِ الأَرْبِعَاءِ

al-Ḥizbu 'th-Thālithu fī Yawmi 'l-Arbi'āi'

Third Chapter on Wednesday

(١) اللَّهُمَّ صَلِّ عَلَى رُوحِ سَيِّدِنَا مُحَمَّدٍ فِي الأَرْوَاحِ وَعَلَى جَسَدِهِ فِي الأَجْسَادِ وَعَلَى قَبْرِهِ فِي القُبُورِ وَعَلَى آلِهِ وَصَحْبِهِ وَسَلِّمْ ❋

(1) Allāhumma ṣalli 'alā rūḥi Sayyīdinā Muḥammadin fī 'l-arwāḥi wa 'alā jasadihi fī 'l-ajsādi wa 'alā qabrihi fī 'l-qubūri wa 'alā ālihi wa ṣaḥbihi wa sallim •

(1) O Allāh, exalt the soul of our master Muḥammad among all souls and exalt his body among all bodies, and exalt his grave from among all graves, and exalt and grant abundant peace to him, his family and his companions! ❋

(٢) اللَّهُمَّ صَلِّ عَلَى سَيِّدِنَا مُحَمَّدٍ كُلَّمَا ذَكَرَهُ الذَّاكِرُونَ

(2) Allāhumma ṣalli 'alā Sayyīdinā Muḥammadin kullamā dhakarahu 'dhākirun

(2) O Allāh, exalt our master Muḥammad whenever those who remember him do so! ➢

اللَّهُمَّ صَلِّ عَلَى سَيِّدِنَا مُحَمَّدٍ كُلَّمَا غَفَلَ عَنْ ذِكْرِهِ الغَافِلُونَ ❋

Allāhumma ṣalli ʿalā Sayyīdinā Muḥammadin kullamā ghafala ʿan dhikrihi 'l-ghāfilūn •

O Allāh, exalt our master Muḥammad whenever those who neglect to remember him do so! ❋

(٣) اللَّهُمَّ صَلِّ عَلَى سَيِّدِنَا مُحَمَّدٍ النَّبِيِّ الأُمِّيِّ وَأَزْوَاجِهِ أُمَّهَاتِ المُؤْمِنِينَ وَذُرِيَّتِهِ وَأَهْلِ بَيْتِهِ صَلَاةً وَسَلَامًا لَا يُحْصَى عَدَدُهُمَا وَلَا يَنقَطِعُ مَدَدُهُمَا ❋

(3) Allāhumma ṣalli wa sallim wa bārik ʿalā Sayyīdinā Muḥammadi 'n-Nabīyyi 'l-ummīyyi wa azwājihi ummahāti 'l-mu'minīna wa dhurrīyatihi wa āhli baytihi ṣalātan wa salāman lā yuḥṣā ʿadaduhumā wa lā yuqṭaʿu madaduhumā •

(3) O Allāh, exalt, grant peace to and bless our master Muḥammad, the Unlettered (not thought to read and write by any human being) Prophet, and also his wives, the Mothers of the Believers, his descendants and the People of his House, such blessings and peace Which are measureless, and which support will never end! ❋

(٤) اللَّهُمَّ صَلِّ عَلَى سَيِّدِنَا مُحَمَّدٍ عَدَدَ مَا أَحَاطَ بِهِ عِلْمُكَ وَأَحْصَاهُ كِتَابُكَ صَلَاةً تَكُونُ لَكَ رِضَاءً وَلِحَقِّهِ أَدَاءً وَاعْطِهِ الْوَسِيلَةَ وَالْفَضِيلَةَ وَالدَّرَجَةَ الرَّفِيعَةَ وَابْعَثْهُ اللَّهُمَّ الْمَقَامَ الْمَحْمُودَ الَّذِي وَعَدْتَهُ وَاجْزِهِ عَنَّا مَا هُوَ أَهْلُهُ وَعَلَى جَمِيعِ إِخْوَانِهِ مِنَ النَّبِيِّينَ وَالصِّدِّيقِينَ وَالشُّهَدَاءِ وَالصَّالِحِينَ ❁

(4) Allāhumma ṣalli ʿalā Sayyīdinā Muḥammadin ʿadada mā aḥāṭa bihi ʿilmuka wa aḥṣāhu kitābuka ṣalātan takūnu laka riḍā'an wa li-ḥaqqihi adā'an wa āʿṭihi 'l-waṣīlata wa 'l-faḍīlata wa 'd-darajata 'r-rafiʿata wa 'bʿathhu 'Llāhumma 'l-maqāma 'l-maḥmūda 'Lladhī waʿadtahu wa 'jzihi ʿannā mā hūwa āhluhu wa ʿalā jamīʿi ikhwānihi mina 'n-nabīyyīnā wa 'ṣ-ṣiddīqīna wa 'sh-shuhadā'i wa 'ṣ-ṣāliḥīn •

(4) O Allāh, exalt our master Muḥammad on the number of things encompassed by Your Knowledge, and accounted for in Your book with such praises that are pleasing to You, and befitting his legitimate right, and grant him the station of *al-Wasīlah* (the means of approach to You), the Pre-eminence and the Lofty Rank, and send him, O Allāh, to the most praised Station which You promised him, and reward his brothers the Prophets, the truthful ones, the martyrs and the righteous ones! ❁

(٥) اللَّهُمَّ صَلِّ عَلَى سَيِّدِنَا مُحَمَّدٍ وَأَنزِلْهُ الْمُنْزَلَ الْمُقَرَّبَ يَوْمَ الْقِيَامَةِ ❋

(5) Allāhumma ṣalli ʿalā Sayyīdinā Muḥammadin wa anzilhu 'l-munzala 'l-muqarraba yawma 'l-qīyāmati •

(5) O Allāh exalt our master Muḥammad and bestow upon him the nearest position to You on the day of Resurrection! ❋

(٦) اللَّهُمَّ صَلِّ عَلَى سَيِّدِنَا مُحَمَّدٍ اللَّهُمَّ تَوِّجْهُ بِتَاجِ الْعِزِّ وَالرِّضَا وَالْكَرَامَةِ ❋

(6) Allāhumma ṣalli ʿalā Sayyīdinā Muḥammadin Allāhumma tawwijhu bitāji 'l-ʿizzi wa 'r-riḍā wa 'l-karāmati •

(6) O Allāh, exalt our master Muḥammad O Allāh, crown him with the crown of might, satisfaction and honour! ❋

(٧) اللَّهُمَّ أَعْطِ لِسَيِّدِنَا مُحَمَّدٍ أَفْضَلَ مَا سَأَلَكَ لِنَفْسِهِ وَأَعْطِ لِسَيِّدِنَا مُحَمَّدٍ أَفْضَلَ مَا سَأَلَكَ لَهُ أَحَدٌ مِنْ خَلْقِكَ

(7)Allāhumma āʿṭi li-Sayyīdinā Muḥammadin afḍala mā sa'alaka li-nafsihi wa āʿṭi li-Sayyīdinā Muḥammadin afḍala mā sa'alaka lahu aḥadun min khalqika

(7) O Allāh, grant our master Muḥammad the best of what he has requested of You for himself and grant our master Muḥammad the best of what creation has requested for him ➢

وَأَعْطِ لِسَيِّدِنَا مُحَمَّدٍ أَفْضَلَ مَا أَنْتَ مَسؤولٌ لَهُ إِلَى يَوْمِ الْقِيَامَةِ ❋

wa āʿṭi li-Sayyīdinā Muḥammadin afḍala mā anta mas'ūlun lahū ilā yawmi 'l-qīyāmati •

and grant our master Muḥammad the best of that which You will be asked until the Day of Resurrection! ❋

(٨) اللَّهُمَّ صَلِّ عَلَى سَيِّدِنَا مُحَمَّدٍ وَسَيِّدِنَا آدَمَ وَسَيِّدِنَا نُوحٍ وَسَيِّدِنَا إِبْرَاهِيمَ وَسَيِّدِنَا مُوسَى وَسَيِّدِنَا عِيسَى وَمَا بَيْنَهُمْ مِنَ النَّبِيِّينَ وَالْمُرْسَلِينَ صَلَوَاتُ اللهِ وَسَلَامُهُ عَلَيْهِمْ أَجْمَعِينَ (ثلاثاً) ❋

(8) Allāhumma ṣalli ʿalā Sayyīdinā Muḥammadin wa Sayyīdinā Ādama wa Sayyīdinā Nūḥin wa Sayyīdinā Ibrāhīma wa Sayyīdinā Mūsā wa Sayyīdinā ʿIsā wa mā baynahum mina 'n-nabīyyīna wa 'l-mursalīna ṣalawātu 'Llāhi wa salāmuhu ʿalayhim ajmaʿīn (3x) •

(8) O Allāh exalt our masters Muḥammad, and Adam, and Abraham, and Moses, and Jesus and all the prophets and messengers between them, may the prayers and peace of Allāh be upon all of them! (3x) ❋

(٩) اللَّهُمَّ صَلِّ عَلَى أَبِينَا سَيِّدِنَا آدَمَ وَأُمِّنَا سَيِّدَتِنَا حَوَّاءَ

(9) Allāhumma ṣalli ʿalā abīna Sayyīdinā Ādam wa umminā Sayyīdatinā Ḥawwā

(9) O Allāh exalt our Father Ādam and our Mother Eve, ➢

صَلاَةَ مَلآَئِكَتِكَ وَأَعْطِهِمَا مِنَ الرِّضْوَانِ حَتَّى تُرْضِيَهُمَا وَاجْزِهِمَا اللَّهُمَّ أَفْضَلَ مَا جَازَيتَ بِهِ أَباً وَأُمّاً عَنْ وَلَدَيهِمَا (ثلاثاً)❋

ṣalāta malā'ikatika wa āʿṭihimā mina 'r-riḍwāni ḥattā turḍīyahumā wa 'jzihimā 'Llāhumma afḍala mā jāzayta bihi aban wa umman ʿan waladayhimā (3x) •

with the praisings of Your angels and grant them Your Pleasure until it pleases them and reward them O Allāh, better than You have rewarded any father and mother on behalf of their children! ❋

(١٠) اللَّهُمَّ صَلِّ عَلَى سَيِّدِنَا جِبْرِيلَ وَسَيِّدِنَا مِيكَائِيلَ وَسَيِّدِنَا إِسْرَافِيلَ وَسَيِّدِنَا عِزْرَائِيلَ وَحَمَلَةِ الْعَرْشِ وَعَلَى المَلآَئِكَةِ وَالْمُقَرَّبِينَ وَعَلَى جَمِيعِ الأَنْبِيَاءِ وَالْمُرْسَلِينَ صَلَوَاتُ اللهِ وَسَلاَمُهُ عَلَيهِمْ أَجْمَعِينْ (ثلاثاً)❋

(10) Allāhumā ṣalli ʿalā Sayyīdinā Jibrīla wa Sayyīdinā Mikā'īla wa Sayyīdinā Isrāfīla wa Sayyīdinā ʿIzrā'īlā wa ḥamalati 'l-ʿarshi wa ʿalā 'l-malā'ikati 'l-muqarrabīna wa ʿalā jamīʿi 'l-anbīyā'i wa 'l-mursalīna ṣalawātu 'Llāhi wa salāmuhu ʿalayhim ajmaʿīn (3x) •

(10) O Allāh, exalt our master Gabriel and Michael and Rafael and Azrael and the Bearers of the Throne, and the Angels brought-nigh, and all the prophets and messengers, and the blessings and peace of Allāh ﷻ be upon them all! (3x) ❋

(١١) اللَّهُمَّ صَلِّ عَلَى سَيِّدِنَا مُحَمَّدٍ عَدَدَ مَا عَلِمْتَ وَمِلْءَ مَا عَلِمْتَ وَزِنَةَ مَا عَلِمْتَ وَمِدَادَ كَلِمَاتِكَ ❋

(11) Allāhumma ṣalli ʿalā Sayyīdinā Muḥammadin ʿadada mā ʿalimta wa milʾā mā ʿalimta wa zīnata mā ʿalimta wa midāda kalimātika •

(11) O Allāh, exalt our master Muḥammad on the number of Your Knowledge, the depth of Your Knowledge and the weight of Your Knowledge and the abundance of Your Words! ❋

(١٢) اللَّهُمَّ صَلِّ عَلَى سَيِّدِنَا مُحَمَّدٍ صَلَاةً مَوْصُولَةً بِالْمَزِيدِ اللَّهُمَّ صَلِّ عَلَى سَيِّدِنَا مُحَمَّدٍ صَلَاةً لَا تَنقَطِعُ أَبَدَ الْأَبَدِ وَلَا تَبِيدُ ❋

(12) Allāhumma ṣalli ʿalā Sayyīdinā Muḥammadin ṣalātan mawṣūlatan bi 'l-mazīd Allāhumma ṣalli ʿalā Sayyīdinā Muḥammadin ṣalātan lā tanqaṭiʿu abad 'l-abadi wa lā tabīdu •

(12) O Allāh, bless our master Muḥammad, with blessings which are continuously abundant! O Allāh, bless our master Muḥammad, with blessings, which are never-ending and unceasing! ❋

(١٣) اللَّهُمَّ صَلِّ عَلَى سَيِّدِنَا مُحَمَّدٍ صَلَاتَكَ الَّتِي صَلَّيْتَ عَلَيْهِ

(13) Allāhumma ṣalli ʿalā Sayyīdinā Muḥammadin ṣalātaka 'Llatī ṣallayta ʿalayhi

(13) O Allāh ❋ exalt our master Muḥammad in the manner of praise which You have praised him with ➢

وسَلِّم عَلَى سَيِّدِنَا مُحَمَّدٍ سَلَامَكَ الَّذِي سَلَّمْتَ عَلَيهِ وَاجْزِهِ عَنْا مَا هُوَ أَهْلُهُ ❋

wa sallim ʿalā Sayyīdinā Muḥammadin salāmaka 'Lladhī sallamta ʿalayhi wa 'jzihi ʿannā mā hūwa āhluh •

and grant peace to our master Muḥammad in the manner of peace You have bestowed upon him and reward him on our behalf as he deserves and reward him on our behalf as he deserves! ❋

(١٤) اللَّهُمَّ صَلِّ عَلَى سَيِّدِنَا مُحَمَّدٍ صَلَاةً تُرْضِيكَ وَتُرْضِيهِ وَتَرضَى بِهَا عَنْا وَاجْزِهِ عَنَّا مَا هُوَ أَهْلُهُ ❋

(14) Allāhumma ṣalli ʿalā Sayyīdinā Muḥammadin ṣalātan turḍīka wa turḍīhi wa tarḍā bihā ʿannā wa 'jzihi ʿannā mā hūwa āhluh •

(14) O Allāh, exalt our master Muḥammad with praise which statisfies You, satisfies him and which makes You pleased with us, and reward him on our behalf with that which befits him! ❋

(١٥) اللَّهُمَّ صَلِّ عَلَى سَيِّدِنَا مُحَمَّدٍ بَحْرِ أَنْوَارِكَ وَمَعْدِنِ أَسْرَارِكَ وَلِسَانِ حُجَّتِكَ

(15) Allāhumma ṣalli ʿalā Sayyīdinā Muḥammadin baḥri anwārika wa maʿdini asrārika wa lisāni ḥujjatika

(15) O Allāh, exalt our master Muḥammad, the ocean of Your Lights, the Mine of Your Secrets, the Tongue of Your Proof, ➢

وَعَرُوسِ مَمْلَكَتِكَ وَإِمَامِ حَضْرَتِكَ وَطِرَازِ مُلْكِكَ وَخَزَائِنِ رَحْمَتِكَ وَطَرِيقِ شَرِيعَتِكَ الْمُتَلَذِّذِ بِتَوْحِيدِكَ إِنْسَانِ عَيْنِ الْوُجُودِ وَالسَّبَبِ فِي كُلِّ مَوْجُودٍ ❋

wa ʿarūsi mamlakatika wa īmāmi ḥaḍratika wa tirāzi mulkika wa khazāʾini raḥmatika wa ṭarīqi sharīʿatika al-mutaladhidhi bi-tawḥīdika insāni ʿayni ʾl-wujūdi

the Bride of Your Kingdom, the Leader of Your Presence, the Embroidery of Your Dominion, the vault of Your Mercy, the Way of Your Law, the Delight of Your Unity, the Pupil of the Eye of Existence, ➢

عَيْنِ أَعيَانِ خَلْقِكَ الْمُتَقَدِّمِ مِنْ نُورِ ضِيَائِكَ صَلَاةً تَدُومُ بِدَوَامِكَ وَتَبقَى بِبَقَائِكَ لَا مُنْتَهَى لَهَا دُونَ عِلْمِكَ صَلَاةً تُرْضِيكَ وَتُرْضِيهِ وَتَرْضَى بِهَا عَنْا يَا رَبَّ الْعَالَمِينَ ❋

wa ʾs-sababi fī kulli mawjūdin ʿayni aʿyāni khalqika ʾl-mutaqaddimi min nūri ḍīyāʾika ṣalātan tadūmu bi-dawāmika wa tabqā bi-baqāʾika lā muntahā lahā dūna ʿilmika ṣalātan turḍīka wa turḍīhi wa tarḍā bihā ʿannā yā rabba ʾl-ʿālamīn •

the Cause of all Existence, the Most Eminent of Your Creation, the Representative of the Light of Your Resplendence, with blessings which last for as long as You last and remain for as long as You remain, blessings which are limitless apart from Your Knowledge thereof, blessings which please You, which please him and by which You are pleased with us, O Allāh, the Lord ❋

(١٦) اللَّهُمَّ صَلِّ عَلَى سَيِّدِنَا مُحَمَّدٍ عَدَدَ مَا فِي عِلْمِ اللهِ صَلَاةً دَائِمَةً بِدَوَامِ مُلْكِ اللهِ ❋

(16) Allāhumma ṣalli ʿalā Sayyīdinā Muḥammadin ʿadada mā fī ʿilmi 'Llāhi ṣalātan dā'imatan bi-dawāmi mulki 'Llāhi •

(16) O Allāh, exalt our master Muḥammad on the number of what is in the Knowledge of Allāh ﷻ, praisings which are eternal and which last as long as Allāh's Kingdom endures! ❋

(١٧) اللَّهُمَّ صَلِّ عَلَى سَيِّدِنَا مُحَمَّدٍ كَمَا صَلَّيْتَ عَلَى سَيِّدِنَا إِبْرَاهِيمَ وَبَارِكْ عَلَى سَيِّدِنَا مُحَمَّدٍ وَعَلَى آلِ سَيِّدِنَا مُحَمَّدٍ كَمَا بَارَكْتَ عَلَى آلِ سَيِّدِنَا إِبْرَاهِيمَ فِي الْعَالَمِينَ إِنَّكَ حَمِيدٌ مَجِيدٌ

(17) Allāhumma ṣalli ʿalā Sayyīdinā Muḥammadin kamā ṣallayta ʿalā Sayyīdinā Ibrāhīma wa bārik ʿalā Sayyīdinā Muḥammadin wa ʿalā āli Sayyīdinā Muḥammadin kamā bārakta ʿalā āli Sayyīdinā Ibrāhīma fī 'l-ʿālamīna innaka Ḥamīdun Majīdun

(17) O Allāh, exalt our master Muḥammad just as You exalted our master Abraham and exalt our master Muḥammad and the family of our master Muḥammad just as You exalted the family of our master Abraham, in all the worlds, for You are The Praiseworthy, The Mighty! ➢

عَدَدَ خَلْقِكَ وَرِضَا نَفْسِكَ وَزِنَةَ عَرْشِكَ وَمِدَادَ كَلِمَاتِكَ وعَدَدَ مَا ذَكَرَكَ بِهِ خَلْقُكَ فِيمَا مَضَى وَعَدَدَ مَا هُمْ ذَاكِرُونَكَ بِهِ فِيمَا بَقِيَ فِي كُلِّ سَنَةٍ وَشَهْرٍ وَجُمُعَةٍ وَيَوْمٍ وَلَيْلَةٍ وَسَاعَةٍ مِنَ السَّاعَاتِ وَشَمٍّ وَنَفَسٍ وَطَرْفَةٍ وَلَمْحَةٍ مِنَ الْأَبَدِ إِلَى الأَبدِ وَآبَادِ الدُّنْيَا وَآبَادِ الْآخِرَةِ وَأَكْثَرَ مِنْ ذَلِكَ لَا يَنْقَطِعُ أَوَّلُهُ وَلَا يَنْفَدُ آخِرُهُ ❋

ʿadada khalqika wa riḍāʼa nafsika wa zinata ʿarshika wa midāda kalimātika wa ʿadada mā dhakaraka bihi khalquka fīmā maḍā wa ʿadada mā hum dhākirūnaka bihi fīmā baqīya fī kulli sannatin wa shahrin wa jumʿuatin wa yawmin wa laylatin wa sāʿatin mina ʼs-sāʿati wa shammin wa nafasin wa ṭarfatin wa lamḥatin mina ʼl-abadi ilā ʼl-abadi wa ābādi ʼd-dunyā wa ābādi ʼl-ākhirati wa akthara min dhālika lā yanqatiʿu āwwaluhu wa lā yanfadu ākhiruh

(And exalt him) as much as all of Your Creation, to the extent of Your pleasure, in the decoration of Your Throne, and in the ink of Your Words and as often as Your Creation has remembered You in the past and (exalt him) as often as Your Creation has remembered You in the past and as often as they will remember You throughout the rest of time. And exalt him in every year, in every month, in every week, in every day, in every night, in every hour, in every sniff, in every breath, in every blink and in every glance, forever and ever, for the duration of this world and the duration of the next, and for longer then this, with a beginning that never ends and an end which never finishes! ➢

(١٨) اللَّهُمَّ صَلِّ عَلَى سَيِّدِنَا مُحَمَّدٍ عَلَى قَدْرِ حُبِّكَ فِيهِ اللَّهُمَّ صَلِّ عَلَى سَيِّدِنَا مُحَمَّدٍ عَلَى قَدْرِ عِنَايَتِكَ بِهِ اللَّهُمَّ صَلِّ عَلَى سَيِّدِنَا مُحَمَّدٍ حَقَّ قَدْرِهِ وَمِقْدَارِهِ ❁

(18) Allāhumma ṣalli ʿalā Sayyīdinā Muḥammadin ʿalā qadri ḥubbika fīhi Allāhumma ṣalli ʿalā Sayyīdinā Muḥammadin ʿalā qadrī ʿināyatika bihi Allāhumma ṣalli ʿalā Sayyīdinā Muḥammadin ḥaqqa qadrihi wa miqdārihi •

(18) O Allāh, exalt our master Muḥammad according to how much You love him! O Allāh, exalt our master Muḥammad according to Your caring for him! O Allāh exalt our master Muḥammad as befits his legitimate rank. ❁

(١٩) اللَّهُمَّ صَلِّ عَلَى سَيِّدِنَا مُحَمَّدٍ صَلَاةً تُنَجِّينَا بِهَا مِنْ جَمِيعِ الْأَهْوَالِ وَالْآفَاتِ وَتَقْضِي لَنَا بِهَا جَمِيعِ الْحَاجَاتِ وَتُطَهِّرُنَا بِهَا مِنْ جَمِيعِ السَّيِّئَاتِ وَتَرْفَعُنَا بِهَا عِنْدَكَ أَعْلَى الدَّرَجَاتِ

(19) Allāhumma ṣalli ʿalā Sayyīdinā Muḥammadin ṣalātan tunjīnā bihā min jamīʿi 'l-ahwāli wa 'l-āfāti wa taqḍī lanā bihā jamīʿi 'l-ḥājāti wa tuṭāhirunā bihā min jamīʿi 's-sayyi'āti wa tarfaʿunā bihā ʿindaka āʿlā 'd-darajāti

(19) O Allāh, raise up our master Muḥammad, with blessings which serve as a sanctuary for us from all terrors and oppression, which takes care of all our needs, which purify us from all sins which raise our rank in Your Presence, ➢

❊وَتُبَلِّغُنَا بِهَا أَقْصَى الْغَايَاتِ مِنْ جَمِيعِ الْخَيْرَاتِ فِي الْحَيَاةِ وَبَعْدَ الْمَمَاتِ

wa tuballighunā bihā aqṣā 'l-ghāyāti min jamī'i 'l-khayrāti fī 'l-ḥayāti wa ba'da 'l-mamāti •

and which allow us to attain ultimate goodness in this life and in the after death! ❊

(٢٠) اللَّهُمَّ صَلِّ عَلَى سَيِّدِنَا مُحَمَّدٍ صَلَاةَ الرِّضَا وَارْضَ عَنْ أَصْحَابِهِ رِضَاءَ الرِّضَا ❊

(20) Allāhumma ṣalli 'alā Sayyīdinā Muḥammadin ṣalāta 'r-riḍā w 'arḍā 'an aṣ-ḥābihi riḍā 'r-riḍā •

(20) O Allāh, raise up our master Muḥammad a blessing of contentment, and be pleased with his companions a pleasure of contentment! ❊

(٢١) اللَّهُمَّ صَلِّ عَلَى سَيِّدِنَا مُحَمَّدٍ السَّابِقِ لِلْخَلْقِ نُورُهُ وَرَحْمَةً لِلْعَالَمِينَ ظُهُورُهُ عَدَدَ مَنْ مَضَى مِنْ خَلْقِكَ وَمَنْ بَقِيَ

(21) Allāhumā ṣalli 'alā Sayyīdinā Muḥammadini 's-sābiqi li 'l-khalqi nūruhu wa raḥmatan li 'l-'ālamīna ẓuhūruhu 'adada man maḍā min khalqika wa man baqīya

(21) O Allāh, exalt our master Muḥammad, whose light preceded all creation, whose appearance is mercy to all the worlds, on the number of Your Creations which have passed before and the number of those which remain, ➢

وَمَنْ سَعِدَ مِنْهُم وَمَنْ شَقِيَ صَلَاةً تَسْتَغْرِقُ الْعَدَّ وَتُحِيطُ بِالْحَدِّ صَلَاةً لَا غَايَةَ لَهَا وَلَا مُنْتَهَى وَلَا انْقِضَاءَ صَلَاةً دَائِمَةً بِدَوَامِكَ وَعَلَى آلِهِ وَصَحْبِهِ وَسَلِّمْ تَسْلِيمًا مِثْلَ ذَلِكَ ❁

wa man sa'ida minhum wa man shaqīya ṣalātan tastaghriqu 'l-'adda wa tuḥīṭu bi 'l-ḥaddi ṣalātan lā ghāyata lahā wa lā muntahā wa lā 'nqiḍā'a ṣalātan dā'imatan bi-dawāmika wa 'alā ālihi wa ṣaḥbihi wa sallim taslīman mithla dhālika •

those who are fortunate and those who are not, with blessings which exceed all count and which encompass all limits, blessings with no limits, no boundaries, ceaseless, blessings which are eternal, enduring as You endure, and likewise bless his family and his companions and grant him and them abundant peace in like measure! ❁

(٢٢) اللَّهُمَّ صَلِّ عَلَى سَيِّدِنَا مُحَمَّدٍ الَّذِي مَلَأْتَ قَلْبَهُ مِنْ جَلَالِكَ وَعَيْنَهُ مِنْ جَمَالِكَ

(22) Allāhumma ṣalli 'alā Sayyīdinā Muḥammadini 'Lladhī malā'ta qalbahu min jalālika wa 'aynahū min jamālika

(22) O Allāh, exalt our master Muḥammad, whose heart was filled with Your Glory, and whose eyes were filled withYour Beauty ➢

فَأَصْبَحَ فَرِحاً مُؤَيَّداً مَنْصُوراً وَعَلَى آلِهِ وَصحبِهِ وَسَلِّم تَسْلِيماً وَالْحَمْدُ لله عَلَى ذَلِكَ ❊

fa-aṣbaḥa fariḥan mu'ayyadan manṣūran wa ʿalā ālihi wa ṣaḥbihi wa sallim taslimān wa 'l-ḥamdu lillāhi ʿalā dhālika •

such that he became overjoyed, supported and victorious, and also exalt his family and Companions and grant him and them abundant peace, and praise be to Allāh ﷻ for all of that! ❊

(٢٣) اللَّهُمَّ صَلِّ عَلَى سَيِّدِنَا وَمَوْلَانَا مُحَمَّدٍ عَدَدَ أَوْرَاقِ الزَّيْتُونِ وَجَمِيعِ الثِّمَارِ اللَّهُمَّ صَلِّ عَلَى سَيِّدِنَا وَمَوْلَانَا مُحَمَّدٍ عَدَدَ مَا كَانَ وَعَدَدَ مَا يَكُونُ وَعَدَدَ مَا أَظْلَمَ عَلَيهِ اللَّيْلُ وَأَضَاءَ عَلَيهِ النَّهَارُ ❊

(23) Allāhumma ṣalli ʿalā Sayyīdinā wa mawlānā Muḥammadin ʿadada awrāqi 'z-zaytūni wa jamīʿi 'th-thimāri Allāhumma ṣalli ʿalā Sayyīdinā wa mawlānā Muḥammadin ʿadada mā kāna wa mā yakūnu wa ʿadada mā aẓlama ʿalayhi 'l-laylu wa aḍā'a ʿalayhi 'n-nahāru •

(23) O Allāh, exalt our master Muḥammad on the number of the leaves of olive trees and all of their fruits! O Allāh, exalt our master Muḥammad on the number of that which existed and that which will exist, and on the number of times nighttime brought darkness and daytime shined forth! ❊

(٢٤) اللَّهُمَّ صَلِّ عَلَى سَيِّدِنَا وَمَوْلَانَا مُحَمَّدٍ وَعَلَى أَزْوَاجِهِ وَذُرِّيَّتِهِ عَدَدَ أَنْفَاسِ أُمَّتِهِ ❊

(24) Allāhumma ṣalli ʿalā Sayyīdinā wa mawlānā Muḥammadin wa ʿalā ālihi wa azwājihi wa dhurrīyatihi ʿadada anfāsi ummatihi •

(24) O Allāh exalt our master and guardian Muḥammad, bless his wives, bless his progeny on the number of the breaths of his nation! ❊

(٢٥) اللَّهُمَّ بِبَرَكَةِ الصَّلَاةِ عَلَيهِ اجْعَلْنَا بِالصَّلَاةِ عَلَيهِ مِنَ الْفَائِزِينَ وَعَلَى حَوضِهِ مِنَ الْوَارِدِينَ الشَّارِبِينَ وَبِسُنَّتِهِ وَطَاعَتِهِ مِنَ العَامِلِينَ وَلَا تَحُلْ بَينَنَا وَبَينَهُ يَوْمَ الْقِيَامَةِ يَا رَبَّ العَالَمِين وَاغْفِرْ لَنَا وَلِوَالِدِينَا وَلِجَمِيعِ الْمُسْلِمِينَ وَالحَمْدُ لله رَبِّ العَالَمِينَ ❊

(25) Allāhumma bi-barakāti 'ṣ-ṣalāti ʿalayhi 'jʿalnā bi 'ṣ-ṣalāti ʿalayhi mina 'l-fā'izīn wa ʿalā ḥawḍihi mina 'l-wāridīna 'sh-shāribīn wa bi sunnatihi wa ṭāʿatihi mina 'l-ʿāmilīn wa lā taḥul baynanā wa baynahu yawma 'l-qīyāmati yā rabba 'l-ʿālamīn wa 'ghfir lanā wa li-wālidīnā wa li-jamīʿi 'l-Muslimīna wa 'l-ḥamdu li 'Llāhi rabbi 'l-ʿālamīn •

(25) O Allāh, through the blessings of praising him, make us through praising him from amongst the successful ones, grant us to visit his heavenly pool, to a apply his way and his obedience in our lives, and do not separate us from him on Resurrection Day, O Lord of all the worlds, and forgive us and forgive our parents and all Muslims, praise be to Allāh, the Lord of the worlds! ❊

ابتِدَاءُ الثُلُثِ الثَانِي

Ibtidā'u 'Thuluthi 'th-Thānī

Beginning of the Second Third

(٢٦) اللَّهُمَّ صَلِّ وسَلِّم وَبَارِكْ عَلَى سَيِّدِنَا مُحَمَّدٍ وَعَلَى آلِ سَيِّدِنَا مُحَمَّدٍ أَكْرَمِ خَلْقِكَ وَسِرَاجِ أُفُقِكَ وَأَفْضَلِ قَائِمٍ بِحَقِّكَ المَبْعُوثِ بِتَيْسِيرِكَ وَرِفقِكِ صَلَاةً يَتَوَالَى تِكْرَارُهَا وَتَلُوحُ عَلَى الْأَكْوَانِ أَنْوَارُهَا ❁

(26) Allāhumma ṣalli wa sallim wa bārik 'alā Sayyīdinā Muḥammadin wa 'alā āli Sayyīdinā Muḥammadin akrami khalqika wa sirāji ufuqika wa afḍali qā'imin bi-ḥaqqika 'l-mab'ūthi bi-taysīrika wa rifqika ṣalātan yatawāla tikrāruhā wa talūḥu 'alā 'l-akwāni anwāruhā •

(26) O Allāh, exalt, grant peace and bless our master Muḥammad and the family of our master, the Noblest of Your Creation, the shining Lamp of the Horizons, the best Upholder of Your Reality, the Envoy of Your Relief and Kindness, with blessings which continue to repeat and let their light permeate throughout the universes! ❁

(٢٧) اللَّهُمَّ صَلِّ وَسَلِّم وَبَارِكْ عَلَى سَيِّدِنَا مُحَمَّدٍ وَعَلَى آلِ سَيِّدِنَا مُحَمَّدٍ أَفْضَلِ مَمْدُوحٍ بِقَولِكَ وَأَشْرَفِ دَاعٍ لِلإِعْتِصَامِ بِحَبْلِكَ وَخَاتَمِ أَنْبِيَائِكَ وَرُسُلِكَ صَلَاةً تُبَلِّغُنَا فِي الدَّارَينِ عَمِيمَ فَضْلِكَ وَكَرَامَةَ رِضْوَانِكَ وَوَصْلِكَ ❋

(27) Allāhumma ṣalli wa sallim wa bārik ʿalā Sayyīdinā Muḥammadin wa ʿalā āli Sayyīdinā Muḥammadin afḍali mamdūḥin bi-qawlika wa ashrafi dāʿin li ʾl-iʿtiṣāmi bi ḥablika wa khātami anbīyāʾika wa rusulika ṣalātan tuballighunā fī ʾd-dārayni ʿamīma faḍlika wa karāmata riḍwānika wa waṣlika •

(27) O Allāh, exalt, grant peace and bless our master Muḥammad and the family of our master Muḥammad, the One praised most by Your Words, the Noblest One calling for adherence to Your Bond, and the Seal of Your prophets and messengers, with blessings which permit us to attain Your general favour both here and hereafter and the honour of Your Pleasure and arrival! ❋

(٢٨) اللَّهُمَّ صَلِّ وسَلِّمْ وَبَارِكْ عَلَى سَيِّدِنَا مُحَمَّدٍ وَعَلَى آلِ سَيِّدِنَا مُحَمَّدٍ أَكْرَمِ الكُرَمَاءِ مِنْ عِبَادِكَ

(28) Allāhumma ṣalli wa sallim wa bārik ʿalā Sayyīdinā Muḥammadin wa ʿalā āli Sayyīdinā Muḥammadin akrami ʾl-kuramāʾi min ʿibādika

(28) O Allāh, bless, grant peace, and exalt our master Muḥammad and the family of our master Muḥammad, the most noble of Your noble servants, ➤

وَأَشْرَفِ الْمُنَادِينَ لِطُرُقِ رَشَادِكَ وَسِرَاجِ أَقْطَارِكَ وَبِلَادِكَ صَلَوَاةً لَا تَفْنَى
وَلَا تَبِيدَ وَتُبَلِّغُنَا بِهَا كَرَامَةَ الْمَزِيدِ ❋

wa ashrafi 'l-munadīna li-ṭuruqi rashādika wa sirāji aqṭārika wa bilādika ṣallatan lā tafnā wa lā tabīdu tuballighunā bihā karāmata 'l-mazīdi •

the most distinguished of the callers to the paths of Your Guidance and the Shining Lamp of all regions and countries, blessings with no end nor beginning through which You grant us great favours! ❋

(٢٩) اللَّهُمَّ صَلِّ وسَلِّمْ وَبَارِكْ عَلَى سَيِّدِنَا مُحَمَّدٍ وَعَلَى آلِ سَيِّدِنَا مُحَمَّدٍ
الرَّفِيعِ مَقَامُهُ الْوَاجِبِ تَعْظِيمُهُ وَاحْتِرَامُهُ صَلَاةً لَا تَنْقَطِعُ أَبَداً وَلَا تَفْنَى
سَرْمَداً وَلَا تَنْحَصِرُ عَدَداً ❋

(29) Allāhumma ṣalli wa sallim wa bārik ʿalā Sayyīdinā Muḥammadin wa ʿalā āli Sayyīdinā Muḥammad 'r-rafīʿi maqāmuhu 'l-wājibi taʿ-ẓīmuhu wa iḥtirāmuhu ṣalātan lā tanqaṭiʿu abadan wa lā tafnā sarmadan wa lā tanḥaṣiru ʿadadan •

(29) O Allāh, exalt, grant peace and bless our master Muḥammad and the family of our master Muḥammad, whose rank is high, whose exaltation and esteem are incumbent upon us, with blessings which are never curtailed and never finish, endless blessings which are immeasurable! ❋

(٣٠) اللَّهُمَّ صَلِّ عَلَى سَيِّدِنَا مُحَمَّدٍ وَعَلَى آلِ سَيِّدِنَا مُحَمَّدٍ كَمَا صَلَّيْتَ عَلَى سَيِّدِنَا إِبْرَاهِيمَ وَعَلَى آلِ سَيِّدِنَا إِبْرَاهِيمَ فِي الْعَالَمِينَ إِنَّكَ حَمِيدٌ مَجِيدٌ

(30) Allāhumma ṣalli ʿalā Sayyīdinā Muḥammadin wa ʿalā āli Sayyīdinā Muḥammadin kamā ṣallayta ʿalā Sayyīdinā Ibrāhīma wa ʿalā āli Sayyīdinā Ibrāhīma fī 'l-ʿālamīna innaka Ḥamīdun Majīd

(30) O Allāh, exalt our master Muḥammad and the family of our master Muḥammad just as You exalted Abraham and the family of Abraham in all the worlds, for You are The Praiseworthy, The Mighty! ➢

وَصَلِّ اللَّهُمَّ عَلَى سَيِّدِنَا مُحَمَّدٍ وَعَلَى آلِ سَيِّدِنَا مُحَمَّدٍ كُلَّمَا ذَكَرَهُ الذَّاكِرُونَ وَغَفَلَ عَنْ ذِكْرِهِ الْغَافِلُونَ ❋

wa ṣalli ʿalā Sayyīdinā Muḥammadin wa ʿalā āli Sayyīdinā Muḥammadin kullamā dhakarahu 'dhākirūna wa ghafala ʿan dhikrihi 'l-ghāfilūn •

And exalt, O Allāh, our master Muḥammad and the family of our master Muḥammad whenever those who remember him do so and whenever those who neglect to remember him do so! ❋

(٣١) اللَّهُمَّ صَلِّ عَلَى سَيِّدِنَا مُحَمَّدٍ وَعَلَى آلِ سَيِّدِنَا مُحَمَّدٍ وَارْحَمْ سَيِّدَنَا مُحَمَّداً وَآلَ سَيِّدِنَا مُحَمَّدٍ وَبَارِكْ عَلَى سَيِّدِنَا مُحَمَّدٍ وَعَلَى آلِ سَيِّدِنَا مُحَمَّدٍ

(31) Allāhumma ṣalli ʿalā Sayyīdinā Muḥammadin wa ʿalā āli Sayyīdinā Muḥammadin wa 'rḥam Sayyidanā Muḥammadin wa āla Sayyīdinā Muḥammadin wa bārik ʿalā Sayyīdinā Muḥammadin wa ʿalā āli Sayyīdinā Muḥammadin

(31) O Allāh, exalt our master Muḥammad and the family of our master Muḥammad, and have mercy upon our master Muḥammad and upon the family of our master Muḥammad, and bless our master Muḥammad and the family of our master Muḥammad ➢

كَمَا صَلَّيْتَ وَرَحِمْتَ وَبَارَكْتَ عَلَى سَيِّدِنَا إِبْرَاهِيمَ وَعَلَى آلِ سَيِّدِنَا إِبْرَاهِيمَ إِنَّكَ حَمِيدٌ مَجِيدٌ ❋

kamā ṣallayta wa rāḥimta wa bārakta ʿalā Sayyīdinā Ibrāhīma wa ʿalā āli Sayyīdinā Ibrāhīma innaka Ḥamīdun Majīd •

just as You exalted, sent your mercy and blessed our master Abraham and the family of our master Abraham, for You are The Praiseworthy, The Mighty! ❋

(٣٢) اللَّهُمَّ صَلِّ عَلَى سَيِّدِنَا مُحَمَّدٍ النَّبِيِّ الأُمِّيِّ الطَّاهِرِ الْمُطَهَّرِ وَعَلَى آلِهِ وَسَلِّمْ ❋

(32) Allāhumma ṣalli ʿalā Sayyīdinā Muḥammadini 'n-nabīyyi 'l-ummīyi 'ṭ-ṭāhirih 'l-muṭahhari wa ʿalā ālihi wa sallim •

(32) O Allāh exalt and grant peace to our master Muḥammad, the Unlettered Prophet, the Pure, the Immaculate, and grant peace and blessings to his family! ❋

(٣٣) اللَّهُمَّ صَلِّ عَلَى مَنْ خَتَمتَ بِهِ الرِّسَالَةَ وَأَيَّدْتَهُ بِالنَّصْرِ وَالْكَوثَرِ وَالشَّفَاعَةِ ❋

(33) Allāhumma ṣalli ʿalā man khatamta bihi 'r-risālata wa ayyadtahu bi 'n-naṣri wa 'l-kawthari wa 'sh-shafāʿatī •

(33) O Allāh, exalt the One with whom You sealed the Message, and the One to whom You granted victory, the Pool known as Kawthar and the Intercession! ❋

(٣٤) اللَّهُمَّ صَلِّ عَلَى سَيِّدِنَا وَمَوْلَانَا مُحَمَّدٍ نَبِيِّ الْحُكْمِ وَالْحِكْمَةِ

(34) Allāhumma ṣalli ʿalā Sayyīdinā wa mawlānā Muḥammadin Nabīyyi 'l-ḥukmi wa 'l-ḥikmati

(34) O Allāh, exalt our master Muḥammad, the Prophet of judiciousness and wisdom, ➢

السِّرَاجِ الوَهَّاجِ المَخْصُوصِ بِالْخُلُقِ الْعَظِيمِ وَخَتْمِ الرُسُلِ ذِي المِعْرَاجِ

's-siraji 'l-wahhāji 'l-makhṣuṣi bi 'l-khuluqi 'l-ʿaẓīmi wa khatmi 'r-rusuli dhi 'l-miʿrāji

the Brilliant Lamp, the One destined for the Greatest character, the seal of the Messengers, the master of the Night journey, and likewise bless his family, ➢

وَعَلَى آلِهِ وَأَصْحَابِهِ وَأَتْبَاعِهِ السَّالِكِينَ عَلَى مَنْهَجِهِ الْقَوِيمِ فَأَعْظِمِ اللَّهُمَّ بِهِ مِنْهَاجَ نُجُومِ الإِسْلامِ وَمَصَابِيحِ الظَّلَامِ المُهْتَدَى بِهِمْ فِي ظُلمَةِ لَيلِ الشَّكِ الدَّاجِ صَلَاةً دَائِمَةً مُستَمِرَّةً مَا تَلَاطَمَتْ فِي الْأَبْحُرِ الْأَمْوَاجُ

wa ʿalā ālihi wa aṣḥābihi wa atbāʿihi 's-sālikina ʿalā manhajihi 'l-qawīm fa aʿẓimi 'llāhumma bihi minhāja nujūmi 'l-Islāmi wa maṣābīḥi 'ẓ-ẓalāmi 'l-muhtadā bihim fī ẓulmati layli 'sh-shakki 'd-dāji ṣalātan dā'imatan mustamirratan mā talāṭamat fī 'l-abḥuri 'l-amwāju

bless his Companions, his Followers, the sincere travelers on the true Path! Magnify, O Allāh, through him, the Path of the Stars of Islām (The Companions) and the Lamps (The Successors) on the path signs posted by them, the path that dispels the darkness in the murky gloom of the night of doubt and send blessing which are eternal and continuous and which last for as long as the waves crash in the oceans! ➢

وَطَافَ بِالْبَيْتِ العَتِيقِ مِنْ كُلِّ فَجٍّ عَمِيقٍ الْحُجَّاجُ ❋

wa ṭāfa bi 'l-bayti 'l-ʿatīqi min kulli fajjin ʿamiqin 'l-ḥujjaju •

and the Ancient House (the Holy Kāʿbah) is circumambulated from all sides by throngs of pilgrims, coming from every deep valley! ❋

(٣٥) وَأَفْضَلُ الصَّلاَةِ وَالتَّسْلِيمِ عَلَى سَيِّدِنَا مُحَمَّدٍ رَسُولِهِ الْكَرِيمِ وَصَفْوَتِهِ مِنَ الْعِبَادِ وَشَفِيعِ الْخَلائِقِ فِي الْمِيعَادِ صَاحِبِ الْمَقَامِ الْمَحْمُودِ وَالْحَوْضِ الْمَوْرُودِ النَّاهِضِ بِأَعْبَاءِ الرِّسَالَةِ وَالتَّبْلِيغِ الْأَعَمِّ وَالْمَخْصُوصِ بِشَرَفِ السِّعَايَةِ فِي الصَّلاَحِ الْأَعْظَمِ

(35) wa afḍalu 'ṣ-ṣalāti wa 't-taslīmi ʿalā Sayyīdinā Muḥammadin Rasūlihi 'l-karīmi wa Ṣafwatihi mina 'l-ʿibādi wa shafiʿi 'l-khalā'iqi fī 'l-miʿadi Ṣāḥibi 'l-Maqāmi 'l-Maḥmūdi wa 'l-Hawḍi 'l-Mawrūdi an-nāhiḍi bi aʿbā'i 'r-risālati wa 't-tablīghi 'l-āʿammi wa 'l-makhṣūṣi bi-sharafi 's-siʿāyati fī 'ṣ-ṣalāḥi 'l-āʿẓam

(35) The best of all praise and peace be upon our master Muḥammad, the Generous Messenger, Allāh's friend among all the devotees, the Intercessor for all created beings at the Appointed Tryst, Owner of the Most-Praised Station and the Oft-Visited Pool, the One who undertook the burden of the Message and the responsibility of spreading it far and wide, the One destined for honor and the One who strove for the greatest righteousness ➢

صَلَّى اللهُ عَلَيهِ وَعَلَى آلِهِ وَأَصْحَابِهِ صَلَاةً دَائِمَةً مُستَمِرَّةَ الدَّوَامِ عَلَى مَرِّ اللَّيَالِي وَالأَيَّامِ

ṣalla 'Llāhu ʿalayhi wa ʿalā ālihi ṣalātan dā'imatan mustamirrata 'd-dawāmi ʿalā marri 'l-layāli wa 'l-ayyāmi

eternal and continuous blessings of Allāh upon him and upon his family, lasting as long as the turning of nights and days ➢

فَهُوَ سَيِّدُ الأَوَّلِينَ وَالآخِرِينَ وَأَفْضَلُ الأَوَّلِينَ وَ الآخِرِينَ عَلَيهِ أَفْضَلُ صَلَاةِ المُصَلِّينَ وَأَزْكَى سَلَامِ المُسَلِّمِينَ وَأَطْيَبُ ذِكْرِ الذَّاكِرِينَ وَأَفْضَلُ صَلَوَاتِ اللهِ وَأَحْسَنُ صَلَوَاتِ اللهِ وَاجَلُّ صَلَوَاتِ اللهِ وَأَجْمَلُ صَلَوَاتِ اللهِ وَأَكْمَلُ صَلَوَاتِ اللهِ

fa hūwa sayyidu 'l-awwalīna wa 'l-ākhirīna wa afḍalu 'l-awwalīna wa 'l-ākhirīn ʿalayhi afḍalu ṣalāti 'l-muṣallīna wa azkā salāmi 'l-musallimīna wa aṭyabu dhikri 'dh-dhākirīna wa afḍalu ṣalawāti 'Llāhi wa āḥsanu ṣalawāti 'Llāh wa ajallu ṣalawāti 'Llāhi wa ajmalu ṣalawāti 'Llāhi wa akmalu ṣalawāti 'Llāhi

For he is the Master of the firsts and the lasts, and the Best of the firsts and the lasts! The best praise of those who invoke blessings on him be for him! The purest peace of those sending peace on him be for him and the finest remembrance of those who remember him and the finest blessings of Allāh and the choicest blessings of Allāh and the greatest blessings of Allāh and the fairest blessings of Allāh and the fullest blessings of Allāh! ➢

وَأَسْبَغُ صَلَوَاتِ اللهِ وَأَتَمُّ صَلَوَاتِ اللهِ وَأَظْهَرُ صَلَواتِ اللهِ وَأَعْظَمُ صَلَوَاتِ اللهِ وَأَزْكَى صَلَوَاتِ اللهِ وَأَطْيَبُ صَلَوَاتِ اللهِ وَأَبْرَكُ صَلَوَاتِ اللهِ وَأَنْمَى صَلَوَاتِ اللهِ وَأَوْفَى صَلَوَاتِ اللهِ وَأَسْمَى صَلَوَاتِ اللهِ وَأَعْلَى صَلَوَاتِ اللهِ وَأَكْثَرُ صَلَوَاتِ اللهِ وَأَجْمَعُ صَلَوَاتِ اللهِ وَأَعَمُّ صَلَوَاتِ اللهِ وَأَدْوَمُ صَلَوَاتِ اللهِ وَأَبْقَى صَلَوَاتِ اللهِ

wa asbaghu ṣalawāti 'Llāhi wa atammu ṣalawāti 'Llāhi wa aẓharu ṣalawāti 'Llāhi wa aʿẓamu ṣalawāti 'Llāhi wa azkā ṣalawāti 'Llāhi wa aṭyabu ṣalawāti 'Llāhi wa abraku ṣalawāti 'Llāhi wa azkā ṣalawāti 'Llāhi wa anmā ṣalawāti 'Llāhi wa awfā ṣalawāti 'Llāhi wa asnā ṣalawāti 'Llāhi wa āʿlā ṣalawāti 'Llāhi wa aktharu ṣalawāti 'Llāhi wa ajmaʿu ṣalawāti 'Llāhi wa aʿammu ṣalawāti 'Llāhi wa adwamu ṣalawāti 'Llāhi wa abqā ṣalawāti 'Llāhi

And the most abundant blessings of Allāh and the utmost blessings of Allāh and the clearest blessings of Allāh and the mightiest blessings of Allāh and the sweetest blessings of Allāh and the freshest blessings of Allāh and the holiest blessings of Allāh and the purest blessings of Allāh and the richest blessings of Allāh and the most sincere blessings of Allāh and the matchless blessing of Allāh and the highest blessings of Allāh and the extravagant blessings of Allāh and the myriad blessings of Allāh and the universal blessings of Allāh and the longest lasting blessings of Allāh and the longest remaining blessings of Allāh! ➢

وَ أَعَزُّ صَلَوَاتِ اللهِ وَأَرْفَعُ صَلَوَاتِ اللهِ وَأَعْظَمُ صَلَوَاتِ اللهِ عَلَى أَفْضَلِ خَلْقِ اللهِ وَأَحْسَنِ خَلْقِ اللهِ وَأَجَلِّ خَلْقِ اللهِ وَأَكْرَمِ خَلْقِ اللهِ وَأَجْمَلِ خَلْقِ اللهِ وَأَكْمَلِ خَلْقِ اللهِ وَاَتَمِّ خَلْقِ اللهِ وَأَعْظَمِ خَلْقِ اللهِ عِنْدَ اللهِ رَسُولِ اللهِ وَنَبِيِّ اللهِ وَحَبِيبِ اللهِ وَصَفِيِّ اللهِ وَنَجِيِّ اللهِ وَخَلِيلِ اللهِ وَوَلِيِّ اللهِ وَأَمِينِ اللهِ

wa aʿazzu ṣalawāti 'Llāhi wa arfaʿu ṣalawāti 'Llāhi wa aʿẓamu ṣalawāti 'Llāhi ʿalā afḍali khalqi 'Llāhi wa āḥsani khalqi 'Llāhi wa ajalli khalqi 'Llāhi wa akrami khalqi 'Llāhi wa ajmali khalqi 'Llāhi wa akmali khalqi 'Llāhi wa atammi khalqi 'Llāhi wa aʿẓami khalqi 'Llāhi ʿinda 'Llāhi Rasūli 'Llāhi wa Nabīyyi 'Llāhi wa Ḥabībi 'Llāhi wa Ṣafīyyi 'Llāhi wa Najīyyi 'Llāhi wa Khalīli 'Llāhi wa Walīyyi 'Llāhi wa Amīni 'Llāhi

And the strongest blessings of Allāh and the loftiest blessings of Allāh and the mightiest blessings of Allāh upon the Best of Allāh's creation, the Finest of Allāh's creation, the Greatest of Allāh's creation, the Noblest of Allāh's creation, the Fairest of Allāh's creation, the Most Perfect of Allāh's creation, the Most Complete of Allāh's creation, the Mightiest of Allāh's creation in Allāh's sight, the Messenger of Allāh, the Beloved of Allāh, the Intimate Friend of Allāh, the Confidante of Allāh, the Friend of Allāh! Allāh's Saint, the One Trusted by Allāh! ➢

وَخِيرَةِ اللهِ مِنْ خَلْقِ اللهِ وَنُخْبَةِ اللهِ مِنْ بَرِيَّةِ اللهِ وَصَفْوَةِ اللهِ مِنْ أَنْبِيَاءِ اللهِ وَعُرْوَةِ اللهِ وَعِصْمَةِ اللهِ وَنِعْمَةِ اللهِ وَمِفْتَاحِ رَحْمَةِ اللهِ الْمُخْتَارِ مِنْ رُسُلِ اللهِ الْمُنْتَخَبِ مِنْ خَلْقِ اللهِ الْفَائِزِ بِالْمَطْلَبِ فِي الْمَرْهَبِ وَالْمَرْغَبِ الْمُخْلِصِ فِيمَا وُهِبَ أَكْرَمِ مَبْعُوثٍ أَصْدَقِ قَائِلٍ أَنْجَحِ شَافِعٍ أَفْضَلِ مُشَفَّعٍ الأَمِينِ فِيمَا اسْتُودِعَ

wa Khiyrati 'Llāhi min khalqi 'Llāhi wa Nukhbati 'Llāhimin barīyyati 'Llāhi wa Ṣafwati 'Llāhi min anbīyā'i 'Llāhi wa ʿUrwati 'Llāhi wa ʿIṣmati 'Llāhi wa Niʿmati 'Llāhi wa Miftāḥi Raḥmati 'Llāhi 'l-Mukhtāri min Rusuli 'Llāhi al-muntakhabi min khalqi 'Llāhi 'l-fā'izi bi 'l-maṭlabi fī 'l-marhabi wa 'l-marghabi 'l-mukhlaṣi fī mā wuhib Akrami mabʿūthin Aṣdaqi qā'ilin Anjaḥi shāfiʿin Afḍali mushaffaʿin 'l-Amīni fīmā 'stūdiʿa

The Boon of Allāh from amongst Allāh's creation, Allāh's Chosen one from amongst Allāh's servants, the Confidante of Allāh from Allāh's prophets, the Handhold of Allāh, the Safety of Allāh, the Favor of Allāh, the Key to Allah's Mercy, the Chosen One among Allāh's messengers, the Elect One from amongst Allāh's creations and the One who succeeded in that which he requested in situations of dread and hope, the Sincere One in what he was granted, the Most Honored Envoy, the Truest Speaker, the Most Successful Intercessor, the Best Intercessor, the One faithful to his pledge ➤

الصَادِقِ فِيمَا بَلَّغَ الصَادِعِ بِأَمْرِ رَبِّهِ الْمُضْطَلِعِ بِمَا حُمِّلَ أَقْرَبِ رُسلِ اللهِ إِلَى اللهِ وَسِيلَةً وَأَعْظَمِهِمْ غَداً عِنْدَ اللهِ مَنْزِلَةً وَفَضِيلَةً وَأَكْرَمِ أَنْبِيَاءِ اللهِ الْكِرَامِ الصَّفْوَةِ عَلَى اللهِ وَأَحَبِّهِمْ إِلَى اللهِ وَأَقْرَبِهِمْ زُلْفَى لَدَى اللهِ وَأَكْرَمِ الْخَلْقِ عَلَى اللهِ وَأَحْظَاهُمْ وَأَرْضَاهُمْ لَدَى اللهِ وَأَعْلَى النَّاسِ قَدْراً وَأَعْظَمِهِمْ مَحَلاً وَأَكْمَلِهِمْ مَحَاسِناً وَفَضْلاً

aṣ-ṣādiqi fī mā ballagha 'ṣ-ṣādiʿi bi amri rabbīhi 'l-muṭṭaliʿi bimā ḥummīl aqrabi rusuli 'Llāhi ilā 'Llāhi wasīlatan wa āʿẓamihim ghadan ʿinda 'Llāhi manzilatan wa faḍīlatan wa akrami anbīyā'i 'Llāhi 'l-kirāmi 'ṣ-Ṣafwati ʿalā 'Llāhi wa aḥabbihim ilā 'Llāhi wa aqrabihim zulfā lada 'l-Lāh wa akrami 'l-khalqi ʿalā 'Llāhi wa aḥẓāhum wa arḍāhum lada 'Llāhi wa āʿlā 'n-nāsi qadran wa āʿẓamihim maḥallan wa akmalihim maḥāsinan wa faḍlan

the One true to his mission, the One who complied with the order of his Lord, and the One who bore his responsibility, the Messenger of Allāh possessing closest access to Allāh ﷺ and the One whose position and pre-eminence in the sight of Allāh is greater than all other prophets! Most honored of prophets honored by Allāh, the Purest before Allāh and Most Beloved to Allāh! Most loved of them by Allāh and closest of them to Allāh, the Most-Honored creation before Allāh! Most fortunate and satisfied of them in Allāh's presence! Highest of mankind in rank attaining their highest position and the most perfect level of conduct and merit among them! ➢

وَأَفْضَلِ الْأَنْبِيَاءِ دَرَجَةً وَأَكْمَلِهِمْ شَرِيعَةً وَأَشْرَفِ الْأَنْبِيَاءِ نِصَاباً وَأَبْيَنِهِم بَيَاناً وَخِطَاباً وَأَفْضَلِهِمْ مَولِداً وَمُهَاجِراً وَعِتْرَةً وَأَصْحَاباً وَأَكْرَمِ النَّاسِ أَرُومَةً وَأَشْرَفِهِمْ جُرْثُومَةً وَخَيْرِهِم نَفَساً وَأَطْهَرِهِمْ قَلْباً وَأَصْدَقِهِم قَولاً وَأَزْكَاهُمْ فِعْلاً وَأَثْبَتِهِمْ أَصْلاً وَأَوْفَاهُمْ عَهْداً وَأَمْكَنِهِمْ مَجْداً وَأَكْرَمِهِمْ طَبْعاً وَأَحْسَنِهِمْ صُنْعاً وَأَطْيَبِهِمْ فَرْعاً

wa afḍali 'l-anbīyā'i darajatan wa akmalihim sharīʿatan wa ashrafi 'l-anbīyā'i nisāban wa abyanihim bayānan wa khiṭāban wa afḍalihim mawlidan wa muhājiran wa ʿitratan wa aṣḥāban wa akrami 'n-nāsi arūmatan wa ashrafihim jurthūmatan wa khayrihim nafsan wa aṭ-harihim qalban wa aṣdaqihim qawlan wa azkāhum fiʿlan wa athbatihim aṣlan wa awfāhum ʿahdan wa amkanihim majdan wa akramihim ṭabʿan wa aḥsanihim ṣunʿan wa aṭyabihim farʿan

best in rank of all the prophets possessing the most perfect of their laws, noblest of them all in ancestry, clearest of them in eloquence and preaching, the best of them in birth, migration, and whose perfumed descendants and companions are most gracious of them all, the most noble human being whose origin was nobler than all others, the best of souls, the purest in heart, the truest in word, the most refined in deeds, firmest of origins, the most faithful to his pledge the most distinguished, most honored in natural disposition, the finest in features, and best in branches of descendents; ➤

وَأَكْثَرِهِمْ طَاعَةً وَسَمْعاً وَأَعْلَاهُمْ مَقَاماً وَأَحْلَاهُمْ كَلَاماً وَأَزْكَاهُمْ سَلَاماً وَأَجَلِّهِمْ قَدْراً وَأَعْظَمِهِم فَخْراً وَأَسْنَاهُمْ فَخْراً وَأَرْفَعِهِمْ فِي الْمَلَإِ الْأَعْلَى ذِكْراً وَأَوْفَاهُمْ عَهْداً وَأَصْدَقِهِم وَعْداً وَأَكْثَرِهِمْ شُكْراً وَأَعْلَاهُمْ امْراً وَأَجْمَلِهِمْ صَبْراً وَأَحْسَنِهِمْ خَيْراً وَأَقْرَبِهِمْ يُسْراً وَأَبْعَدِهِمْ مَكَاناً وَأَعْظَمِهِمْ شَأْناً وَأَثْبَتِهِمْ بُرْهَاناً وَأَرْجَحِهِمْ مِيزَاناً وَأَوَّلِهِمْ إِيمَاناً وَأَوْضَحِهِمْ بَيَاناً وَأَفْصَحِهِمْ لِسَاناً وأَظْهَرِهِمْ سُلْطَاناً ❋

wa aktharihim ṭā'atan wa sam'an wa ā'lāhum maqāman wa aḥlāhum kalāman wa azkāhum salāman wa ajallihim qadran wa ā'ẓamihim fakhran wa asnāhum fakhran wa arfa'ihim fī 'l-mala'i 'l-ā'lā dhikran wa aṣdaqihim w'adan wa aktharihim shukran wa ā'lāhum amran wa ajmalihim ṣabran wa aḥsanihim khayran wa aqrabihim yusran wa ab'adihim makānan wa a'ẓamihim shā'nan wa athbatihim burhānan wa arjaḥihim mīzānan wa āwwalihim īmānan wa awḍaḥihim bayānan wa afṣaḥihim lisānan wa aẓharihim sulṭānan •

most obedient and dutiful of all, the highest in station, the sweetest in speech, the purest in peace, the most resplendent in rank, highest in glory, loftiest in mention in the High Hosts, most profusely sincere in his promise, most grateful of them all, highest in authority, most beautifully patient, finest in goodness, closest to ease, most balanced in judgment, most advanced in faith, clearest in evidence, most eloquent in speaking, possessing the strongest authority amongst them! ❋

Thursday

الحِزْبُ الرَّابِعُ فِي يَوْمِ الخَمِيسِ

Al-Ḥizbu 'r-Rābi'u fī Yawmi 'l-Khamīs

The Fourth Chapter to Be Read on Thursday

(1)اللَّهُمَّ صَلِّ عَلَى سَيِّدِنَا مُحَمَّدٍ عَبْدِكَ وَرَسُولِكَ النَّبِيِّ الأُمِّيِّ وَعَلَى آلِ سَيِّدِنَا مُحَمَّدٍ ❋

(1) Allāhumma ṣalli 'alā Sayyīdinā Muḥammadin 'abdika wa Rasūlika 'n-Nabīyyi 'l-'Ummīyi wa 'alā āli Sayyīdinā Muḥammadin •

(1) O Allāh, bless our master Muḥammad, Your slave and Your Messenger, the Unlettered Prophet, and the family of our master Muḥammad! ❋

(٢) اللَّهُمَّ صَلِّ عَلَى سَيِّدِنَا مُحَمَّدٍ صَلَاةً تَكُونُ لَكَ رِضَاءً وَلَهُ جَزَاءً وَلِحَقِّهِ أَدَاءً

(2) Allāhumma ṣalli 'alā Sayyīdinā Muḥammadin wa 'alā āli Sayyīdinā Muḥammadin ṣalātan takūnu laka riḍā'an wa lāhu jazā'an wa li-ḥaqqihi ādā'an

(2) O Allāh, exalt our master Muḥammad and the family of our master Muḥammad, exaltation pleasing to You, a reward for him which is his deserved right ➤

وَأَعْطِهِ الوَسِيلَةَ وَالفَضِيلَةَ وَالمَقَامَ المَحْمُودَ الَّذِي وَعَدْتَهُ وَاجْزِهِ عَنَّا مَا هُوَ أَهْلُهُ وَاجْزِهِ أَفْضَلَ مَا جَازَيتَ نَبِياً عَنْ قَومِهِ وَرسُولاً عَنْ أُمَّتِهِ وَصَلِّ عَلَى جَمِيعِ إِخوَانِهِ مِنَ النَّبِيِّينَ وَالصَّالِحِينَ يَا ارْحَمْ الرَّاحِمِينَ ❋

wa āʿṭihi 'l-wasīlata wa 'l-faḍīlata wa 'l-Maqām 'l-Maḥmūda 'Lladhī wʿadtahu wa 'jzihi ʿannā mā hūwa āhluhu wa 'jzihi afḍala mā jāzayta nabīyyan ʿan qawmihi wa rasūlan ʿan ummatihi wa ṣalli ʿalā jamīʿi ikhwānihi mina 'n-nabīyyīna wa 'ṣ-ṣāliḥīna yā arḥama 'r-rāḥimīn •

and grant him the Closest access, the Pre-eminence and the Praised Station which You promised him. and reward him on our behalf of his people Any other Prophet or on behalf of his nation any other Messengers, and bless all his brothers, the Prophet and righteous ones, Most Merciful of the Merciful! ❋

(٣) اللَّهُمَّ اجْعَلْ فَضَائِلَ صَلَوَاتِكَ وَشَرَائِفَ زَكَوَاتِكَ وَنَوَامِيَ بَرَكَاتِكَ وَعَوَاطِفَ رَأْفَتِكَ وَرَحْمَتِكَ وَتَحِيَّتِكَ

(3) Allāhumma 'jʿal faḍā'ilā ṣalawātika wa sharā'ifa zakawātika wa nawāmīya barakātika wa ʿawāṭifa rāfatika wa raḥmatika wa taḥīyyatika

(3) O Allāh, bestow the favors of Your noble blessings and virtues, and the increase of Your benedictions, and the benevolence of Your Compassion and Your Mercy, and Your Salutation ➢

وَفَضَائِلَ آلاَئِكَ عَلَى سَيِّدِنَا مُحَمَّدٍ سَيِّدِ الْمُرْسَلِينَ وَرَسُولِ رَبِّ الْعَالَمِينَ

wa faḍā'ilā ālā'ika ʿalā Sayyīdinā Muḥammadin sayyidi 'l-mursalīna wa rasūli Rabbi 'l-ʿālamīna

and the favors of Your bounties, upon our master Muḥammad, the Master of the Messengers, the Messenger of the lord of the worlds ➤

قَائِدِ الْخَيْرِ وَفَاتِحِ الْبِرِّ وَنَبِيِّ الرَّحْمَةِ وَسَيِّدِ الْأُمَّةِ ❁

qā'idi 'l-khayri wa fātiḥi 'l-birri wa Nabīyyi 'r-Raḥmati wa Sayyidi 'l-ummati •

the Guide to the Goodness, the Opener of Piety, the Prophet of Mercy and the master of the nation! ❁

(٤) اللَّهُمَّ ابْعَثْهُ مَقَاماً مَحْمُوداً تُزْلِفُ بِهِ قُرْبَهُ وَتُقِرُّ بِهِ عَيْنَهُ يَغْبِطُهُ فِيهِ الْأَوَّلُونَ وَالْآخِرُونَ ❁

(4) Allāhumma 'b-ʿathhu maqāman maḥmūdan tuzlifu bihi qurbahu wa tuqirru bihi ʿaynahu yaghbiṭuhu fīhi 'l-awālūna wa 'l-'ākhirūna •

(4) O Allāh send him to the Most-Praised Station, thereby advancing his nearness, comforting his eyes, Of those who came first and those who came last! ❁

(٥) اللَّهُمَّ أَعْطِهِ الفَضْلَ وَالفَضِيلَةَ وَالشَّرَفَ وَالْوَسِيلَةَ وَالدَّرَجَةَ الرَّفِيعَةَ وَالمَنْزِلَةَ الشَّامِخَةَ ❋

(5) Allāhumma 'āʿṭihi 'l-faḍla wa 'l-faḍīlata wa 'sh-sharafa wa 'l-wasīlata wa 'd-darajata 'r-rafī-ʿata wa 'l-manzilata 'sh-shāmikhata •

(5) O Allāh, grant him Divine Favour, Divine Grace, Divine Honour, the closest access, the lofty rank and the high standing! ❋

(٦) اللَّهُمَّ أَعْطِ سَيِّدِنَا مُحَمَّداً الْوَسِيلَةَ وَبَلِّغْهُ مَأْمُولَهُ وَاجْعَلْهُ أَوَّلَ شَافِعٍ وَأَوَّلَ مُشَفَّعٍ ❋

(6) Allāhumma aʿti Sayyīdinā Muḥammadan 'l-wasīlata wa ballighu māmūlahu wa 'jʿalhu āwwala shāfiʿin wa āwwala mushaffaʿin •

(6) O Allāh grant our master Muḥammad the closest Access and send him what he hopes for and make him the first intercessor and the first whose intercession is accepted! ❋

(٧) اللَّهُمَّ عَظِّمْ بُرْهَانَهُ وَثَقِّلْ مِيزَانَهُ وَأَبْلِجْ حُجَّتَهُ

(7) Allāhumma ʿaẓ-ẓim burhānahu wa tḥaqqil mīzānahu wa ablij ḥujjatuhu

(7) O Allāh! Strengthen his proof, make his judgment sound, make his argument shine ➤

وَارْفَعْ فِي أَهْلِ عِلِّيِّينَ دَرَجَتَهُ وَفِي أَعْلَى الْمُقَرَّبِينَ مَنْزِلَتَهُ ❋

wa 'rfa' fī āhli 'illiyīna darajatahu wa fī ā'lā 'l-muqarrabīna manzilatahu •

and raise his rank among the dwellers of the Uppermost Heaven and uplift his standing among the heights of those who are closest! ❋

(٨) اللَّهُمَّ أَحْيِنَا عَلَى سُنَّتِهِ وَتَوَفَّنَا عَلَى مِلَّتِهِ وَاجْعَلْنَا مِنْ أَهْلِ شَفَاعَتِهِ

(8) Allāhumma aḥyinā 'alā sunnatihi wa tawaffanā 'alā millatihi wa 'j'alnā min āhli shafā'atīhi

(8) O Allāh, cause us to live according to his way and Pass us away following his religion and make us among the people of his intercession! ➢

وَاحْشُرْنَا فِي زُمْرَتِهِ وَأَوْرِدْنَا حَوضَهُ وَاسْقِنَا مِنْ كَأسِهِ غَيرَ خَزَايَا وَلَا نَادِمِينَ وَلَا شَاكِّينَ وَلَا مُبَدِّلِينَ وَلَا مُغَيِّرِينَ وَلَا فَاتِنِينَ وَلَا مَفْتُونِينَ آمِينْ يَا رَبَّ الْعَالَمِينَ ❋

wa 'ḥshurnā fī zumratihi wa 'awridnā ḥawḍahu wasqinā min kā'sihi ghayra khazāyā wa lā nādimīna wa lā shākīna wa lā mubaddilīna wa lā mughayyirīna wa lā fātinīna wa lā maftunīna āmīn yā rabba 'l-'ālamīn

And resurrect us in his company and make us to be watered from his pool and to drink from his drinking bowl with no disgrace, no regrets, no doubts, and no temptations, amen, O Allāh the Lord of the worlds! ➢

(٩) اللَّهُمَّ صَلِّ عَلَى سَيِّدِنَا مُحَمَّدٍ وَعَلَى آلِ سَيِّدِنَا مُحَمَّدٍ وَأَعْطِهِ الوَسِيلَةَ وَالْفَضِيلَةَ وَالدَّرَجَةَ الرَّفِيعَةَ وَابْعَثْهُ المَقَامَ المَحْمُودَ الَّذِي وَعَدْتَهُ مَعَ إِخْوَانِهِ النَّبِيِّينَ ❊

(9) Allāhumma ṣalli ʿalā Sayyīdinā Muḥammadin wa ʿalā āli Sayyīdinā Muḥammaddin wa aʿṭihi 'l-wasīlata wa 'l-faḍīlata wa 'd-darajata 'r-rafīʿata wa 'bʿath-hu 'l-Maqāma 'l-Maḥmūda 'Lladhī waʿadtahu maʿa ikhwānihi 'n-Nabīyyīn •

(9) O Allāh exalt our master Muḥammad and the family of master Muḥammad and grant him the closest access, the pre-eminence and Lofty Rank and send him to the Most Praised Station which You promised him with his brother Prophets! ❊

(١٠) صَلَّى اللهُ عَلَى سَيِّدِنَا مُحَمَّدٍ نَبِيِّ الرَّحْمَةِ وَسَيِّدِ الأُمَّةِ وَعَلَى أَبِينَا آدَمَ وَأُمِّنَا حَوَّاءَ وَمَنْ وَلَدَا مِنَ النَّبِيِّينَ وَالصِّدِّيقِينَ وَالشُّهَدَاءِ وَالصَّالِحِينَ

(10) ṣalla 'Llāhu ʿalā Muḥammadin Nabīyyi 'r-raḥmati wa Sayyidi 'l-ummati wa ʿalā abinā Ādama wa ummīna Ḥawwāʿ wa man waladā mina 'n-nabīyyīnā wa 'ṣ-ṣiddīqīna wa 'sh-shuhadā'i wa 'ṣ-ṣāliḥīna

(10) The blessings of Allāh ﷻ be upon our master Muḥammad, the Prophet of Mercy and the master of the nation, and upon our Father, our master Ādam and upon our Mother, our lady Eve, and upon all the offspring of the Prophets, the truthful ones, the martyrs and all the righteous ones, ➢

وَصَلِّ عَلَى مَلَآئِكَتِكَ أَجْمَعِينَ مِنْ أَهْلِ السَّمَاوَاتِ وَالْأَرَضِينَ وَعَلَيْنَا مَعْهُم
يَا ارْحَمْ الرَّاحِمِينَ ❁

wa ṣalli ʿalā malā'ikatika ajmaʿīna min āhli 's-samāwāti wa 'l-araḍīna wa ʿalaynā maʿahum yā Arḥama 'r-Rāḥimīna •

and raise up all Your angels among the folk of the heavens and the Earths and upon us along with them, O Allāh the Most Merciful of the Merciful! ❁

(١١) اللَّهُمَّ اغْفِرْ لِي ذُنُوبِي وَلِوَالِدَيَّ وَارْحَمْهُمَا كَمَا رَبَّيَانِي صَغِيراً

(11) Allāhumma 'ighfir lī dhunūbi wa li-wālidayya wa 'rḥamhumā kamā rabbayāni ṣaghīran

(11) O Allāh forgive me my sins and my parents', and bestow mercy upon them even as they cherished me in childhood, ➢

وَلِجَمِيعِ الْمُؤْمِنِينَ والْمُؤْمِنَاتِ وَالْمُسْلِمِينَ وَالْمُسْلِمَاتِ اَلأَحْياءِ مِنْهُمْ وَالأَمْوَاتِ

wa li-jamiʿī 'l-mu'minīna wa 'l-mu'mināti wa 'l-muslimīna wa 'l-muslimāti 'l-'aḥyā'i minhum wa 'l-'amwāti

and to all the believing men and women, the Muslim men and Muslim women, the living and the dead, ➢

وَتَابِعْ بَيْنَنَا وَبَيْنَهُم بِالْخَيْرَاتِ رَبِّ اغْفِرْ وَارْحَمْ وَأَنْتَ خَيرُ الرَّاحِمِينَ وَلا حَوْلَ وَلَا قُوَّةَ إِلاَّ بِاللهِ العَلِيِّ العَظِيمِ ❁

wa tābiʿ baynanā wa baynahum bi 'l-khayrāti Rabbī 'ghfir wa 'rḥam wa anta khayru 'r-Rāḥimīn wa lā ḥawla wa lā quwwata illā bi-'Llāhi 'l-ʿAlīyyi 'l-ʿAẓīm •

and many blessings ensure for us, forgive, bestow, mercy, and You are the best of those who grant mercy! Lord, forgive, bestow mercy, and You are the Best of those who give mercy. And there is no help nor power save through Allāh the High, and the Great! ❁

(١٢) اللَّهُمَّ صَلِّ عَلَى سَيِّدِنَا مُحَمَّدٍ نُورِ الْأَنْوَارِ وَسِرِّ الأَسْرَارِ وَسَيِّدِ الأَبْرَارِ وَزَيْنِ الْمُرْسَلِينَ الأَخْيَارِ وَأَكْرَمِ مَنْ أَظْلَمَ عَلَيهِ اللَّيلُ وَأَشْرَقَ عَلَيهِ النَّهَارُ عَدَدَ مَا نَزَلَ مِنْ أَوَّلِ الدُّنْيَا إِلَىٰ آخِرِهَا مِنْ قَطْرِ الأَمْطَارِ

(12) Allāhumma ṣalli ʿalā Sayyīdinā Muḥammadin nūri 'l-anwāri wa sirri 'l-asrāri wa Sayyidi 'l-abrāri wa zayni 'l-mursalīna 'l-akhyāri wa akrami man aẓlama ʿalayhi 'l-laylu wa ashraqa ʿalayhi 'n-nahāru ʿadada mā nazala min āwwali 'd-dunyā ilā ākhirihā min qaṭri 'l-'amṭāri

(12) O Allāh, exalt our master Muḥammad, the Light of Light, the Secret of Secret, the Master of the Pious, the Adornment of the Messengers, the Chosen One, the Most Noble One the night has ever clocked and the day has ever bathed in light, in every drop of rain which has fallen from the beginning of this world until its end, ➤

وَعَدَدَ مَا نَبَتَ مِنْ أَوَّلِ الدُّنْيَا إِلَى آخِرِهَا مِنَ النَّبَاتِ وَالْأَشْجَارِ صَلَاةً دَائِمَةً بِدَوَامِ مُلْكِ اللهِ الْوَاحِدِ الْقَهَّارِ ❋

wa 'adada mā nabata min āwwali 'd-dunyā ilā ākhirihā mina 'n-nabāti wa 'l-'ashjāri ṣalātan dā'imatan bi-dawāmi mulki 'Llāhi'l-Wāḥidi 'l-Qahhāri •

and in every plant and in every tree which have grow from the beginning of this world to its end, blessings which are eternal, lasting as long as The Dominion of Allāh, the One, the Powerful! ❋

(١٣) اللَّهُمَّ صَلِّ عَلَى سَيِّدِنَا مُحَمَّدٍ صَلَاةً تُكَرِّمُ بِهَا مَثْوَاهُ وَتُشَرِّفُ بِهَا عُقْبَاهُ وَتُبَلِّغُ بِهَا يَوْمَ الْقِيَامَةِ مُنَاهُ وَرِضَاهُ هَذِهِ الصَّلَاةُ تَعْظِيمًا لِحَقِّكَ يَا سَيِّدَنَا مُحَمَّداً (x٣) ❋

(13) Allāhumma ṣalli 'alā Sayyīdinā Muḥammadin ṣalātan tukarrimu bihā mathwāhu wa tusharrifu bihā 'uqbāhu wa tuballighu bihā yawma 'l-qīyāmati munāhu wa riḍāhu hādhihi 'ṣ-ṣalātu ta-'ẓīman li-ḥaqqika yā Sayyīdanā Muḥammadan (3x) •

(13) O Allāh, exalt our master Muḥammad, blessings which ennoble his Place of Rest, his final destination, and on the day of Resurrection bring him his heart's desire and contentment, these great blessings are You right, O Our master Muḥammad, (3x) ❋

(١٤) اللَّهُمَّ صَلِّ عَلَى سَيِّدِنَا مُحَمَّدٍ حَاءِ الرَّحْمَةِ وَمِيمِ الْمُلْكِ وَدَالِ الدَّوَامِ
السَّيِّدِ الكَامِلِ الفَاتِحِ الْخَاتِمِ عَدَدَ مَا فِي عِلْمِكَ كَائِنٌ أَوْ قَدْ كَانَ كُلَّمَا ذَكَرَكَ
وَذَكَرَهُ الذَّاكِرُونَ وَكُلَّمَا غَفَلَ عَنْ ذِكْرِكَ وَذِكْرِهِ الغَافِلُونَ صَلَاةً دَائِمَةً
بِدَوَامِكَ بَاقِيَةً بِبَقَائِكَ لَا مُنْتَهَى لَهَا دُونَ عِلْمِكَ إِنَّكَ عَلَى كُلِّ شَيْءٍ قَدِيرٌ
(x٣) ❋

(14) Allāhumma ṣalli ʿalā Sayyīdinā Muḥammadin ḥā'i 'r-raḥmati wa mīm al-mulki wa dāl ad-dawāmi 's-sayyidi 'l-kāmili 'l-fātiḥi 'l-khātimi ʿadada mā fī ʿilmika kā'inun aw qad kāna kullamā dhakaraka wa dhakarahu 'dh-dhākirūna wa kullamā ghafala ʿan dhikrika wa dhikrihi 'l-ghāfilūn ṣalātan dā'imatam bi-dawāmika bāqiyatan bi-baqā'ika lā muntahā lahā dūna ʿilmika innaka ʿalā kulli shayin qadīrun (3x) •

(14) O Allāh, bless our master Muḥammad, the *'ha'* of Mercy, the *'mim'* of Sovereignty, and the *'dal'* of Eternity, [29] the Perfect Master, the Opener, the Seal, as much as Your Knowledge, now or before, and whenever You are remembered and he is remember by those who remember and whenever You are forgotten and he is forgotten by those who forget! Blessings which are eternal, lasting as long as You last, enduring as long as You endure, and without end without Your Knowledge, for You have the Power over all things! (3x) ❋

---

[29] *'ḥā'* is the middle letter of *Raḥmān, 'mīm'* is the first letter of *Mulk, 'dāl'* the first letter of *Dā'im.*

(١٥) اللَّهُمَّ صَلِّ عَلَى سَيِّدِنَا مُحَمَّدٍ النَّبِيِّ الأُمِّيِّ وَعَلَى آلِ سَيِّدِنَا مُحَمَّدٍ الَّذِي هُوَ أَبْهَى شُمُوسِ الْهُدَى نُوراً وَأَبْهَرُهَا وَأَسيَرُ الْأَنْبِيَاءِ فَخْراً وَأَشْهَرُهَا وَنُورُهُ أَزْهَرُ أَنوَارِ الْأَنْبِيَاءِ وَأَشْرَقُهَا وَأَوْضَحُهَا وَأَزْكَى الْخَلِيقَةِ أَخْلَاقاً وَأَطْهَرُهَا وَأَكْرَمُهَا خُلُقاً وَأَعْدَلُهَا ❋

(15) Allāhumma ṣalli ʿalā Sayyīdinā Muḥammadini 'n-Nabīyyi 'l-ummīyi wa ʿalā āli Sayyīdinā Muḥammadin 'Lladhī hūwa abhā shumūsi 'l-hudā nūran wa abharuhā wa asyaru 'l-anbīyā'i fakhran wa ash-haruhā wa nūruhu azharu anwāri 'l-anbīyā'i wa ashrafuhā wa awḍaḥuhā wa azkā 'l-khalīqati akhlāqan wa aẓharuhā wa akramuhā khuluqan wa āʿdaluhā •

(15) O Allāh, bless our master Muḥammad, the Unlettered (not thought to read and write by any human being) Prophet, and the family of our master Muḥammad, him whose light is the most beautiful and most dazzling of all the suns of Guidence and whose conduct and glory are the best and most renowed of all the Prophets and whose light is more radiant, nobler and more brilliant than the lights of the Prophets, and who has the purest and most immaculate in creation, and who is the most just and generous creature! ❋

(١٦) اللَّهُمَّ صَلِّ عَلَى سَيِّدِنَا مُحَمَّدٍ النَّبِيِّ الأُمِّيِّ وَعَلَى آلِ سَيِّدِنَا مُحَمَّدٍ الَّذِي
هُوَ أَبْهَى مِنَ القَمَرِ التَّامِّ وَأَكْرَمُ مِنَ السَّحَابِ المُرْسَلَةِ وَالبَحْرِ الخِضَّمِّ ❋

(16) Allāhumma ṣalli ʿalā Sayyīdinā Muḥammadin 'Lladhī hūwa abhā mina 'l-qamari 't-tāmmi wa akramu mina 's-saḥḥābi 'l-mursalati wa 'l-baḥri 'l-khiḍḍam •

(16) The family of our master Muḥammad, him who is more beautiful than the full moon, more noble than the following clouds and the raging sea! ❋

(١٧) اللَّهُمَّ صَلِّ عَلَى سَيِّدِنَا مُحَمَّدٍ النَّبِيِّ الأُمِّيِّ وَعَلَى آلِ سَيِّدِنَا مُحَمَّدٍ الَّذِي
قُرِنَتِ الْبَرَكَةُ بِذَاتِهِ وَمُحَيَّاهُ وَتَعَطَّرَتِ العَوَالِمُ بِطِيبِ ذِكْرِهِ وَرَيَّاهُ ❋

(17) Allāhumma ṣalli ʿalā Sayyīdinā Muḥammadini 'n-Nabīyyi 'l-ummīyyi wa ʿalā āli Sayyīdinā Muḥammadin 'Lladhī qurinat 'l-barakātu bi-dhātihi wa muḥayyāhu wa ta-ʿaṭṭarati 'l-ʿawālimu bi-ṭībi dhikrihi wa rayyāhu •

(17) O Allāh, exalt our master Muḥammad, the Unlettered Prophet, and the family of our master Muḥammad, to whose essence and countenance blessing is joined, and the worlds are scented by the fragrance and perfume of his *dhikr*. ❋

(١٨) اللَّهُمَّ صَلِّ عَلَى سَيِّدِنَا مُحَمَّدٍ وَعَلَى آلِهِ وَسَلِّمْ ❁

(18) Allāhumma ṣalli ʿalā Sayyīdinā Muḥammadin wa ʿalā ālihi wa sallim •

(18) O Allāh exalt and grant peace to our master Muḥammad and his family! ❁

(١٩) اللَّهُمَّ صَلِّ عَلَى سَيِّدِنَا مُحَمَّدٍ وَعَلَى آلِ سَيِّدِنَا مُحَمَّدٍ وَبَارِكْ عَلَى سَيِّدِنَا مُحَمَّدٍ وَعَلَى آلِ سَيِّدِنَا مُحَمَّدٍ وَارْحَمْ سَيِّدَنَا مُحَمَّداً و آلَ سَيِّدِنَا مُحَمَّدٍ كَمَا صَلَّيْتَ وَبَارَكْتَ وَتَرَحَّمتَ عَلَى سَيِّدِنَا إِبرَاهِيمَ وَعَلَى آلِ سَيِّدِنَا إِبْرَاهِيمَ إِنَّكَ حَمِيدٌ مَجِيدٌ ❁

(19) Allāhumma ṣalli ʿalā Sayyīdinā Muḥammadin wa ʿalā āli Sayyīdinā Muḥammadin wa bārik ʿalā Sayyīdinā Muḥammadin wa ʿalā āli Sayyīdinā Muḥammadin wa 'rḥam Sayyīdanā Muḥammadan wa āla Sayyīdinā Muḥammadin kamā ṣallayta wa bārakta wa taraḥḥamta ʿalā Sayyīdinā Ibrāhīma wa ʿalā āli Sayyīdinā Ibrāhīma innaka Ḥamīdun Majīd •

(19) O Allāh, exalt our master Muḥammad and the family of our master Muḥammad, and bless our master Muḥammad and the family of master Muḥammad, and bestow mercy upon our master Muḥammad and the family of our master Muḥammad just as You exalted, blessed and bestowed mercy upon our master Abraham and the family of our master Abraham, for You are The Praiseworthy, The Mighty! ❁

(٢٠) اللَّهُمَّ صَلِّ عَلَى سَيِّدِنَا مُحَمَّدٍ عَبْدِكَ وَنَبِيِّكَ وَرَسُولِكَ النَّبِيِّ الأُمِّيِّ وَعَلَى آلِ سَيِّدِنَا مُحَمَّدٍ ❋

(20) Allāhumma ṣalli ʿalā Sayyīdinā Muḥammadin ʿabdika wa Nabīyyika wa Rasūlika 'n-nabīyyi 'l-ummīyyi wa ʿalā āli Sayyīdinā Muḥammad •

(20) O Allāh, exalt our master Muḥammad, Your Servant, Your Prophet and Your Messenger, the Unlettered Prophet, and the family of our master Muḥammad! ❋

(٢١) اللَّهُمَّ صَلِّ عَلَى سَيِّدِنَا مُحَمَّدٍ وَعَلَى آلِ سَيِّدِنَا مُحَمَّدٍ مِلْءَ الدُّنْيَا وَمِلْءَ الْآخِرَةِ وَبَارِكْ عَلَى سَيِّدِنَا مُحَمَّدٍ وَعَلَى آلِ سَيِّدِنَا مُحَمَّدٍ مِلْءَ الدُّنْيَا وَمِلْءَ الْآخِرَةِ

(21) Allāhumma ṣalli ʿalā Sayyīdinā Muḥammadin wa ʿalā āli Sayyīdinā Muḥammadin mila 'd-dunyā wa mila 'l-ākhirati wa bārik ʿalā Muḥammadin wa ʿāla āli Sayyīdinā Muḥammadin mila 'd-dunyā wa mila 'l-ākhirati

(21) O Allāh, exalt our master Muḥammad and the family of our master Muḥammad to the fullness of this world and to the fullness of the next! O Allāh, bless our master Muḥammad ﷺ and the family of our master Muḥammad to the fullness of this world and the fullness of the next world! O Allāh, bestow mercy upon our master Muḥammad and the family of our master Muḥammad to the fullness of this world and to the fullness of the next world! ➤

وَارْحَمْ سَيِّدَنَا مُحَمَّداً وَ آلَ سَيِّدِنَا مُحَمَّدٍ مِلْءَ الدُّنْيَا وَمِلْءَ الْآخِرَة وَاجْزِ سَيِّدَنَا مُحَمَّداً وآلَ سَيِّدِنَا مُحَمَّدٍ مِلْءَ الدُّنْيَا وَمِلْءَ الْآخِرَةِ وَسَلِّمْ عَلَى سَيِّدِنَا مُحَمَّدٍ وَعَلَى آلِ سَيِّدِنَا مُحَمَّدٍ مِلْءَ الدُّنْيَا وَمِلْءَ الْآخِرَةِ ❋

wa 'rḥam Sayyīdanā Muḥammadan wa āla Sayyīdinā Muḥammadin mila 'd-dunyā wa mila 'l-ākhirati wa 'jzi Sayyīdanā Muḥammadan wa āla Sayyīdinā Muḥammadin mila 'd-dunyā wa mila 'l-ākhirati wa sallim 'alā Sayyīdinā Muḥammadin wa 'alā āli Sayyīdinā Muḥammadin mila 'd-dunyā wa mila 'l-ākhirati •

O Allāh, reward our master Muḥammad and the family of our master Muḥammad to the fullness of this world and to the fullness of the next! O Allāh, grant peace to our master Muḥammad and the family of our master Muḥammad to the fullness of this world and to the fullness of the next! ❋

(٢٢) اللَّهُمَّ صَلِّ عَلَى سَيِّدِنَا مُحَمَّدٍ كَمَا أَمَرْتَنَا أَنْ نُصَلِّيَ عَلَيهِ وَصَلِّ عَلَى سَيِّدِنَا مُحَمَّدٍ كَمَا يَنْبَغِي أَنْ يُصَلَّى عَلَيهِ ❋

(22) Allāhumma ṣalli 'alā Sayyīdinā Muḥammadin kamā amartanā an nuṣalliya 'alayhi wa ṣalli 'alā Sayyīdinā Muḥammadin kamā yambaghī an yuṣallā 'alayhi •

(22) O Allāh, exalt our master Muḥammad as You ordered us to exalt him and bless our master Muḥammad as he should be blessed! ❋

(٢٣) اللَّهُمَّ صَلِّ عَلَى نَبِيِّكَ الْمُصْطَفَى وَرَسُولِكَ الْمُرْتَضَى وَوَلِيِّكَ الْمُجْتَبَى وَأَمِينِكَ عَلَى وَحْيِ السَّمَاءِ ❋

(23) Allāhumma ṣalli ʿalā nabīyyika 'l-Musṭafā wa rasūlika 'l-Murtaḍā wa walīyyika 'l-Mujtabā wa amīnika ʿalā waḥīy as-samā'i •

(23) O Allāh, exalt Your Prophet, the chosen One, Your Messenger, the Satisfied One, Your Friend, the Elected One, and Your Custodian of the celestial Revelation! ❋

(٢٤) اللَّهُمَّ صَلِّ عَلَى سَيِّدِنَا مُحَمَّدٍ أَكْرَمِ الْأَسْلَافِ الْقَائِمِ بِالْعَدْلِ وَالْإِنْصَافِ الْمَنْعُوتِ فِي سُورَةِ الْأَعْرَافِ الْمُنْتَخَبِ مِنْ أَصْلَابِ الشِّرَافِ وَالْبُطُونِ الظِّرَافِ الْمُصَفَّى مِنْ مُصَاصِ عَبْدِ الْمُطَّلِبِ بْنِ عَبدِ مَنَافٍ الَّذِي هَدَيتَ بِهِ مِنَ الخِلَافِ وَبَيَّنْتَ بِهِ سَبِيلَ العَفَافِ ❋

(24) Allāhumma ṣalli ʿalā Sayyīdinā Muḥammadin akrami 'l-aslāfi 'l-qā'imi bi 'l-ʿadli wa 'l-inṣāfi 'l-man-ʿūti fī sūrati 'l-āʿrāfi 'l-muntakhabi min aṣlābi 'sh-shirāfi wa 'l-buṭūni 'ẓ-ẓhirāfi 'l-muṣaffā min muṣāṣi ʿAbdi 'l-Muṭṭalibi 'bni ʿAbdi Manāfin 'Lladhī hadayta bihi mina 'l-khilāfi wa bayyanta bihi sabīla 'l-ʿafāfi •

(24) O Allāh, exalt our master Muḥammad, the most noble ancestor, the upholder of justice and equity, the one described in Sūrat al-ʿArāf, the one chosen from the noble loins and refined wombs and the one purified by suckling, from ʿAbdul Muṭṭalib son of ʿAbdi Manāf through whom You guided from conflict and by whom You made clear the path of virtue and chastity! ❋

(٢٥) اللَّهُمَّ إِنِّي أَسْأَلُكَ بِأَفْضَلِ مَسْأَلَتِكَ وَبِأَحَبِّ أَسْمَائِكَ إِلَيْكَ وَأَكْرَمِهَا عَلَيْكَ وَبِمَا مَنَنْتَ عَلَيْنَا بِمُحَمَّدٍ نَبِيِّنَا صَلَّى اللهُ عَلَيهِ وَسَلَّمَ فَاسْتَنْقَذْتَنَا بِهِ مِنَ الضَّلَالَةِ وَأَمَرْتَنَا بِالصَّلَاةِ عَلَيهِ وَجَعَلْتَ صَلَاتَنَا عَلَيهِ دَرَجَةً وَكَفَّارَةً وَلُطْفاً وَمَنّاً مِنْ إِعْطَائِكَ فَأَدْعُوكَ تَعْظِيماً لِأَمْرِكَ وَاتِّبَاعاً لِوَصِيَّتِكَ وَمُنْتَجِزاً لِمَوْعُودِكَ

(25) Allāhumma innī as'aluka bi afḍali mas'alatika wa bi aḥabbi asmā'ika ilayka wa akramihā ʿalayka wa bimā mananta ʿalaynā bi Sayyīdinā Muḥammadin nabīyyīnā ṣalla 'Llāhu ʿalayhi wa sallāma fa 'stanqadh-tanā bihi mina 'ḍ-ḍalālata wa amartanā bi 'ṣ-ṣalāti ʿalayhi wa jaʿalta ṣalātanā ʿalayhi darajatan wa kaffāratan wa luṭfan wa mannan min iʿṭā'ika fa adʿūka taʿẓīman li amrika wa 't-tibāʿan li-waṣīyyatika wa muntajazan limawʿūdika

(25) O Allāh, I beseech You by most superior beseeching, in the most loved of Your Names, in the most noble of Your Names, and for the sake of the fact that You blessed us with our master Muḥammad upon whom be of Allāh's blessings and peace, saving us through him from error and for the sake of the fact that You ordered us to ask for blessing upon him, And for the sake of the fact that You made our asking for blessings upon him a means of raising our rank, a expiation for our sins, and grace and favor for us, Out of obedience to You, I call on You, exalting Your command, following Your instruction and fulfilling Your Promise, ➢

لِمَا يَجِبُ لِنَبِيِّنَا سَيِّدِنَا مُحَمَّدٍ صَلَّى اللهُ عَلَيهِ وَسَلَّم فِي أَدَاءِ حَقِّهِ قِبَلَنَا إِذْ آمَنَّا بِهِ وَصَدَّقْنَاهُ وَاتَّبَعْنَا النُّورَ الَّذِي أُنْزِلَ مَعَهُ وَقُلْتَ إِنَّ اللهَ وَمَلَآئِكَتَهُ يُصَلُّونَ عَلَى النَّبِيِّ يَا أَيُّهَا الَّذِينَ آمَنُوا صَلُّوا عَلَيهِ وَسَلِّمُوا تَسْلِيماً وَأَمَرْتَ العِبَادَ بِالصَّلَاةِ عَلَى نَبِيِّهِمْ فَرِيضَةً اِفْتَرَضْتَهَا وَأَمَرْتَهُم بِهَا فَنَسأَلُكَ بِجَلَالِ وَجْهِكَ وَنُورِ عَظَمَتِكَ وَبِمَا أَوْجَبْتَ عَلَى نَفْسِكَ

limā yajibu li nabīyyinā Sayyīdinā Muḥammadin ﷺ fī adā'i ḥaqqihi qibalanā idh āmannā bihi wa ṣaddaqnāhu wa 't-taba'nā 'n-nūra 'Lladhī unzila ma'ahu wa qulta wa qawluka 'l-ḥaqqu inna 'Llāha wa malā'ikatahu yuṣallūna 'alā 'n-nabī Yā ayyuha 'Lladhīna āmanū ṣallū 'alayhi wa sallimū taslīma wa amarta 'l-'ibāda bi 'ṣ-ṣalāti 'alā nabīyyihim farīḍatan iftaraḍ-tahā wa amratahum bihā fa-nas'aluka bijalāli wajhika wa nūri 'aẓamatika wa bimā awjabta 'alā nafsika

to render unto our Prophet, our master Muḥammad, the blessings and peace of Allāh be upon him, what is his due from us, for we have faith in him and we believe in him and we follow the light which came down with him and You said, and Your word is the Truth, Allāh ﷻ and His angels bless the Prophet. O Allāh You who believe, ask (Allāh) to bless and grant him abundant peace and for the sake of the fact that You made obligatory for the servant to invoke blessings upon their Prophet, making it an obligation and making it binding on them, I ask You for the sake of the Majesty of Your Face and the Light of Your Greatness, and for the sake of that which You have made binding on Yourself in respect of the virtuous, ➢

أَنْ تُصَلِّيَ أَنْتَ وَمَلَآئِكَتُكَ عَلَى سَيِّدِنَا مُحَمَّدٍ عَبْدِكَ وَرَسُولِكَ وَنَبِيِّكَ وَصَفِيِّكَ وَخِيرَتِكَ مِنْ خَلْقِكَ أَفْضَلَ مَا صَلَّيْتَ عَلَى أَحَدٍ مِنْ خَلْقِكَ إِنَّكَ حَمِيدٌ مَجِيدٌ ❋

an tuṣallīya anta wa malā'ikatuka ʻalā Sayyīdinā Muḥammadin ʻabdika wa rasūlika wa nabīyyika wa ṣafīyyika wa khīratika min khalqika afḍala mā ṣallayta ʻalā aḥadin min khalqika innaka Ḥamīdun Majīd •

that You and Your angels bless our master Muḥammad, Your slaves, Your Messenger, Your Prophet, Your Pure One and Your Treasure from Your Creation, the Best blessing ever bestowed upon any one of Your Creation, for You are The Praiseworthy, The Mighty! ❋

(٢٦) اللّٰهُمَّ ارْفَعْ دَرَجَتَهُ وَأَكْرِمْ مَقَامَهُ وَثَقِّلْ مِيزَانَهُ وَأَبْلِجْ حُجَّتَهُ وَأَظْهِرْ مِلَّتَهُ وَأَجْزِلْ ثَوَابَهُ وَأَضِيءْ نُورَهُ وَأَدِمْ كَرَامَتَهُ وَأَلْحِقْ بِهِ ذُرِّيَّتَهُ وَأَهْلَ بَيْتِهِ

(26) Allāhumma 'rfaʻ darajatahu wa akrim maqāmahu wa tḥaqqil mīzānahu wa ablij ḥujjatahu wa aẓhir millatahu wa ajzil thawābahu wa aḍī' nūrahu wa adim karāmatahu wa alḥiq bihi min dhurrīyyatahu wa āhla baytihi;

(26) O Allāh, raise his rank, ennoble his station, increase the weight in his balnce, refine his proof, make his community triumphant, increase his reward, brighten his light and perpetuate his nobility and join him with his descendants and the People of his House ➢

مَا تُقِرُّ بِهِ عَينَهُ وَعَظِّمْهُ فِي النَّبِيينَ الَّذِينَ خَلَوا قَبْلَهُ ❁

mā tuqirru bihi ʿaynahu wa ʿaẓ-ẓimhu fī 'n-nabīyyīni 'Lladhīna khalaw qablahu •

which will be a comfort for his eyes and exalt him among all the prophets who passed before him. ❁

(٢٧) اللَّهُمَّ اجْعَلْ سَيِّدَنا مُحَمَّدًا أَكْثَرَ النَّبِيِّينَ تَبعاً وَ أَكْثَرَهُمْ أُزَرَاءَ وَأَفْضَلَهُمْ كَرَامَةً وَنُوراً وَأَعْلَاهُم دَرَجَةً وَأَفْسَحَهُمْ فِي الْجَنَّة مَنزِلاً ❁

(27) Allāhumma 'jʿal Sayyidanā Muḥammadan akthara 'n-nabīyyīna tabaʿan wa aktharahum uzarā'a wa afḍalahum karāmatan wa nūran wa āʿlāhum darajatan wa afsaḥahum fī 'l-jannati manzilan •

(27) O Allāh, of all the Prophets make our master Muḥammad have the greatest number of followers, the greatest in strength, and give them the most perfect nobility and light and raise their Ranks and widen their abodes in the Garden! ❁

(٢٨) اللَّهُمَّ اجْعَلْ فِي السَّابِقِينَ غَايَتَهُ وَفِي الْمُنْتَخَبِينَ مَنْزِلَهُ وَفِي الْمُقَرَّبِينَ دَارَهُ وَفِي الْمُصْطَفَيْنَ مَنْزِلَتهُ ❁

(28) Allāhumma 'jʿal fī 's-sābiqīna ghāyatahu wa fī 'l-muntakhabīna manzilahu wa fī 'l-muqarrabīna dārahu wa fī 'l-musṭafayna manzilatahu •

(28) O Allāh, make his final destination among the foremost and his abode among the elite and his dwelling place among those who are close and his abode among the chosen ones! ❁

(٢٩) اللَّهُمَّ أَجْعَلْهُ أَكْرَمَ الأَكْرَمِينَ عِنْدِكَ مَنْزِلاً وَأَفْضَلَهُمْ ثَواباً وَأَقْرَبَهُمْ مَجْلِساً وَأَثْبَتَهُمْ مَقَاماً وَأَصْوَبَهُمْ كَلَاماً وَأَنْجَحَهُمْ مَسْأَلَةً وَأَفْضَلَهُمْ لَدَيكَ نَصِيبًا وَأَعْظَمَهُمْ فِيمَا عِنْدَكَ رَغْبَةً وَأَنْزِلْهُ فِي غُرُفَاتِ الفِرْدَوسِ مِنَ الدَّرَجَاتِ العُلْيَا الَّتِي لَا دَرَجَةَ فَوقَهَا ❋

(29) Allāhumma 'j-ʿalhu akrama 'l-akramīna ʿindaka manzilan wa afḍalahum thawāban wa aqrabahum majlisan wa athbatahum maqāman wa aṣwabahum kalāman wa anjaḥahum mas'alatan wa afḍalahum ladayka naṣīban wa āʿẓamahum fīmā ʿindaka raghbatan wa anzilhu fī ghurufāti 'l-firdawsi mina 'd-darajāti 'l-ʿulyā 'Llatī lā darajata fawqahā •

(29) O Allāh, make his abode the most noble of the Noble in Your Presence and favor him with Your reward, make him sit close to You, strengthen his Station, reward him with Your Word, give his entries success, favor his share in Your Presence, strengthen his longing for what is with You and bring him into the chambers of Firdaws in the most elevated ranks above which there is no higher rank! ❋

(٣٠) اللَّهُمَّ أَجْعَل سَيِّدَنا مُحَمَّداً أَصْدَقَ قَائِلٍ وَأَنْجَحَ سَائِلٍ وَأَوَّلَ شَافِعٍ

(30) Allāhumma 'jʿal Sayyīdanā Muḥammadan aṣdaqa qā'ilin wa anjaḥa sā'ilin wa awwala shāfiʿin

(30) O Allāh, grant our master Muḥammad the truest word, the most successful petitioning, the first intercession, ➢

وَأَفْضَلَ مُشَفَّعٍ وَشَفِّعْهُ فِي أُمَّتِهِ بِشَفَاعَةٍ يَغْبِطُهُ بِهَا الْأَوَّلُونَ وَالْآخِرُونَ وَإِذَا مَيَّزْتَ عِبَادَكَ بِفَصْلِ قَضَائِكَ فَاجْعَلْ سَيِّدَنَا مُحَمَّداً فِي الْأَصْدَقِينَ قِيلاً وَالْأَحْسَنِينَ عَمَلاً وَفِي الْمَهْدِيِّينَ سَبِيلاً

wa afḍala mushaffaʿin wa shaffiʿhu fī ummatihi bi-shafāʿatin yaghbiṭuhu bihā 'l-awwalūna wa 'l-ākhirūna wa idhā mayyazta ʿibādaka bi-faḍli qaḍā'ika fajʿal Sayyīdanā Muḥammadan fī 'l aṣdaqīna qīlan wa 'l-aḥṣanīna ʿamalan wa fī 'l-mahdīyyīna sabīla

and the best intercession, and intercede on his behalf for his nation, an intercession that will be the envy of the first to come and those who came last, and distinguish Your Servant in the discharge of Your Decree, and make our master Muḥammad among the Speakers of Truth, the Doers of Good and the Guides to the Path! ➢

وأَجْعَلْ نَبِيَّنَا لَنَا فَرَطاً وَاجْعَلْ حَوضَهُ لَنَا مَوعِداً لِأَوَّلِنَا وَآخِرِنَا ❋

wa 'jʿal nabīyyanā lanā faraṭan wa 'jʿal ḥawḍahu lanā mawʿidan li awwalinā wa ākhirinā •

O Allāh, grant our Prophet to excess and make his Pool the tryst for the first of us and the last of us! ❋

(٣١) اللَّهُمَّ احْشُرْنَا فِي زُمْرَتِهِ وَاسْتَعْمِلْنَا فِي سُنَّتِهِ وَتَوَفَّنَا عَلَى مِلَّتِهِ

(31) Allāhumma 'ḥshurnā fī zumratihi wa 'staʿmilnā bi sunnatihi wa tawaffanā ʿalā millatihi

(31) O Allāh, resurrect us in his company, establish us on his way and cause us to die following his tradition, ➢

وَعَرِّفْنَا وَجْهَهُ وَاجْعَلْنَا فِي زُمْرَتِهِ وَحِزْبِهِ ❋

wa ʿarrifnā wajhahu wa 'jʿalnā fī zumratihi wa hizbihi •

acquaint us with face and make us among his company and party! ❋

(٣٢) اللَّهُمَّ اجْمَعْ بَيْنَنَا وَبَيْنَهُ كَمَا آمَنَّا بِهِ وَلَمْ نَرَهُ وَلَا تُفَرِّقْ بَيْنَنَا وَبَيْنَهُ حَتَّى تُدْخِلَنَا مُدْخَلَهُ وَتُورِدَنَا حَوضَهُ وَتَجْعَلَنَا مِنْ رُفَقَائِهِ الْمُنْعَمِ عَلَيهِمْ مِنَ النَّبِيِّينَ وَالصِّدِّيقِينَ وَالشُّهَدَاءِ وَالصَّالِحِينَ وَحَسُنَ أُولَئِكَ رَفِيقاً وَالْحَمْدُ لله رَبِّ الْعَالَمِينَ ❋

(32) Allāhumma 'jmaʿ baynanā wa baynahu kamā āmannā bihi wa lam narahu wa lā tufarriq baynanā wa baynahu ḥattā tud-khilanā mud-khalahu wa tūwridanā ḥawḍahu wa taj-ʿalanā min-rufaqā'ihi al-munʿami ʿalayhim mina 'n-nabīyyīna wa 'ṣ-ṣiddīqīna wa 'sh-shuhadā'i wa 'ṣ-ṣāliḥīna wa ḥasuna ūlā'ika rafīqā wa 'l-ḥamdu li 'Llāhi rabbi 'l-ʿĀlamīn •

(32) O Allāh, unite us with him for we believed in him without seeing him and do not separate us from him until the day You cause us to enter into his entrance hall, quench us at his Pool, and put us in his company along with those favored from among the prophets, the truthful ones, the martyrs and the righteous ones, and what a beautiful company that is and praise be to Allāh, the Lord of the Worlds! ❋

إِبْتِدَاءُ الرُّبْعِ الثَّالِثِ

Ibtidā' ar-Rub'i 'th-Thālith

Beginning of the Third Quarter

(٣٣) اللَّهُمَّ صَلِّ عَلَى سَيِّدِنَا مُحَمَّدٍ نُورِ الْهُدَى وَالْقَائِدِ إِلَى الْخَيْرِ وَالدَّاعِي إِلَى الرُّشْدِ نَبِيِّ الرَّحْمَةِ وَإِمَامِ الْمُتَّقِينَ وَرَسُولِ رَبِّ الْعَالَمِينَ

(33) Allāhumma ṣalli 'alā Sayyīdinā Muḥammadin nūri 'l-hudā wa 'l-qā'idi ilā 'l-khayri wa 'd-dā'ī ilā 'r-rushdi nabīyyi 'r-raḥmati wa imāmi 'l-muttaqīna wa rasūli rabbi 'l-'ālamīna

(33) O Allāh, exalt our master Muḥammad, the Light of Guidence, the Guide to Goodness, the caller to Spiritual Direction, the Prophet of Mercy, the Leader of the Pious, the Messenger of the Lord of the Worlds, ➢

لا نَبِيَّ بَعْدَهُ كَمَا بَلَّغَ رِسَالَتَكَ وَنَصَحَ لِعِبَادِكَ وَتَلَا آيَاتِكَ وَأَقَامَ حُدُودَكَ وَوَفَّى بِعَهْدِكَ وَأَنْفَذَ حُكْمَكَ

lā nabīyya ba'dahu kamā ballagha risālataka wa naṣaḥa li-'ibādika wa talā āyātika wa aqāma ḥudūdaka wa waffā bi 'ahdika wa anfadha ḥukmaka

there being no prophet after him, as he conveyed Your Message, advised Your Servants, recited Your Verses, upheld Your Divine Statutes, faithfully discharged Your Covenant, carried out Your Judgment, ➢

وَأَمَرَ بِطَاعَتِكَ وَنَهَى عَنْ مَعْصِيَتِكَ وَوَالَى وَلِيَّكَ الَّذِي تُحِبُّ أَنْ تُوَالِيَهُ
وَعَادَى عَدُوَّكَ الَّذِي تُحِبُّ أَنْ تُعَادِيَهُ وَ صَلَّى اللهُ عَلَى سَيِّدِنَا مُحَمَّدٍ ❁

wa amara bi ṭā-'atika wa nahā 'an ma'ṣīyatika wa wālā walīyyaka 'Lladhī tuḥibbu an tuwāliyahu wa 'ādā 'aduwwaka 'Lladhī tuḥibbu an tu'ādiyahu wa ṣalla 'Llāhu 'alā Sayyīdinā Muḥammadin •

enjoined obedience to You, forbade disobedience to You, befriended the friends whom You chose to befriend, and opposed Your enemy whom You chose to oppose and the blessings and peace of Allāh be upon him! ❁

(٣٤) اللَّهُمَّ صَلِّ عَلَى جَسَدِهِ فِي الْأَجْسَادِ وَعَلَى رُوحِهِ فِي الْأَرْوَاحِ وَعَلَى
مَوقِفِهِ فِي الْمَوَاقِفِ وَعَلَى مَشْهَدِهِ فِي الْمَشَاهِدِ وَعَلَى ذِكْرِهِ إِذَا ذُكِرَ صَلَاةً مِنَّا
عَلَى نَبِيِّنَا ❁

(34) Allāhumma ṣalli 'alā jasadihi fī 'l-ajsādi wa 'alā rūḥihi fī 'l-arwāḥī wa 'alā qabrihi fī 'l-qubūri wa 'alā mawqifihi fī 'l-mawāqifi wa 'alā mash-hadihi fī 'l-mashāhidi wa 'alā dhikrihi idhā dhukira ṣalātan minnā 'alā nabīyyinā •

(34) O Allāh, bless his body among all the bodies in existence and among all the souls bless his soul; bless his tomb among all tombs, bless his place among all places in existence, and bless his memory whenever he is remembered, blessings from us upon our Prophet! ❁

(٣٥) اللَّهُمَّ بَلِّغْهُ مِنَّا السَّلَامَ كَمَا ذُكِرَ السَّلَامُ وَالسَّلَامُ عَلَى النَّبِيِّ وَرَحمَةُ اللهِ وَبَرَكَاتُهُ ❁

(35) Allāhumma abligh-hu minna 's-salāma kamā dhukira 's-salāmu wa 's-salāmu ʿalā 'n-nabīyyi wa raḥmatu 'Llāhi taʿālā wa barakātuhu •

(35) O Allāh, convey to him from us peace just as he invoked peace, and peace, Allāh's Mercy and blessings be upon the Prophet! ❁

(٣٦) اللَّهُمَّ صَلِّ عَلَى مَلآئِكَتِكَ الْمُقَرَّبِينَ وَعَلَى أَنْبِيَائِكَ الْمُطَهَّرِينَ وَعَلَى رُسُلِكَ الْمُرْسَلِينَ وَعَلَى حَمَلَةِ عَرْشِكَ وَعَلَى سَيِّدِنَا جِبْرِيلَ و سَيِّدِنَا مِيكَائِيلَ وَ سَيِّدِنَا إِسْرَافِيلَ وَمَلَكِ المَوتِ و سَيِّدِنَا رِضْوَان خَازِنِ جَنَّتِكَ وَ سَيِّدِنَا مَالِكٍ

(36) Allāhumma ṣalli ʿalā malā'ikatika 'l-muqarrabīn wa ʿalā anbīyā'ika 'l-muṭahharīna wa ʿalā rusulika 'l-mursalīna wa ʿalā ḥamalati ʿarshika wa ʿalā Sayyīdinā Jibrīla wa Sayyīdinā Mikā'īla wa Sayyīdinā Isrāfīla wa Malaki 'l-Mawti wa Sayyīdinā Riḍwāna khāzini jannatika wa Sayyīdinā Mālik

(36) O Allāh, bless Your closest angels, Your purest prophets, Your divine messengers, the Bearers of Your Throne, our master Gabriel, our master Michael, our master Rafael, the Angel of Death, our master Riḍwān, the Guardian of Your Garden, our master Mālikin, ➢

وَصَلِّ عَلَى الْكِرَامِ الكَاتِبِينَ وَصَلِّ عَلَى أَهْلِ طَاعَتِكَ أَجْمَعِينَ مِنْ أَهْلِ السَّمَاوَاتِ وَالْأَرَضِينَ ❋

wa ṣalli ʿalā 'l-Kirāmi 'l-Kātibīna wa ṣalli ʿalā āhli ṭāʿatika ajmaʿīna min āhli 's-samāwāti wa 'l-araḍīn •

and bless the noble recording angels, and bless all the obedient folk, from among the people of the heavens and the earths. ❋

(٣٧) اللَّهُمَّ آتِ أَهْلَ بَيتِ نَبِيِّكَ أَفْضَلَ مَا آتَيتَ أَحَداً مِنْ أَهْلِ بُيوتِ المُرْسَلِينَ وَاجْزِ أَصْحَابَ نَبِيِّكَ أَفْضَلَ مَا جَازَيتَ بِهِ أَحَداً مِنْ أَصْحَابِ المُرْسَلِينَ ❋

(37) Allāhumma āti āhla bayti nabīyyika afḍala mā ātayta aḥadan min āhli buyūti 'l-mursalīna wa 'jzi aṣ-ḥāba nabīyyika afḍala mā jāzayta aḥadan min aṣ-hābi 'l-mursalīn •

(37) O Allāh, give the people of the House of Your Prophet the best ever given to any of people of the houses of the messengers, and reward the companions of Your Prophet the best ever given to any of the companions of the messengers! ❋

(٣٨) اللَّهُمَّ اغفِر لِلْمُؤمِنِينَ وَالمُؤْمِنَاتِ

(38) Allāhumma ighfir li 'l-mu'minīna wa 'l-mu'mināti

(38) O Allāh, forgive the believing men and women ➢

وَالْمُسلِمِينَ وَالْمُسلِمَاتِ الْأَحْيَاءِ مِنْهُمْ وَالْأَمْوَاتِ

wa 'l-muslimīna wa 'l-muslimāti 'l-aḥyā'i minhum wa 'l-amwāti

and the surrendering men and women, the living among them and the dead! ➢

وَاغْفِرْ لَنَا وَلِإِخْوَانِنَا الَّذِينَ سَبَقُونَا بِالإِيمَانِ وَلَا تَجْعَلْ فِي قُلُوبِنَا غِلّاً لِلَّذِينَ آمَنُوا رَبَّنَا إِنَّكَ رَؤُوفٌ رَحِيمٌ ❋

wa 'ghfir lanā wa li ikhwāninā 'Lladhīna sabaqūnā bi 'l-īmāni wa lā taj'al fī qulūbinā ghillan li 'Lladhīna āmanū rabbanā innaka ra'ūfun raḥīmun •

And forgive us and our brothers who came before us in faith and leave not in our hearts any rancor against those who believe, O our Lord, You are full of Pity, Most Merciful!

(٣٩) اللَّهُمَّ صَلِّ عَلَى النَّبِيِّ الهَاشِمِيِّ سَيِّدِنَا مُحَمَّدٍ وَعَلَى آلِهِ وَصَحْبِهِ وَسَلِّمْ تَسْلِيمًا ❋

(39) Allāhumma ṣalli 'alā 'n-nabīyyi 'l-hāshimīyyi Sayyīdinā Muḥammadin wa 'alā ālihi wa ṣaḥbihi wa sallim taslīman •

(39) O Allāh bless and grant abundant peace to the Hāshimī Prophet, our master Muḥammad, and to his family and companions! ❋

(٤٠) اللَّهُمَّ صَلِّ عَلَى سَيِّدِنَا مُحَمَّدٍ خَيْرِ الْبَرِيَّةِ صَلَاةً تُرْضِيكَ وَتُرْضِيهِ وَتَرْضَى بِهَا عَنَّا يَا أَرْحَمَ الرَّاحِمِينَ ❋

(40) Allāhumma ṣalli ʿalā Sayyīdinā Muḥammadin khayri 'l-barīyyati ṣalātan turḍīka wa turḍīhi wa tarḍā bihā ʿannā yā Arḥama 'r-Rāḥimīn •

(40) O Allāh exalt our master Muḥammad, the Best of Creation, with praise which is pleasing to You, pleasing to him and by which You are pleased with us, O Allāh, Most Merciful of those who show mercy! ❋

(٤١) اللَّهُمَّ صَلِّ عَلَى سَيِّدِنَا مُحَمَّدٍ وَعَلَى آلِهِ وَصَحْبِهِ وسَلِّم تَسْلِيماً كَثِيراً طَيِّباً مُبَارَكاً فِيهِ جَزِيلاً جَمِيلاً دَائِماً بِدَوَامِ مُلْكِ الله ❋

(41) Allāhumma ṣalli ʿalā Sayyīdinā Muḥammadin wa ʿalā ālihi wa ṣaḥbihi wa sallim taslīman kathīran ṭayyiban mubārakan fīhi jazīlan jamīlan dā'iman bi-dawāmi mulki 'L-lāh •

(41) O Allāh bless our master Muḥammad and his family, and companions, and grant them peace, abundantly, profusely, agreeably, graciously, beautifully, and eternally for as long Allāh's Kingdom endures! ❋

(٤٢) اللَّهُمَّ صَلِّ عَلَى سَيِّدِنَا مُحَمَّدٍ وَعَلَى آلِهِ

(42) Allāhumma ṣalli ʿalā Sayyīdinā Muḥammadin wa ʿalā ālihi

(42) O Allāh, bless our master Muḥammad and the family of our master Muḥammad, ➢

مِلْءَ الفَضَاءِ وَعَدَدَ النُّجُومِ فِي السَّمَاءِ صَلاةً تُوازِنُ السَّمَاوَاتِ وَالأَرْضِ وعَدَدَ مَا خَلَقْتَ وَمَا أَنْتَ خَالِقُهُ إِلَى يَوْمِ الْقِيَامَةِ ❋

mila 'l-faḍā'i wa ʿadada 'n-nujūmi fī 's-samā'i ṣalātan tuwāzinu 's-samāwāti wa 'l-arḍi wa ʿadada mā khalaqta wa mā anta khāliquhu ilā yawmi 'l-qīyāmati •

to the fullness of cosmic space, and on the number of stars in the sky, blessings which outweigh the heavens and the earth, on the number of what You have created and as much as You will create until the Day of Resurrection! ❋

(٤٣) اللَّهُمَّ صَلِّ عَلَى سَيِّدِنَا مُحَمَّدٍ وَعَلَى آلِ سَيِّدِنَا مُحَمَّدٍ كَمَا صَلَّيْتَ عَلَى سَيِّدِنَا إِبْرَاهِيمَ وَبَارِكْ عَلَى سَيِّدِنَا مُحَمَّدٍ وَعَلَى آلِ سَيِّدِنَا مُحَمَّدٍ كَمَا بَارَكْتَ سَيِّدِنَا إِبْرَاهِيمَ وَعَلَى آلِ سَيِّدِنَا إِبْرَاهِيمَ فِي الْعَالَمِينَ إِنَّكَ حَمِيدٌ مَجِيدٌ ❋

(43) Allāhumma ṣalli ʿalā Sayyīdinā Muḥammadin wa ʿalā āli Sayyīdinā Muḥammadin kamā ṣallayta ʿalā Sayyīdinā Ibrāhīma wa bārik ʿalā Sayyīdinā Muḥammadin wa ʿalā āli Sayyīdinā Muḥammadin kamā bārakta ʿalā Sayyīdinā Ibrāhīma wa ʿalā āli Sayyīdinā Ibrāhīma fī 'l-ʿĀlamīna innaka Ḥamīdun Majīd •

(43) O Allāh, exalt our master Muḥammad and the family of our master Muḥammad just as You exalted our master Abraham and bless our master Muḥammad and the family of our master Muḥammad just as blessed Abraham and the family of Abraham in the worlds, for You are The Praiseworthy, The Mighty! ❋

(٤٤) اللَّهُمَّ إِنِّي أَسْأَلُكَ الْعَفْوَ وَالْعَافِيَةَ فِي الدِّينِ وَالدُّنْيَا وَالآخِرَة (٣x) اللَّهُمَّ اسْتُرْنَا بِسَتْرِكَ الْجَمِيلِ (٣x) ❋

(44) Allāhumma innī as'aluka 'l-ʿafwa wa 'l-ʿāfiyata fī 'd-dīni wa 'd-dunyā wa 'l-ākhirah ﷺ (3x) Allāhumma 'sturnā bi-satrika 'l-jamīl (3x) •

(44) O Allāh, I beg You for forgiveness and well being in my religion, in this life and the next! (3x) O Allāh, veil my faults with Your beautiful cover ! (3x) ❋

(٤٥) اللَّهُمَّ إِنِّي أَسْأَلُكَ بِحَقِّكَ الْعَظِيمِ وَبِحَقِّ نُورِ وَجْهِكَ الْكَرِيمِ وَبِحَقِّ عَرْشِكَ الْعَظِيمِ وَبِمَا حَمَلَ كُرْسِيُّكَ مِنْ عَظَمَتِكَ وَجَلَالِكَ وَجَمَالِكَ وَبَهَائِكَ وَقُدْرَتِكَ وَسُلْطَانِكَ

(45) Allāhumma innī as'aluka bi-ḥaqqika 'l-ʿaẓīm wa bi-ḥaqqi nūri wajhika 'l-karīm wa bi-ḥaqqi ʿarshika 'l-ʿaẓīm wa bimā ḥamala kursīyyuka min ʿaẓamatika wa jalālika wa jamālika wa bahā'ika wa qudratika wa sulṭānika

(45) O Allāh, I ask You for the sake of Great Truth and for the sake of the Truth of the light of Your Noble Face and for the sake of the Truth of Your Tremendous Throne and for the sake of which bears Your Chair from Your Oceans of Greatness, from Your Oceans of Majesty, from Your Beauty Oceans, Your Pride Oceans, Your Power Oceans and Your Oceans of Majesty ➢

وَبِحَقِّ أَسْمَائِكَ الْمَخْزُونَةِ الْمَكْنُونَةِ الَّتِي لَمْ يَطَّلِعْ عَلَيهَا أَحَدُ مِنْ خَلْقِكَ اللَّهُمَّ
وَأَسْأَلُكَ بِالإِسْمِ الَّذِي وَضَعْتَهُ عَلَى اللَّيلِ فَأَظْلَم وَعَلَى النَّهَارِ فَاسْتَنَارَ

wa biḥaqqi asmā'ika 'l-makhzūnati 'l-maknūnati 'Llatī lam yaṭṭaliʿ ʿalayhā aḥadun min khalqika Allāhumma as'aluka bi 'l-ismi 'Lladhī waḍaʿtahu ʿalā 'l-layli fa aẓlama wa ʿalā 'n-nahāri fa 'stanāra

and for the sake of the Truth of Your Preserved and Hidden Names which no one from Your Creation will ever come to know! O Allāh, I ask You by the Name which when laid upon the night makes darkness fall and when laid upon the day makes light appear, ➤

وَعَلَى السَّمَاوَاتِ فَاسْتَقَلَّتْ وَعَلَى الأَرْضِ فَاسْتَقَرَّتْ وَعَلَى الْجِبَالِ فَأَرْسَتْ
وَعَلَى البِحَارِ وَالأَوْدِيَةِ فَجَرَتْ

wa ʿalā 's-samāwāti fa 'staqallat wa ʿalā 'l-arḍi fa'staqarrat wa ʿalā 'l-jibāli fa arsat wa ʿalā 'l-bihāri wa 'l-awdīyati fajarat

and when laid upon the Heavens, they are raised on high and when laid upon the Earth, it becomes firm and when laid upon the mountains, they become fixed and when laid upon oceans and rivers, they begin to flow, ➤

وَعَلَى الْعُيُونِ فَنبَعَتْ وَعَلَى السَّحَابِ فَأَمْطَرَتْ وَأَسْأَلُكَ اللَّهُمَّ بِالأَسْمَاءِ
المَكْتُوبَةِ فِي جَبْهَةِ سَيِّدِنَا إِسْرَافِيلَ ﷺ وَبِالْأَسْمَاءِ المَكْتُوبَةِ فِي جبهَةِ سَيِّدِنَا
جِبْرِيلَ ﷺ وَعَلَى المَلاَئِكَةِ المُقَرَّبِينَ

wa ʿalā 'l-ʿuyūni fa nabaʿat wa ʿalā 's-saḥābi fa amṭarat wa as'aluka 'l-Lāhumma bi 'l-asmā'i 'l-maktūbati fī jab-hati Sayyīdinā Isrāfīla ﷺ *wa bi 'l-asmā'i 'l-maktūbati fī jabhati Sayyīdinā Jibrīla* ﷺ *wa ʿalā 'l-malā'ikati 'l-muqarrabīn*

and when laid upon springs, they burst forth and when laid upon the clouds, they shed their rain and I ask You by the Names written upon the forehead of our master Raphael ﷺ, and by the Names written on the forehead of our master Gabriel ﷺ and upon all the angels of intimacy! ➢

وَأَسْأَلُكَ اللَّهُمَّ بِالأَسْمَاءِ المَكْتُوبَةِ حَولَ العَرْش وبِالأَسْمَاءِ المَكْتُوبَةِ حَوْلَ
الْكُرْسِيِّ وَأَسْأَلُكَ اللَّهُمَّ بِالإِسْمِ المَكْتُوبِ عَلَى وَرَقِ الزَّيْتُونِ ❋

wa as'aluka 'l-Lāhumma bi 'l-asmā'i 'l-maktūbati ḥawla l-ʿarshi wa bi 'l-asmā'i 'l-maktūbati ḥawla 'l-kursīyyi wa as'aluka 'l-Lāhumma bi 'l-ismi 'l-maktūbi ʿalā waraqi 'z-zaytūn •

And I ask You by the Names written around the Throne and by the Divine Names inscribed around the Footstool and I ask You by the Divine Name inscribed on the olive leaf. ❋

الجُمُعَةُ

Friday

الحِزْبُ الخَامِسُ فِي يَوْمِ الجُمُعَةِ

Al-Ḥizbu 'l-Khāmisu fī Yawmi 'l-Jumu'ati

The Fifth Chapter to be Read on Friday

(١) وَأَسْأَلُكَ اللَّهُمَّ بِالْأَسْمَاءِ الْعِظَامِ الَّتِي سَمَّيتَ بِهَا نَفْسَكَ مَا عَلِمْتُ مِنْهَا وَمَا لَمْ أَعْلَمْ وأَسْأَلُكَ اللَّهُمَّ بِالْأَسْمَاءِ الَّتِي دَعَاكَ بِهَا سَيِّدُنَا آدَمُ ﵇ وبِالْأَسْمَاءِ الَّتِي دَعَاكَ بِهَا سَيِّدُنَا نُوحٌ ﵇ وبِالْأَسْمَاءِ الَّتِي دَعَاكَ بِهَا سَيِّدُنَا هُودٌ ﵇ وبِالْأَسْمَاءِ الَّتِي دَعَاكَ بِهَا سَيِّدُنَا إِبْرَاهِيمُ ﵇

(1) as'aluka 'l-Lāhumma bi 'l-asmā'i 'l-'iẓāmi 'Llatī sammayta bihā nafsaka mā 'alimta minhā wa mā lam a'lam wa as'aluka 'l-Lāhumma bi 'l-asmā'i 'Llatī da'āka bihā Sayyīdunā Ādamu ﵇ wa bi 'l-'asmā'i 'Llatī da'āka bihā Sayyīdunā Nūḥun ﵇ wa bi 'l-asmā'i 'Llatī da'aka bihā Sayyīdunā Hūdun ﵇ wa bi 'l-asmā'i 'Llatī da'āka bihā Sayyīdunā Ibrāhīmu ﵇

(1) O Allāh, I ask You by the Majestic Names by which You have named Yourself, those which I know and those I do not and I ask You by the Name by which our master Ādam ﵇ called You and I ask You by the Name by which our master Noah ﵇ called You and I ask You by the Name by which our master Hūd ﵇ called You and I ask You by the Name by which our master Abraham ﵇ called You ➢

وبِالْأَسْمَاءِ الَّتِي دَعَاكَ بِهَا سَيِّدُنَا صَالِحٌ ﷺ وبِالْأَسْمَاءِ الَّتِي دَعَاكَ بِهَا سَيِّدُنَا يُونُس ﷺ وبِالْأَسْمَاءِ الَّتِي دَعَاكَ بِهَا سَيِّدُنَا أَيُّوبُ ﷺ وبِالْأَسْمَاءِ الَّتِي دَعَاكَ بِهَا سَيِّدُنَا يَعْقُوبُ ﷺ وبِالْأَسْمَاءِ الَّتِي دَعَاكَ بِهَا سَيِّدُنَا يُوسُفُ ﷺ وبِالْأَسْمَاءِ الَّتِي دَعَاكَ بِهَا سَيِّدُنَا مُوسَى ﷺ وبِالْأَسْمَاءِ الَّتِي دَعَاكَ بِهَا سَيِّدُنَا هَارُونُ ﷺ وبِالْأَسْمَاءِ الَّتِي دَعَاكَ بِهَا سَيِّدُنَا شُعَيبٌ ﷺ

wa bi 'l-asmā'i 'Llatī daʿāka bihā Sayyīdunā Ṣāliḥun ﷺ wa bi 'l-asmā'i 'Llatī daʿāka bihā Sayyīdunā Yūsuf ﷺ wa bi 'l-asmā'i 'Llatī daʿāka bihā Sayyīdunā Ayyūbu ﷺ wa bi 'l-asmā'i 'Llatī daʿāka bihā Sayyīdunā Yaʿqūbu ﷺ wa bi 'l-asmā'i 'Llatī daʿāka bihā Sayyīdunā Yūsūfu ﷺ wa bi 'l-asmā'i 'Llatī daʿāka bihā Sayyīdunā Mūsā ﷺ wa bi 'l-asmā'i 'Llatī daʿāka bihā Sayyīdunā Hārūn ﷺ wa bi 'l-asmā'i 'Llatī daʿāka bihā Sayyīdunā Shuʿaybun ﷺ

and I ask You by the Name by which our master Ṣāliḥ ﷺ called You and I ask You by the Name by which our master Jonah ﷺ called You and I ask You by the Name by which our master Job ﷺ called You and I ask You by the Name by which our master Jacob ﷺ called You and I ask You by the Name by which our master Joseph ﷺ called You and I ask You, by the Name by which our master Moses ﷺ called You and I ask You by the Name by which our master Aaron ﷺ, called You and I ask You by the Name by which our master Shuʿayb ﷺ called You ➢

وبِالْأَسْماءِ الَّتِي دَعاكَ بِها سَيِّدُنا إِسْماعِيلُ ﷺ وبِالْأَسْماءِ الَّتِي دَعاكَ بِها سَيِّدُنا داوُودُ ﷺ وَبِالْأَسْماءِ الَّتِي دَعاكَ بِها سَيِّدُنا سُلَيْمانُ ﷺ وبِالْأَسْماءِ الَّتِي دَعاكَ بِها سَيِّدُنا زَكَرِيَّا ﷺ وبِالْأَسْماءِ الَّتِي دَعاكَ بِها سَيِّدُنا يَحْيَ ﷺ وبِالْأَسْماءِ الَّتِي دَعاكَ بِها سَيِّدُنا أَرْمِياءُ ﷺ وبِالْأَسْماءِ الَّتِي دَعاكَ بِها سَيِّدُنا شَعْياءُ ﷺ وَبِالْأَسْماءِ الَّتِي دَعاكَ بِها سَيِّدُنا إِلْياسُ ﷺ

wa bi 'l-asmāʼi 'Llatī daʻaka bihā Sayyīdunā Ismāʻīlu ﷺ *wa bi 'l-asmāʼi 'Llatī daʻaka bihā Sayyīdunā Dawūdu* ﷺ *wa bi 'l-asmāʼi 'Llatī daʻāka bihā Sayyīdunā Sulaymān* ﷺ *wa bi 'l-asmāʼi 'Llatī daʻāka bihā Sayyīdunā Zakarīyyā* ﷺ *wa bi 'l-asmāʼi 'Llatī daʻāka bihā Sayyīdunā Yaḥyā* ﷺ *wa bi 'l-asmāʼi 'Llatī daʻāka bihā Sayyīdunā Armīyāʻu* ﷺ *wa bi 'l-asmāʼi 'Llatī daʻāka bihā Sayyīdunā Shaʻyāʻu* ﷺ *wa bi 'l-asmāʼi 'Llatī daʻāka bihā Sayyīdunā Ilyāsu* ﷺ

and I ask You by the Name by which our master Ishmael ﷺ called You and I ask You by the Name by which our master David ﷺ called You and I ask You by the Name by which our master Solomon, ﷺ called You and I ask You by the Name by which our master Zechariah ﷺ called You and I ask You by the Name by which our master Jonah ﷺ called You and I ask You by the Name in which out master Jeremiah ﷺ called You and I ask You by the Name by which our master Shaʻyāʻu ﷺ called You and I ask You by the Name by which our master Elias ﷺ called You ➢

وبِالْأَسْمَاءِ الَّتِي دَعَاكَ بِهَا سَيِّدُنَا الْيَسَعُ ﷺ وبِالْأَسْمَاءِ الَّتِي دَعَاكَ بِهَا سَيِّدُنَا ذُو الْكِفْلِ ﷺ وَبِالْأَسْمَاءِ الَّتِي دَعَاكَ بِهَا سَيِّدُنَا يُوشَعُ ﷺ وبِالْأَسْمَاءِ الَّتِي دَعَاكَ بِهَا سَيِّدُنَا عِيسَى ﷺ وبِالْأَسْمَاءِ الَّتِي دَعَاكَ بِهَا سَيِّدُنَا مُحَمَّدٌ ﷺ وَعَلَى جَمِيعِ النَّبِيِّينَ وَالْمُرْسَلِينَ أَنْ تُصَلِّيَ عَلَى سَيِّدِنَا مُحَمَّدٍ نَبِيِّكَ عَدَدَ مَا خَلَقْتَهُ مِنْ قَبْلِ أَنْ تَكُونَ السَّمَاءُ مَبْنِيَّةً وَالْأَرْضُ مَدْحِيَّةً

wa bi 'l-asmā'i'Llatī daʿāka bihā Sayyīdunā Alyasaʿu ﷺ wa bi 'l-asmā'i 'Llatī daʿāka bihā Sayyīdunā Dhul-Kifli ﷺ wa bi 'l-asmā'i 'Llatī daʿāka bihā Sayyīdunā Yushāʿu ﷺ wa bi 'l-asmā'i 'Llatī daʿāka bihā Sayyīdunā ʿĪsā ﷺ wa bi 'l-asmā'i 'Llatī daʿāka bihā Sayyīdunā Muḥammadun ﷺ wa ʿalā jamīʿi 'n-nabīyyina wa 'l-mursalīna an tuṣalliya ʿalā Sayyīdinā Muḥammadin nabīyyika ʿadada mā khalaqtahu min qabli an takūna 's-samā'u mabnīyyatan wa 'l-arḍu madḥīyyatan

and I ask You by the Name by which our master Esau ﷺ called You and I ask You by the Name by which our master Dhu'l-Kifl ﷺ called You and I ask You by the Name by which our master Joshua ﷺ called You and I ask You by the Name by which our master Jesus ﷺ called You and I ask You by the Name by which our master Muḥammad, the blessings and peace of Allāh be upon him and all the Prophets and Messengers, called You that You exalt our master Muḥammad, Your Prophet, in all that You created before the sky was built, the earth was spread out, ➢

وَالْجِبَالُ مُرسِيَةً وَالْبِحَارُ مُجْرَاةً وَالْعُيونُ مِنْفَجِرَةً وَالأَنهارُ مُنْهَمِرَةً وَالشَّمْسُ مُضْحِيَةً وَالْقَمرُ مُضِيئاً وَالْكَوَاكِبُ مُسْتَنِيرَةً كُنْتَ حَيْثُ كُنْتَ لا يَعْلَمُ أَحَدٌ حَيْثُ كُنْتَ إِلَّا أَنْتَ وَحْدَكَ لا شَرِيكَ لَكَ ❋

wa 'l-jibālu mursiyyatan wa 'l-bīḥāru mujrātan wa 'l-ʿuyūnu munfajiratan wa 'l-anhāru munhamiratan wa 'sh-shamsu muḍhīyatan wa 'l-qamaru muḍīyyan wa 'l-kawākibu mustanīratan kunta haythu kunta lā yaʿlamu aḥadun haythu kunta illā anta waḥdaka lā sharīka lak •

the mountains were made stable, the seas began to flow, the springs burst forth, the rivers streamed forth, the sun shone forth, the moon beamed forth and the planets were lit up and there where You were, You were, and no one knows where You were except You Alone, O Allāh, Who exists without partner! ❋

(٢) اللَّهُمَّ صَلِّ عَلَى سَيِّدِنَا مُحَمَّدٍ عَدَدَ حِلْمِكَ وَصَلِّ عَلَى سَيِّدِنَا مُحَمَّدٍ عَدَدَ عِلْمِكَ وَصَلِّ عَلَى سَيِّدِنَا مُحَمَّدٍ عَدَدَ كَلِمَاتِكَ

(2) Allāhumma ṣalli ʿalā Sayyīdinā Muḥammadin ʿadada ḥilmika wa ṣalli ʿalā Sayyīdinā Muḥammadin ʿadada ʿilmika wa ṣalli ʿalā Sayyīdinā Muḥammadin ʿadada kalimātika

(2) O Allāh, exalt our master Muḥammad to the extent of Your Forbearance! O Allāh, exalt our master Muḥammad to the extent of Your Knowledge! O Allāh, exalt our master Muḥammad on the number of Your Words! ➢

وَصَلِّ عَلَى سَيِّدِنَا مُحَمَّدٍ عَدَدَ نِعْمَتِكَ وَصَلِّ عَلَى سَيِّدِنَا مُحَمَّدٍ مِلْءَ سَمَاوَاتِكَ
وَصَلِّ عَلَى سَيِّدِنَا مُحَمَّدٍ مِلْءَ أَرْضِكَ وَصَلِّ عَلَى سَيِّدِنَا مُحَمَّدٍ مِلْءَ عَرْشِكَ
وَصَلِّ عَلَى سَيِّدِنَا مُحَمَّدٍ عَدَدَ مَا جَرَى بِهِ الْقَلَمُ فِي أُمِّ الْكِتَابِ وَصَلِّ عَلَى سَيِّدِنَا
مُحَمَّدٍ عَدَدَ مَا خَلَقْتَ فِي سَبْعِ سَمَاوَاتِكَ وَصَلِّ عَلَى سَيِّدِنَا مُحَمَّدٍ عَدَدَ مَا أَنْتَ
خَالِقُهُ فِيهِنَّ إِلَى يَوْمِ الْقِيَامَةِ فِي كُلِّ يَوْمٍ أَلْفَ مَرَّةٍ ❋

wa ṣalli ʿalā Sayyīdinā Muḥammadin ʿadada niʿmatika wa ṣalli ʿalā Sayyīdinā Muḥammadin mila' samawātika wa ṣalli ʿalā Sayyīdinā Muḥammadin mila' arḍika wa ṣalli ʿalā Sayyīdinā Muḥammadin mila' ʿarshika wa ṣalli ʿalā Sayyīdinā Muḥammadin mila' zinata ʿarshika wa ṣalli ʿalā Sayyīdinā Muḥammadin ʿadada mā jarā bihi 'l-qalamu fī ummi 'l-kitāb wa ṣalli ʿalā Sayyīdinā Muḥammadin ʿadada mā khalaqta fī sabʿi samāwātika wa ṣalli ʿalā Sayyīdinā Muḥammadin ʿadada mā Anta khāliqun fī-hinna ilā yawmi 'l-qīyāmati fī kulli yawmin alfa marratin •

Bless, O Allāh, our master Muḥammad, to the extent of Your favor! Bless our master Muḥammad to the fullness Your skies! Bless our master Muḥammad to the fullness of Your earth! Bless our master Muḥammad to the fullness of Your Throne! Bless our master Muḥammad in the decoration of Your Throne! Bless our master Muḥammad in all The Pen has written in the Mother of the Book! Bless our master Muḥammad as much as You have created in Your Seven Heavens! Bless our master Muḥammad as much as You will create in them until the Day of Resurrection and every day a thousand times! ❋

(٣) اللَّهُمَّ صَلِّ عَلَى سَيِّدِنَا مُحَمَّدٍ عَدَدَ كُلِّ قَطْرَةٍ قَطَرَتْ مِنْ سَمَاوَاتِكَ إِلَى أَرْضِكَ مِنْ يَوْمِ خَلَقْتَ الدُّنْيَا إِلَى يَوْمِ الْقِيَامَةِ فِي كُلِّ يَوْمٍ أَلْفَ مَرَّةٍ ❋

(3) Allāhumma ṣalli ʿalā Sayyīdinā Muḥammadin ʿadada kulli qaṭratin qaṭarat min samāwātika ilā arḍika min yawmi khalaqta 'd-dunyā ilā yawmi 'l-qīyāmati fī kulli yawmin alfa marratin •

(3) O Allāh, bless our master Muḥammad In every drop of rain that has fallen from Your heavens to Your earth from the Day You created the world to the Day of Resurrection and every day a thousand! ❋

(٤) اللَّهُمَّ صَلِّ عَلَى سَيِّدِنَا مُحَمَّدٍ عَدَدَ مَنْ يُسَبِّحُكَ وَيُهَلِّلُكَ وَيُكَبِّرُكَ وَيُعَظِّمُكَ مِنْ يَوْمِ خَلَقْتَ الدُّنْيَا إِلَى يَوْمِ الْقِيَامَةِ فِي كُلِّ يَوْمٍ أَلْفَ مَرَّةٍ ❋

(4) Allāhumma ṣalli ʿalā Sayyīdinā Muḥammadin ʿadada man yusabbiḥuka wa yuhalliluka wa yukabbiruka wa yuʿaẓẓimuka min yawmi khalaqta 'd-dunyā ilā yawmi 'l-qīyāmati fī kulli yawmin alfa marratin •

(4) O Allāh, bless our master Muḥammad as many times as those who have glorified You, declared Your unity, magnified You and extolled You from the Day You created the world to the Day of Resurrection in every day a thousand times! ❋

(٥) اللَّهُمَّ صَلِّ عَلَى سَيِّدِنَا مُحَمَّدٍ عَدَدَ أَنْفَاسِهِمْ وَأَلْفَاظِهِمْ وَصَلِّ عَلَى سَيِّدِنَا مُحَمَّدٍ عَدَدَ كُلِّ نَسْمَةٍ خَلَقْتَهَا فِيهِمْ مِنْ يَوْمِ خَلَقْتَ الدُّنْيَا إِلَى يَوْمِ الْقِيَامَةِ فِي كُلِّ يَوْمٍ أَلْفَ مَرَّةٍ ❋

(5) Allāhumma ṣalli ʿalā Sayyīdinā Muḥammadin ʿadada anfāsihim wa alfāẓihim wa ṣalli ʿalā Sayyīdinā Muḥammadin ʿadada kulli nasamatin khalaqtahā fīhim min yawmi khalaqta 'd-dunyā ilā yawmi 'l-qīyāmati fī kulli yawmin alfa marratin •

(5) O Allāh, bless our master Muḥammad in every one of their breaths and their utterances and bless our master Muḥammad in each of their fragrant exhalations from the Day You created the world to the Day of Resurrection in every day a thousand times! ❋

(٦) اللَّهُمَّ صَلِّ عَلَى سَيِّدِنَا مُحَمَّدٍ عَدَدَ السَّحَابِ الْجَارِيَةِ وَصَلِّ عَلَى سَيِّدِنَا مُحَمَّدٍ عَدَدَ الرِّيَاحِ الذَّارِيَةِ مِنْ يَوْمِ خَلَقْتَ الدُّنْيَا إِلَى يَوْمِ الْقِيَامَةِ فِي كُلِّ يَوْمٍ أَلْفَ مَرَّةٍ ❋

(6) Allāhumma ṣalli ʿalā Sayyīdinā Muḥammadin ʿadada 's-sahābi 'l-jāriyati wa ṣalli ʿalā Sayyīdinā Muḥammadin ʿadada 'r-riyāḥi 'dh-dhārīyati min yawmi khalaqta 'd-dunyā ilā yawmi 'l-qīyāmati fī kulli yawmin alfa marratin •

(6) O Allāh bless our master Muḥammad in every rolling cloud and bless our master Muḥammad in every sweeping wind from the Day You created the world the Day of Resurrection in every day a thousand times! ❋

(٧) اللَّهُمَّ صَلِّ عَلَى سَيِّدِنَا مُحَمَّدٍ عَدَدَ مَا هَبَّت عَلَيهِ الرِّيَاحُ وَحَرَّكَتْهُ مِنَ الأَغْصَانِ وَالْأَشْجَارِ وَالْأَوْرَاقِ وَالثِّمَارِ وَجَمِيعِ مَا خَلَقْتَ عَلَى أَرْضِكَ وَمَا بَيْنَ سَمَاوَاتِكَ مِنْ يَوْمِ خَلَقْتَ الدُّنْيَا إِلَى يَوْمِ الْقِيَامَةِ فِي كُلِّ يَوْمٍ أَلْفَ مَرَّةٍ ❋

(7) Allāhumma ṣalli ʿalā Sayyīdinā Muḥammadin ʿadad mā habbat ʿalayhi 'r-riyāḥu wa ḥarrakathu mina 'l-aghsāni wa 'l-ashjāri wa 'l-awrāqi wa 'th-thimāri wa jamīʿi mā khalaqta ʿalā arḍika wa bayna samāwātika min yawmi khalaqta 'd-dunyā ilā yawmi 'l-qīyāmati fī kulli yawmin alfa marratin •

(7) O Allāh, bless our master Muḥammad in the movement of every branch, every tree, every leaf and every fruit stirred by the wind and in every wind-stirred movement of all else that You have created on your earth and between Your Heavens from the Day You created the world to the Day of Resurrection in every day a thousand times! ❋

(٨) اللَّهُمَّ صَلِّ عَلَى سَيِّدِنَا مُحَمَّدٍ عَدَدَ نُجُومِ السَّمَاءِ مِنْ يَوْمِ خَلَقْتَ الدُّنْيَا إِلَى يَوْمِ الْقِيَامَةِ فِي كُلِّ يَوْمٍ الْفَ مَرَّةٍ ❋

(8) Allāhumma ṣalli ʿalā Sayyīdinā Muḥammadin ʿadada nujūmi 's-samā'i min yawmi khalaqta 'd-dunyā ilā yawmi 'l-qīyāmati fī kulli yawmin alfa marratin •

(8) O Allāh, bless Our master Muḥammad on the number of every star in the sky from the Day You created the world to the Day of Resurrection in every day a thousand times! ❋

(٩) اللَّهُمَّ صَلِّ عَلَى سَيِّدِنَا مُحَمَّدٍ مِلْءَ أَرْضِكَ مِمَّا حَمَلَت وَأَقَلَّتْ مِنْ قُدْرَتِكَ اللَّهُمَّ صَلِّ عَلَى سَيِّدِنَا مُحَمَّدٍ عَدَدَ مَا خَلَقْتَ فِي سَبْعِ بِحَارِكَ مِمَّا لَا يَعْلَمُ عِلْمُهُ إِلَّا أَنْتَ وَمَا أَنْتَ خَالِقُهُ فِيهَا إِلَى يَوْمِ الْقِيَامَةِ فِي كُلِّ يَوْمٍ أَلْفَ مَرَّةٍ ❋

(9) Allāhumma ṣalli ʿalā Sayyīdinā Muḥammadin mil'a arḍika mimmā ḥamalat wa aqallat min qudratika Allāhumma ṣalli ʿalā Sayyīdinā Muḥammadin ʿadada mā khalaqta fī sabʿi biḥārika mimmā lā yāʿ-lamu ʿilmuhu illā Anta wa mā anta khāliquhu fīhā ilā yawmi 'l-qīyāmati fī kulli yawmin alfa marratin •

(9) O Allāh, exalt our master Muḥammad filling the earth and what it holds and what it bears of Your Power! O Allāh exalt our master Muḥammad in everything You have created in the seven seas from what You Alone know and in everything You created within them until the Day of Resurrection in every day a thousand times! ❋

(١٠) اللَّهُمَّ صَلِّ عَلَى سَيِّدِنَا مُحَمَّدٍ عَدَدَ مِلْءِ سَبْعِ بِحَارِكَ وَصَلِّ عَلَى سَيِّدِنَا مُحَمَّدٍ زِنَةَ سَبْعِ بِحَارِكَ مِمَّا حَمَلَتْ وَأَقَلَّتْ مِنْ قُدْرَتِكَ

(10) Allāhumma ṣalli ʿalā Sayyīdinā Muḥammadin ʿadada mil'a sabʿi biḥārika wa ṣalli ʿalā Sayyīdinā Muḥammadin zinata sabʿi bihārika mimmā ḥamalat wa aqallat min qudratika

(10) O Allāh, exalt our master Muḥammad to the fullness of Your Seven Seas and exalt our master Muḥammad in the adornment of Your Seven Seas in that which they hold and bear of Your Power, ➢

اللَّهُمَّ وَصَلِّ عَلَى سَيِّدِنَا مُحَمَّدٍ عَدَدَ أَمْوَاجِ بِحَارِكَ مِنْ يَوْمِ خَلَقْتَ الدُّنْيَا إِلَى يَوْمِ الْقِيَامَةِ فِي كُلِّ يَوْمٍ أَلْفَ مَرَّةٍ ❋

Allāhumma wa ṣalli 'alā Sayyīdinā Muḥammadin 'adada amwāji biḥārika min yawmi khalaqta 'd-dunyā ilā yawmi 'l-qīyāmati fī kulli yawmin alfa marratin •

O Allāh, exalt our master Muḥammad in every wave on Your seas from the Day You created the world to the Day of Resurrection in every day a thousand times! ❋

(١١) اللَّهُمَّ وَصَلِّ عَلَى سَيِّدِنَا مُحَمَّدٍ عَدَدَ الرَّمْلِ وَالْحَصَى فِي مُسْتَقَرِّ الْأَرَضِينَ شَرْقِهَا وَغَرْبِهَا وَسَهْلِهَا وَجِبَالِهَا مِنْ يَوْمِ خَلَقْتَ الدُّنْيَا إِلَى يَوْمِ الْقِيَامَةِ فِي كُلِّ يَوْمٍ أَلْفَ مَرَّةٍ ❋

(11) Allāhumma wa ṣalli 'alā Sayyīdinā Muḥammadin 'adada 'r-ramli wa 'l-ḥaṣā fī mustaqarri 'l-araḍīna sharqihā wa gharbihā wa sahlihā wa jibālihā min yawmi khalaqta 'd-dunyā ilā yawmi 'l-qīyāmati fī kulli alfa marratin •

(11) O Allāh, exalt our master Muḥammad in every grain of sand in every pebble on the solid ground of the earth, the soft ground of the earth and the mountains of the earth from the Day You created the world to the Day of Resurrection in every day a thousand times! ❋

(١٢) اللَّهُمَّ وَصَلِّ عَلَى سَيِّدِنَا مُحَمَّدٍ عَدَدَ اضْطِرَابِ الْمِيَاهِ الْعَذْبَةِ وَالْمِلْحَةِ مِنْ يَوْمِ خَلَقْتَ الدُّنْيَا إِلَى يَوْمِ الْقِيَامَةِ فِي كُلِّ يَوْمٍ أَلْفَ مَرَّةٍ ❋

(12) Allāhumma wa ṣalli ʿalā Sayyīdinā Muḥammadin ʿadada 'ḍ-ṭirābi 'l-miyāhi 'l-ʿadhbati wa 'l-milḥati min yawmi khalaqta 'd-dunyā ilā yawmi 'l-qīyāmati fī kulli yawmi alfa marratin •

(12) O Allāh, bless our master Muḥammad in the turbidity between the saltwater and the fresh from the Day You created the world to the Day of Resurrection in every day a thousand times! ❋

(١٣) اللَّهُمَّ وَصَلِّ عَلَى سَيِّدِنَا مُحَمَّدٍ عَدَدَ مَا خَلَقْتَهُ عَلَى جَدِيدِ أَرْضِكَ فِي مُسْتَقَرِّ الْأَرَضِينَ شَرْقِهَا وَغَرْبِهَا وَسَهْلِهَا وَجِبَالِهَا وَأَوْدِيَتِهَا وَطَرِيقِهَا وَعَامِرِهَا وَغَامِرِهَا

(13) Allāhumma wa ṣalli ʿalā Sayyīdinā Muḥammadin ʿadada mā khalaqtahu ʿalā jadīdi arḍika fī mustaqarri 'l-araḍīn sharqihā wa gharbihā wa sahlihā wa jibālihā wa awdiyatihā wa ṭarīqihā wa ʿāmirihā wa ghāmirihā

(13) O Allāh, bless our master Muḥammad on the number of everything You have created on the face of Your earth, on solid land, East and West, on soft ground, in the mountains, in the streets and on the paths, in populated areas and in wastelands ➤

إِلَى سَائِرِ مَا خَلَقْتَهُ عَلَيهَا وَمَا فِيهَا مِنْ حَصَاةٍ وَمَدَرٍ وَحَجَرٍ مِنْ يَوْمِ خَلَقْتَ الدُّنْيَا إِلَى يَوْمِ الْقِيَامَةِ فِي كُلِّ يَوْمٍ أَلْفَ مَرَّةٍ ۞

ilā sā'iri mā khalaqtahu 'alayhā wa mā fīhā min ḥaṣātin wa madarin wa ḥajarin min yawmi khalāqta 'd-dunyā ilā yawmi 'l-qīyāmati fī-kulli yaumin alfa marratin •

and in what You have created on it and in it, every pebble, in every lump of mud and in every stone, from the Day You created the world to the Day of Resurrection in every day a thousand times! ۞

(١٤) اللَّهُمَّ صَلِّ عَلَى سَيِّدِنَا مُحَمَّدٍ النَّبِيِّ عَدَدَ نَبَاتِ الْأَرْضِ مِنْ قِبْلَتِهَا شَرْقِهَا وَغَرْبِهَا وَسَهْلِهَا وَجِبَالِهَا وَأَوْدِيَتِهَا وَأَشْجَارِهَا وَثِمَارِهَا وَأَوْرَاقِهَا

(14) Allāhumma ṣalli 'alā Sayyīdinā Muḥammadin 'n-nabīyyi 'adada nabāti 'l-arḍi min qiblatihā wa sharqihā wa gharbihā wa sahlihā wa jibālihā wa awdiyatihā wa ashjārihā wa thimārihā wa awrāqihā

(14) O Allāh, exalt our master Muḥammad, the Prophet, on the number of every plant on the earth in its East and in its West, on soft ground, on mountains and in valleys, and may there be blessings in every tree, in every fruit, in every leaf ➢

وَزُرُوعِهَا وَجَمِيعِ مَا يَخْرُجُ مِنْ نَبَاتِهَا وَبَرَكَاتِهَا مِنْ يَوْمِ خَلَقْتَ الدُّنْيَا إِلَى يَوْمِ الْقِيَامَةِ فِي كُلِّ يَوْمٍ أَلْفَ مَرَّةٍ ❋

wa zurūʿihā wa jamīʿi mā yakhruju min nabātihā wa barakātihā min yawmi khalaqta 'd-dunyā ilā yawmi 'l-qīyāmati fī kulli yawmin alfa marratin •

and in every plant, and in all other vegetation or verdure that grows from the Day You created the world to the Day of Resurrection in every day a thousand times. ❋

(١٥) اللَّهُمَّ وَصَلِّ عَلَى سَيِّدِنَا مُحَمَّدٍ عَدَدَ مَا خَلَقْتَ مِنَ الْجِنِّ وَالإِنْسِ وَالشَّيَاطِينِ وَمَا أَنْتَ خَالِقُهُ مِنْهُم إِلَى يَوْمِ الْقِيَامَةِ فِي كُلِّ يَوْمٍ أَلْفَ مَرَّةٍ ❋

(15) Allāhumma wa ṣalli ʿalā Sayyīdinā Muḥammadin ʿadada mā khalaqta mina 'l-jinni wa 'l-insi wa 'sh-shayāṭīni wa mā anta khāliquhu minhum ilā yawmi 'l-qīyāmati fī kulli yawmin alfa marratin •

(15) O Allāh bless our master Muḥammad on the number of every Jinn, human being and devil You have created and every one of them You will create until the Day of Resurrection in every day a thousand times! ❋

(١٦) اللَّهُمَّ وَصَلِّ عَلَى سَيِّدِنَا مُحَمَّدٍ عَدَدَ كُلِّ شَعْرَةٍ فِي أَبْدَانِهِم وَفِي وُجُوهِهِم وَعَلَى رُؤُسِهِمْ مُنْذُ خَلَقْتَ الدُّنْيَا إِلَى يَوْمِ الْقِيَامَةِ فِي كُلِّ يَوْمٍ أَلْفَ مَرَّةٍ ❋

(16) Allāhumma wa ṣalli ʿalā Sayyīdinā Muḥammadin ʿadada kulli shaʿratin fī abdānihim wa fī wujūhihim wa ʿalā ru'ūsihim mundhu khalaqta 'd-dunyā ilā yawmi 'l-qīyāmati fī kulli yawmin alfa marratin •

(16) O Allāh bless our master Muḥammad, in the number of the hairs on their bodies, on their faces, and on their heads, from the moment You created the world to the Day of Resurrection in every day a thousand times! ❋

(١٧) اللَّهُمَّ وَصَلِّ عَلَى سَيِّدِنَا مُحَمَّدٍ عَدَدَ خَفَقَانِ الطَّيرِ وَطَيَرَانِ الْجِنِّ وَالشَّيَاطِينِ مِنْ يَوْمِ خَلَقْتَ الدُّنْيَا إِلَى يَوْمِ الْقِيَامَةِ فِي كُلِّ يَوْمٍ أَلْفَ مَرَّةٍ ❋

(17) Allāhumma wa ṣalli ʿalā Sayyīdinā Muḥammadin ʿadada khafaqāni 'ṭ-ṭayri wa ṭayrāni 'l-jinni wa 'sh-shayāṭīni min yawmi khalaqta 'd-dunyā ilā yawmi 'l-qīyāmati fī kulli yawmi alfa marratin. •

(17) O Allāh, Bless our master Muḥammad on the number of times birds flapped their wings, and the flying of the jinn and devils from the Day You created the world to the Day of Resurrection in every day a thousand times! ❋

(١٨) اللَّهُمَّ وَصَلِّ عَلَى سَيِّدِنَا مُحَمَّدٍ عَدَدَ كُلِّ بَهِيمَةٍ خَلَقْتَهَا عَلَى جَدِيدِ أَرْضِكَ مِنْ صَغِيرٍ أَوْ كَبِيرٍ فِي مَشَارِقِ الْأَرْضِ وَمَغَارِبِهَا مِنْ إِنْسِهَا وَجِنِّهَا وَمِمَّا لَا يَعْلَمُ عِلْمَهُ إِلَّا أَنْتَ مِنْ يَوْمِ خَلَقْتَ الدُّنْيَا إِلَى يَوْمِ الْقِيَامَةِ فِي كُلِّ يَوْمٍ أَلْفَ مَرَّةٍ ❋

(18) Allāhumma wa ṣalli ʿalā Sayyīdinā Muḥammadin ʿadada kulli bahīmatin khalaqtahā ʿalā jadīdi arḍika min ṣaghīrin aw kabīrin fī mashāriqi 'l-arḍi wa maghāribihā min insihā wa jinnihā wa mimmā lā yaʿlamu ʿilmahu illā Anta min yawmi khalaqta 'd-dunyā ilā yawmi 'l-qīyāmati fī kulli yawmin alfa marratin •

(18) O Allāh, exalt our master Muḥammad in all the cattle You have created on the surface of Your earth, both big and small, in the East of the earth and in the West, and on the count of all the men and the jinn and in all that of which there is no knowledge expect Yours from the Day You created the world to the Day of Resurrection in every day a thousand times! ❋

(١٩) اللَّهُمَّ وَصَلِّ عَلَى سَيِّدِنَا مُحَمَّدٍ عَدَدَ خُطَاهُمْ عَلَى وَجْهِ الْأَرْضِ مِنْ يَوْمِ خَلَقْتَ الدُّنْيَا إِلَى يَوْمِ الْقِيَامَةِ فِي كُلِّ يَوْمٍ أَلْفَ مَرَّةٍ ❋

(19) Allāhumma wa ṣalli ʿalā Sayyīdinā Muḥammadin ʿadada khuṭāhum ʿalā wajhi 'l-arḍi min yawmi khalaqta 'd-dunyā ilā yawmi 'l-qīyāmati fī kulli yawmin alfa marrah •

(19) O Allāh, exalt our master Muḥammad in every ridge on the face of the earth From the Day You created the world to the Day of Resurrection in every day a thousand times! ❋

(٢٠) اللَّهُمَّ وَصَلِّ عَلَى سَيِّدِنَا مُحَمَّدٍ عَدَدَ مَنْ يُصَلِّي عَلَيْهِ وَصَلِّ عَلَى سَيِّدِنَا مُحَمَّدٍ عَدَدَ مَنْ لَمْ يُصَلِّ عَلَيْهِ وَصَلِّ عَلَى سَيِّدِنَا مُحَمَّدٍ عَدَدَ الْقَطْرِ وَالْمَطَرِ وَالنَّبَاتِ وَصَلِّ عَلَى سَيِّدِنَا مُحَمَّدٍ عَدَدَ كُلِّ شَيْءٍ ❋

(20) Allāhumma wa ṣalli 'alā Sayyīdinā Muḥammadin 'adada man yuṣalli 'alayhi wa ṣalli 'alā Sayyīdinā Muḥammadin 'adada man lam yuṣalli 'alayhi wa ṣalli 'alā Sayyīdinā Muḥammadin 'adada 'l-qaṭri wa 'l-maṭari wa 'n-nabāti wa ṣalli 'alā Sayyīdinā Muḥammadin 'adada kulli shay'in •

(20) O Allāh, bless our master Muḥammad as many times as those invoked blessings on him and bless our master Muḥammad, as many times who do not invoke blessings on him and bless our master Muḥammad in every raindrop, in every rainfall and in every plant and bless our master Muḥammad in everything which exists. ❋

(٢١) اللَّهُمَّ وَصَلِّ عَلَى سَيِّدِنَا مُحَمَّدٍ فِي اللَّيْلِ إِذَا يَغْشَى وَصَلِّ عَلَى سَيِّدِنَا مُحَمَّدٍ فِي النَّهَارِ إِذَا تَجَلَّى

(21) Allāhumma wa ṣalli 'alā Sayyīdinā Muḥammadin fī 'l-layli idhā yaghshā wa ṣalli 'alā Sayyīdinā Muḥammadin fī 'n-nahāri idhā tajallā

(21) And exalt our master Muḥammad at night when it grows dark and exalt our master Muḥammad in the day when it grows light ➢

وَصَلِّ عَلَى سَيِّدِنَا مُحَمَّدٍ فِي الْآخِرَةِ وَالْأُولَى وَصَلِّ عَلَى سَيِّدِنَا مُحَمَّدٍ شَابّاً زَكِيّاً وَصَلِّ عَلَى سَيِّدِنَا مُحَمَّدٍ كَهْلاً مَرضِيّاً وَصَلِّ عَلَى سَيِّدِنَا مُحَمَّدٍ مُنْذُ كَانَ فِي الْمَهْدِ صَبِيّاً وَصَلِّ عَلَى سَيِّدِنَا مُحَمَّدٍ حَتَّى لا يَبْقَى مِنَ الصَّلاةِ شَيْءٌ اللَّهُمَّ وَأَعْطِ سَيِّدِنَا مُحَمَّداً الْمَقَامَ الْمَحْمُودَ الَّذِي وَعَدْتَهُ الَّذِي إِذَا قَالَ صَدَّقْتَهُ وَإِذَا سَأَلَ أَعْطَيْتَهُ ❋

wa ṣalli ʿalā Sayyīdinā Muḥammadin fī 'l-ākhirati wa 'l-ūla wa ṣalli ʿalā Sayyīdinā Muḥammadin shābban zakīyyan wa ṣalli ʿalā Sayyīdinā Muḥammadin kahlan marḍīyyan wa ṣalli ʿalā Sayyīdinā Muḥammadin mundhu kāna fī 'l-mahdi ṣabīyyan wa ṣalli ʿalā Sayyīdinā Muḥammadin ḥattā lā yabqā mina 'ṣ-ṣalāti shay'un Allāhumma wa āʿṭi Sayyīdanā Muḥammadan 'l-Maqāma al-Maḥmūda 'Lladhī waʿadtahu 'Lladhī idhā qāla ṣaddaqtahu wa idhā sa'ala āʿṭaytahu •

And exalt our master Muḥammad in the end and at the beginning and exalt our master Muḥammad in his youth, in his purity and bless our master Muḥammad in his middle age and bless our master Muḥammad even in the cradle and bless our master Muḥammad until there remains naught from blessings. O Allāh, grant our master Muḥammad the most-Praised Station, which You promised to him, the place where when he speaks, You vindicate him and when he ask, You give to him. ❋

(٢٢) اللَّهُمَّ وَاعظِم بُرهَانَهُ وَشَرِّف بُنيَانَهُ وَابلِج حُجَّتَهُ وَبَيِّن فَضِيلَتَهُ اللَّهُمَّ وَتَقَبَّل شَفَاعَتَهُ فِي أُمَّتِهُ وَاستَعمِلنَا بِسُنَّتِهِ وَتَوَفَّنَا عَلَى مِلَّتِهِ وَاحشُرنَا فِي زُمرَتِهِ وَتَحتَ لِوَائِهِ وَاجعَلنَا مِنْ رُفَقَائِهِ وَاوِردنَا حَوضَهُ وَاسقِنَا بِكَأسِهِ وَانفَعنَا بِمَحَبَّتِهِ اللَّهُمَّ آمين ❋

(22) Allāhumma wa ʿaẓim burhānahu wa sharrif bunyānahu wa ablij ḥujjatahu wa bayyin faḍīlatahu Allāhumma wa taqabbal shafāʿatahu fī ummatihi wa 'staʿmilnā bi-sunnatihi wa tawaffanā ʿalā millatihi wa 'ḥshurnā fī zumratihi wa taḥta liwā'ihi wa 'jʿalnā min rufaqā'ihi wa awridnā ḥawḍahu wa 'sqinā bikā'sihi wa 'nfaʿnā bi maḥabbatihi Allāhumma āmīn •

(22) O Allāh, accept his intercession for his nation and establish us on his way, allow us to die in his sunnah, resurrect us in his company beneath his flag, and make us among his associates, water us at his pool, allow us to drink from his drinking bowl, and cause us to enjoy his love! O Allāh, Amen! ❋

(٢٣) وَأَسْأَلُكَ بِأَسْمَائِكَ الَّتِي دَعَوْتُكَ بِهَا أَنْ تُصَلِّيَ عَلَى سَيِّدِنَا مُحَمَّدٍ عَدَدَ مَا وَصَفْتَ وَمِمَّا لَا يَعْلَمُ عِلْمُهُ إِلَّا أَنْتَ

(23) Wa as'aluka bi-asmāika 'Llatī daʿawtuka bihā an tuṣallīya ʿalā Sayyīdinā Muḥammadin ʿadada mā waṣafta mimmā lā yāʿlamu ʿilmahu illā Anta

(23) And I ask You, by the Names in which I have called on You to bless our master Muḥammad, as much as I have outlined and as much as that of which You have knowledge ➢

وَأَنْ تَرْحَمَنِي وَتَتُوبَ عَلَيَّ وَتُعَافِيَنِي مِنْ جَمِيعِ البَلَاءِ وَالْبَلْوَاءِ وَأَن تَغْفِرَ لِي وَلِوَالِدَيَّ وَتَرْحَمَ الْمُؤْمِنِينَ وَالْمُؤْمِنَاتِ وَالْمُسْلِمِينَ وَالْمُسْلِمَاتِ الأَحْيَاءَ مِنْهُمْ وَالأَمْوَاتَ وَأَنْ تَغْفِرَ لِعَبْدِكَ فُلَانِ بْنِ فُلَانٍ (إِسْمُكَ ....) الْمُذْنِبِ الْخَاطِيءِ الضَّعِيفِ وَأَنْ تَتُوبَ عَلَيهِ إِنَّكَ غَفُورٌ رَحِيمٌ اللَّهُمَّ آمِين يَا رَبَّ العَالَمِينَ ❋

wa an tarḥamanī wa tatūba ʿalayya wa tuʿāfiyanī min jamīʿi 'l-balā'i wa 'l-balwā'i wa an taghfira lī wa li-wālidayya wa tarḥam 'l-mu'minīna wa 'l-mu'mināti wa 'l-muslimīna wa 'l-muslimāti 'l-aḥyā'a minhum wa 'l-amwāta wa an taghfira li-ʿabdika fulānin-ibni fulāni (your name -------- Ibni - Your father's name ----------) 'l-mudhnibi 'l-khāṭī'i 'ḍ-ḍaʿīf wa an tatūba ʿalayhi innaka Ghafūrun Raḥīmun Allāhumma āmīn yā Rabba 'l-ʿālamīn •

to have mercy on me and accept my repentance, absolve me of all trials and tribulations and to forgive me and my parents and have mercy on the believing men and women, and the Muslim men and women, the living among them and the dead, and forgive the reader of this book (your name) the sincere, the erroneous, the weak, and accept his repentance, for You are The Forgiver, The Merciful! O Allāh, Amen, O Lord of the worlds! ❋

Hadith about the benefits of invoking blessings on the Prophet ﷺ on Friday:

قَالَ رَسُولُ اللهِ صَلَّى اللهُ عَلَيْهِ وسَلَّم : مَنْ قَرأَ هَذِهِ الصَلاَةَ مَرَّةً وَاحِدَةً كَتَبَ اللهُ لَهُ ثَوَابَ حَجَّةٍ مَقبُولَةٍ وَثَوَابَ مَنْ أَعْتَقَ رَقَبَةً مِنْ وَلَدِ إِسْمَاعِيلَ عليه السلام فَيَقُولُ اللهُ تَعَالَى يَا مَلآئِكَتِي هَذَا عَبدٌ مِنْ عِبَادِي أَكْثَرَ الصَّلاَةَ عَلَى حَبِيبِي مُحَمَّدٍ فَوَعِزَّتِي وَجَلاَلِي وَجُودِي وَمَجْدِي وَارْتِفَاعِي لَأُعْطِيَنَّهُ بِكُلِّ حَرْفٍ صَلَّى قَصْراً فِي الْجَنَّةِ

Qāla Rasūlu 'Llāhi ﷺ: man qarā'a hādhihi 'ṣ-ṣalāta marratan wāḥidatan kataba 'Llāhu lahu thawāba ḥajjatin maqbūlatin wa thawāba man a'taqa raqabatan min waladi Ismā'īla عليه السلام fa-yaqūlu 'Llāhu ta'ālā: yā malā'ikatī hādhā 'abdun min 'ibādī akthara 'ṣ-ṣalāta 'alā ḥabībī Muḥammadin fa wa 'izzatī wa jalālī wa jūdī wa majdī wa 'rtifā'ī la-u'ṭīyannahu bi kulli ḥarfin ṣallā bihi 'alā Ḥabībī qaṣran fī 'l-jannati

The Prophet of Allāh ﷺ said, "Whoever read this blessing once, Allāh will write for him the reward of an accepted pilgrimage and the reward of freeing a slave from among the descendants of Ishmael عليه السلام. And Allāh the Exalted says, "O My angels, this is one of my servants who has sought abundant blessings upon my Beloved Muḥammad Verily by My Power, My Glory, My Generosity, My Splendor and My Sublimity, I grant him for every letter of his words invoking blessings upon My Beloved, a castle in Paradise. ➢

وَلَيَأْتِيَنِّي يَوْمَ الْقِيَامَةِ تَحْتَ لِوَاءِ الْحَمْدِ نُورُ وَجْهِهِ كَالْقَمَرِ لَيْلَةَ الْبَدْرِ وَكَفُّهُ فِي كَفِّ حَبِيبِي مُحَمَّدٍ هَذَا لِمَنْ قَالَهَا كُلَّ يَوْمِ جُمُعَةٍ لَهُ هَذَا الفَضْلُ وَاللهُ ذُو الفَضْلِ الْعَظِيمِ ۞

wa la-yā'tīyannī yawma 'l-qīyāmati taḥta liwā'i 'l-ḥamdi wa nūru wajhihi ka 'l-qamari laylata 'l-badri wa kaffuhu fī kaffi ḥabībī Muḥammadin hādhā liman qālahā fī kulli yawmi Jumuʿuatin lahu hādhā 'l-faḍlu wa 'Llāhu dhu 'l-faḍli 'l-ʿaẓīm •

And he will come to me on the Day of Resurrection beneath the Flag of Praise, and the light of his face will be like the full moon and he will be hand-in-hand with My Beloved Muḥammad! This is for whoever recites this on Friday, this great reward, and Allāh is Lord of ever-abounding grace. ۞

(وَفِي رِوَايَةٍ):

wa fī riwāyatin:

And in another narration:

(٢٤) اللَّهُمَّ إِنِّي أَسْأَلُكَ بِحَقِّ مَا حَمَلَ كُرْسِيُّكَ مِنْ عَظَمَتِكَ وَقُدْرَتِكَ وَجَلَالِكَ وَبَهَائِكَ وَسُلْطَانِكَ

(24) Allāhumma innī as'aluka bi-ḥaqqi mā ḥamala kursīyyuka min ʿaẓamatika wa qudratika wa jalālika wa bahā'ika wa sulṭānika

(24) O Allāh, I ask You for the sake of the truth that carries Your Throne from Your Might, Your Power, Your Glory Oceans, Your Splendor Oceans and Your Authority, ➢

وَبِحَقِّ إِسْمِكَ الْمَخْزُونِ الْمَكْنُونِ الَّذِي سَمَّيتَ بِهِ نَفْسَكَ وَأَنْزَلْتَهُ فِي كِتَابِكَ وَاسْتَأْثَرْتَ بِهِ فِي عِلْمِ الْغَيبِ عِنْدَكَ أَنْ تُصَلِّيَ عَلَى سَيِّدِنَا مُحَمَّدٍ عَبْدِكَ وَرَسُولِكَ ❋

wa bi-ḥaqqi ismika ʾl-makhzūni ʾl-maknūni ʿLladhī sammayta bihi nafsaka wa anzaltahu fī kitābika wa ʾstaʾtharta bihi fī ʿilmi ʾl-ghaybi ʿindaka an tuṣallīya ʿalā Sayyīdinā Muḥammadin ʿabdika wa Rasūlika •

and for the sake of the truth of Your Name, secret and hidden, which You named Yourself and which You revealed in Your Book and which You alone took for Yourself in the unseen world, that You bless our master Muḥammad Your Servant and Your Messenger! ❋

(٢٥) وَأَسْأَلُكَ بِإِسْمِكَ الَّذِي إِذَا دُعِيتَ بِهِ أَجَبْتَ وَإِذَا سُئِلْتَ بِهِ أَعْطَيتَ وَأَسْأَلُكَ بِإِسْمِكَ الَّذِي وَضَعْتَهُ عَلَى اللَّيلِ فَأَظْلَمَ وَعَلَى النَّهَارِ فَاسْتَنَارَ

(25) Wa asʾaluka bi ismika ʿLladhī idhā duʿīta bihi ajabta wa idhā suʾilta bihi āʿ-ṭayt wa asʾaluka bi ismika ʿLladhī waḍaʿ-tahu ʿalā ʾl-layli fa aẓlama wa ʿalā ʾn-nahāri fa ʾstanāra

(25) and I ask You by the Name in which were one to call upon You, You would answer, and in which were one to ask You something, You would grant it and I ask You by Your Name which when laid upon the night darkness falls and when laid upon the day light arises ➢

وَعَلَى السَّمَاوَاتِ فَاسْتَقَلَّتْ وَعَلَى الْأَرْضِ فَاسْتَقَرَّتْ وَعَلَى الجِبَالِ فَرَسَتْ وَعَلَى الصَّعْبَةِ فَذَلَّتْ وَعَلَى مَاءِ السَّمَاءِ فَسَكَبَتْ وَعَلَى السَّحَابِ فَأَمْطَرَتْ وَأَسْأَلُكَ بِمَا سَأَلَكَ بِهِ سَيِّدُنَا مُحَمَّدٌ نَبِيُّكَ وَأَسْأَلُكَ بِمَا سَأَلَكَ بِهِ سَيِّدُنَا آدَمُ نَبِيُّكَ وَأَسْأَلُكَ بِمَا سَأَلَكَ بِهِ أَنْبِيَاؤُكَ وَرُسُلُكَ وَمَلَائِكَتُكَ الْمُقَرَّبُونَ صَلَّى اللهُ عَلَيهِمْ أَجْمَعِينَ

wa ʿalā 's-samāwāti fa 'staqallat wa ʿalā 'l-arḍi fa 'staqarrat wa ʿalā 'l-jibāli fa-rasat wa ʿalā 'ṣ-ṣaʿbati fadhallat wa ʿalā mā'i 's-samā'i fa sakabat wa ʿalā 's-saḥābi fa amṭarat wa as'aluka bimā sa'alaka bihi Sayyīdunā Muḥammadun 'n-nabīyyuka wa as'aluka bimā sa'alaka bihi Sayyīdunā Ādamu nabīyyuka wa as'aluka bimā sa'alaka bihi anbīyā'uka wa rusuluka wa malā'ikatuk al-muqarrabūn ṣalla 'Llāhu ʿalayhim ajmaʿīn

and when laid upon the heavens they are raised up and when laid upon the earth it becomes solid and firm and when laid upon the mountains they form summits and when laid upon difficulties they are overcome and when laid upon the water of the sky it pours forth and when laid upon the clouds they rain and I ask You for the sake of what our master Muḥammad, Your Prophet, asked You and I ask You for the sake of what our master Ādam ﵇, Your Prophet, asked You and I ask You, for the sake of what Your Prophet and Your Messenger and Your Closest Angels asked You Allāh's blessings upon them all ➤

وَأَسْأَلُكَ بِمَا سَأَلَكَ بِهِ أَهْلُ طَاعَتِكَ أَجْمَعِينَ أَنْ تُصَلِّيَ عَلَى سَيِّدِنَا مُحَمَّدٍ وَعَلَى آلِ سَيِّدِنَا مُحَمَّدٍ عَدَدَ مَا خَلَقْتَ مِنْ قَبْلِ أَنْ تَكُونَ السَّمَاءُ مَبْنِيَّةً وَالْأَرْضُ مَدْحِيَّةً وَالْجِبَالُ مَرسِيَةً وَالعُيُونُ مُنْفَجِرَةً وَالْأَنْهَارُ مُنْهَمِرَةً وَالشَّمْسُ مُضْحِيَةً وَالقَمَرُ مُضِيئاً وَالكَوَاكِبُ مُنِيرَةً ❋

wa as'aluka bimā sa'alaka bihi āhlu ṭāʿatika ajmaʿīn an tuṣallīya ʿalā Sayyīdinā Muḥammadin wa ʿalā āli Sayyīdinā Muḥammadin ʿadada mā khalaqta min qabli an takūna 's-samā'u mabnīyyatan wa 'l-arḍu madḥīyyatan wa 'l-jibālu mursīyatan wa 'l-ʿuyūnu munfajiratan wa 'l-anhāru munhamiratan wa 'sh-shamsu muḍ-ḥīyatan wa 'l-qamaru muḍīyan wa 'l-kawākibu munīratan •

and I ask You, for the sake of what Your Prophet and Your Messenger and Your Closest Angels asked You, upon all of them Allāh's blessings, and I ask You for the sake of what all the Folk of Your obedience asked You, that You bless our master Muḥammad and the family of our master Muḥammad in all that You created before the sky was built and the earth was spread out and the mountains were made stable and the seas began to flow and the springs burst open and the rivers poured forth and the sun shone forth and the moon beamed and the planets were illuminated. ❋

(٢٦) اللَّهُمَّ صَلِّ عَلَى سَيِّدِنَا مُحَمَّدٍ وَعَلَى آلِ سَيِّدِنَا مُحَمَّدٍ عَدَدَ عِلْمِكَ وَصَلِّ عَلَى سَيِّدِنَا مُحَمَّدٍ وَعَلَى آلِ سَيِّدِنَا مُحَمَّدٍ عَدَدَ حِلْمِكَ وَصَلِّ عَلَى سَيِّدِنَا مُحَمَّدٍ وَعَلَى آلِ سَيِّدِنَا مُحَمَّدٍ عَدَدَ مَا أَحْصَاهُ اللَّوحُ المَحْفُوظُ مِنْ عِلْمِكَ وَصَلِّ عَلَى سَيِّدِنَا مُحَمَّدٍ وَعَلَى آلِ سَيِّدِنَا مُحَمَّدٍ عَدَدَ مَا جَرَى بِهِ القَلَمُ فِي أُمِّ الكِتَابِ عِنْدَكَ

(26) Allāhumma ṣalli ʿalā Sayyīdinā Muḥammadin wa ʿalā āli Sayyīdinā Muḥammadin ʿadada ʿilmika wa ṣalli ʿalā Sayyīdinā Muḥammadin wa ʿalā āli Sayyīdinā Muḥammadin ʿadada ḥilmika wa ṣalli ʿalā Sayyīdinā Muḥammadin wa ʿalā āli Sayyīdinā Muḥammadin ʿadada mā aḥṣāhu 'l-lawḥu 'l-maḥfūẓu min ʿilmika Allāhumma ṣalli ʿalā Sayyīdinā Muḥammadin wa ʿalā āli Sayyīdinā Muḥammadin ʿadada mā jarā bihi 'l-qalamu fī ummī 'l-kitābi ʿindaka

(26) O Allāh, exalt our master Muḥammad and the family of our master Muḥammad as much as Your Knowledge! O Allāh, exalt our master Muḥammad and the family of our master Muḥammad as much as Your forbearance! O Allāh, exalt our master Muḥammad and the family of our master Muḥammad as much as Your Knowledge is registered on the Preserved Table! O Allāh, exalt our master Muḥammad and the family of our master Muḥammad as much as the Pen has written in the Mother of Books lodged with You! ➢

وَصَلِّ عَلَى سَيِّدِنَا مُحَمَّدٍ وَعَلَى آلِ سَيِّدِنَا مُحَمَّدٍ مِلْءَ سَمَاوَاتِكَ وَصَلِّ عَلَى سَيِّدِنَا مُحَمَّدٍ وَعَلَى آلِ سَيِّدِنَا مُحَمَّدٍ مِلْءَ أَرْضِكَ وَصَلِّ عَلَى سَيِّدِنَا مُحَمَّدٍ وَعَلَى آلِ سَيِّدِنَا مُحَمَّدٍ مِلْءَ مَا أَنْتَ خَالِقُهُ مِنْ يَوْمِ خَلَقْتَ الدُّنْيَا إِلَى يَوْمِ الْقِيَامَةِ ❁

wa ṣalli 'alā Sayyīdinā Muḥammadin wa 'alā āli Sayyīdinā Muḥammadin mila' samāwātika wa ṣalli 'alā Sayyīdinā Muḥammadin wa 'alā āli Sayyīdinā Muḥammadin mila' arḍika wa ṣalli 'alā Sayyīdinā Muḥammadin wa 'alā āli Sayyīdinā Muḥammadin mila' mā anta khāliquhu min yawmi khalaqta 'd-dunyā ilā yawmi 'l-qīyāmati •

And exalt our master Muḥammad and the family of our master Muḥammad to the fullness of Your heavens and exalt our master Muḥammad and the family of our master Muḥammad to the fullness of Your earth and exalt our master Muḥammad and the family of our master Muḥammad in all that You have created from the Day You created this world until the Day of Resurrection! ❁

(٢٧) اللَّهُمَّ صَلِّ عَلَى سَيِّدِنَا مُحَمَّدٍ وَعَلَى آلِ سَيِّدِنَا مُحَمَّدٍ عَدَدَ صُفُوفِ الْمَلَائِكَةِ

(27) Allāhumma ṣalli 'alā Sayyīdinā Muḥammadin wa 'alā āli Sayyīdinā Muḥammadin 'adada ṣufūfi 'l-malā'ikati

(27) O Allāh, bless our master Muḥammad and the family of our master Muḥammad on the number of the ranks of the angels ➢

وَتَسْبِيحِهِمْ وَتَقْدِيسِهِمْ وَتَحْمِيدِهِمْ وَتَمْجِيدِهِمْ وَتَكْبِيرِهِمْ وَتَهْلِيلِهِمْ مِنْ يَوْمِ خَلَقْتَ الدُّنْيَا إِلَى يَوْمِ الْقِيَامَةِ ❋

wa tasbīḥihim wa taqdīsihim wa taḥmīdihim wa tamjīdihim wa takbīrihim wa tahlīlihim min yawmi khalaqta 'd-dunyā ilā yawmi 'l-qīyāmati •

and the count of their glorification, their sanctification, their praise, their magnification, their declarations of Your greatness and their declarations of Your Unity from the Day You created this world until the Day of Resurrection! ❋

(٢٨) اللَّهُمَّ صَلِّ عَلَى سَيِّدِنَا مُحَمَّدٍ وَعَلَى آلِ سَيِّدِنَا مُحَمَّدٍ عَدَدَ السَّحَابِ الْجَارِيَةِ وَالرِّيَاحِ الذَّارِيَةِ مِنْ يَوْمِ خَلَقْتَ الدُّنْيَا إِلَى يَوْمِ الْقِيَامَةِ ❋

(28) Allāhumma ṣalli ʿalā Sayyīdinā Muḥammadin wa ʿalā āli Sayyīdinā Muḥammadin ʿadada 's-saḥābi 'l-jārīyati wa 'r-riyāḥi 'dh-dhārīyati min yawmi khalaqta 'd-dunyā ilā yawmi 'l-qīyāmati •

(28) O Allāh, exalt our master Muḥammad and the family of our master Muḥammad on the number of every rolling cloud and sweeping wind from the Day You created this world until the Day of Resurrection! ❋

(٢٩) اللَّهُمَّ صَلِّ عَلَى سَيِّدِنَا مُحَمَّدٍ وَعَلَى آلِ سَيِّدِنَا مُحَمَّدٍ عَدَدَ كُلِّ قَطْرَةٍ تَقْطُرُ مِنْ سَمَاوَاتِكَ إِلَى أَرْضِكَ وَمَا تَقْطُرُ إِلَى يَوْمِ الْقِيَامَةِ ❋

(29) Allāhumma ṣalli ʿalā Sayyīdinā Muḥammadin wa ʿalā āli Sayyīdinā Muḥammadin ʿadada kulli qaṭratin taqṭuru min samāwātika ilā arḍika wa mā taqṭuru ilā yawmi 'l-qīyāmati •

(29) O Allāh, exalt our master Muḥammad and the family of our master Muḥammad in every drop of rain falling from the Your heavens to Your earth and in all the rain that will fall until the Day of Resurrection! ❋

(٣٠) اللَّهُمَّ صَلِّ عَلَى سَيِّدِنَا مُحَمَّدٍ وَعَلَى آلِ سَيِّدِنَا مُحَمَّدٍ عَدَدَ مَا هَبَّتْ الرِّيَاحُ وَعَدَدَ مَا تَحَرَّكَتِ الْأَشْجَارُ والْأَوْرَاقُ والزُّرُوعُ وَجَمِيعُ مَا خَلَقْتَ فِي قَرَارِ الحِفْظِ مِنْ يَوْمِ خَلَقْتَ الدُّنْيَا إِلَى يَوْمِ الْقِيَامَةِ ❋

(30) Allāhumma ṣalli ʿalā Sayyīdinā Muḥammadin wa ʿalā āli Sayyīdinā Muḥammadin ʿadada mā habbati 'r-rīyāḥu wa ʿadada mā taḥarrakati 'l-ashjāru wa 'l-awrāqu wa 'z-zurūʿu wa jamīʿu mā khalaqta fī qarāri 'l-ḥifẓi min yawmi khalaqta 'd-dunyā ilā yawmi 'l-qīyāmati •

(30) O Allāh, exalt our master Muḥammad on the count of movements of every branch, every tree, every leaf and every plant stirred by the wind and in the wind-stirred movement of everything else that You have created in the Abode of Safety from the Day You created the world up to the Day of Resurrection! ❋

(٣١) اللّٰهُمَّ صَلِّ عَلَى سَيِّدِنَا مُحَمَّدٍ وَعَلَى آلِ سَيِّدِنَا مُحَمَّدٍ عَدَدَ الْقَطْرِ وَالْمَطَرِ وَالنَّبَاتِ مِنْ يَوْمِ خَلَقْتَ الدُّنْيَا إِلَى يَوْمِ الْقِيَامَةِ ❋

(31) Allāhumma ṣalli ʿalā Sayyīdinā Muḥammadin wa ʿalā āli Sayyīdinā Muḥammadin ʿadada 'l-qaṭri wa 'l-maṭari wa 'n-nabāti min yawmi khalaqta 'd-dunyā ilā yawmi 'l-qīyāmati •

(31) O Allāh, exalt our master Muḥammad and the family of our master Muḥammad on the number every bead of dew, every drop of rain and every plant growing from the Day You created this world until the Day of Resurrection! ❋

(٣٢) اللّٰهُمَّ صَلِّ عَلَى سَيِّدِنَا مُحَمَّدٍ وَعَلَى آلِ سَيِّدِنَا مُحَمَّدٍ عَدَدَ النُّجُومِ فِي السَّمَاءِ مِنْ يَوْمِ خَلَقْتَ الدُّنْيَا إِلَى يَوْمِ الْقِيَامَةِ ❋

(32) Allāhumma ṣalli ʿalā Sayyīdinā Muḥammadin wa ʿalā āli Sayyīdinā Muḥammadin ʿadada 'n-nujūmu fī 's-samā'i min yawmi khalaqta 'd-dunyā ilā yawmi 'l-qīyāmati •

(32) O Allāh exalt our master Muḥammad and the family of our master Muḥammad on the count of every star in the sky from the Day You created this world until the Day of Resurrection. ❋

(٣٣) اللَّهُمَّ صَلِّ عَلَى سَيِّدِنَا مُحَمَّدٍ وَعَلَى آلِ سَيِّدِنَا مُحَمَّدٍ عَدَدَ مَا خَلَقْتَ فِي بِحَارِكَ السَّبْعَةِ مِمَّا لَا يَعْلَمُ عِلْمُهُ إِلَّا أَنْتَ وَمَا أَنْتَ خَالِقُهُ إِلَى يَوْمِ الْقِيَامَةِ ❋

(33) Allāhumma ṣalli ʿalā Sayyīdinā Muḥammadin wa ʿalā āli Sayyīdinā Muḥammadin ʿadada mā khalaqta fī biḥārika 's-sabʿati mimmā lā yāʿlamu ʿilmahū illā anta wa mā anta khāliquhū ilā yawmi 'l-qīyāmati •

(33) O Allāh, exalt our master Muḥammad and the family of our master Muḥammad on the number of what You have created in Your Seven Seas, knowledge of which is Yours alone, and as much as that which You will create until the Day of Resurrection! ❋

(٣٤) اللَّهُمَّ صَلِّ عَلَى سَيِّدِنَا مُحَمَّدٍ وَعَلَى آلِ سَيِّدِنَا مُحَمَّدٍ عَدَدَ الرَّمْلِ وَالْحَصَى فِي مَشَارِقِ الْأَرْضِ وَمَغَارِبِهَا

(34) Allāhumma ṣalli ʿalā Sayyīdinā Muḥammadin wa ʿalā āli Sayyīdinā Muḥammadin ʿadada 'r-ramli wa 'l-ḥaṣā fī mashāriqi 'l-arḍi wa maghāribihā

(34) O Allāh, exalt our master Muḥammad and the family of our master Muḥammad in every grain of sand and in every pebble on the earth, East and West! ➢

اللَّهُمَّ صَلِّ عَلَى سَيِّدِنَا مُحَمَّدٍ وَعَلَى آلِ سَيِّدِنَا مُحَمَّدٍ عَدَدَ مَا خَلَقْتَ مِنَ الجِنِّ وَالْإِنسِ وَمَا أَنْتَ خَالِقُهُ إِلَى يَوْمِ الْقِيَامَةِ ❋

Allāhumma ṣalli ʿalā Sayyīdinā Muḥammadin wa ʿalā āli Sayyīdinā Muḥammadin ʿadada mā khlaqta mina 'l-jinni wa 'l-insi wa mā anta khāliquhu ilā yawmi 'l-qīyāmati •

O Allāh, exalt our master Muḥammad and the family of our master Muḥammad on the number of every Jinn and every human being You have created and every one of them that You will create until the Day of Resurrection! ❋

(٣٥) اللَّهُمَّ صَلِّ عَلَى سَيِّدِنَا مُحَمَّدٍ وَعَلَى آلِ سَيِّدِنَا مُحَمَّدٍ عَدَدَ أَنْفَاسِهِمْ وَأَلْفَاظِهِمْ وَأَلْحَاظِهِمْ مِنْ يَوْمِ خَلَقْتَ الدُّنْيَا إِلَى يَوْمِ الْقِيَامَةِ ❋

(35) Allāhumma ṣalli ʿalā Sayyīdinā Muḥammadin wa ʿalā āli Sayyīdinā Muḥammadin ʿadada anfāsihim wa alfāẓihim wa alḥāẓihim min yawmi khalaqta 'd-dunyā ilā yawmi 'l-qīyāmati •

(35) O Allāh, exalt our master Muḥammad and the family of our master Muḥammad in every one of their breaths, their utterances and their glances from the Day You created this world until the Day of Resurrection! ❋

(٣٦) اللَّهُمَّ صَلِّ عَلَى سَيِّدِنَا مُحَمَّدٍ وَعَلَى آلِ سَيِّدِنَا مُحَمَّدٍ عَدَدَ طَيَرَانِ الْجِنِّ وَالْمَلَآئِكَةِ مِنْ يَوْمِ خَلَقْتَ الدُّنْيَا إِلَى يَوْمِ الْقِيَامَةِ ❋

(36) Allāhumma ṣalli 'alā Sayyīdinā Muḥammadin wa 'alā āli Sayyīdinā Muḥammadin 'adada ṭayarāni 'l-jinni wa 'l-malā'ikati min yawmi khalaqta 'd-dunyā ilā yawmi 'l-qīyāmati •

(36) O Allāh exalt our master Muḥammad and the family of our master Muḥammad in the flying of the Jinn and the angels from the Day You created this world until the Day of Resurrection! ❋

(٣٧) اللَّهُمَّ صَلِّ عَلَى سَيِّدِنَا مُحَمَّدٍ وَعَلَى آلِ سَيِّدِنَا مُحَمَّدٍ عَدَدَ الطُّيُورِ وَالْهَوَامِّ وَعَدَدَ الْوُحُوشِ وَالْآكَامِ فِي مَشَارِقِ الْأَرْضِ وَمَغَارِبِهَا

(37) Allāhumma ṣalli 'alā Sayyīdinā Muḥammadin wa 'alā āli Sayyīdinā Muḥammadin 'adada 'ṭ-ṭuyūri wa 'l-hawāmmi wa 'adada 'l-wuḥūshi wa 'l-ākāmi fī mashāriqi 'l-arḍi wa maghāribihā

(37) O Allāh, exalt Our master Muḥammad and the family of our master Muḥammad in every bird and pest, in every wild beast and in every hill on earth, East and West! ➢

اللَّهُمَّ صَلِّ عَلَى سَيِّدِنَا مُحَمَّدٍ وَعَلَى آلِ سَيِّدِنَا مُحَمَّدٍ عَدَدَ الْأَحْيَاءِ وَالْأَمْوَاتِ اللَّهُمَّ صَلِّ عَلَى سَيِّدِنَا مُحَمَّدٍ وَعَلَى آلِ سَيِّدِنَا مُحَمَّدٍ عَدَدَ مَا أَظْلَمَ عَلَيْهِ اللَّيْلُ وَمَا أَشْرَقَ عَلَيْهِ النَّهَارُ مِنْ يَوْمِ خَلَقْتَ الدُّنْيَا إِلَى يَوْمِ الْقِيَامَةِ ❁

Allāhumma ṣalli ʿalā Sayyīdinā Muḥammadin wa ʿalā āli Sayyīdinā Muḥammadin ʿadada 'l-aḥyā'i wa 'l-amwāti Allāhumma ṣalli ʿalā Sayyīdinā Muḥammadin wa ʿalā āli Sayyīdinā Muḥammadin ʿadada mā aẓlama ʿalayhi 'l-laylu wa ashraqa ʿalayhi 'n-nahāru min yawmi khalaqta 'd-dunyā ilā yawmi 'l-qīyāmati •

O Allāh, exalt our master Muḥammad and the family of our master Muḥammad in the living and the dead! O Allāh, exalt our master Muḥammad as much as the night has covered with darkness and as much as the day has illuminated from the Day You created this world until the Day of Resurrection! ❁

(٣٨) اللَّهُمَّ صَلِّ عَلَى سَيِّدِنَا مُحَمَّدٍ وَعَلَى آلِ سَيِّدِنَا مُحَمَّدٍ عَدَدَ مَنْ يَمْشِي عَلَى رِجْلَيْنِ وَمَنْ يَمْشِي عَلَى أَرْبَعٍ مِنْ يَوْمِ خَلَقْتَ الدُّنْيَا إِلَى يَوْمِ الْقِيَامَةِ ❁

(38) Allāhumma ṣalli ʿalā Sayyīdinā Muḥammadin wa ʿalā āli Sayyīdinā Muḥammadin ʿadada man-yamshī ʿalā rijlayni wa man yamshī ʿalā arbaʿin min yawmi khalaqta 'd-dunyā ilā yawmi 'l-qīyāmati •

(38) O Allāh, exalt our master Muḥammad and the family of our master Muḥammad on the count of every two-legged creature and every four-legged one from the Day You created this world until the Day of Resurrection! ❁

(٣٩) اللَّهُمَّ صَلِّ عَلَى سَيِّدِنَا مُحَمَّدٍ وَعَلَى آلِ سَيِّدِنَا مُحَمَّدٍ عَدَدَ مَنْ صَلَّى عَلَيْهِ مِنَ الْجِنِّ وَالْإِنْسِ وَالْمَلَآئِكَةِ مِنْ يَوْمِ خَلَقْتَ الدُّنْيَا إِلَى يَوْمِ الْقِيَامَةِ ❋

(39) Allāhumma ṣalli ʿalā Sayyīdinā Muḥammadin wa ʿalā āli Sayyīdinā Muḥammadin ʿadada man ṣalla ʿalayhi mina 'l-jinni wa 'l-insi wa 'l-malā'ikati min yawmi khalaqta 'd-dunyā ilā yawmi 'l-qīyāmati •

(39) O Allāh, exalt our master Muḥammad and the family of our master Muḥammad as many times as the jinn, the human beings and the angels have asked You to exalt him from the Day You created this world until the Day of Resurrection! ❋

(٤٠) اللَّهُمَّ صَلِّ عَلَى سَيِّدِنَا مُحَمَّدٍ وَعَلَى آلِ سَيِّدِنَا مُحَمَّدٍ عَدَدَ مَنْ يُصَلِّي عَلَيْهِ اللَّهُمَّ صَلِّ عَلَى سَيِّدِنَا مُحَمَّدٍ وَعَلَى آلِ سَيِّدِنَا مُحَمَّدٍ عَدَدَ مَنْ لَمْ يُصَلِّ عَلَيْهِ

(40) Allāhumma ṣalli ʿalā Sayyīdinā Muḥammadin wa ʿalā āli Sayyīdinā Muḥammadin ʿadada man yuṣallī ʿalayhi Allāhumā ṣalli ʿalā Sayyīdinā Muḥammadin wa ʿalā āli Sayyīdinā Muḥammadin ʿadada man lam yuṣalli ʿalayhi

(40) O Allāh, exalt our master Muḥammad and the family of our master Muḥammad on the count of those who invoked blessings upon him, and, O Allāh, exalt our master Muḥammad and the family of our master Muḥammad on the count of those who have not asked for blessings upon him. ➢

اللَّهُمَّ صَلِّ عَلَى سَيِّدِنَا مُحَمَّدٍ وَعَلَى آلِ سَيِّدِنَا مُحَمَّدٍ كَمَا يَجِبُ أَنْ يُصَلَّى عَلَيهِ اللَّهُمَّ صَلِّ عَلَى سَيِّدِنَا مُحَمَّدٍ وَعَلَى آلِ سَيِّدِنَا مُحَمَّدٍ كَمَا يَنْبَغِي أَنْ يُصَلَّى عَلَيهِ اللَّهُمَّ صَلِّ عَلَى سَيِّدِنَا مُحَمَّدٍ وَعَلَى آلِ سَيِّدِنَا مُحَمَّدٍ حَتَّى لَا يَبْقَى شَيءٌ مِنَ الصَّلَاةِ عَلَيهِ ❋

Allāhumma ṣalli ʿalā Sayyīdinā Muḥammadin wa ʿalā āli Sayyīdinā Muḥammadin kamā yajibu an yuṣallā ʿalayhi Allāhumma ṣalli ʿalā Sayyīdinā Muḥammadin wa ʿalā āli Sayyīdinā Muḥammadin kamā yambaghī an yuṣalla ʿalayhi Allāhumma ṣalli ʿalā Sayyīdinā Muḥammadin wa ʿalā āli Sayyīdinā Muḥammadin ḥattā lā yabqā shayun mina 'ṣ-ṣalāti ʿalayhi •

O Allāh, exalt our master Muḥammad and the family of our master Muḥammad as it is incumbent upon us to invoke Your blessings on him. O Allāh, exalt our master Muḥammad and the family of our master Muḥammad as it is fitting for him. O Allāh, exalt our master Muḥammad and the family of our master Muḥammad until not one thing remains from praises and blessings on him. ❋

(٤١)اللَّهُمَّ صَلِّ عَلَى سَيِّدِنَا مُحَمَّدٍ فِي الْأَوَّلِينَ

(41) Allāhumma ṣalli ʿalā Sayyīdinā Muḥammadin fī 'l-awwalīn

(41) O Allāh, exalt our master Muḥammad among the firsts. ➢

وَصَلِّ عَلَى سَيِّدِنَا مُحَمَّدٍ فِي الْآخِرِينَ اللَّهُمَّ صَلِّ عَلَى سَيِّدِنَا مُحَمَّدٍ فِي الْمَلَإِ الْأَعْلَى إِلَى يَوْمِ الدِّين مَا شَاءَ اللهُ لَا قُوَّةَ إِلَّا بِاللهِ الْعَلِيِّ الْعَظِيمِ ❋

wa ṣalli ʿalā Sayyīdinā Muḥammadin fī 'l-'ākhirīn Allāhumma ṣalli ʿalā Sayyīdinā Muḥammadin fī 'l-malā'i 'l-āʿlā ilā yawmi 'd-dīni mā shā'a 'Llāhu lā quwwata illā bi-'Llāhi 'l-ʿAlīyyi 'l-ʿAẓīmi •

O Allāh, exalt our master Muḥammad among the lasts. O Allāh, exalt our master Muḥammad in the Heavenly Assembly until the Day of Reckoning and as much as Allāh Wills.There is no might and no power save through Allāh The High, The Tremendous. ❋

الحِزْبُ ٱلسَّادِسُ فِي يَوْمِ السَّبْتِ

Saturday

Al-Ḥizbu 's-Sādisu fī Yawmi 's-Sabt

The Sixth Chapter on Saturday

(١) اللَّهُمَّ صَلِّ عَلَى سَيِّدِنَا مُحَمَّدٍ وَعَلَى آلِ سَيِّدِنَا مُحَمَّدٍ وَأَعْطِهِ الْوَسِيلَةَ وَالْفَضِيلَةَ وَالدَّرَجَةَ الرَّفِيعَةَ وَابْعَثْهُ مَقَاماً مَحْمُوداً الَّذِي وَعَدْتَهُ إِنَّكَ لَا تُخْلِفُ الْمِيعَادَ اللَّهُمَّ عَظِّمْ شَأْنَهُ وَبَيِّنْ بُرْهَانَهُ وَأَبْلِجْ حُجَّتَهُ وَبَيِّنْ فَضِيلَتَهُ وَتَقَبَّلْ شَفَاعَتَهُ فِي أُمَّتِهِ وَاسْتَعْمِلْنَا بِسُنَّتِهِ يَا رَبَّ الْعَالَمِينَ وَيَا رَبَّ الْعَرْشِ الْعَظِيمِ

Allāhumma ṣalli ʿalā Sayyīdinā Muḥammadin wa ʿalā āli Sayyīdinā Muḥammadin wa āʿṭihi 'l-wasīlata wa 'l-faḍīlata wa 'd-darajata 'r-rafīʿata wa 'bʿath-hu 'l-maqāma 'l-Maḥmūda 'Lladhī waʿadtahū innaka lā tukhlifu 'l-mīʿād Allāhumma aʿẓẓim sha'nahu wa bayyin burhānahu wa ablij ḥujjatahu wa bayyin faḍīlatahu wa taqabbal shafāʿatahu fī ummatihi wa 'staʿmilnā bi sunnatihi yā Rabba 'l-ʿālamīn wa yā Rabba 'l-ʿarshi 'l-ʿaẓīm

O Allāh, exalt our master Muḥammad and the family of Muḥammad, and grant him with the Closest Access, the Pre-eminence, the Lofty Rank, and send him to the Most-Praised Station which You promised him for You do not break Your Word! O Allāh, magnify his value, clarify his argument, embellish his proof, makes evident his excellence and accept his intercession for his Nation and establish us on his way, O Lord of the Worlds and O Lord of the Tremendous Throne. ➤

اللَّهُمَّ يَا رَبِّ احْشُرْنَا فِي زُمْرَتِهِ وَتَحْتَ لِوَائِهِ وَاسْقِنَا بِكَأْسِهِ وَانْفَعْنَا بِمَحَبَّتِهِ آمِين يَا رَبَّ الْعَالَمِينَ اللَّهُمَّ يَا رَبِّ بَلِّغْهُ عَنَّا أَفْضَلَ السَّلَام وَاجْزِهِ عَنَّا أَفْضَلَ مَا جَازَيْتَ بِهِ نَبِيّاً عَنْ أُمَّتِهِ يَا رَبَّ الْعَالَمِينَ اللَّهُمَّ يَا رَبِّ إِنِّي أَسْأَلُكَ أَنْ تَغْفِرَ لِي وَتَرْحَمَنِي وَتَتُوبَ عَلَيَّ وَتُعَافِيَنِي مِنْ جَمِيعِ الْبَلَاءِ وَالْبَلْوَاءِ الْخَارِجِ مِنَ الْأَرْضِ وَالنَّازِلِ مِنَ السَّمَاءِ إِنَّكَ عَلَى كُلِّ شَيْءٍ قَدِيرٌ بِرَحْمَتِكَ

Allāhumma yā rabbī 'ḥ-shurnā fī zumratihi wa taḥta liwā'ihi wa 'sqinā bika'sihi wa 'nfaʿnā bi-maḥabbatihi āmīn yā Rabba 'l-ʿālamīn Allāhumma yā rabbī balligh-hu ʿannā afḍala 's-salām wa 'jzihi ʿannā afḍala mā jāzayta bihi nabīyyan ʿan ummatihi yā Rabba 'l-ʿālamīn Allāhumma yā rabbī innī as'aluka an taghfira lī wa tarḥamanī wa tatūba ʿalayya wa tuʿafīyanī min jamīʿi 'l-balā'i wa 'l-balwā'i 'l-khāriji mina 'l-arḍi wa 'n-nāzili mina 's-samā'i innaka ʿalā kulli shayin qadīr bi raḥmatika

O Allāh, our Lord, gather us in his company and beneath his flag, let us drink from his drinking bowl and avail us of his love, Amen, O Allāh, Lord of the Worlds! O Allāh, the Lord, bestow upon him, on our behalf, a better reward than You have bestowed upon any Prophet on behalf of his Nation, O Allāh, Lord of the Worlds. O Allāh, O my Lord, I beseech You to forgive me, have mercy on me, accept my repentance and remove from me all trials and tribulations, earthly and heavenly, for You have power over all things, through Your Mercy ➢

وَأَنْ تَغْفِرَ لِلْمُؤْمِنِينَ وَالْمُؤْمِنَاتِ وَالْمُسْلِمِينَ وَالْمُسْلِمَاتِ الْأَحْيَاءِ مِنْهُمْ وَالْأَمْوَاتِ وَرَضِيَ اللهُ عَنْ أَزْوَاجِهِ الطَّاهِرَاتِ أُمَّهَاتِ الْمُؤْمِنِينَ وَرَضِيَ اللهُ عَنْ أَصْحَابِهِ الْأَعْلَامِ أَئِمَّةِ الْهُدَى وَمَصَابِيحِ الدُّنْيَا وَعَنِ التَّابِعِينَ وَتَابِعِ التَّابِعِينَ لَهُمْ بِإِحْسَانٍ إِلَى يَوْمِ الدِّينِ وَالْحَمْدُ للهِ رَبِّ الْعَالَمِينَ ❁

wa an taghfira li ʾl-muʾminīna wa ʾl-muʾmināti wa ʾl-muslimīna wa ʾl-muslimāti ʾl-aḥyāʾi minhum wa ʾl-amwāti wa raḍīya ʾLlāhu ʿan azwājihi ʾṭ-ṭāhirāti ummahāti ʾl-muʾminīna wa raḍīya ʾLlāhu ʿan aṣḥābihi ʾl-āʿlāmi aʾimmati ʾl-hudā wa māṣabīḥi ʾd-dunyā wa ʿani ʾt-tābiʿīna wa tābiʿi ʾt-tābiʿīna lahum bi iḥsānin ilā yawmi ʾd-dīni wa ʾl-ḥamdu liʾLlāhi Rabbi ʾl-ʿālamīn •

and for You to forgive the believing men and women and the Muslim men and women, the living and the dead, and the Pleasure of Allāh ﷻ be upon his pure wives, the Mothers of the Believers, and the pleasure of Allāh ﷻ be upon his Companions, the Eminent Leaders of Guidance and Lamps of this Lower Life, and also with the Successors and the Successors of the Successors, salutations upon them until the Day of Resurrection, and praise be to Allāh ﷻ the Lord of Worlds! ❁

إِبْتِدَاءُ الثُّلُثِ الثَّالِثِ

Ibtidā'u 'th-Thuluthi 'th-Thālithi

Beginning of the Third Third

(٢) اللَّهُمَّ رَبَّ الأَرْوَاحِ وَالأَجسَادِ الْبَالِيَةِ أَسْأَلُكَ بِطَاعَةِ الأَرْوَاحِ الرَّاجِعَةِ إِلَى أَجْسَادِهَا وَبِطَاعَةِ الأَجْسَادِ الْمُلْتَئِمَةِ بِعُرُوقِهَا وَبِكَلِمَاتِكَ النَّافِذَةِ فِيهِمْ وَأَخْذِكَ الْحَقَّ مِنْهُمْ وَالْخَلَائِقُ بَيْنَ يَدَيْكَ يَنْتَظِرُونَ فَصْلَ قَضَائِكَ وَيَرْجُونَ رَحْمَتَكَ وَيَخَافُونَ عِقَابَكَ

(2) Allāhumma Rabba 'l-arwāḥi wa 'l-ajsādi 'l-bālīyati as'aluka biṭā'ati 'l-arwāḥi 'r-raji'ati ilā ajsādihā wa biṭā'ati 'l-ajsādi 'l-multa'imati bi 'urūqihā wa bi kalimātika 'n-nāfidhāti fīhim wa akhdhika 'l-ḥaqqa minhum wa 'l-khalā'iqu bayna yadayka yantaẓirūna faṣla qaḍā'ika wa yarjūna raḥmataka wa yakhāfūna 'iqābaka

(2) O Allāh, Lord of souls and mortal flesh, I ask You for the sake of the obedience of souls returning to their bodies (on the Day for Resurrection), and for the sake of the obedience of bodies becoming whole once again, and for the sake of Your Words which will order this and for the sake of Your exacting of Your rights over them, and for the sake of Your creatures who are before You waiting for the apportioning of Your decree, hoping for Your Mercy and fearing Your punishment, ➢

أَنْ تَجْعَلَ النُّورَ فِي بَصَرِي وَذِكْرَكَ بِاللَّيلِ وَالنَّهَارِ عَلَى لِسَانِي وَعَمَلاً صَالِحاً فَارْزُقنِي ❁

an taj'alā 'n-nūra fī baṣarī wa dhikraka bi 'l-layli wa 'n-nahāri 'alā lisānī wa 'amalan ṣāliḥan fa 'rzuqnī •

I ask You that bestow light in my eyes, remembrance of You during the day and the light upon my tongue, and provide me with good actions. ❁

(٣) اللَّهُمَّ صَلِّ عَلَى سَيِّدِنَا مُحَمَّدٍ كَمَا صَلَّيْتَ عَلَى سَيِّدِنَا إِبْرَاهِيمَ وَبَارِكْ عَلَى سَيِّدِنَا مُحَمَّدٍ كَمَا بَارَكْتَ عَلَى سَيِّدِنَا إِبْرَاهِيمَ اللَّهُمَّ اجْعَلْ صَلَوَاتِكَ وَبَرَكَاتِكَ عَلَى سَيِّدِنَا مُحَمَّدٍ وَعَلَى آلِ سَيِّدِنَا مُحَمَّدٍ

(3) Allāhumma ṣalli 'alā Sayyīdinā Muḥammadin kamā ṣallayta 'alā Sayyīdinā Ibrāhīma wa bārik 'alā Sayyīdinā Muḥammadin kamā bārakta 'alā Sayyīdinā Ibrāhīma Allāhumma 'ja'al ṣalawātika wa barakātika 'alā Sayyīdinā Muḥammadin wa 'alā āli Sayyīdinā Muḥammadin

(3) O Allāh, exalt our master Muḥammad just as You exalted our master Abraham and bless our master Muḥammad just as You blessed our master Abraham! O Allāh, grant Your blessings and Your favors to our master Muḥammad and the family of our master Muḥammad ➢

كَمَا جَعَلْتَهَا عَلَى سَيِّدِنَا إِبْرَاهِيمَ وَعَلَى آلِ سَيِّدِنَا إِبْرَاهِيمَ إِنَّكَ حَمِيدٌ مَجِيدٌ
وَبَارِكْ عَلَى سَيِّدِنَا مُحَمَّدٍ وَعَلَى آلِ سَيِّدِنَا مُحَمَّدٍ كَمَا بَارَكْتَ عَلَى سَيِّدِنَا إبراهِيمَ
وَعَلَى آلِ سَيِّدِنَا إِبْرَاهِيمَ إِنَّكَ حَمِيدٌ مَجِيدٌ ❁

kamā jaʿaltahā ʿalā Sayyīdinā Ibrāhīma wa ʿalā āli Sayyīdinā Ibrāhīma innaka Ḥamīdun Majīdwa bārik ʿalā Sayyīdinā Muḥammadin wa ʿalā āli Sayyīdinā Muḥammadin kamā bārakta ʿalā Sayyīdinā Ibrāhīma wa ʿalā āli Sayyīdinā Ibrāhīma innaka Ḥamīdun Majīd •

just as You granted them to our master Abraham and the family of our master Abraham, for You are The Praiseworthy, The Mighty and bless our master Muḥammad and the family of our master Muḥammad just as You blessed our master Abraham and the family of our master Abraham, for You are The Praiseworthy, The Mighty! ❁

(٤) اللَّهُمَّ صَلِّ عَلَى سَيِّدِنَا مُحَمَّدٍ عَبْدِكَ وَرَسُولِكَ وَصَلِّ عَلَى الْمُؤْمِنِينَ
وَالْمُؤْمِنَاتِ وَالْمُسْلِمِينَ وَالْمُسْلِمَاتِ ❁

(4) Allāhumma ṣalli ʿalā Sayyīdinā Muḥammadin ʿabdika wa rasūlika wa ṣalli ʿalā 'l-mu'minīna wa 'l-mu'mināti wa 'l-muslimīna wa 'l-muslimāti •

(4) O Allāh, exalt our master Muḥammad, Your Servant and Your Messenger, and bless the believing men and women and Muslim men and women! ❁

(٥) اللَّهُمَّ صَلِّ عَلَى سَيِّدِنَا مُحَمَّدٍ وَعَلَى آلِهِ عَدَدَ مَا أَحَاطَ بِهِ عِلْمُكَ وَأَحْصَاهُ كِتَابُكَ وَشَهِدَتْ بِهِ مَلَآئِكَتُكَ صَلَاةً دَائِمَةً تَدُومُ بِدَوَامِ مُلْكِ اللهِ ❋

(5) Allāhumma ṣalli ʿalā Sayyīdinā Muḥammadin wa ʿalā ālihi ʿadada mā aḥāṭa bihi ʿilmuka wa aḥṣāhu kitābuka wa shahidat bihi malā'ikatuka ṣalātan dā'imatan tadūmu bi dawāmi mulki 'Llāhi •

(5) O Allāh, exalt our master Muḥammad and his family as much as all that is encompassed by Your Knowledge, all that is contained in Your Book and all that is witnessed by Your angels, blessings which are eternal and which endures as long as Allāh's Kingdom endures! ❋

(٦) اللَّهُمَّ إِنِّي أَسْأَلُكَ بِأَسْمَائِكَ الْعِظَامِ مَا عَلِمْتُ مِنْهَا وَمَا لَمْ أَعْلَمْ وَبِالْأَسْمَاءِ الَّتِي سَمَّيتَ بِهَا نَفْسَكَ مَا عَلِمْتُ مِنْهَا وَمَا لَمْ أَعْلَمْ أَنْ تُصَلِّيَ عَلَى سَيِّدِنَا مُحَمَّدٍ

(6) Allāhumma innī as'aluka bi asmā'ika 'l-ʿiẓāmi mā ʿalimtu minhā wa mā lam aʿlam wa bi 'l-asmā'i 'l-latī sammayta bihā nafsaka mā ʿalimtu minhā wa mā lam āʿlam an tuṣallīya ʿalā Sayyīdinā Muḥammadin

(6) I beseech You by Your Greatest Names, those, which I know and those which I do not know, and by the Names that You have named Yourself, Names I know not and Names I shall never know, that You exalt our master Muḥammad, ➤

عَبْدِكَ وَنَبِيِّكَ وَرَسُولِكَ عَدَدَ مَا خَلَقْتَ مِنْ قَبْلِ أَنْ تَكُونَ السَّمَاءُ مَبْنِيَّةً وَالْأَرْضُ مَدْحِيَّةً وَالْجِبَالُ مُرْسِيَةً وَالعُيونُ مُنْفَجِرَةً وَالْأَنْهَارُ مُنْهَمِرَةً وَالشَّمْسُ مُشْرِقَةً وَالقَمَرُ مُضِيئاً وَالكَواكِبُ مُسْتَنِيرَةً وَالبِحَارُ مَجْرِيَّةً وَالْأَشْجَارُ مُثْمِرَةً ❋

'abdika wa nabīyyika wa rasūlika 'adada mā khalaqta min qabli an takūna 's-samā'u mabnīyyatan wa 'l-arḍu madḥīyyatan wa 'l-jibālu mursīyyatan wa 'l-'uyūnu munfajiratan wa 'l-anhāru munhamiratan wa 'sh-shamsu mushriqatan wa 'l-qamaru muḍīyan wa 'l-kawākibu mustanīratan wa 'l-bihāru mujrīyyatan wa 'l-ashjāru muthmiratan •

Your Servant, Your Prophet, and Your Messenger, in all that You created before the sky was built and the earth was spread out and the mountains were anchored down and the springs burst forth and the river flowed out and the sun blazed forth and the moon shone forth and the planets illuminated the sky and the oceans began to flow and the trees gave their fruit. ❋

(٧) اللَّهُمَّ صَلِّ عَلَى سَيِّدِنَا مُحَمَّدٍ عَدَدَ عِلْمِكَ وَصَلِّ عَلَى سَيِّدِنَا مُحَمَّدٍ عَدَدَ حِلْمِكَ

(7) Allāhumma ṣalli 'alā Sayyīdinā Muḥammadin 'adada 'ilmika wa ṣalli 'alā Sayyīdinā Muḥammadin 'adada ḥīlmika

(7) O Allāh, exalt our master Muḥammad to the extent Of Your Knowledge! O Allāh, exalt our master Muḥammad to the extent of Your forbearance! ➤

وَصَلِّ عَلَى سَيِّدِنَا مُحَمَّدٍ عَدَدَ كَلِمَاتِكَ وَصَلِّ عَلَى سَيِّدِنَا مُحَمَّدٍ عَدَدَ نِعْمَتِكَ وَصَلِّ عَلَى سَيِّدِنَا مُحَمَّدٍ عَدَدَ فَضْلِكَ وَصَلِّ عَلَى سَيِّدِنَا مُحَمَّدٍ عَدَدَ جُودِكَ وَصَلِّ عَلَى سَيِّدِنَا مُحَمَّدٍ عَدَدَ سَمَاوَاتِكَ وَصَلِّ عَلَى سَيِّدِنَا مُحَمَّدٍ عَدَدَ أَرْضِكَ وَصَلِّ عَلَى سَيِّدِنَا مُحَمَّدٍ عَدَدَ مَا خَلَقْتَ فِي سَبْعِ سَمَاوَاتِكَ مِنْ مَلَآئِكَتِكَ وَصَلِّ عَلَى سَيِّدِنَا مُحَمَّدٍ عَدَدَ مَا خَلَقْتَ فِي أَرْضِكَ مِنَ الْجِنِّ وَالْإِنْسِ وَغَيْرِهِمَا

wa ṣalli ʻalā Sayyīdinā Muḥammadin ʻadada kalimātika wa ṣalli ʻalā Sayyīdinā Muḥammadin ʻadada niʻmatika wa ṣalli ʻalā Sayyīdinā Muḥammadin ʻadada jūdika wa ṣalli ʻalā Sayyīdinā Muḥammadin ʻadada samāwātika wa ṣalli ʻalā Sayyīdinā Muḥammadin ʻadada arḍika wa ṣalli ʻalā Sayyīdinā Muḥammadin ʻadada mā khalaqta fī sabʻi samāwātika min malā'ikatika wa ṣalli ʻalā Sayyīdinā Muḥammadin ʻadada mā khalaqta fī arḍika mina 'l-Jinni wa 'l-insi wa ghayrihimā

O Allāh, exalt our master Muḥammad on the number of Your Words! O Allāh, exalt our master Muḥammad as the number of Your Favors! O Allāh, exalt our master Muḥammad to the extent of Your Grace! O Allāh, exalt our master Muḥammad to the extent of Your Generosity! O Allāh, exalt our master Muḥammad to the extent of Your Heavens! O Allāh, exalt our master Muḥammad to the extent of Your Earth! O Allāh, exalt our master Muḥammad on the number of all the angels You have created in Your Seven Heavens! O Allāh, exalt our master on the number of all the Jinn and humans and beings other than them, ➢

مِنَ الْوَحْشِ وَالطَّيرِ وَغَيرِهِمَا وَصَلِّ عَلَى سَيِّدِنَا مُحَمَّدٍ عَدَدَ مَا جَرَى بِهِ الْقَلَمُ فِي عِلْمِ غَيبِكَ وَمَا يَجْرِي بِهِ إِلَى يَوْمِ الْقِيَامَةِ وَصَلِّ عَلَى سَيِّدِنَا مُحَمَّدٍ عَدَدَ الْقَطْرِ وَالمَطَرِ وَصَلِّ عَلَى سَيِّدِنَا مُحَمَّدٍ عَدَدَ مَنْ يَحْمَدُكَ وَيَشْكُرُكَ وَيُهَلِّلُكَ وَيُمَجِّدُكَ وَيَشْهَدُ أَنَّكَ أَنْتَ اللهُ وَصَلِّ عَلَى سَيِّدِنَا مُحَمَّدٍ عَدَدَ مَا صَلَّيْتَ عَلَيهِ أَنْتَ وَمَلَآئِكَتُكَ

mina 'l-waḥshi wa 'ṭ-ṭayri wa ghayrihimā wa ṣalli ʿalā Sayyīdinā Muḥammadin ʿadada mā jarā bihi 'l-qalamu fī ʿilmi ghaybika wa mā yajrī bihi ilā yawmi 'l-qīyāmati wa ṣalli ʿalā Sayyīdinā Muḥammadin ʿadada 'l-qaṭri wa 'l-maṭari wa ṣalli ʿalā Sayyīdinā Muḥammadin ʿadada man yaḥmaduka wa yashkuruka wa yuhalliluka wa yumajjiduka wa yashhadu annaka anta 'Llāhu wa ṣalli ʿalā Sayyīdinā Muḥammadin ʿadada mā ṣallayta ʿalayhi anta wa malā'ikatuka

and beast and the birds, and beings other then them, that You have Created on Your earth and exalt our master Muḥammad as much as all that the Pen has written of Knowledge of the Unseen and in all that the Pen will write until the Day of Resurrection and bless our master Muḥammad as the number of every dewdrop and every raindrop and exalt our master Muḥammad as often as You are praised, as often as You are thanked, as often as Your Unity is declared, as often as You are magnified, as often as it is witnessed that You are indeed Allāh and bless our master Muḥammad as many times as You and Your angels have invoked blessings on him! ➢

وَصَلِّ عَلَى سَيِّدِنَا مُحَمَّدٍ عَدَدَ مَنْ صَلَّى عَلَيهِ مِنْ خَلْقِكَ وَصَلِّ عَلَى سَيِّدِنَا مُحَمَّدٍ عَدَدَ مَنْ لَمْ يُصَلِّ عَلَيهِ مِنْ خَلْقِكَ وَصَلِّ عَلَى سَيِّدِنَا مُحَمَّدٍ عَدَدَ الْجِبَالِ وَالرِّمَالِ وَالْحَصَى وَصَلِّ عَلَى سَيِّدِنَا مُحَمَّدٍ عَدَدَ الشَّجَرِ وَأَوْرَاقِهَا وَالْمَدَرِ وَأَثْقَالِهَا وَصَلِّ عَلَى سَيِّدِنَا مُحَمَّدٍ عَدَدَ كُلِّ سَنَةٍ وَمَا تَخْلُقُ فِيهَا وَمَا يَمُوتُ فِيهَا وَصَلِّ عَلَى سَيِّدِنَا مُحَمَّدٍ عَدَدَ مَا تَخْلُقُ كُلَّ يَوْمٍ وَمَا يَمُوتُ إِلَى يَوْمِ الْقِيَامَةِ ❋

wa ṣalli ʿalā Sayyīdinā Muḥammadin ʿadada man ṣalla ʿalayhi min khalqika wa ṣalli ʿalā Sayyīdinā Muḥammadin ʿadada man lam yuṣalli ʿalayhi min khalqika wa ṣalli ʿalā Sayyīdinā Muḥammadin ʿadad 'l-jibāli wa 'r-rimāli wa 'l-ḥaṣā wa ṣalli ʿalā Sayyīdinā Muḥammadin ʿadada 'sh-shajāri wa awrāqihā wa 'l-madari wa athqāliha wa ṣalli ʿalā Sayyīdinā Muḥammadin ʿadada kulli sanatin wa mā takhluqu fīhā wa mā yamūtu fīhā wa ṣalli ʿalā Sayyīdinā Muḥammadin ʿadada mā takhluqu kulla yawmin wa mā yamūtu ilā yawmi 'l-qīyāmati •

And exalt our master Muḥammad as many times as all those from Your Creation invoked blessings on him and as many times as all those who have not sought blessings on him and exalt our master Muḥammad on the number of every mountain, of every grain of sand and of every stone and exalt our master Muḥammad on the count of the trees and each of their leaves and on the amount of soil and its weight and exalt our master Muḥammad on the number of years and whatever You have created in them and those who died in them and exalt our master Muḥammad in all You create every day and in all that dies as well, until the Day of Rising! ❋

(٨) اللَّهُمَّ وَصَلِّ عَلَى سَيِّدِنَا مُحَمَّدٍ عَدَدَ السَّحَابِ الْجَارِيَةِ مَا بَيْنَ السَّمَاءِ وَ الْأَرْضِ وَمَا تَمْطُرُ مِنَ الْمِيَاهِ وَصَلِّ عَلَى سَيِّدِنَا مُحَمَّدٍ عَدَدَ الرِّيَاحِ الْمُسَخَّرَاتِ فِي مَشَارِقِ الْأَرْضِ وَمَغَارِبِهَا وَجَوفِهَا وَقِبْلَتِهَا وَصَلِّ عَلَى سَيِّدِنَا مُحَمَّدٍ عَدَدَ نُجُومِ السَّمَاءِ وَصَلِّ عَلَى سَيِّدِنَا مُحَمَّدٍ عَدَدَ مَا خَلَقْتَ فِي بِحَارِكَ مِنَ الْحِيتَانِ وَالدَّوَابِّ وَالْمِيَاهِ وَالرِّمَالَ وَغَيرِ ذَلِكَ وَصَلِّ عَلَى سَيِّدِنَا مُحَمَّدٍ عَدَدَ النَّبَاتِ وَالْحَصَى

(8) Allāhumma wa ṣalli ʿalā Sayyīdinā Muḥammadin ʿadada 's-sahābi 'l-jārīyati mā bayna 's-samā'i wa 'l-arḍi wa mā tamṭuru mina 'l-mīyāh wa ṣalli ʿalā Sayyīdinā Muḥammadin ʿadada 'r-rīyāḥi 'l-musakh-kharāti fī mashāriqi 'l-arḍi wa maghāribihā wa jawfihā wa qiblatihā wa ṣalli ʿalā Sayyīdinā Muḥammadin ʿadada nujūmi 's-samā'i wa ṣalli ʿalā Sayyīdinā Muḥammadin ʿadada mā khalaqta fī biḥārika mina 'l-ḥītāni wa 'd-dawābbi wa 'l-mīyāhi wa 'r-rimāli wa ghayri dhālika wa ṣalli ʿalā Sayyīdinā Muḥammadin ʿadada 'n-nabāti wa 'l-ḥaṣā

(8) And exalt our master Muḥammad in every clouds sailing between the Heavens and the Earth and in every drop of their rain and exalt our master Muḥammad in every Swirling wind in the East of the Earth and in the West, in the North and in the South and exalt our master Muḥammad as many times as there are stars in the sky and exalt our master Muḥammad as many times as all the fish and all the creatures in the sea and all the water and all the grains of sand and whatever else there is and exalt our master Muḥammad in every plant and in every stone ➢

وَصَلِّ عَلَى سَيِّدِنَا مُحَمَّدٍ عَدَدَ النَّمْلِ وَصَلِّ عَلَى سَيِّدِنَا مُحَمَّدٍ عَدَدَ الْمِيَاهِ الْعَذْبَةِ وَصَلِّ عَلَى سَيِّدِنَا مُحَمَّدٍ عَدَدَ الْمِيَاهِ الْمِلْحَةِ وَصَلِّ عَلَى سَيِّدِنَا مُحَمَّدٍ عَدَدَ نِعْمَتِكَ عَلَى جَمِيعِ خَلْقِكَ وَصَلِّ عَلَى سَيِّدِنَا مُحَمَّدٍ عَدَدَ نِقْمَتِكَ وَعَذَابِكَ عَلَى مَنْ كَفَرَ بِسَيِّدِنَا مُحَمَّدٍ ﷺ وَصَلِّ عَلَى سَيِّدِنَا مُحَمَّدٍ عَدَدَ مَا دَامَتِ الدُّنْيَا وَالْآخِرَةُ

wa ṣalli ʿalā Sayyīdinā Muḥammadin ʿadada 'n-namli wa ṣalli ʿalā Sayyīdinā Muḥammadinʿadada 'l-mīyāhi 'l-ʿadhbati wa ṣalli ʿalā Sayyīdinā Muḥammadin ʿadada 'l-mīyāhi 'l-milḥati wa ṣalli ʿalā Sayyīdinā Muḥammadin ʿadada niʿmatika ʿalā jamīʿi khalqika wa ṣalli ʿalā Sayyīdinā Muḥammadin ʿadada niqmatika wa ʿadhābika ʿalā man kafara bi Sayyīdinā Muḥammadin ﷺ wa ṣalli ʿalā Sayyīdinā Muḥammadin ʿadada mā dāmati 'd-dunyā wa 'l-ākhiratu

and exalt our master Muḥammad as the number of ants, and exalt our master Muḥammad as abundantly as saltwater, and exalt our master Muḥammad as abundantly as there is fresh water and bless our master Muḥammad as abundantly as there is saltwater and exalt our master Muḥammad as much as the entire Favour You have shown to the whole of Your Creation and exalt our master Muḥammad as much as Your vengeance and Your punishment on those who deny our master Muḥammad, ﷺ and exalt our master Muḥammad as long as the this world endures and as long as does the afterlife! ➢

وَصَلِّ عَلَى سَيِّدِنَا مُحَمَّدٍ عَدَدَ مَا دَامَتِ الْخَلَائِقُ فِي الْجَنَّةِ وَصَلِّ عَلَى سَيِّدِنَا مُحَمَّدٍ عَدَدَ مَا دَامَتِ الْخَلَائِقُ فِي النَّارِ وَصَلِّ عَلَى سَيِّدِنَا مُحَمَّدٍ عَلَى قَدْرِ مَا تُحِبُّهُ وَتَرْضَاهُ وَصَلِّ عَلَى سَيِّدِنَا مُحَمَّدٍ عَلَى قَدْرِ مَا يُحِبُّكَ وَيَرْضَاكَ وَصَلِّ عَلَى سَيِّدِنَا مُحَمَّدٍ أَبَدَ الآبِدِينَ وَأَنزِلْهُ الْمَنْزِلَ الْمُقَرَّبَ عِنْدَكَ وَأَعْطِهِ الْوَسِيلَةَ وَالْفَضِيلَةَ وَالشَّفَاعَةَ

wa ṣalli ʿalā Sayyīdinā Muḥammadin ʿadada mā dāmati ʾl-khalāʾiqu fī ʾl-jannati wa ṣalli ʿalā Sayyīdinā Muḥammadin ʿadada mā dāmati ʾl-khalāʾiqu fī ʾn-nāri wa ṣalli ʿalā Sayyīdinā Muḥammadin ʿalā qadri mā tuḥibbuhu wa tarḍāhu wa ṣalli ʿalā Sayyīdinā Muḥammadin ʿalā qadri mā yuḥibbuka wa yarḍāka wa ṣalli ʿalā Sayyīdinā Muḥammadin abada ʾl-ābidīna wa anzilhu ʾl-manzila ʾl-muqarraba ʿindaka wa aʿṭihi ʾl-wasīlata wa ʾl-faḍīlata wa ʾsh-shafāʿata

And exalt our master Muḥammad for as long as Your creatures remain in the Garden and exalt our master Muḥammad as long as Your creatures remain in the Fire! And exalt our master Muḥammad equal to Your love for him and Your good pleasure with him and exalt our master Muḥammad equal to his love for You and his good pleasure with You and exalt our master Muḥammad Forever and ever and award him the Closest Position in Your Presence and grant him the Closest Access, the Station of Pre-eminence and the Station of Intercession ➢

وَالدَّرَجَةَ الرَّفِيعَةَ وَالْمَقَامَ الْمَحْمُودَ الَّذِي وَعَدْتَهُ إِنَّكَ لَا تُخْلِفُ الْمِيعَادَ ❁

wa 'd-darajata 'r-rafīʿata wa 'bʿath-hu 'l-maqāma 'l-maḥmūda 'Lladhī wa ʿadtahū innaka lā tukhlifu 'l-mīʿād •

and the Lofty Rank and send him to the Most Praised Station which You promised him, for You do not break Your Word! ❁

(٩) اللَّهُمَّ إِنِّي أَسْأَلُكَ بِأَنَّكَ مَالِكِي وَسَيِّدِي وَمَوْلَايَ وَثِقَتِي وَرَجَائِي أَسْأَلُكَ بِحُرْمَةِ الشَّهْرِ الْحَرَامِ وَالْبَلَدِ الْحَرَامِ وَالْمَشْعَرِ الْحَرَامِ وَقَبْرِ نَبِيِّكَ ﷺ أَنْ تَهَبَ لِي مِنَ الْخَيْرِ مَا لَا يَعْلَمُ عِلْمَهُ إِلَّا أَنْتَ وَتَصْرِفَ عَنِّي مِنَ السُّوءِ مَا لَا يَعْلَمُ عِلْمَهُ إِلَّا أَنْتَ ❁

(9) Allāhumma innī as'aluka bi annaka mālikī wa Sayyīdī wa mawlāya wa thiqatī wa rajā'ī as'aluka bi-ḥurmati 'sh-shahri 'l-ḥarāmi wa 'l-baladi 'l-ḥarāmi wa 'l-mashʿari 'l-ḥarāmi wa qabri nabīyyika ﷺ an tahaba lī mina 'l-khayri mā lā yāʿlamu ʿilmahu illā anta wa taṣrifa ʿannī mina 's-sūw'i mā lā yāʿlamu ʿilmahu illā Anta

(9) O Allāh, I beseech You, for the sake of the fact that You are my King, my Lord, my Master, my Trust, and my Hope, and I beseech You for the honor of the Holy Month, the Holy Land, the Holy Sanctuary, and the tomb of the Prophet ﷺ that You bestow upon me Good, knowledge of which is Yours alone, and that You remove from me Evil, knowledge of which is Yours alone! ➢

(١٠) اللَّهُمَّ يَا مَنْ وَهَبَ لِسَيِّدِنَا آدَمَ سَيِّدَنَا شَيثاً وَلِسَيِّدِنَا إِبْرَاهِيمَ سَيِّدَنَا إِسْمَاعِيلَ وَ سَيِّدَنَا إِسْحَاقَ وَرَدَّ سَيِّدَنَا يُوسُفَ عَلَى سَيِّدِنَا يَعْقُوبَ وَيَا مَنْ كَشَفَ الْبَلَاءَ عَنْ سَيِّدِنَا أَيُّوبَ وَيا مَنْ رَدَّ سَيِّدِنَا مُوسَى إِلَى أُمِّهِ وَيَا زَائِدَ سَيِّدِنَا الْخَضِرِ فِي عِلْمِهِ وَ يَا مَنْ وَهَبَ لِسَيِّدِنَا دَاوُودَ سَيِّدَنَا سُلَيْمَانَ وَلِسَيِّدِنَا زَكَرِيَّا سَيِّدَنَا يَحْيَى

(10) Allāhumma yā man wahaba li Sayyīdinā Ādama Sayyīdanā Shīthan wa li Sayyīdinā Ibrāhīma Sayyīdanā Ismāʿīla wa Sayyīdanā Isḥāq wa radda Sayyīdanā Yūsufa ʿalā Sayyīdinā Yaʿqūba wa yā man kashafa 'l-balā'a ʿan Sayyīdinā Ayyūba Wa yā man radda Sayyīdanā Mūsā ilā ummihi wa yā zā'ida Sayyīdinā l-Khaḍiri fī ʿilmihi wa yā man wahaba li Sayyīdinā Dawūda Sayyīdanā Sulaymāna wa li Sayyīdinā Zakarīyya Sayyīdanā Yaḥyā

(10) O Allāh, Who bestowed on our master Adam our master Seth and on our master Abraham our master Ishmael and our master Isaac, and Who returned our master Joseph to our master Jacob and O You Who removed the trials from our master Job and O You Who returned our master Moses to his mother and O You Who increased our master Khidr in knowledge and Who bestowed on our master David our master Solomon and on our master Zechariah our master John the Baptist ➤

وَ لِسَيِّدَتِنَا مَرْيَمَ سَيِّدَنَا عِيسَى وَيَا حَافِظَ اِبْنَةِ سَيِّدِنَا شُعَيبٍ أَسْأَلُكَ أَنْ تُصَلِّيَ عَلَى سَيِّدِنَا مُحَمَّدٍ وَعَلَى جَمِيعِ النَّبِيِّينَ وَالْمُرْسَلِينَ وَيَا مَنْ وَهَبَ لِسَيِّدِنَا مُحَمَّدٍ ﷺ الشَّفَاعَةَ وَالدَّرَجَةَ الرَّفِيعَةَ أَنْ تَغْفِرَ لِي ذُنُوبِي وَتَسْتُرَ لِي عُيوبِي كُلَّهَا وَتُجِيرَنِي مِنَ النَّارِ وَتُوجِبَ لِي رِضْوَانَكَ وَأَمَانَكَ وَغُفْرَانَكَ وَإِحْسَانَكَ وَتُمَتِّعَنِي فِي جَنَّتِكَ مَعَ الَّذِينَ أَنْعَمْتَ عَلَيهِمْ

wa li Sayyīdatinā Maryama Sayyīdanā ʿĪsa wa yā ḥāfiẓa 'bnati Sayyīdinā Shuʿaybin as'aluka an tuṣalliya ʿāla Sayyīdinā Muḥammadin wa ʿalā jamīʿi 'n-nabīyyīnā wa 'l-mursalīna wa yā man wahaba li-Sayyīdinā Muḥammadin ﷺ ash-shafāʿata wa 'd-darajata 'r-rafīʿata an taghfira lī dhunūbī wa tastura lī ʿuyūbi kullahā wa tujīranī mina 'n-nāri wa tūwjiba lī riḍwānika wa amānika wa ghufrānika wa iḥsānika wa tumattiʿanī fī jannatika maʿa 'Lladhīna anʿamta ʿalayhim

and Who gave to our lady Mary our master Jesus and Who protected the daughter of Shuʿayb, I ask You to exalt our master Muḥammad and all the prophets and messengers. And You who gave to our master Muḥammad ﷺ, the Station of Intercession and the Lofty Rank, I ask You to forgive my sins, conceal all my failings, give me sanctuary from the Fire, grant me Your Pleasure and Your Safety and Your Forgiveness and Your Beneficence and admit me into Your Garden long with those whom You have Favored ➢

مِنَ النَّبِيِّينَ وَالصِّدِّيقِينَ وَالشُّهَدَاءِ وَالصَّالِحِينِ إِنَّكَ عَلَى كُلِّ شَيْءٍ قَدِيرٌ وَ صَلَّى اللهُ
عَلَى سَيِّدِنَا مُحَمَّدٍ وَعَلَى آلِهِ مَا أَزْعَجَتِ الرِّيَاحُ سَحَاباً رُكَاماً وَذَاقَ كُلُّ ذِي رُوحٍ حِمَامًا
وَأَوْصِلِ السَّلَامَ لِأَهْلِ السَّلَامِ فِي دَارِ السَّلَامِ تَحِيَّةً وَسَلَامًا ❋

mina 'n-nabīyyīnā wa 'ṣ-ṣiddīqīna wa 'sh-shuhadā'i wa 's-ṣāliḥīna innaka ʿalā kulli shayin qadīr wa ṣalla 'Llāhu ʿalā Sayyīdinā Muḥammadin wa ʿalā ālihi mā azʿajati 'r-riyāḥu saḥāban rukāman wa dhāqa kullu dhi rūḥin ḥimāman wa awṣili 's-salāma li āhli 's-salāmi fī dāri 's-salāmi taḥīyyatan wa salāman •

from the prophets, the true ones, the martyrs and the righteous, for You have Power over all things. Exalt O Allāh, our master Muḥammad and his family as often as the wind has stirred the gathered clouds and as often as everything possessing a soul has tasted death, and convey peace and salutations to the People of Peace in the Abode of Peace! ❋

(١١) اللَّهُمَّ أَفْرِدْنِي لِمَا خَلَقْتَنِي لَهُ وَلَا تَشْغِلْنِي بِمَا تَكَفَّلْتَ لِي بِهِ وَلَا تَحْرِمْنِي
وَأَنَا أَسْأَلُكَ وَلَا تُعذِّبْنِي وَأَنَا أَسْتَغْفِرُكَ (٣x) ❋

(11) Allāhumma 'fridnī limā khalaqtanī lahu wa lā tashghilnī bimā takaffalta lī bihi wa lā taḥrimnī wa anā as'aluka wa lā tuʿadh-dhibnī wa anā astaghfiruk (3x) •

(11) O Allāh, make me single-hearted on the purpose for which You created me and busy me with what You hold me answerable and do not deprive me while I ask You and do not to punish me while I seek Your forgiveness! (3x) ❋

(١٢) اللَّهُمَّ صَلِّ عَلَى سَيِّدِنَا مُحَمَّدٍ وَعَلَى آلِهِ وسَلِّمْ اللَّهُمَّ إِنِّي أَسْأَلُكَ وَأَتَوَجَّهُ إِلَيْكَ بِحَبِيبِكَ الْمُصْطَفَى عِنْدَكَ يَا حَبِيبَنَا يَا سَيِّدَنَا مُحَمَّدٍ إِنَّا نَتَوَسَّلُ بِكَ إِلَى رَبِّكَ فَاشْفَعْ لَنَا عِنْدَ الْمَوْلَى الْعَظِيمِ يَا نِعمَ الرَّسُولُ الطَّاهِرُ اللَّهُمَّ شَفِّعْهُ فِينَا بِجَاهِهِ عِنْدَكَ (x٣)

(12) Allāhumma ṣalli ʿalā Sayyīdinā Muḥammadin wa ʿalā ālihi wa sallim Allāhumma innī as'aluka wa atawajjahu ilayka bi ḥabībika 'l-Musṭafā ʿindaka yā ḥabībanā yā Sayyīdanā Muḥammadan innā natawassalu bika ilā rabbika fa 'shfaʿ lanā ʿinda 'l-mawla 'l-ʿaẓīm yā niʿma 'r-rasūlu 'ṭ-ṭāhiru Allāhumma shaffiʿhu fīnā bi-jāhihi ʿindaka (3x)

(12) O Allāh, exalt and grant peace to our master Muḥammad and his family! O Allāh, I ask You and turn my face to You, by means of Your Beloved Chosen One ﷺ in Your Presence! O our beloved, our master Muḥammad, we seek your mediation to your Lord so intercede for us in the Presence of our Tremendous Guardian Lord, O Most Excellent and Pure Messenger! O Allāh, grant us his intercession for the sake of his honor in Your Presence! (3x) ➢

وَاجْعَلْنَا مِنْ خَيْرِ الْمُصَلِّينَ وَالْمُسَلِّمِينَ عَلَيهِ

wa 'jʿalnā min khayri 'l-muṣṣallīna wa 'l-musallimmīna ʿalayhi

and make us the best of those invoking blessings and peace upon him ➢

وَمِنْ خَيْرِ الْمُقَرَّبِينَ مِنْهُ وَالْوَارِدِينَ عَلَيهِ وَمِنْ اَخْيارِ الْمُحِبِّينَ فِيهِ وَالْمَحْبُوبِينَ لَدَيهِ وَفَرِّحْنَا بِهِ فِي عَرَصَاتِ الْقِيَامَةِ وَاجْعَلهُ لَنَا دَلِيلاً إِلَى جَنَّةِ النَّعِيمِ بِلَا مَؤُونَةٍ وَلَا مَشَقَّةٍ وَلَا مُنَاقَشَةِ الْحِسَابِ وَاجْعَلْهُ مُقبِلًا عَلَينَا وَلَا تَجْعَلْهُ غَاضِباً عَلَيْنَا وَاغْفِرْ لَنَا وَلِوَالِدِينَا وَلِجَمِيعِ الْمُسْلِمِينَ الْأَحْيَاءِ مِنْهُمْ وَالْمَيِّتِينْ وَآخِرُ دَعْوَانَا أَنْ الْحَمْدُ لله رَبِّ الْعَالَمِينَ ❁

wa min khayri 'l-muqarrabīna minhu wa 'l-wāridīna ʿalayhi wa min akhyāri 'l-muḥibbīna fīhi wa 'l-maḥbubīna ladayhi, wa farriḥnā bihi fī ʿaraṣāti 'l-qīyāmati wa 'jʿalhu lanā dalīlan ilā jannati 'n-naʿīmi bilā maʿūnatin wa lā mashaqqatin wa lā munāqashati 'l-ḥisābi wa 'jʿalhu muqbilan ʿalaynā wa lā tajʿalhu ghāḍiban ʿalaynā wa 'ghfir lanā wa li-wālidaynā wa li-jamīʿi 'l-muslimīna 'l-aḥyā'i minhum wa 'l-mayyitīna wa ākhiru daʿwānā ani 'l-ḥamdu li 'Llāhi rabbi 'l-ʿĀlamīn •

and the best of those who are near to him and who are received by him and the best of those who are in love with him and are loved in his presence and have mercy on us because of him in the fields of the Day of Rising and make him a guide for us to the Garden of Delights, burdenless, troublefree, unopposed and make him welcoming to us and let him not be angry with us and forgive us and our parents and all those submitted before Allāh, (the Muslims), the living among them and the dead, and our final invocation is praise be to Allāh ﷻ the Lord of the Worlds! ❁

إِبْتِدَاءُ الرُّبْعِ الرَّابِعِ

Ibtida'u 'r-Rub'i 'r-Rābi'i
Beginning of the Fourth Quarter

(١٣) فَأَسْأَلُكَ يَا اللهُ يَا اللهُ يَا اللهُ يَا حَيُّ يَا قَيُّومُ يَا ذَا الْجَلَالِ وَالْإِكْرَامِ لَا اِلَهَ إِلَّا أَنْتَ سُبْحَانَكَ إِنِّي كُنْتُ مِنَ الظَّالِمِينَ أَسْأَلُكَ بِمَا حَمَلَ كُرْسِيُّكَ مِنْ عَظَمَتِكَ وَجَلَالِكَ وَبَهَائِكَ وَقُدْرَتِكَ وَسُلْطَانِكَ وَبِحَقِّ أَسْمَائِكَ الْمَخْزُونَةِ الْمَكْنُونَةِ الْمُطَهَّرَةِ الَّتِي لَمْ يَطَّلِعْ عَلَيْهَا أَحَدٌ مِنْ خَلْقِكَ

(13) Fa as'aluka yā Allāhu yā Allāhu yā Allāhu yā Ḥayyu yā Qayyūmu yā dha 'l-Jalāli wa 'l-Ikrāmi lā ilāha illā anta subḥānaka innī kuntu mina 'z-ẓālimīn as'aluka bimā ḥamala kursīyyuka min 'aẓamatika wa jalālika wa bahā'ika wa qudratika wa sulṭānika wa bi-ḥaqqi asmā'ika 'l-makhzhūnati 'l-maknūnati 'l-muṭahharati 'Llatī lam yaṭ-ṭali' 'alayhā aḥadun min khalqika

(13) So I ask You O Allāh, O Allāh, O Allāh, O Living One, O Everlasting, O Possessor of Majesty and Honor, there is no god but You, Glory be to You. Verily I was one of those who oppresssed themselves! I ask You for the sake of that which bears Your Footstool from Your Oceans of Might, Your Oceans of Majesty, Your Oceans of Beauty, Your Oceans of Power and Your Oceans of Lordship, and for the right of Your Guarded, Hidden and Pure Names, to which no created being can attain, ➢

وَبِحَقِّ الإِسْمِ الَّذِي وَضَعْتَهُ عَلَى اللَّيلِ فَأَظْلَمَ وَعَلَى النَّهارِ فَاسْتَنَارَ وَعَلَى السَّماوَاتِ فَاسْتَقَلَّتْ وَعَلَى الْأَرْضِ فَاستَقَرَّتْ وَعَلَى الْبِحَارِ فَانْفَجَرَتْ وَعَلَى العُيُونِ فَنَبَعَتْ وَعَلَى السَّحَابِ فَأَمْطَرَتْ وَأَسْأَلُكَ بِالْأَسْمَاءِ المَكْتُوبَةِ فِي جَبْهَةِ سَيِّدِنَا جِبْرِيلَ ﷵ وَبِالْأَسْمَاءِ المَكْتُوبَةِ فِي جَبهَةِ سَيِّدِنَا إِسْرَافِيل ﷵ وَعَلَى جَمِيعِ المَلَائِكَةِ وَأَسْأَلُكَ بِالْأَسْمَاءِ المَكتوبَةِ حَولَ العَرْشِ وَبِالْأَسْمَاءِ المَكْتُوبَةِ حَولَ الْكُرْسِيِّ وَأَسْأَلُكَ بِاسمِكَ العَظِيمِ الأَعْظَمِ

wa bi-ḥaqqi 'l-ismi 'Lladhī wadaʿtahu ʿalā 'l-layli fa aẓlama wa ʿalā 'n-nahāri fa 'stanāra wa ʿalā 's-samāwāti fa 'staqallat wa ʿalā 'l-arḍi fa 'staqarrat wa ʿalā 'l-bihāri fa 'nfajarat wa ʿalā 'l-ʿuyūni fa nabaʿat wa ʿalā 's-saḥābi fa amṭarat wa as'aluka bi 'l-asmā'i 'l-maktūbati fī jabhati Sayyīdinā Isrāfīla ﷵ wa bi'l-asmā'i 'l-maktūbati fī jabhati Sayyīdinā Jibrīla ﷵ wa ʿalā jamīʿi 'l-malā'ikati wa asʿaluka bi 'l-asmā'i 'l-maktūbati ḥawla 'l-ʿarshi wa bi 'l-asma'i 'l-maktūbati ḥawla l-kursīyyi wa as'aluka bi ismika'l-ʿaẓīmi 'l-ʿaẓam

and for the sake of the reality of the Name which when laid upon the night makes it darken and when laid upon the day makes it light, when laid upon the heavens they rise, when laid upon the earth it is made firm, when laid upon the seas they roll, when laid upon the springs they burst forth and when laid upon the clouds they rain! I ask You by the Names written in the forehead of our master Raphael ﷵ, and I ask You by the Names inscribed in the forehead of our master Gabriel ﷵ and upon all the angels, and I ask You by the Names written around the Throne and in the Names written around the Footstool. O Allāh, I ask You by the Greatest Name ➢

الَّذِيْ سَمَّيتَ بِهِ نَفسَكَ وَأَسْأَلُكَ بِحَقِّ اَسمَائِكَ كُلِّها مَا عَلِمْتُ مِنْهَا وَمَا لَمْ أَعْلَمْ وَأَسْأَلُكَ بِالْأَسْمَاءِ الَّتِي دَعَاكَ بِهَا سَيِّدُنَا آدَمُ ﵇ وَبِالْأَسْمَاءِ الَّتِي دَعَاكَ بِهَا سَيِّدُنَا نُوحٌ ﵇ وَبِالْأَسْمَاءِ الَّتِي دَعَاكَ بِهَا سَيِّدُنَا صَالِحٌ ﵇ وَبِالْأَسْمَاءِ التي دَعَاكَ بِهَا سَيِّدُنَا يعقُوبُ ﵇ وَبِالْأَسْمَاءِ التي دَعَاكَ بِهَا سَيِّدُنَا يُوسُفُ ﵇ وَبِالْأَسْمَاءِ التي دَعَاكَ بِهَا سَيِّدُنَا يُونُسُ ﵇ وَبِالْأَسْمَاءِ الَّتِي دَعَاكَ بِهَا سَيِّدُنَا مُوسَى ﵇

alladhī sammayta bihi nafsaka wa as'aluka bi ḥāqqi asmā'ika kullihā mā ʿalimtu minhā wa mā lam aʿlam wa as'aluka bi 'l-asmā'i 'Llatī daʿāka bihā Sayyīdunā Ādamu ﵇ wa bi 'l-asmā'i 'Llatī daʿāka bihā Sayyīdunā Nūḥun ﵇ wa bi 'l-asmā'i 'Llatī daʿāka bihā Sayyīdunā Ṣāliḥun ﵇ wa bi 'l-asmā'i 'Llatī daʿāka bihā Sayyīdunā Yaʿqūbun ﵇ wa bi 'l-asmā'i 'Llatī daʿāka bihā Sayyīdunā Yūsufu ﵇ wa bi 'l-asmā'i 'Llatī daʿāka bihā Sayyīdunā Yūnusu ﵇ wa bi 'l-asmā'i 'Llatī daʿāka bihā Sayyīdunā Mūsā ﵇

by which You named Yourself, and by the right of all Your Names, those I know and those I do not, and I ask You by the Name by which our master Adam ﵇ invoked You and I ask You by the Name by which our master Noah ﵇ invoked You and I ask You by the Name by which our master Ṣāliḥ ﵇ invoked You and I ask You by the Name by which our master Jacob ﵇ invoked You and I ask You by the Name by which our master Joseph ﵇ invoked You and I ask You by the Name by which our master Jonah ﵇ invoked You And I ask You by the Name which our master Moses ﵇ invoked You ➢

وَبِالْأَسْمَاءِ الَّتِي دَعَاكَ بِهَا سَيِّدُنَا هَارُون عليه السلام وَبِالْأَسْمَاءِ الَّتِي دَعَاكَ بِهَا سَيِّدُنَا شُعَيب عليه السلام وَبِالْأَسْمَاءِ الَّتِي دَعَاكَ بِهَا سَيِّدُنَا إِبرَاهِيمُ عليه السلام وبِالْأَسْمَاءِ التي دَعَاكَ بِهَا سَيِّدُنَا إِسْمَاعِيل عليه السلام وَبِالْأَسْمَاءِ الَّتِي دَعَاكَ بِهَا سَيِّدُنَا دَاوودُ عليه السلام وَبِالْأَسْمَاءِ الَّتِي دَعَاكَ بِهَا سَيِّدُنَا سُلَيمَانَ عليه السلام وَبِالْأَسْمَاءِ الَّتِي دَعَاكَ بِهَا سَيِّدُنَا زَكَرِيَّا عليه السلام وَبِالْأَسْمَاءِ الَّتِي دَعَاكَ بِهَا سَيِّدُنَا يَحيَى عليه السلام

wa bi 'l-asmā'i 'Llatī daʿāka bihā Sayyīdunā Hārūn عليه السلام *wa bi 'l-asmā'i 'Llatī daʿāka bihā Sayyīdunā Shuʿaybun* عليه السلام *wa bi 'l-asmā'i 'Llatī daʿāka bihā Sayyīdunā Ibrāhīma* عليه السلام *wa bi 'l-asmā'i 'Llatī daʿāka bihā Sayyīdunā Ismāʿīlu* عليه السلام *wa bi 'l-asmā'i 'Llatī daʿāka bihā Sayyīdunā Dāwūdu* عليه السلام *wa bi 'l-asmā'i 'Llatī daʿāka bihā Sayyīdunā Sulaymānu* عليه السلام *wa bi 'l-asmā'i 'Llatī daʿāka bihā Sayyīdunā Zakarīyya* عليه السلام *wa bi 'l-asmā'i 'Llatī daʿāka bihā Sayyīdunā Yaḥyā* عليه السلام

and I ask You by the Name by which our master Aaron عليه السلام invoked You and I ask You by the Name by which our master Shuʿayb عليه السلام invoked You and I ask You by the Name by which our master Abraham invoked You, and I ask You by the Name by which our master Ishmael عليه السلام invoked You and I ask You by the Name by which our master David عليه السلام invoked You and I ask You by the Name by which our master Solomon عليه السلام invoked You and I ask You by the Name by which our master Zechariah عليه السلام invoked You and I ask You by the Name by which our master John the Baptist, عليه السلام invoked You ➢

وَبِالْأَسْمَاءِ الَّتِي دَعَاكَ بِهَا سَيِّدُنَا يُوشَعُ ﵇ وَبِالْأَسْمَاءِ الَّتِي دَعَاكَ بِهَا سَيِّدُنَا الخَضِرُ ﵇ وَبِالْأَسْمَاءِ الَّتِي دَعَاكَ بِهَا سَيِّدُنَا اليَسَعُ ﵇ وَبِالْأَسْمَاءِ الَّتِي دَعَاكَ بِهَا سَيِّدُنَا ذُو الكِفْلِ ﵇ وَبِالْأَسْمَاءِ الَّتِي دَعَاكَ بِهَا سَيِّدُنَا عِيسَى ﵇ وَبِالْأَسْمَاءِ الَّتِي دَعَاكَ بِهَا سَيِّدُنَا مُحَمَّدٌ ﷺ نَبِيُّكَ وَرَسُولُكَ وَحَبِيبُكَ وَصَفِيُّكَ يَا مَنْ قَالَ وَقَوْلُهُ الحَقُّ وَاللهُ خَلَقَكُمْ وَمَا تَعْمَلُونَ

wa bi ʾl-asmāʾi ʿLlatī daʿāka bihā Sayyīdunā Yūshaʿu ﵇ wa bi ʾl-asmāʾi ʿLlatī daʿāka bihā Sayyīdunā Khaḍiru ﵇ wa bi ʾl-asmāʾi ʿLlatī daʿāka bihā Sayyīdunā al-Yasaʿu ﵇ wa bi ʾl-asmāʾi ʿLlatī daʿāka bihā Sayyīdunā Dhu ʾl-Kifli ﵇ wa bi ʾl-asmāʾi ʿLlatī daʿāka bihā Sayyīdunā ʿĪsā ﵇ wa bi ʾl-asmāʾi ʿLlatī daʿāka bihā Sayyīdunā Muḥammadun ﷺ Nabīyyuka wa Rasūluka wa Ḥabībuka wa Ṣafiyyuka yā man qāla wa qawluhu ʾl-ḥaqqu: "wa ʾLlāhu khalaqakum wa mā taʿmalūn"

and I ask You by the Name by which our master Yūshaʿu, invoked You and I ask You by the Name by which our master Khaḍir ﵇ invoked You and I ask You by the Name by which our master Elias ﵇ invoked You and I ask You by the Name by which our master Esau ﵇ invoked You and I ask You by the Name by which our master Dhu'l-Kifl ﵇ invoked You and I ask You by the Name by which our master Jesus son of Mary ﵇ invoked You and I ask You by the Name by which our master Muḥammad ﷺ, Your Prophet, Your Messenger, Your Friend, invoked You. O You Who said, and His Word is true: "*And Allāh created You and what You do*" ➢

وَلَا يَصْدُرُ عَنْ أَحَدٍ مِنْ عَبِيدِهِ قَوْلٌ وَلَا فِعْلٌ وَلَا حَرَكَةٌ وَلَا سُكُونٌ إِلَّا وَقَدْ سَبَقَ فِي عِلْمِهِ وَقَضَائِهِ وَقَدَرِهِ كَيْفَ يَكُونُ كَمَا أَلْهَمْتَنِي وَقَضَيْتَ لِي بِجَمْعِ هَذَا الكِتَابِ وَيَسَّرْتَ عَلَيَّ فِيهِ الطَّرِيقَ وَالأَسْبَابَ وَنَفَيْتَ عَنْ قَلْبِي فِي هَذَا النَّبِيِّ الكَرِيمِ الشَّكَ وَالِارْتِيَابَ وَغَلَّبْتَ حُبَّهُ عِنْدِي عَلَى حُبِّ جَمِيعِ الْأَقْرِبَاءِ وَالْأَحِبَّاءِ أَسْأَلُكَ يَا اللهُ يَا اللهُ يَا اللهُ أَنْ تَرْزُقَنِي وَكُلَّ مَنْ أَحَبَّهُ وَاتَّبَعَهُ شَفَاعَتَهُ وَمُرَافَقَتَهُ يَوْمَ الْحِسَابِ

wa lā yaṣduru ʿan aḥadin min ʿabīdihi qawlun wa lā fiʿlun wa lā ḥarakatun wa lā sukūnun illā wa qad sabaqa fī ʿilmihi wa qaḍā'ihi wa qadarihi kayfa yakūnu kamā alhamtanī wa qaḍayta lī bi jamʿi hādhā 'l-kitāb wa yassarta ʿalayya fīhi 'ṭ-ṭarīqa wa 'l-asbāba wa nafayt ʿan qalbī fī hādhā 'n-nabīyya 'l-karīma 'sh-shakka wa 'l-irtīyāba wa ghallabta ḥubbahu ʿindī ʿalā ḥubbi jamīʿi 'l-aqribāi wa 'l-aḥibbā'i as'aluka yā Allāhu yā Allāhu yā Allāhu an tarzuqanī wa kulla man aḥabbahu wa 't-tabaʿahu shafāʿatahu wa murāfaqatahu yawma 'l-ḥisābi

there is no action, no word, no movement and no inactivity, which originates from His slaves, but that it has already been preordained in His knowledge, His destiny and His Decree; as I was inspired and destined to compile this book and the method and means were facilitated for me, and all doubts, and misgiving about this noble Prophet were removed from my heart and my love for him overwhelmed all loves for other relations and loved ones, I ask You O Allāh, O Allāh, O Allāh, that You grant me and all who love him and follow him, his intercession and his company on the Day of Account ➢

مِنْ غَيرِ مُنَاقَشَةٍ وَلَا عَذَابٍ وَلَا تَوبِيخٍ وَلَا عِتَابٍ وَأَنْ تَغْفِرَ لِي ذُنُوبِي وَتَسْتُرَ عُيُوبِي يَا وَهَّابُ يَا غَفَّارُ وَأَنْ تُنَعِّمَنِي بِالنَّظَرِ إِلَى وَجْهِكَ الْكَرِيمِ فِي جُمْلَةِ الْأَحْبَابِ يَوْمَ الْمَزِيدِ وَالثَّوابِ وَأَنْ تَتَقَبَّلَ مِنِّي عَمَلِي وَأَنْ تَعْفُوَ عَمَّا أَحَاطَ عِلْمُكَ بِهِ مِنْ خَطِيئَتِي وَنِسْيَانِي وَزَلَلِي وَأَنْ تُبَلِّغَنِي مِنْ زِيَارَةِ قَبْرِهِ وَالتَّسْلِيمِ عَلَيهِ وَعَلَى صَاحِبَيهِ غَايَةَ أَمَلِي بِمَنِّكَ وَفَضْلِكَ وَجُودِكَ وَكَرَمِكَ يَا رَؤُوفُ يَا رَحِيمُ يَا وَلِيُّ

min ghayri munāqashatin wa lā ʿadhābin wa lā tawbīkhin wa lā ʿitābin wa an taghfira lī dhunūbī wa tastura ʿuyūbī, yā Wahhābu yā Ghaffāru wa an tunaʿimanī bi 'n-naẓari ilā wajhika 'l-karīmi fī jumlati 'l-aḥbābi yawma 'l-mazīdi wa 'th-thawābi wa an tataqabbala minnī ʿamalī wa an taʿfuwa ʿammā aḥāta ʿilmuka bihi min khaṭīyatī wa nisyānī wa zalalī wa an tuballighanī min ziyārati qabrihi wa 't-taslīmi ʿalayhi wa ʿalā ṣāḥibayhi ghāyata amlī bi-mannika wa faḍlika wa jūdika wa karamika yā Ra'ūfu yā Raḥīmu yā Walīyyu

with no dispute, no punishment, no reproach, no censure, and that You forgive me my sins and You conceal my failings, O Granter, O Forgiver, and that You favor me with a glance at Your Noble Countenance among the dear ones on the Day of Excess and Reward and accept from me my actions and annul all of my failings, lapses and mistakes of which You have knowledge and grant me a visit to his tomb and to greet him and his two companions is the utmost limit of my hope from Your Favor, Your grace, Your generosity, Your Nobility, O Gracious, O Merciful, O Sovereign, ➢

وَأَنْ تُجَازِيَهُ عَنِّي وَعَنْ كُلِّ مَنْ آمَنَ بِهِ وَاتَّبَعَهُ مِنَ الْمُسْلِمِينَ وَالْمُسْلِمَاتِ الْأَحْيَاءِ مِنْهُم وَالْأَمْوَاتِ أَفْضَلَ وَأَتَمَّ وَأَعَمَّ مَا جَازَيتَ بِهِ أَحداً مِنْ خَلْقِكَ يَا قَوِيُّ يَا عَزِيزُ يَا عَلِيُّ وَأَسْأَلُكَ اللَّهُمَّ بِحَقِّ مَا اَقْسَمتُ بِهِ عَلَيكَ أَنْ تُصَلِّيَ عَلَى سَيِّدِنَا مُحَمَّدٍ وَعَلَى آلِ سَيِّدِنَا مُحَمَّدٍ عَدَدَ مَا خَلَقْتَ مِنْ قَبْلِ أَنْ تَكُونَ السَّمَاءُ مَبنِيَّةً وَالْأَرْض مَدْحِيَّةً

wa an tujāziyahu ʿannī wa ʿann kulli man āmana bihi wa 't-tabaʿahu mina 'l-muslimīna wa 'l-muslimāti 'l-aḥyā'i minhum wa 'l-amwāti afḍala wa atamma wa aʿamma mā jāzayta bihi aḥadan min khalqika yā Qawīyyu yā ʿAzīzu yā ʿAlīyyu wa as'aluka Allāhumma bi-ḥaqqi mā aqsamtu bihi ʿalayka an tuṣallīya ʿalā Sayyīdinā Muḥammadin wa ʿalā āli Sayyīdinā Muḥammadin ʿadada mā khalaqta min qabli an takūna 's-samā'u mabnīyyatan wa 'l-arḍu madḥīyyatan

and reward him on my behalf and on behalf of everyone who believed in him and followed him from the Muslims, men and women, their living and their dead, who believe in him and follow him, better than, more perfect than, and more extensively than You have rewarded anyone from Your Creation, O Allāh, The Powerful, O Allāh, The Mighty, O Allāh, The Sublime. And I ask You by the reality of my swearing an oath by You, that You bless our master Muḥammad and the family of our master Muḥammad in all that You created before the sky was built, the earth was spread out, ➤

وَالجِبَالُ عُلوِيَّةً وَالعُيُونُ مُنْفَجِرَةً وَالْبِحَارُ مُسَخَّرَةً وَالْأَنهَارُ مُنْهَمِرَةً وَالشَّمْسُ مُضْحِيَةً وَالقَمَرُ مُضِيئاً وَالنَّجْمُ مُنِيراً وَلَا يَعْلَمُ أَحَدٌ حَيْثُ تَكُونُ إِلَّا أَنْتَ وَأَنْ تُصَلِّيَ عَلَيهِ وَعَلَى آلِهِ عَدَدَ كَلَامِكَ وَأَنْ تُصَلِّيَ عَلَيهِ وَعَلَى آلِهِ عَدَدَ آيَاتِ الْقُرْآنِ وَحُرُوفِهِ وَأَنْ تُصَلِّيَ عَلَيهِ وَعَلَى آلِهِ عَدَدَ مَنْ يُصَلِّ عَلَيهِ وَأَنْ تُصَلِّيَ عَلَيهِ وَعَلَى آلِهِ عَدَدَ مَنْ لَمْ يُصَلِّ عَلَيهِ وَأَنْ تُصَلِّيَ عَلَيهِ وَعَلَى آلِهِ مِلْءَ أَرْضِكَ

wa 'l-jibālu 'ulwīyyatan wa 'l-'uyūnu munfajiratan wa 'l-bihāru musakharatan wa 'l-anhāru munhamiratan wa 'sh-shamsu muḍḥīyatan wa 'l-qamaru muḍī'an wa 'n-najmu munīran wa lā yā'lamu aḥadun ḥaythu takūnu illā anta wa an tuṣallīya 'alayhi wa 'alā ālihi 'adada kalāmika wa an tuṣallīya 'alayhi wa 'alā ālihi 'adada āyāti 'l-qur'āni wa ḥurūfihi wa an tuṣallīya 'alayhi wa 'alā ālihi 'adada man yuṣallī 'alayhi wa an tuṣallīya 'alayhi wa 'alā ālihi 'adada man lam yuṣalli 'alayhi wa an tuṣallīya 'alayhi wa 'alā ālihi mila' arḍika

the mountains were raised, the spring burst forth, the oceans were subdued, the rivers streamed forth, the sun shone forth, the moon beamed and the stars illuminated the sky, and no one knew where You were but Yourself and exalt him and his family on the numbers of verses and letters in the Quran, and exalt him and his family as many times as those who ask You to exalt him and exalt him and his family as many time as those who neglect to ask You to exalt him, and exalt him and his family as much as the earth contains ➢

وَأَنْ تُصَلِّيَ عَلَيهِ وَعَلَى آلِهِ عَدَدَ مَا جَرَى بِهِ القَلَمُ فِي أُمِّ الْكِتَابِ وَأَنْ تُصَلِّيَ عَلَيهِ وَعَلَى آلِهِ عَدَدَ مَا خَلَقْتَ فِي سَبْعِ سَمَاوَاتِكَ وَأَنْ تُصَلِّيَ عَلَيهِ وَعَلَى آلِهِ عَدَدَ مَا أَنْتَ خَالِقُهُ فِيهِنَّ إِلَى يَوْمِ الْقِيَامَةِ فِي كُلِّ يَوْمٍ أَلْفَ مَرَّةٍ وَأَنْ تُصَلِّيَ عَلَيهِ وَعَلَى آلِهِ عَدَدَ قَطْرِ الْمَطَرِ وَكُلِّ قَطْرَةٍ قَطَرَتْ مِنْ سَمَائِكَ إِلَى أَرْضِكَ مِنْ يَوْمِ خَلَقْتَ الدُّنْيَا إِلَى يَوْمِ الْقِيَامَةِ فِي كُلِّ يَوْمٍ أَلْفَ مَرَّةٍ ❋

wa an tuṣallīya ʿalayhi wa ʿalā ālihi ʿadada mā jarā bihi 'l-qalamu fī ummi 'l-kitābi wa an tuṣallīya ʿalayhi wa ʿalā ālihi ʿadada mā khalaqta fī sabʿi samāwātik wa an tuṣallīya ʿalayhi wa ʿalā ālihi ʿadada mā anta khāliquhu fīhinna ilā yawmi 'l-qīyāmati fī kulli yawmin alfa marratin wa an tuṣallīya ʿalayhi wa ʿalā ālihi ʿadada qaṭri 'l-maṭari wa kulli qaṭratin qaṭarat min samā'ika ilā arḍika min yawmi khalaqta 'd-dunyā ilā yawmi 'l-qīyāmati fī kulli yawmin alfa marratin •

and exalt him and his family as great as the Pen has written the Mother of Books and exalt him and his family as much as You have created in Your Seven Heavens! and exalt him and is family as much as You will create in them until the Day of Resurrection and every day a thousand times, and bless him and his family in every single drop of rain and in the total of all the rain which has fallen from Your sky to the earth from the Day You created this world until the Day of Resurrection and every day a thousand times! ❋

يَوْمُ الأَحَدِ

Sunday

الحِزْبُ السَّابِعُ فِي يَوْمِ الأَحَدِ

Al-Ḥizbu 's-Sābi'u fī Yawmi 'l-Āḥadi

Chapter Seven to be read on Sunday

(١) وَأَنْ تُصَلِّيَ عَلَيهِ وَعَلَى آلِهِ عَدَدَ مَنْ سَبَّحَكَ وَقَدَّسَكَ وَسَجَدَ لَكَ وَعَظَّمَكَ مِنْ يَوْمِ خَلَقْتَ الدُّنْيَا إِلَى يَوْمِ الْقِيَامَةِ فِي كُلِّ يَوْمٍ أَلْفَ مَرَّةٍ ❁

(1) wa ann tuṣallīya 'alayhi wa 'alā ālihi 'adada man sabbaḥaka wa qaddasaka wa sajada laka wa 'aẓẓamaka min yawmi khalaqta 'd-dunyā ilā yawmi 'l-qīyāmati fī kulli yawmin alfa marratin •

(1) And exalt him and his family as many times as Your Glorifiers, Your Worshippers, Your Prostrating Servants and Your Magnifiers, from the Day You created this world until the Day of Resurrection in every day a thousand times. ❁

(٢) وَأَنْ تُصَلِّيَ عَلَيهِ وَعَلَى آلِهِ عَدَدَ كُلِّ سَنَةٍ خَلَقْتَهُمْ فِيهَا مِنْ يَوْمِ خَلَقْتَ الدُّنْيَا إِلَى يَوْمِ الْقِيَامَةِ فِي كُلِّ يَوْمٍ أَلْفَ مَرَّةٍ ❋

(2) Wa ann tuṣallīya ʿalayhi wa ʿalā ālihi ʿadada kulli sanatin khalaqtahum fīhā min yawmi khalaqta 'd-dunyā ilā yawmi 'l-qīyāmati fī kulli yawmin alfa marratin •

(2) and exalt him and his family as many times as the years in which You created them, from the Day You created this world until the Day of Resurrection in every day a thousand times! ❋

(٣) وَأَنْ تُصَلِّيَ عَلَيهِ وَعَلَى آلِهِ عَدَدَ السَّحَابِ الْجَارِيَةِ وَأَنْ تُصَلِّيَ عَلَيهِ وَعَلَى آلِهِ عَدَدَ الرِّيَاحِ الذَّارِيَةِ مِنْ يَوْمِ خَلَقْتَ الدُّنْيَا إِلَى يَوْمِ الْقِيَامَةِ فِي كُلِّ يَوْمٍ أَلْفَ مَرَّةٍ ❋

(3) Wa ann tuṣallīya ʿalayhi wa ʿalā ālihi ʿadada 's-saḥābi 'l-jārīyati wa an tuṣallīya ʿalayhi wa ʿalā ālihi ʿadada 'r-riyāḥi 'dh-dhāriyati min yawmi khalaqta 'd-dunyā ilā yawmi 'l-qīyāmati fī kulli yawmin alfa marratin •

(3) And exalt him and his family in every sweeping cloud and exalt him and his family in every gusting wind from the Day You created this world until the Day of Resurrection in every day a thousand times! ❋

(٤) وَأَنْ تُصَلِّيَ عَلَيهِ وَعَلَى آلِهِ عَدَدَ مَا هَبَّتِ الرِّيَاحُ عَلَيهِ وَحَرَّكَتْهُ مِنَ الْأَغْصَانِ وَالْأَشْجَارِ وَأَوْرَاقِ الثِّمَارِ وَالْأَزْهَارِ وَعَدَدَ مَا خَلَقْتَ عَلَى قَرَارِ أَرْضِكَ وَمَا بَيْنَ سَمَاوَاتِكَ مِنْ يَوْمِ خَلَقْتَ الدُّنْيَا إِلَى يَوْمِ الْقِيَامَةِ فِي كُلِّ يَوْمٍ أَلْفَ مَرَّةٍ ❋

(4) Wa ann tuṣallīya ʿalayhi wa ʿalā ālihi ʿadada mā habbati 'r-riyāḥu ʿalayhi wa ḥarrakat-hu mina 'l-aghṣāni wa 'l-ashjāri wa awrāqi 'th-thimāri wa 'l-azhāri wa ʿadada mā khalaqta ʿalā qarāri arḍika wa mā bayna samāwātika min yawmi khalaqta 'd-dunyā ilā yawmi 'l-qīyāmati fī kulli yawmin alfa marratin •

(4) And exalt him and his family in the movement of every branch, every tree, every leaf, every fruit and every flower stirred by the wind, and in amount of all things created on the surface of the earth and within Your heavens from the Day You created this world until the Day of Resurrection in every day a thousand times. ❋

(٥) وَأَنْ تُصَلِّيَ عَلَيهِ وَعَلَى آلِهِ عَدَدَ أَمْوَاجِ بِحَارِكَ مِنْ يَوْمِ خَلَقْتَ الدُّنْيَا إِلَى يَوْمِ الْقِيَامَةِ فِي كُلِّ يَوْمٍ أَلْفَ مَرَّةٍ ❋

(5) Wa ann tuṣallīya ʿalayhi wa ʿalā ālihi ʿadada amwāji biḥārika min yawmi khalaqta 'd-dunyā ilā yawmi 'l-qīyāmati fī kulli yawmin alfa marratin •

(5) And bless him and his family in every ocean wave from the Day You created this world until the Day of Resurrection in every day a thousand times! ❋

(٦) وَأَنْ تُصَلِّيَ عَلَيهِ وَعَلَى آلِهِ عَدَدَ الرِّمَالِ وَالْحَصَى وَكُلِّ حَجَرٍ وَمَدَرٍ خَلَقْتَهُ فِي مَشَارِقِ الْأَرْضِ وَمَغَارِبِهَا سَهْلِهَا وَجِبَالِهَا وَأَوْدِيَتِهَا مِنْ يَوْمِ خَلَقْتَ الدُّنْيَا إِلَى يَوْمِ الْقِيَامَةِ فِي كُلِّ يَوْمٍ أَلْفَ مَرَّةٍ ❁

(6) Wa ann tuṣallīya ʿalayhi wa ʿalā ālihi ʿadada ʾr-ramli wa ʾl-ḥaṣā wa kulli ḥajrin wa madarin khalaqtahu fī mashāriqi ʾl-arḍi wa maghāribihā sahlihā wa jibālihā wa awdīyatihā min yawmi khalaqta ʾd-dunyā ilā yawmi ʾl-qīyāmati fī kulli yawmin alfa marratin •

(6) And exalt him and his family on the number of every grain of sand, of every stone, of every rock and of every cloud You created in the East and in the West, on lowlands, on highlands and in the valleys from the Day You created this world until the Day of Resurrection in every day a thousand times. ❁

(٧) وَأَنْ تُصَلِّيَ عَلَيهِ وَعَلَى آلِهِ عَدَدَ نَبَاتِ الْأَرْضِ فِي قِبْلَتِهَا وَجَوفِهَا وَشَرْقِهَا وَغَرْبِهَا وَسَهْلِهَا وَجِبَالِهَا مِنْ شَجَرٍ وَثَمَرٍ وَأَوْرَاقٍ وَزَرْعٍ

(7) Wa ann tuṣallīya ʿalayhi wa ʿalā ālihi ʿadada nabāti ʾl-arḍi fī qiblatihā wa jawfihā wa sharqihā wa gharbihā wa sahlihā wa jibālihā min shajarin wa thamarin wa awrāqin wa zarʿin

(7) And exalt him and his family on the number of every plant of the earth, in the north and south, in the east and west, on the plains and in the mountains, and in every tree, every fruit, every leaf and everything growing from it ➢

وَجَمِيعِ مَا أَخْرَجَتْ مِنْهَا وَمَا يَخْرُجُ مِنْ نَبَاتِهَا وَبَرَكَاتِهَا مِنْ يَوْمِ خَلَقْتَ الدُّنْيَا
إِلَى يَوْمِ الْقِيَامَةِ فِي كُلِّ يَوْمٍ الفَ مَرَّةٍ ❋

wa jamīʿi mā akhrajat wa mā yakhruju minhā min nabātihā wa barakātihā min yawmi khalaqta 'd-dunyā ilā yawmi 'l-qīyāmati fī kulli yawmin alfa marratin •

and in everything produced and in whatever will be produced of its plants and its provisions growing from it from the Day You created this world until the Day of Resurrection in every day a thousand times! ❋

(٨) وَأَنْ تُصَلِّيَ عَلَيْهِ وَعَلَى آلِهِ عَدَدَ مَا خَلَقْتَ مِنَ الْإِنْسِ وَالْجِنِّ
وَالشَّيَاطِينِ وَمَا أَنْتَ خَالِقُهُ مِنْهُمْ إِلَى يَوْمِ الْقِيَامَةِ فِي كُلِّ يَوْمٍ أَلْفَ مَرَّةٍ ❋

(8) Wa ann tuṣallīya ʿalayhi wa ʿalā ālihi ʿadada mā khalaqta mina 'l-insi wa 'l-jinni wa 'sh-shayāṭīni wa mā anta khāliquhu minhum ilā yawmi 'l-qīyāmati fī kulli yawmin alfa marratin •

(8) And exalt him and his family on the number of whatever You created of human beings, of jinn and of devils from the Day You created this world until the Day of Resurrection in every day a thousand times! ❋

(٩) وَأَنْ تُصَلِّيَ عَلَيهِ وَعَلَى آلِهِ عَدَدَ كُلِّ شَعْرَةٍ فِي أَبْدَانِهِمْ وَوُجُوهِهِمْ وَعَلَى رُؤُوسِهِمْ مُنْذُ خَلَقْتَ الدُّنْيَا إِلَى يَوْمِ الْقِيَامَةِ فِي كُلِّ يَوْمٍ أَلْفَ مَرَّةٍ

❋

(9) Wa ann tuṣallīya ʿalayhi wa ʿalā ālihi ʿadada kulli shaʿratin fī abdānihim wa wujūhihim wa ʿalā ruʾūsihim mundhu khalaqta 'd-dunyā ilā yawmi 'l-qīyāmati fī kulli yawmin alfa marratin •

(9) And exalt him and his family as the number of every hair on their bodies, on their faces and on their heads since the time You created this world until the Day of Resurrection in every day a thousand times! ❋

(١٠) وَأَنْ تُصَلِّيَ عَلَيهِ وَعَلَى آلِهِ عَدَدَ أَنْفَاسِهِمْ وَأَلْفَاظِهِمْ وَأَلْحَاظِهِمْ مِنْ يَوْمِ خَلَقْتَ الدُّنْيَا إِلَى يَوْمِ الْقِيَامَةِ فِي كُلِّ يَوْمٍ أَلْفَ مَرَّةٍ ❋

(10) Wa ann tuṣalliya ʿalayhi wa ʿalā ālihi ʿadada anfāsihim wa alfāẓihim wa alḥāẓihim min yawmi khalaqta 'd-dunyā ilā yawmi 'l-qīyāmati fī kulli yawmin alfa marratin •

(10) And exalt him and his family as the number of every one of their breaths, their utterances and every one of their glances, from the Day You created this world until the Day of Resurrection in every day a thousand times! ❋

(١١) وَأَنْ تُصَلِّيَ عَلَيهِ وَعَلَى آلِهِ عَدَدَ طَيَرَانِ الْجِنِّ وَخَفقَانِ الْإِنسِ مِنْ يَوْمِ خَلَقْتَ الدُّنْيَا إِلَى يَوْمِ الْقِيَامَةِ فِي كُلِّ يَوْمٍ أَلْفَ مَرَّةٍ ❋

(11) Wa ann tuṣallīya ʿalayhi wa ʿalā ālihi ʿadada ṭayarāni 'l-jinni wa khafaqāni 'l-insi min yawmi khalaqta 'd-dunyā ilā yawmi 'l-qīyāmati fī kulli yawmin alfa marratin •

(11) And exalt him and his family on the count of every flight of Jinn and the beating of every human heart from the Day You created this world until the Day of Resurrection in every day a thousand times! ❋

(١٢) وَأَنْ تُصَلِّيَ عَلَيهِ وَعَلَى آلِهِ عَدَدَ كُلِّ بَهِيمَةٍ خَلَقْتَهَا عَلَى أَرْضِكَ صَغِيرَةً أَوْ كَبِيرَةً فِي مَشَارِقِ الْأَرْضِ وَمَغَارِبِهَا مِمَّا عُلِمَ وَمِمَّا لَا يَعْلَمُ عِلْمَهُ إِلَّا أَنْتَ مِنْ يَوْمِ خَلَقْتَ الدُّنْيَا إِلَى يَوْمِ الْقِيَامَةِ فِي كُلِّ يَوْمٍ أَلْفَ مَرَّةٍ ❋

(12) Wa ann tuṣallīya ʿalayhi wa ʿalā ālihi ʿadada kulli bahīmatin khalaqtahā ʿalā arḍika ṣaghīratan wa kabīratan fī mashāriqi 'l-arḍi wa maghāribihā mimmā ʿulima wa mimmā lā yaʿlamu ʿilmahu illā anta min yawmi khalaqta 'd-dunyā ilā yawmi 'l-qīyāmati fī kulli yawmin alfa marratin •

(12) And exalt him and his family on the number of every beast and every small creature created by You in the west and in the east of those which are known and those which are not known except by You Alone from the Day You created this world until the Day of Resurrection in every day a thousand times! ❋

(١٣) وَأَنْ تُصَلِّيَ عَلَيهِ وَعَلَى آلِهِ عَدَدَ مَنْ صَلَّى عَلَيهِ وَعَدَدَ مَنْ لَمْ يُصَلِّ عَلَيْهِ وَعَدَدَ مَنْ يُصَلِّي عَلَيهِ إِلَىٰ يَوْمِ الْقِيَامَةِ فِي كُلِّ يَوْمٍ أَلْفَ مَرَّةٍ ❋

(13) Wa ann tuṣallīya ʿalayhi wa ʿalā ālihi ʿadada man ṣalla ʿalayhi wa ʿadād man lam yuṣalli ʿalayhi wa ʿadada man yuṣalli ʿalayhi ilā yawmi 'l-qīyāmati fī kulli yawmin alfa marratin •

(13) And exalt him and his family as many times as those who haved invoked blessings upon him and as many times as those who have not and as many times as those who will invoke them until the Day of Resurrection in every day a thousand times! ❋

(١٤) وَأَنْ تُصَلِّيَ عَلَيهِ عَدَدَ الْأَحْيَاءِ و الاَموَاتِ وَعَدَدَ مَا خَلَقْتَ مِنْ حِيتَانٍ وَطَيرٍ وَنَملٍ وَ نَحْلٍ وَحَشَرَاتٍ ❋

(14) Wa ann tuṣallīya ʿalayhi wa ʿalā ālihi ʿadad al-aḥyāʾi wa 'l-amwāti wa ʿadada mā khalaqta min ḥitānin wa ṭayrin wa namlin wa naḥlin wa ḥasharātin •

(14) And exalt him and his family on the number of every soul, alive and dead, and on the number of whatever You created of whales, birds, ants, bees and from every insect! ❋

(١٥) وَأَنْ تُصَلِّيَ عَلَيهِ وَعَلَى آلِهِ فِي اللَّيلِ إِذَا يَغْشَى وَالنَّهَارِ إِذَا تَجَلَّى وَأَنْ تُصَلِّيَ عَلَيهِ وَعَلَى آلِهِ فِي الْآخِرَةِ وَالْأُولَى ❋

(15) Wa an tuṣallīya ʿalayhi wa ʿalā ālihi fī 'l-layli idhā yaghshā wa 'n-nahāri idhā tajallā wa an tuṣallīya ʿalayhi wa ʿalā ālihi fī 'l-ākhirati wa 'l-ūla •

(15) And exalt him and his family in every darkening night and in every brightening day and exalt him and his family in the end and in the beginning! ❋

(١٦) وَأَنْ تُصَلِّيَ عَلَيهِ وَعَلَى آلِهِ مُنْذُ كَانَ فِي المَهْدِ صَبِيًّا إِلَى أَنْ صَارَ كَهْلاً مَهْدِيًّا فَقَبَضْتَهُ إِلَيكَ عَدْلاً مَرْضِيًّا لِتَبْعَثَهُ شَفِيعاً حَفِيًّا❋

(16) Wa an tuṣallīya ʿalayhi wa ʿalā ālihi mundhu kāna fī 'l-mahdi ṣabīyyan ilā an ṣāra kahlan mahdīyyan fa-qabaḍtahu ilayka ʿadlan marḍīyyan li-tabʿathahu shafīʿan ḥafīyyan •

(16) And exalt him and his family from the time he was in the cradle until his full maturity when You took him to Yourself, justly satisfied, and until You finally send him as a welcome intercessor! ❋

(١٧) وَأَنْ تُصَلِّيَ عَلَيهِ وَعَلَى آلِهِ عَدَدَ خَلْقِكَ وَرِضَاءَ نَفْسِكَ وَزِنَةَ عَرْشِكَ

(17) Wa ann tuṣallīya ʿalayhi wa ʿalā ālihi ʿadada khalqika wa riḍā' nafsika wa zinata ʿarshika

(17) And exalt him and his family on the number of all Your Creation, to the extent of Your Pleasure and the Adornment of Your Throne ➢

وَمِدَادَ كَلِمَاتِكَ وَأَن تُعْطِيَهُ الْوَسِيلَةَ وَالْفَضِيلَةَ وَالدَّرَجَةَ الرَّفِيعَةَ وَالْحَوْضَ الْمَوْرُودَ وَالْمَقَامَ الْمَحْمُودَ وَالْعِزَّ الْمَمْدُودَ وَأَن تُعَظِّمَ بُرهَانَهُ وَأَنْ تُشَرِّفَ بُنْيَانَهُ وَأَنْ تَرفَعَ مَكَانَهُ وَأَنْ تَسْتَعْمِلَنَا يَا مَوْلَانَا بِسُنَّتِهِ وَأَنْ تُمِيتَنَا عَلَى مِلَّتِهِ وَأَنْ تَحْشُرَنَا فِي زُمْرَتِهِ وَتَحْتَ لِوَائِهِ وَأَنْ تَجْعَلَنَا مِنْ رُفَقَائِهِ وَأَنْ تُورِدَنَا حَوضَهُ

wa midāda kalimātika wa an tuʿṭiyahu 'l-wasīlata wa 'l-faḍīlata wa 'd-darajata 'r-rafīʿata wa 'l-ḥawḍa 'l-mawrūda wa 'l-maqāma 'l-maḥmūda wa 'l-ʿizza 'l-mamdūda wa an tuʿaẓẓima burhānahu wa an tusharrifa bunyānahu wa an tarfaʿa makānahu wa an tastaʿmillnā yā mawlānā bi sunnatihi wa an tumītanā ʿalā millatih wa an taḥshuranā fī zumratihi wa taḥta liwā'ihi wa an tajʿalanā min rufaqā'ihi wa an tūridanā ḥawḍahu

in the ink of Your Words, and grant him the Closest Access, the Pre-eminence, the Lofty Rank, the Oft-visited Pool, the Most Praised Station, and the Greatest Standing, and enhance his proof, ennoble his stature, raise his station, and have us, O Lord, follow his way and let us die following his religion and resurrect us in his company, and underneath his flag, and to make us from his comrades and to quench our thirst at his Pool ➢

مَا ظَهَرَ مِنْهَا وَمَا بَطَنَ وَأَنْ تَرْحَمَنَا وَأَنْ تَعْفُوَ عَنَّا وَتَغْفِرَ لَنَا وَلِجَمِيعِ الْمُؤْمِنِينَ وَالْمُؤْمِنَاتِ وَالْمُسْلِمِينَ وَالْمُسْلِمَاتِ الْأَحْيَاءِ مِنْهُمْ وَالْأَمْوَاتِ وَالْحَمْدُ لِلّٰهِ رَبِّ الْعَالَمِينَ وَهُوَ حَسْبِي وَنِعْمَ الْوَكِيلُ وَلَا حَوْلَ وَلَا قُوَّةَ إِلَّا بِاللهِ الْعَلِيِّ الْعَظِيمِ ❋

wa an tusqīnā bika'sihi wa an tanfaʿanā bi maḥabbatihi wa an tatūba ʿalaynā wa an tuʿāfiyanā min jamīʿi 'l-balā'i wa 'l-balwā'i wa 'l-fitani mā ẓahara minhā wa mā baṭana wa an tarḥamanā wa an taʿfua ʿannā wa taghfira lanā wa li-jamīʿi 'l-mu'minīna wa 'l-mu'mināti wa 'l-muslimīna wa 'l-muslimāti 'l-aḥyā'i minhum wa 'l-amwāti wa 'l-ḥamdu lillāhi rabbi 'l-ʿĀlamīn wa hūwa ḥasbī wa niʿma 'l-wakīlu wa lā ḥawla wa lā quwwata illā bi 'Llāhi 'l-ʿAlīyyi 'l-ʿAẓīm •

and to quench our thirst with his cup, and to benefit us by granting us his love, and to forgive us and to remove from us all trials and tribulations, whatever is apparent as well as what is hidden, and to have mercy on us, and to pardon us and to forgive us and all believers, men and women, and all Muslims, men and women, the living and the dead, and praise be to Allāh Lord of the Worlds, and He suffices me and He is the best of Protectors and there is no help and power save with Allāh The High, The Mighty! ❋

(١٨) اللَّهُمَّ صَلِّ عَلَى سَيِّدِنَا مُحَمَّدٍ وَعَلَى آلِ سَيِّدِنَا مُحَمَّدٍ مَا سَجَعَتِ الْحَمَائِمُ وَحَمَتِ الْحَوَائِمُ وَسَرَحَتِ الْبَهَائِمُ وَنَفَعَتِ التَّمَائِمُ وَشُدَّتِ الْعَمَائِمُ وَنَمَتِ التَّوَائِمُ ❋

(18) Allāhumma ṣalli ʿalā Sayyīdinā Muḥammadin wa ʿalā āli Sayyīdinā Muḥammadin mā sajaʿati 'l-ḥamā'imu wa ḥamati 'l-ḥawā'imu wa saraḥāṭi 'l-bahā'imu wa nafaʿati 't-tamā'imu wa shuddati 'l-ʿamā'imu wa namati 't-tawā'imu •

(18) O Allāh, exalt our master Muḥammad and the family of our master Muḥammad for as long as doves are cooing, beasts are circling around waterholes, cattle are grazing, amulets benefit, turbans are tied and vegetation grows! ❋

(١٩) اللَّهُمَّ صَلِّ عَلَى سَيِّدِنَا مُحَمَّدٍ وَعَلَى آلِ سَيِّدِنَا مُحَمَّدٍ مَا أَبْلَجَ الإِصْبَاحُ وَهَبَّتِ الرِّيَاحُ وَدَبَّتِ الْأَشْبَاحُ وَتَعَاقَبَ الغُدُوُّ وَالرَّوَاحُ وَتُقُلِّدَتِ الصِّفَاحُ وَاعْتُقِلَتِ الرِّمَاحُ وَصَحَّتِ الْأَجْسَادُ وَالْأَرْوَاحُ ❋

(19) Allāhumma ṣalli ʿalā Sayyīdinā Muḥammadin wa ʿalā āli Sayyīdinā Muḥammadin mā ablaja 'l-iṣbāḥu wa habbati 'r-riyāḥu wa dabbati 'l-ashbāḥu wa taʿāqaba 'l-ghudūwwu wa 'r-rawāḥu wa tuqullidati 'ṣ-ṣifāḥu wa āʿtuqilati 'r-rimāḥu wa ṣaḥḥati 'l-ajsādu wa 'l-arwāḥu •

(19) O Allāh, bless our master Muḥammad and the family of our master Muḥammad in the breaking dawns, in the blowing winds, in the creeping shades, in the succeeding morns and eves, in the girding of armor, in the grasping of lances, and in the healing of bodies and souls! ❋

(٢٠) اللَّهُمَّ صَلِّ عَلَى سَيِّدِنَا مُحَمَّدٍ وَعَلَى آلِ سَيِّدِنَا مُحَمَّدٍ مَا دَارَتِ الْأَفْلَاكُ وَدَجَتِ الْأَحْلَاكُ وَسَبَحَتِ الْأَمْلَاكُ ❋

(20) Allāhumma ṣalli ʿalā Sayyīdinā Muḥammadin wa ʿalā āli Sayyīdinā Muḥammadin mā dārati 'l-aflāku wa dajati 'l-aḥlāku wa sabaḥati 'l-amlāku •

(20) O Allāh, exalt our master Muḥammad and the family of our master Muḥammad in the rotation of the celestial bodies, in the overshadowing of darkness and in the glorifying of angels! ❋

(٢١) اللَّهُمَّ صَلِّ عَلَى سَيِّدِنَا مُحَمَّدٍ وَعَلَى آلِ سَيِّدِنَا مُحَمَّدٍ كَمَا صَلَّيْتَ عَلَى سَيِّدِنَا إِبْرَاهِيمَ وَبَارِكْ عَلَى سَيِّدِنَا مُحَمَّدٍ وَعَلَى آلِ سَيِّدِنَا مُحَمَّدٍ كَمَا بَارَكْتَ عَلَى سَيِّدِنَا إِبْرَاهِيمَ فِي الْعَالَمِينَ إِنَّكَ حَمِيدٌ مَجِيدٌ ❋

(21) Allāhumma ṣalli ʿalā Sayyīdinā Muḥammadin wa ʿalā āli Sayyīdinā Muḥammadin kamā ṣallayta ʿalā Sayyīdinā Ibrāhīma wa bārik ʿalā Sayyīdinā Muḥammadin wa ʿalā āli Sayyīdinā Muḥammadin kamā bārakta ʿalā Sayyīdinā Ibrāhīma fī 'l-ʿālamīna innaka Ḥamīdun Majīd •

(21) O Allāh, exalt our master Muḥammad and the family of our master Muḥammad just as You exalted our master Abraham, and bless our master Muḥammad and the family just as You blessed our master Abraham in all the worlds, for You are The Praiseworthy, The Mighty! ❋

(٢٢) اللَّهُمَّ صَلِّ عَلَى سَيِّدِنَا مُحَمَّدٍ وَعَلَى آلِ سَيِّدِنَا مُحَمَّدٍ مَا طَلَعَتِ الشَّمْسُ وَمَا صُلِّيَتِ الْخَمْسُ وَمَا تَأَلَّقَ بَرْقٌ وَمَا تَدَفَّقَ وَدْقٌ وَمَا سَبَّحَ رَعْدٌ ❋

(22) Allāhumma ṣalli ʿalā Sayyīdinā Muḥammadin wa ʿalā āli Sayyīdinā Muḥammadin mā ṭalaʿati 'sh-shamsu wa mā ṣullīyati 'l-khamsu wa mā tā'llaqa barqun wa tadaffaqa wadqun wa mā sabbaḥa rʿadun •

(22) O Allāh, exalt our master Muḥammad and the family of our master Muḥammad in the rising sun, in the observance of the five daily prayers, in lighting which strikes, in the falling rain and in the pealing of thunder! ❋

(٢٣) اللَّهُمَّ صَلِّ عَلَى سَيِّدِنَا مُحَمَّدٍ وَعَلَى آلِ سَيِّدِنَا مُحَمَّدٍ مِلْءَ السَّمَاوَاتِ وَالْأَرْضِ وَمِلْءَ مَا بَيْنَهُمَا وَمِلْءَ مَا شِئْتَ مِنْ شَيْءٍ بَعْدُ ❋

(23) Allāhumma ṣalli ʿalā Sayyīdinā Muḥammadin wa ʿalā āli Sayyīdinā Muḥammadin mila 's-samāwāti wa 'l-arḍi wa mila' mā baynahumā wa mila' mā shi'ta min shay'in bʿadu •

(23) O Allāh exalt our master Muḥammad and the family of our master Muḥammad to the fullness of the heavens and the earth and to the fullness of whatever is between them and to the fullness of whatever You may have created elsewhere! ❋

(٢٤) اللَّهُمَّ كَمَا قَامَ بِأَعبَاءِ الرِّسَالَةِ وَاسْتَنْقَذَ الْخَلْقَ مِنَ الْجَهَالَةِ وَجَاهَدَ أَهْلَ الْكُفْرِ وَالضَّلَالَةِ وَدَعَا إِلَى تَوْحِيدِكَ وَقَاسَى الشَّدَائِدَ فِي إِرْشَادِ عَبِيدِكَ فَأَعْطِهِ اللَّهُمَّ سُؤْلَهُ وَبَلِّغْهُ مَأْمُولَهُ وَآتِهِ الوَسِيلَةَ وَالفَضِيلَةَ وَالدَّرَجَةَ الرَّفِيعَةَ وَابْعَثْهُ الْمَقَامَ الْمَحْمُودَ الَّذِي وَعَدْتَهُ إِنَّكَ لَا تُخْلِفُ الْمِيعَادَ ❋

(24) Allāhumma kamā qāma bi āʿbāʾi 'r-risālati wa 'stanqadha 'l-khalqi mina 'l-jahālati wa jāhada āhla 'l-kufri wa 'ḍ-ḍalālati wa daʿā ilā tawḥīdika wa qāsa 'sh-shadāʾida fī irshādi ʿabīdika fa-aʿtihi 'llāhumma sū'lahu wa balligh-hu mā'mūlahu wa ātihi 'l-wasīlata wa 'l-faḍīlata wa 'd-darajata 'r-rafīʿata wa 'bʿath-hu 'l-maqāma 'l-maḥmūda 'Lladhī waʿadtahū innaka lā tukhlifu 'l-mīʿād •

(24) O Allāh, as he bore the responsibility of the Message, and as he delivered creation from ignorance, and as he struggled against the people of unbelief and error, and called to Your Unity, and endured hardships in guiding Your servants, then grant him, O Allāh, his wishes, fulfill his hopes, and give him the Closest Access, the Pre-eminence, the Lofty Rank, and send him to the most Praised Station which You have promised him, for You never break a promise! ❋

(٢٥) اللَّهُمَّ وَاجْعَلْنَا مِنَ الْمُتَّبِعِينَ لِشَرِيعَتِهِ وَالْمُتَّصِفِّينَ بِمَحَبَّتِهِ الْمُهْتَدِينَ بِهَدْيِهِ وَسِيرَتِهِ وَتَوَفَّنَا عَلَى سُنَّتِهِ وَلَا تَحْرِمْنَا فَضْلَ شَفَاعَتِهِ وَاحْشُرْنَا فِي أَتْبَاعِهِ الْغُرِّ الْمُحَجَّلِينَ وَأَشْيَاعِهِ السَّابِقِينَ وَأَصْحَابِ الْيَمِينِ يَا أَرْحَمَ الرَّاحِمِينَ ❋

(25) Allāhumma wa 'j'alna mina 'l-muttabi'īna li-sharī'atihi 'l-muttaṣifīna bi maḥabbatihi 'l-muhtadīna bi hadyihi wa sīratihi wa tawaffana 'alā sunnatihi wa lā taḥrimnā faḍla shafā'atīhī wa 'ḥshurnā fī atbā'ihi 'l-ghurri 'l-muḥajjalīna wa ashyā'ihi 's-sābiqīna wa aṣḥābi 'l-yamīni yā Arḥama 'r-Rāhimīn •

(25) O Allāh, make us the followers of his law, those known and described by their love for him, those guided by his guidance and life, and let us die following his way and do not deny us the favour of his intercession, and resurrect us among his followers, those shining with light, his foremost companions, the Companions of the Right Hand, O Allāh The Most Merciful of Those Who Show Mercy! ❋

(٢٦) اللَّهُمَّ صَلِّ عَلَى مَلَآئِكَتِكَ وَالْمُقَرَّبِينَ وَعَلَى أَنْبِيَائِكَ وَالْمُرْسَلِينَ وَعَلَى أَهْلِ طَاعَتِكَ أَجْمَعِينَ وَاجْعَلْنَا بِالصَّلَاةِ عَلَيْهِمْ مِنَ الْمَرْحُومِينَ ❋

(26) Allāhumma ṣalli 'alā malā'ikatika wa 'l-muqarrabīna wa 'alā anbīyā'ika wa 'l-mursalīna wa 'alā āhli ṭā'atika ajma'īna wa 'j'alna bi-'ṣ-ṣalāti 'alayhim mina 'l-marḥūmīn •

(26) O Allāh, bless Your angels, Your archangels, Your Prophets and Your Messengers, and all the People obedient to You, and may our asking for such blessings be a mercy for us! ❋

(٢٧) اللَّهُمَّ صَلِّ عَلَى سَيِّدِنَا مُحَمَّدٍ الْمَبْعُوثِ مِنْ تِهَامَةَ وَالْآمِرِ بِالْمَعْرُوفِ وَالْإِسْتِقَامَةِ وَالشَّفِيعِ لِأَهْلِ الذُّنُوبِ فِي عَرَصَاتِ الْقِيَامَةِ ❋

(27) Allāhumma ṣalli ʿalā Sayyīdinā Muḥammadini 'l-mabʿūthi min Tihāmata wa 'l-āmiri bi 'l-maʿrūfi wa 'l-istaqāmati wa 'sh-shafīʿi li āhli 'dh-dhunūbi fī ʿaraṣāti 'l-qīyāmati •

(27) O Allāh, exalt our master Muḥammad, the Envoy from Tihama, the Commander and Upholder of Justice, the Intercessor of the Sinners in the Fields of the Day of Rising! ❋

(٢٨) اللَّهُمَّ بَلِّغ عَنَّا نَبِيَّنَا وَشَفِيعَنَا وَحَبِيبَنَا أَفْضَلَ الصَّلَاةِ وَالتَّسْلِيمِ وَأَبْعَثْهُ الْمَقَامَ الْمَحْمُودَ الْكَرِيمَ وَآتِهِ الْوَسِيلَةَ وَالْفَضِيلَةَ وَالدَّرَجَةَ الرَّفِيعَةَ الَّتِي وَعَدْتَهُ فِي الْمَوْقِفِ الْعَظِيمِ وَصَلِّ اللَّهُمَّ عَلَيهِ صَلَاةً دَائِمَةً مُتَّصِلَةً تَتَوَالَى وَتَدُومُ ❋

(28) Allāhumma abligh ʿannā nabīyyanā wa shafīʿyanā wa ḥabībanā afḍala 'ṣ-ṣalāti wa 't-taslīmi wa 'bʿathhu 'l-maqāma 'l-maḥmūda 'l-karīma wa ātihi 'l-faḍīlata wa 'l-wasīlata wa 'd-darajata 'r-rafīʿata 'Llatī waʿadtahu fī 'l-mawqifi 'l-ʿaẓīmi wa ṣalli 'llāhumma ʿalayhi ṣalātan dā'imatan muttaṣilatan tatawālā wa tadūm •

(28) O Allāh, send to our Prophet, our Advocate and our Beloved, on our behalf, the finest blessings and greetings and send him to the Most Praised and Noble Station, and grant him the Pre-eminence, the Closest Access and the Lofty Rank which You have Promised him on the great Day of Rising and bless him, O Allāh, with eternal, continual, continuous and everlasting blessings. ❋

(٢٩) اللَّهُمَّ صَلِّ عَلَيهِ وَعَلَى آلِهِ مَا لَاحَ بَارِقٌ وَذَرَّ شَارِقٌ وَوَقَبَ غَاسِقٌ وَانْهَمَرَ وَادِقٌ وَصَلِّ عَلَيهِ وَعَلَى آلِهِ مِلْءَ اللَّوْحِ وَالْفَضَاء وَمِثْلَ نُجُومِ السَّمَاءِ وَعَدَدَ القَطْرِ وَالمَطَرِ وَالحَصَى وَصَلِّ عَلَيهِ وَعَلَى آلِهِ صَلَاةً لَا تُعَدُّ وَلَا تُحصَى ❋

(29) Allāhumma ṣalli ʿalayhi wa ʿalā ālihi mā lāḥa bāriqun wa dharra shāriqun wa waqaba ghāsiqun wa 'nhamara wādiqun wa ṣalli ʿalayhi wa ʿalā ālihi mila 'l-lawḥi wa 'l-faḍā'i wa mithla nujūmi 's-samā'i wa ʿadada 'l-qaṭari wa 'l-maṭari wa 'l-ḥaṣā wa ṣalli ʿalayhi wa ʿalā ālihi ṣalātan lā tuʿaddu wa lā tuḥṣā •

(29) O Allāh, exalt him and his family as long as lightning glimmers, day dawns, night obscures and rain pours, and bless him and his family to the fullness of the Preserved Tablet and the cosmos and as every star in the sky and on the count of every dewdrop and every raindrop and every pebble, and bless him and his family with blessings countless and unrestricted! ❋

(٣٠) اللَّهُمَّ صَلِّ عَلَيهِ زِنَةَ عَرْشِكَ وَمَبْلَغَ رِضَاكَ وَمِدَادَ كَلِمَاتِكَ وَمُنْتَهَى رَحْمَتِكَ ❋

(30) Allāhumma ṣalli ʿalayhi zinata ʿarshika wa mablagha riḍāka wa midāda kalimātika wa muntahā raḥmatika •

(30) O Allāh, exalt him to the adornment of Your Throne, to the full extent of Your Pleasure, to the ink of Your Words and to the bounds of Your Mercy! ❋

(٣١) اللَّهُمَّ صَلِّ عَلَيهِ وَعَلَى آلِهِ وَأَزْوَاجِهِ وَذُرِيَّتِهِ كَمَا صَلَّيْتَ وَبَارَكْتَ عَلَى سَيِّدِنَا إِبْرَاهِيمَ وَعَلَى آلِ سَيِّدِنَا إِبْرَاهِيمَ إِنَّكَ حَمِيدٌ مَجِيدٌ وَجَازِهِ عَنَّا أَفْضَلَ مَا جَازَيتَ نَبِيّاً عَنْ أُمَّتِهِ وَاجْعَلنَا مِنَ الْمُهْتَدِينَ بِمِنْهَاجِ شَرِيعَتِهِ وَاهْدِنَا بِهَدْيِهِ وَتَوَفَّنَا عَلَى مِلَّتِهِ وَاحشُرنَا يَوْمَ الفَزَعِ الأكبرِ مِنَ الآمِنِينَ فِي زُمْرَتِهِ وَأَمِتْنَا عَلَى حُبِّهِ وَحُبِّ آلِهِ وَأَصْحَابِهِ وَذُرِيَّتِه ❋

(31) Allāhumma ṣalli 'alayhi wa 'alā ālihi wa azwājihi wa dhurrīyyatihi wa bārik 'alayhi wa 'alā ālihi wa azwājihi wa dhurrīyyatihi kamā ṣallayta wa bārakta 'alā Sayyīdinā Ibrāhīma wa 'alā āli Sayyīdinā Ibrāhīma innaka Ḥamīdun Majīdwa jāzihi 'annā afḍala mā jāzayta Nabīyyan 'an ummatihi wa 'j'alnā mina 'l-muhtadīna bi-minhāji sharī'atihi wa 'hdinā bi hadyihi wa tawaffanā 'alā millatihi wa 'ḥshurnā yawma 'l-faz'ai 'l-akbari mina 'l-āminīna fī zumratihi wa amitnā 'alā ḥubbihi wa ḥubbi ālihi wa aṣḥābihi wa dhurrīyyatih •

(31) O Allāh, exalt him and his family, his wives and his descendants, and bless him and his family, his wives and his descendants just as You exalted and blessed our master Abraham and the family of our master Abraham for You are indeed The Praiseworthy, The Mighty and reward him, on our behalf, better than You have rewarded any prophet on behalf of his nation, and make us among those guided by following his religion, and resurrect us on the Day of Greatest Terror among the faithful, in his company and have us die loving him and loving his family, his companions and his descendants! ❋

(٣٢) اللَّهُمَّ صَلِّ عَلَى سَيِّدِنَا مُحَمَّدٍ أَفْضَلِ أَنْبِيَائِكَ وَأَكْرَمِ أَصْفِيَائِكَ وَإِمَامِ أَوْلِيَائِكَ وَخَاتَمِ أَنْبِيَائِكَ وَحَبِيبِ رَبِّ العَالَمِينَ ، وَشَهِيدِ المُرْسَلِينَ ، وَشَفِيعِ المُذْنِبِينَ ، وَسَيِّدِ وَلَدِ آدَمَ أَجْمَعِينَ المَرفُوعِ الذِّكْرِ فِي المَلَآئِكَةِ المُقَرَّبِينَ البَشِيرِ النَّذِيرِ السِّرَاجِ المُنِيرِ الصَّادِقِ الوَعْدِ الأَمِينِ الحَقِّ المُبِينِ الرَّؤُوفِ الرَحِيمِ الهَادِي إِلَى الصِّرَاطِ المُسْتَقِيمِ

(32) Allāhumma ṣalli ʿalā Sayyīdinā Muḥammadin afḍali anbīyā'ika wa akrami aṣfīyā'ika wa imāmi awlīyā'ika wa khātami anbīyā'ika wa ḥabībi rabbi 'l-ʿĀlamīna wa shahīdi 'l-mursalīna wa shafiʿi 'l-mudhnibīna wa Sayyīdi waladi Ādama ajmāʿina 'l-marfūʿi 'dh-dhikri fī 'l-mālā'ikati 'l-muqarrabīna 'l-bashīri 'n-nadhīri 's-sirāji 'l-munīri 'ṣ-ṣādiqi 'l-wʿadi 'l-amīni 'l-ḥaqqi 'l-mubīni 'r-ra'ūfi 'r-raḥīmi 'l-hādī ilā 'ṣ-ṣirāti 'l-mustaqīmi

(32) O Allāh, exalt our master Muḥammad, the Finest of Your prophets, the Noblest of Your friends, the Leader of Your saints, the Seal of Your prophets, Beloved of the Lord of the Worlds, Witness for the messengers, Advocate of the sinners, Master of the Children of Ādam ﷺ, the One mentioned with inestimable regard among the Highest Angels, the Bearer of good-tidings the Warner, the Shining Lamp, the Truthful One, the Trustworthy One, the Clear Truth, the Compassionate, the Merciful, the Guide to the Straight Path ➢

الَّذِي آتَيتَهُ سَبْعاً مِنَ المَثَانِي وَالْقُرْآنِ العَظِيمِ نَبِيِّ الرَّحْمَةِ وَهَادِي الْأُمَّةِ أَوَّلُ مَنْ تَنْشَقُّ عَنْهُ الْأَرْضُ وَيَدْخُلُ الْجَنَّةَ المُؤَيَّدِ بِسَيِّدِنَا جِبْرِيلَ ﷺ وَ سَيِّدِنَا مِيكَائِيلَ ﷺ المُبَشَّرِ بِهِ فِي التَّوْرَاةِ وَالْإِنْجِيلِ المُصْطَفَى المُجْتَبَى المُنْتَخَبِ أَبِي الْقَاسِمِ سَيِّدِنَا مُحَمَّدِ بْنِ عَبْدِ اللهِ بْنِ عَبْدِ المُطَّلِبِ بْنِ هَاشِمٍ ❁

'Lladhī ātaytatu sab'an mina 'l-mathāni wa 'l-Qur'āni 'l-'aẓīm nabīyyi 'r-raḥmati wa hādi 'l-ummati awwalu man tansḥaqqu 'anhu 'l-arḍu wa yadkhulu 'l-jannata wa 'l-mu'ayyadi bi-Sayyīdinā Jibrīla ﷺ *wa Sayyīdinā Mīkā'īla 'l-mubashshari bihi fī 't-Tawrāti wa 'l-Injīli 'l-Muṣṭafā 'l-Mujtabā 'l-Muntakhabi abi 'l-Qāsimi Sayyīdinā Muḥammadi 'bni 'Abdi 'Llāhi 'bni 'Abdi 'l-Muṭṭalibi 'bni Hāshim* •

The one You granted the Seven oft-mentioned verses and the Tremendous Qur'an, the Prophet of Mercy, the Guide of the Nation, the First to arise from the Earth (on Judgment Day) and the First to enter the Garden, the One supported by our master Gabriel ﷺ and our master Michael ﷺ The One announced in the Torah and in the Gospel, the chosen One, the Elect One, the Select One, Father of Qāsim, our master Muḥammad, son of 'Abdullāh, son of 'Abdul-Muṭṭalib, son of Hāshim! ❁

(٣٣) اللَّهُمَّ صَلِّ عَلَى مَلَآئِكَتِكَ الْمُقَرَّبِينَ الَّذِين يُسَبِّحُونَ اللَّيلَ وَالنَّهَارِ لَا يَفتَرُونَ وَلاَ يَعْصُونَ اللهَ مَا أَمَرَهُمْ وَيَفْعَلُونَ مَا يُؤْمَرُونَ اللَّهُمَّ وَكَمَا اصْطَفَيتَهُمْ سُفَرَاءَ إِلَى رُسُلِكَ وَأُمَنَاءَ عَلَى وَحيِكَ وَشُهَدَاءَ عَلَى خَلْقِكَ وَخَرَقْتَ لَهُم كَنَفَ حُجُبِكَ وَاَطْلَعْتَهُمْ عَلَى مَكْنُونِ غَيبِكَ وَاخْتَرتَ مِنهُمْ خَزَنَةً لِجَنَّتِكَ وَحَمَلَةً لِعَرْشِكَ وَجَعَلتَهُمْ مِنْ أَكْثَرِ جُنُودِكَ

(33) Allāhumma ṣalli ʿalā malā'ikatika wa 'l-muqarrabīni 'Lladhīna yusabbiḥūna 'l-layla wa 'n-nahāra wa lā yafturūna wa lā yʿasūna 'Llāha mā amarahum wa yafʿalūna mā yu'marūn Allāhumma wa kamā 'ṣṭafaytahum sufarā'a ilā rusulika wa umanā'a ʿalā waḥyīka wa shuhadā'a ʿalā khalqika wa kharaqta lahum kanafa ḥujubika wa aṭlʿatahum ʿalā maknūni ghaybika wa 'khtarta minhum khazanatan li-jannatika wa ḥamalatan li-ʿarshika wa jaʿaltahum min akthari junūdika

(33) O Allāh, bless Your highest angels who glorify You ceaselessly, night and day, and who never disobey Allāh ﷻ in what He has ordered and who carry out what they have been ordered to do! O Allāh, just as You have chosen them to be envoys to Your Messengers, Guardians of Your Revelation and Witnesses over Your Creation, and have allowed them to pass the folds of Your Veils, and have given them access to Your hidden unseen Realms, And have chosen them to be the Guardians of Your Garden and Bearers of Your Throne, and have made them the most numerous of Your Soldiers ➢

وَفَضَّلْتَهُمْ عَلَى الْوَرَى وَاَسْكَنْتَهُمُ السَّمَاوَاتِ العُلَى وَنَزَّهْتَهُم عَنْ المَعَاصِي وَالدَّنَاءَاتِ وَقَدَّسْتَهُمْ عَنْ النَّقَائِصِ وَالْآفَاتِ فَصَلِّ عَلَيهِمْ صَلَاةً دَائِمَةً تَزِيدُهُمّ بِهَا فَضْلاً وَتَجْعَلُنَا لِاسْتِغْفَارِهِم بِهَا أَهْلاً ❋

wa faḍḍaltahum 'alā 'l-warā wa askantahumu 's-samāwāti 'l-'ulā wa nazzahtahum 'ani 'l-ma'āṣī wa 'd-danā'āti wa qaddastahum 'ani 'l-naqā'iṣi wa 'l-āfāti fa ṣalli 'alayhim ṣalātan dā'imatan tazīduhum bihā faḍlan wa taj'alunā li 'stighfārihim bihā āhlan •

and have favored them over mortal men, and have populated the High Heavens with them, and have freed them from disobedience and baseness, and have exalted them from short coming and misfortunes, so bless them eternally and may this request serve as a means of increasing their favour and a means of their asking forgiveness for us. ❋

(٣٤) اللَّهُمَّ وَصَلِّ عَلَى جَمِيعِ أَنْبِيَائِكَ وَرُسُلِكَ الَّذِينَ شَرَحْتَ صُدُورَهُمْ وَأَوْدَعْتَهُمْ حِكْمَتَكَ وَطَوَّقْتَهُمْ نُبُوَّتَكَ

(34) Allāhumma wa ṣalli 'alā jamī'i anbīyā'ika wa Rusulaka 'Lladhīna sharaḥta ṣudūrahum wa awda'tahum ḥikmataka wa ṭawwaqtahum nubūwwataka

(34) O Allāh, exalt all of Your prophets and messengers whose hearts You have opened, to whom You have entrusted Your wisdom, whom You have empowered with Your Prophethood ➢

وَأَنْزَلتَ عَلَيهِمْ كُتُبَكَ وَهَدَيتَ بِهِمْ خَلْقَكَ وَدَعَوا إِلَى تَوْحِيدِكَ وَشَوَّقُوا إِلَى وَعْدِكَ وَخَوَّفُوا مِنْ وَعِيدِكَ وَأَرشَدُوا إِلَى سَبِيلِكَ وَقَامُوا بِحُجَّتِكَ وَدَلِيلِكَ وَسَلِّمِ اللَّهُمَّ عَلَيهِمْ تَسْلِيماً وَهَبْ لَنَا بِالصَّلَاةِ عَلَيهِمْ أَجْرًا عَظِيماً ❋

wa anzalta ʿalayhim kutubaka wa hadayta bihim khalqaka wa daʿaw ilā tawḥīdika wa shawwaqū ilā wʿadika wa khawwafū min waʿīdika wa arshadū ilā sabīlika wa qāmū bi ḥujjatika wa dalīlika wa sallimi 'Llāhumma ʿalayhim taslīman wa hab lanā bi 'ṣ-ṣalāti ʿalayhim ajran ʿaẓīmā •

To whom You have revealed Your Books, by whom Your Creation have been guided, who have called to Your Unicity, who have looked forward to Your promise and feared Your Threat, who have guided to Your Path, who have upheld Your Proof and Your Evidence, and grant them abundant peace, O Allāh, and through this request for them bestow upon us a mighty reward! ❋

(٣٥) اللَّهُمَّ صَلِّ عَلَى سَيِّدِنَا مُحَمَّدٍ وَعَلَى آلِ سَيِّدِنَا مُحَمَّدٍ صَلَاةً دَائِمَةً مَقْبُولَةً تُؤَدِّي بِهَا عَنَّا حَقَّهُ العَظِيمَ ❋

(35) Allāhumma ṣalli ʿalā Sayyīdinā Muḥammadin wa ʿalā āli Sayyīdinā Muḥammadin ṣalātan dā'imatan maqbūlatan tu'addi bihā ʿannā ḥaqqahu 'l-ʿaẓīma •

(35) O Allāh, exalt our master Muḥammad and the family of our master Muḥammad blessing eternally acceptable and which discharge us of his overwhelming rights over us! ❋

(٣٦) اللَّهُمَّ صَلِّ عَلَى سَيِّدِنَا مُحَمَّدٍ صَاحِبِ الْحُسنِ وَالْجَمَالِ وَالبَهْجَةِ وَالْكَمَالِ وَالْبَهَاءِ وَالنُّورِ وَالْوِلْدَانِ وَالْحُورِ وَالْغُرَفِ وَالْقُصُورِ وَاللِّسَانِ الشَّكُورِ وَالْقَلْبِ الْمَشْكُورِ وَالْعِلْمِ الْمَشْهُورِ وَالْجَيْشِ الْمَنْصُورِ وَالْبَنِينَ وَالبَنَاتِ وَالْأَزْوَاجِ الطَّاهِرَاتِ وَالْعُلُوِّ عَلَى الدَّرَجَاتِ وَالزَمْزَمِ وَالْمَقَامِ وَالْمَشْعَرِ الْحَرَامِ وَاجْتِنَابِ الآثَامِ وَتَرْبِيَةِ الْأَيْتَامِ وَالْحَجِّ وَتِلَاوَةِ الْقُرْآنِ وَتَسْبِيحِ الرَّحْمَنِ وَصِيَامِ رَمَضَانَ

(36) Allāhumma ṣalli ʿalā Sayyīdinā Muḥammadin ṣāḥibi 'l-ḥusni wa 'l-jamāli wa 'l-bahjati wa 'l-kamāli wa 'l-bahā'i wa 'n-nūri wa 'l-wildāni wa 'l-ḥūri wa 'l-ghurafi wa 'l-quṣūri wa 'l-lisāni 'sh-shakūri wa 'l-qalbi 'l-mashkūri wa 'l-ʿilmi 'l-mash-hūri wa 'l-jayshi 'l-manṣūri wa 'l-banīna wa 'l-banāti wa 'l-azwāji 'ṭ-ṭāhirāti wa 'l-ʿulūwwi ʿalā 'd-darajāti wa 'z-zamzami wa 'l-maqāmi wa 'l-mashʿari 'l-ḥarāmi wa 'jtinābi 'l-āthāmi wa tarbīyati 'l-aytāmi wa 'l-ḥajji wa tilāwati 'l-Qur'āni wa tasbīḥi 'r-Raḥmāni wa ṣiyāmi Ramaḍāna

(36) O Allāh, bless our master Muḥammad, the Possessor of beauty and handsomeness, splendor and perfection, radiance and light, youthful servants and maidens, chambers and palaces, a grateful tongue and a praising heart, renowned knowledge and the victorious army, sons and daughters, pure wives, the highest ranks, the spring of Zamzam, the Station of Abraham, the Holy Sanctuary, infallibility, an orphan's upbringing, the Hajj, Quranic recitation, glorification of the All-Merciful, and the Ramadan fast, ➤

وَاللِّوَاءِ المَعْقُودِ والْكَرَمِ وَالْجُودِ وَالْوَفَاءِ بِالْعُهُودِ صَاحِبِ الرَّغْبَةِ وَالتَّرْغِيبِ وَالْبَغْلَةِ وَالنَجِيبِ وَالْحَوْضِ وَالقَضِيبِ النَّبِيِّ الْأَوَّابِ النَّاطِقِ بِالصَّوَابِ المَنْعُوتِ فِي الْكِتَابِ النَّبِيِّ عَبْدِ اللهِ النَّبِيِّ كَنْزِ اللهِ النَّبِيِّ حُجَّةِ اللهِ النَّبِيِّ مَنْ أَطَاعَهُ فَقَدْ أَطَاعَ اللهَ وَمَنْ عَصَاهُ فَقَدْ عَصَى اللهَ النَّبِيِّ الْعَرَبِيِّ الْقُرَشِيِّ الزَمزَمِي المَكِّيِّ التِّهَامِيِّ *

wa 'l-liwā'i 'l-mʿaqūdi wa 'l-karami wa 'l-jūdi wa 'l-wafā'i bi 'l-ʿuhūdi ṣāḥibi 'r-raghbati wa 't-targhībi wa 'l-baghlati wa 'n-najībi wa 'l-ḥawḍi wa 'l-qaḍībi an-nabīyyi 'l-awwābi 'n-nāṭiqi bi 'ṣ-ṣawābi 'l-manʿūti fī 'l-kitābi 'n-nabīyyi ʿabdi 'Llāhi 'n-nabīyyi kanzi 'Llāhi 'n-nabīyyi ḥujjati 'Llāhi 'n-nabīyyi man aṭāʿahu faqad aṭāʿ Allāha wa man ʿaṣāhu faqad ʿaṣa 'Llāha 'n-nabīyyi 'l-ʿarabīyyi 'l-qurashīyyi 'z-zamzamīyyi 'l-makkīyyi 't-tihāmīyyi

Possessor of the Flag, nobility and generosity, Fulfiller of promises, possessor of longing for Allāh ﷻ, the Kindler of such longing in others, Owner of the mule, of noble birth, Owner of the Pool and the scepter, the Prophet of Return, the speaker with Reward, the One mentioned in the Book, the Prophet of Allāh, the Prophet-servant of Allāh, the Prophet-Treasure of Allāh the Prophet-Proof of Allāh, the Prophet that whoever obeyed, in truth obeyed Allāh and that whoever disobeyed, in truth disobeyed Allāh; the Arabian Prophet, the Qurayshī Prophet, the Zamzamī prophet, the Meccan prophet , the Tihamī prophet, ➢

صَاحِبِ الوَجْهِ الْجَمِيلِ وَالطَّرْفِ الكَحِيلِ وَالْخَدِّ الأَسِيلِ وَالْكَوثَرِ وَالسَّلْسَبِيلِ قَاهِرِ الْمُضَادِّينَ مُبِيدِ الْكَافِرِينَ وَقَاتِلِ الْمُشْرِكِينَ قَائِدِ الغُرِّ الْمُحَجَّلِينَ إِلَى جَنَّاتِ النَّعِيمِ وَجِوَارِ الْكَرِيمِ صَاحِبِ سَيِّدِنَا جِبْرِيلَ ﷺ وَرَسُولِ رَبِّ العَالَمِينَ وَشَفِيعِ الْمُذْنِبِينَ وَغَايَةِ الغَمَامِ وَمِصْبَاحِ الظَّلَامِ وَقَمَرِ التَّمَامِ

ṣāḥibi 'l-wajhi 'l-jamīli wa 'ṭ-ṭarfi 'l-kaḥīli wa 'l-khaddi 'l-assīli wa 'l-kawthari wa 's-salsabīli qāhiri 'l-muḍāddīna mubīdi 'l-kāfirina wa qātili 'l-mushrikīna qā'idi 'l-ghurri 'l-muḥajjalīna ilā jannāti 'n-naʿīmi wa jiwāri 'l-karīmi ṣāḥibi Sayyīdinā Jibrīla ﷺ *wa Rasūli Rabbi 'l-ʿĀlamīna wa shafīʿi 'l-mudhnibīna wa ghāyati 'l-ghamām wa misbāḥi 'ẓ-ẓalāmi wa qamari 't-tamāmi*

Possessor of the handsome face, the naturally-mascaraed eyebrows, the noble cheeks, and Owner of the Springs of Kawthar and Salsabīl, conqueror of the adversaries to Truth, the Destroyer of unbelief, the one who fought idolaters' false belief, general for those possessing shining faces and shining limbs (from the light of ablution), the Guide to the Divine Garden and the Vicinity of the Allāh, The Most Generous, Companion of our master Gabriel ﷺ, the Messenger of the Lord of the worlds, Advocate for sinners though their sins reached the heights of the clouds, the Lamp of the Darkness and the full moon, ➢

صَلَّى اللهُ عَلَيهِ وَعَلَى آلِهِ الْمُصْطَفَينَ مِنْ أَطْهَرِ جِبلَةٍ صَلَاةً دَائِمَةً يَتَجَدَّدُ بِهَا حُبُورُهُ وَيُشَرَّفُ بِهَا فِي الْمِيعَادِ بَعْثُهُ وَنُشُورُهُ صَلَّى اللهُ عَلَيهِ وَعَلَى آلِهِ الْأَنْجُمِ الطَّوَالِعِ صَلَاةً تَجُودُ عَلَيهِمْ بِهَا أَجوَدَ الْغُيُوثِ وَالْهَوامِعِ أَرْسَلَهُ مِنْ أَرْجَحِ الْعَرَبِ مِيزَاناً وَأَوضَحِهَا بَيَاناً وَأَفْصَحِهَا لِسَاناً وَأَشْمَخِهَا إِيمَاناً وَأَعْلَاهَا مَقَاماً وَأَحْلَاهَا كَلَاماً وَأَوْفَاهَا ذِمَاماً وَأَصْفَاهَا رَغَاماً

ṣalla-'Llāhu ʿalayhi wa ʿalā ālihi 'l-muṣṭafayna min aṭ-hari jibillatin ṣalātan dā'imatan ʿalā 'l-abadi ghayra muḍmaḥillatan ṣalla 'Llāhu ʿalayhi wa ʿalā ālihi ṣalātan yatajaddadu bihā ḥubūruhu wa yusharrafu bihā fī 'l-mīʿādi baʿthuhu wa nushūruhu faṣalla 'Llāhu ʿalayhi wa ʿalā ālihi 'l-anjumi 'ṭ-ṭawaliʿi ṣalātan tajūdu ʿalayhim ajwada 'l-ghuyūthi wa 'l-hawāmiʿi arsalahu min arjaḥi 'l-ʿarabī mīzānan wa awḍaḥihā bayānan wa afṣaḥihā lisānan wa ashmakhihā īmānan wa āʿlāhā maqāman wa aḥlāhā kalāman wa awfāhā dhimāman wa aṣfāhā raghāman

may Allāh's blessings be upon him and his more purely chosen family blessings eternal and everlasting, never diminishing, the blessings of Allāh be upon him and his family! Blessing by means of which his happiness is renewed, his sending and his resurrection on the Promised Day are honored! Bless him and his family, the Rising Stars, blessings more generous than abundant pouring rains! Send them to the one who of all the Arabs is more just, more eloquent, Greater in faith, higher in station, more articulate in words, more careful of the rights of others and purer in his aversion for others ➢

فَأَوْضَحَ الطَّرِيقَةَ وَنَصَحَ الْخَلِيقَةَ وَشَهَرَ الإِسْلَامَ وَكَسَّرَ الأَصْنَامَ وَأَظْهَرَ الْأَحْكَامَ وَحَظَّرَ الْحَرَامَ وَعَمَّ بِالإِنْعَامِ صَلَّى اللهُ عَلَيهِ وَعَلَى آلِهِ فِي كُلِّ مَحْفَلٍ وَمَقَامٍ أَفْضَلَ الصَّلَواةِ وَالسَّلَامِ صَلَّى اللهُ عَلَيهِ وَعَلَى آلِهِ صَلَاةً تَامَّةً زَاكِيَةً وَ صَلَّى اللهُ عَلَيهِ وَعَلَى آلِهِ صَلَاةً يَتْبَعُهَا رَوحٌ وَرَيحَانٌ وَيَعْقِبُهَا مَغْفِرَةٌ وَرِضْوَانٌ

fa awḍaḥa 't-ṭarīqaṭa wa naṣaḥa 'l-khalīqaṭa wa shahara 'l-Islāma wa kassara 'l-aṣnāma wa aẓhara 'l-aḥkāma wa ḥaẓẓara 'l-ḥarāma wa 'amma bi 'l-in'āmi ṣalla 'Llāhu 'alayhi wa 'alā ālihi fī kulli maḥfilin wa maqāmin afḍala 'ṣ-ṣalāti wa 's-salāmi ṣalla 'Llāhu 'alayhi wa 'alā ālihi 'awdan wa bad'an ṣalātan takūnu dhakhīratan wa wirdan ṣalla 'Llāhu 'alayhi wa 'alā ālihi ṣalātan tāmmatan zākīyatan wa ṣalla 'Llāhu 'alayhi wa 'alā ālihi ṣalātan yatba'uhā rawḥun wa rayḥānun wa yā'qubuhā maghfiratun wa riḍwān

For he made the Path clear and he advised creation, he made Islām reknowned and smashed the idols, he made justice appear, he forbade the prohibited, and spread favours to all the worlds, the blessings of Allāh be upon him and his family at every gathering and every spot, the best of peace and blessings upon him and his family over and over again, blessings, which are a source of treasure, the blessings of Allāh be upon him and his family, complete and pure blessings, and the blessings of Allāh be upon him and his family, blessings trailed by fragrances and scents and succeeded by forgiveness and satisfaction! ➢

وَ صَلَّى اللهُ عَلَى أَفْضَلِ مَنْ طَابَ مِنْهُ النَّجَارُ وَسَمَا بِهِ الفَخَارُ وَاسْتَنَارَتْ بِنُورِ جَبِينِهِ الْأَقْمَارُ وَتَضَاءَلَتْ عِنْدَ جُودِ يَمِينِهِ الْغَمَائِمُ وَالبِحَارُ سَيِّدِنَا وَنَبِيِّنَا مُحَمَّدٍ الَّذِي بِبَاهِرِ آيَاتِهِ أَضَاءَتِ الْأَنْجَادُ وَالْأَغْوَارُ وَبِمُعْجِزَاتِ آيَاتِهِ نَطَقَ الْكِتَابُ وَتَوَاتَرَتِ الْأَخْبَارُ صَلَّى اللهُ عَلَيهِ وَعَلَى آلِهِ وَأَصْحَابِهِ الَّذِينَ هَاجَرُوا لِنُصْرَتِهِ وَنَصَرُوهُ فِي هِجْرَتِهِ

wa ṣalla 'Llāhu ʿalā afḍala man ṭāba minhu 'n-najāru wa samā bihi 'l-fakhāru wa 'stanārat bi-nūri jabīnihi 'l-aqmār wa taḍā'alat ʿinda jūdi yamīnihi 'l-ghamā'imu wa 'l-bihāru Sayyīdinā wa nabīyyinā Muḥammadini 'Lladhī bi bāhiri āyātihi aḍā'ati 'l-anjādu wa 'l-aghwāru wa bi-muʿjizāti āyātihi naṭaqa 'l-kitābu wa tawātarati 'l-'akhbāru ṣalla-'Llāhu ʿalayhi wa ʿalā ālihi wa aṣḥābihi 'Lladhīna hājarū li-nuṣratihi wa naṣarūḥu fī hijratihi

And the blessing of Allāh be upon the One whose lineage was most permeated with goodness, and was cause for its exaltation, and through the light of whose cheeks the moons were illuminated and by the generosity of his right hand the clouds and seas were illuminated, our master and prophet Muḥammad by the splendor of whose signs the highlands and lowlands were illuminated and by the miracles of his signs the Book was enunciated and the Good News was transmitted, blessings of Allāh be upon him and his family, and his companions who emigrated to help him and helped him to emigrate, ➢

فَنِعْمَ الْمُهَاجِرُونَ وَنِعْمَ الْأَنْصَارُ صَلَاةً نَامِيَةً دَائِمَةً مَا سَجَعَتْ فِي أَيْكِهَا الْأَطْيَارُ وَهَمَعَتْ بِوَبْلِهَا الدِّيَمَةُ الْمِدْرَارُ ضَاعَفَ اللهُ عَلَيْهِ دَائِمَ صَلَوَاتِهِ اللَّهُمَّ صَلِّ عَلَى سَيِّدِنَا مُحَمَّدٍ وَعَلَى آلِهِ الطَّيِّبِينَ الْكِرَامِ صَلَاةً مَوْصُولَةً دَائِمَةَ الْإِتِّصَالِ بِدَوَامِ ذِي الْجَلَالِ وَالْإِكْرَامِ *

fa-ni'mā 'l-muhājirūna wa ni'mā 'l-anṣāru ṣalātan nāmīyatan dā'imatan mā saja'at fī aykihā 'l-aṭyāru wa hama't bi wablihā 'd-diyamatu 'l-midrāru ḍā'afa 'Llāhu 'alayhi dā'ima ṣalawātihi Allāhumma ṣalli 'alā Sayyīdinā Muḥammadin wa 'alā ālihi 'ṭ-ṭayyibīna 'l-kirāmi ṣalātan mawsūlatan dā'imata 'l-ittiṣāli bi dawāmi dhi 'l-jalāli wa 'l-ikrāmi •

and blessed be the Emigrants and blessed be the Helpers blessings which grow and are the eternal for as long as birds cool themselves in the forests, rain streams down in abundance, and multiply the eternal blessings upon him. O Allāh, bless our master Muḥammad and his good and noble family with blessing which are perpetual and eternally bound up with the duration of the Owner of Majesty and Nobility! *

(٣٧) اللَّهُمَّ صَلِّ عَلَى سَيِّدِنَا مُحَمَّدٍ الَّذِي هُوَ قُطْبُ الْجَلَالَةِ

(37) Allāhumma ṣalli 'alā Sayyīdinā Muḥammadin 'Lladhī hūwa qutbu 'l-jalālati

(37) O Allāh, bless our master Muḥammad who is the Pole of Majesty, ➤

وَشَمْسُ النُّبُوَّةِ وَالرِّسَالَةِ الْهَادِي مِنَ الضَّلَالَةِ وَالْمُنْقِذُ مِنَ الْجَهَالَةِ ﷺ صَلَاةً دَائِمَةَ الْإِتِّصَالِ وَالتَّوَالِي مُتَعَاقِبَةً بِتَعَاقُبِ الْأَيَّامِ وَاللَّيَالِي ❋

wa shamsu 'n-nubūwwati wa 'r-Risālati wa 'l-hādi mina 'ḍ-ḍalālati wa 'l-munqidhu mina 'l-jahālati ﷺ *ṣalātan dā'imata 'l-ittiṣāli wa 't-tawāli muta-ʿāqibatan bitaʿāqubi 'l-ayyāmi wa 'l-layāli* •

the sun of Prophethood ﷺ and the Message, the Guide away from error and the savior from ignorance, may the blessings and peace of Allāh be upon him, eternal blessings connected with and successively repeating with the alternation of days and nights! ❋

الإثْنَيْن

Monday

الحِزبُ الثَّامِنْ فِي يَوْمِ الإِثْنَيْنِ

Al-Ḥizbu 'th-Thāminu fī Yawmi 'l-Ithnayni

The Eighth Chapter to be Read on Monday

(١) اللَّهُمَّ صَلِّ عَلَى سَيِّدِنَا مُحَمَّدٍ النَّبِيِّ الزَّاهِدِ رَسُولِ المَلِكِ الصَّمَدِ الْوَاحِدِ ﷺ صَلَاةً دَائِمَةً إِلَى مُنْتَهَى الْأَبَدِ بِلَا انْقِطَاعٍ وَلَا نَفَاذٍ صَلَاةً تُنْجِينَا مِنْ حَرِّ جَهَنَّمَ وَبِئْسَ الْمِهَادُ ❋

(1) Allāhumma ṣalli ʿalā Sayyīdinā Muḥammadin 'n-nabīyyi 'z-zāhidi Rasūli 'l-Malki 'ṣ-Ṣamadi 'l-Wāḥidi ﷺ ṣalātan dā'imatan ilā muntahā 'l-abadi bilā inqiṭāʿin wa lā nafādhin ṣalātan tunjīnā bihā min ḥarri jaḥannama wa bi'sa 'l-mihād •

(1) O Allāh, bless our master Muḥammad, the aesthetic Prophet, the Messenger of only Eternal King, and Allāh ﷻ s blessing and peace be upon him, blessings which are eternal, and which reach the farthest limit of eternity, with no break and depletion, blessings which save us from the heat of Helfire, an evil resting place! ❋

(٢) اللَّهُمَّ صَلِّ عَلَى سَيِّدِنَا مُحَمَّدٍ النَّبِيِّ الْأُمِّيِّ وَعَلَى آلِهِ وَسَلِّمْ صَلَاةً لَا يُحْصَىٰ لَهَا عَدَدٌ وَلَا يُعَدُّ لَهَا مَدَدٌ ❁

(2) Allāhumma ṣalli ʿalā Sayyīdinā Muḥammidini 'n-nabīyyi 'l-ummīyi wa ʿalā ālihi wa sallim ṣalātan lā yuḥsā lahā ʿadadun wa lā yuʿaddu lahā madadun •

(2) O Allāh, bless and grant peace to our master Muḥammad, the Unlettered Prophet, and his family, blessing which are uncountable and blessing whose supply is not impeded! ❁

(٣) اللَّهُمَّ صَلِّ عَلَى سَيِّدِنَا مُحَمَّدٍ صَلَاةً تُكَرِّمُ بِهَا مَثْوَاهُ وَتُبَلِّغُ بِهَا يَوْمَ الْقِيَامَةِ مِنَ الشَّفَاعَةِ رِضَاهُ ❁

(3) Allāhumma ṣalli ʿalā Sayyīdinā Muḥammadin ṣalātan tukkarimu bihā mathwāhu wa tuballighu bihā yawma 'l-qīyāmati mina 'sh-shafāʿatī riḍāhu •

(3) O Allāh, bless our master Muḥammad, blessing which which enable his abode and blessings, which procure on the Day of Judgment pleasure from his intercession! ❁

(٤) اللَّهُمَّ صَلِّ عَلَى سَيِّدِنَا مُحَمَّدٍ النَّبِيِّ الْأَصِيلِ السَّيِّدِ النَّبِيلِ

(4) Allāhumma ṣalli ʿalā Sayyīdinā Muḥammadin 'n-nabīyyi 'l-aṣīli 's-Sayyidi 'n-nabīl

(4) O Allāh, bless our master Muḥammad, the Prophet of noble origin, the highbred master ➤

الَّذِي جَاءَ بِالوَحْيِ وَالتَّنْزِيلِ وَأَوْضَحَ بَيَانَ التَّأْوِيلِ وَجَاءَهُ الأَمِينُ سَيِّدُنَا جِبْرِيلُ ﵇ بِالكَرَامَةِ وَالتَّفْضِيلِ وَأَسْرَى بِهِ المَلِكُ الجَلِيلُ فِي اللَّيلِ البَهِيمِ الطَّوِيلِ فَكَشَفَ لَهُ عَنْ أَعْلَى المَلَكُوتِ وَأَرَاهُ سَنَاءَ الجَبَرُوتِ وَنَظَرَ إِلَى قُدْرَةِ الحَيِّ الدَّائِمِ البَاقِي الَّذِي لَا يَمُوتُ ﷺ صَلَاةً مَقْرُونَةً بِالجَمَالِ وَالحُسْنِ وَالكَمَالِ وَالخَيْرِ وَالإِفْضَالِ ❋

Alladhī jā'a bi 'l-waḥyī wa 't-tanzīli wa awḍaḥa bayāna 't-tāwīli wa jā'ahu 'l-amīnu Sayyīdunā Jibrīlu 'alayhi 's-salām bi 'l-karāmati wa 't-tafḍīli wa asrā bihi 'l-maliku 'l-jalīlu fī 'l-layli 'l-bahīmi 'ṭ-ṭawīli fa kashafa lahu 'an 'alā 'l-malakūti wa arāhu sanā'a 'l-jabarūti wa naẓara ilā qudrati 'l-ḥayyi 'd-dā'imi 'l-bāqī 'Lladhī lā yamūt ﷺ ṣalātan maqrūnatan bi 'l-jamāli wa 'l-ḥusni wa 'l-kamāli wa 'l-khayri wa 'l-ifḍāli •

who came with inspired revelation, and who clarified the meaning of interpretation, and to whom came the faithful one, our master Gabriel ﵇ with honour and dignity, and who journeyed with him to the King, the Glorious One, on the long dark night and revealed to him the heights of the Kingdoms of Heavens, and showed him the supremacy of the omnipotence of the Heavens, and who saw the Power of The Living, The Eternal, The Abiding, the One who never dies! Allāh's blessing and peace be upon him, blessings which are permeated with beauty, with perfection, with goodness and with favour! ❋

(٥) اللَّهُمَّ صَلِّ عَلَى سَيِّدِنَا مُحَمَّدٍ وَعَلَى آلِ سَيِّدِنَا مُحَمَّدٍ عَدَدَ الْأَقْطَار وَصَلِّ عَلَى سَيِّدِنَا مُحَمَّدٍ وَعَلَى آلِ سَيِّدِنَا مُحَمَّدٍ عَدَدَ وَرَقِ الْأَشجَارِ وَصَلِّ عَلَى سَيِّدِنَا مُحَمَّدٍ وَعَلَى آلِ سَيِّدِنَا مُحَمَّدٍ عَدَدَ زَبَدِ الْبِحَارِ وَصَلِّ عَلَى سَيِّدِنَا مُحَمَّدٍ وَعَلَى آلِ سَيِّدِنَا مُحَمَّدٍ عَدَدَ الْأَنهَارِ وَصَلِّ عَلَى سَيِّدِنَا مُحَمَّدٍ وَعَلَى آلِ سَيِّدِنَا مُحَمَّدٍ عَدَدَ رَمْلِ الصَّحَارِي وَالقِفَارِ

(5) Allāhumma ṣalli ʿalā Sayyīdinā Muḥammadin wa ʿalā āli Sayyīdinā Muḥammadin ʿadada 'l-aqṭāri wa ṣalli ʿalā Sayyīdinā Muḥammadin wa ʿalā Sayyīdinā Muḥammadin ʿadada waraqi 'l-ashjār wa ṣalli ʿalā Sayyīdinā Muḥammadin wa ʿalā āli Sayyīdinā Muḥammadin ʿadada zabadi 'l-bihār wa ṣalli ʿalā Muḥammadin ʿadada 'l-anhār wa ṣalli ʿāla Sayyīdinā Muḥammadin wa ʿalā Sayyīdinā Muḥammadin ʿadada ramli 'ṣ-ṣaḥārī wa 'l-qifār

(5) O Allāh, bless our master Muḥammad and the family of our master Muḥammad as many times as there are drops of rain! O Allāh bless our master Muḥammad and the family of master Muḥammad as many times as they are leaves of rain and bless our master Muḥammad and the family of master Muḥammad in as much abundance as there is foam upon the sea and bless our master Muḥammad and the family of master Muḥammad as many times as there are rivers and bless our master Muḥammad and family of our master Muḥammad as there are grains of send in the desert and in the wilderness! ➢

وَصَلِّ عَلَى سَيِّدِنَا مُحَمَّدٍ وَعَلَى آلِ سَيِّدِنَا مُحَمَّدٍ عَدَدَ ثِقْلِ الْجِبَالِ وَالْأَحْجَارِ
وَصَلِّ عَلَى سَيِّدِنَا مُحَمَّدٍ وَعَلَى آلِ سَيِّدِنَا مُحَمَّدٍ عَدَدَ أَهْلِ الْجَنَّةِ وَأَهْلِ النَّارِ
وَصَلِّ عَلَى سَيِّدِنَا مُحَمَّدٍ وَعَلَى آلِ سَيِّدِنَا مُحَمَّدٍ عَدَدَ الْأَبْرَارِ وَالْفُجَّارِ وَصَلِّ
عَلَى سَيِّدِنَا مُحَمَّدٍ وَعَلَى آلِ سَيِّدِنَا مُحَمَّدٍ عَدَدَ مَا يَخْتَلِفُ بِهِ اللَّيْلُ وَالنَّهَارُ
وَاجْعَلِ اللَّهُمَّ صَلَاتَنَا عَلَيْهِ حِجَاباً مِنْ عَذَابِ النَّارِ

wa ṣalli ʿalā Sayyīdinā Muḥammadin wa ʿalā āli Sayyīdinā Muḥammadin ʿadada thiqli 'l-jibāli wa 'l-aḥjār wa ṣalli ʿalā Sayyīdinā Muḥammadin wa ʿalā āli Sayyīdinā Muḥammadin ʿadada āhli 'l-jannati wa āhli 'n-nāri wa ṣalli ʿalā Sayyīdinā Muḥammadin wa ʿalā āli Sayyīdinā Muḥammadin ʿadada 'l-abrāri wa 'l-fujjāri wa ṣalli ʿalā Sayyīdinā Muḥammadin wa ʿalā āli Sayyīdinā Muḥammadin ʿadada mā yakhtalifu bihi 'l-laylu wa 'n-nahār wa 'jʿali 'Llāhiumma ṣalātanā ʿalayhi ḥijāban min ʿadhābi 'n-nāri

And bless our master Muḥammad and the family of master Muḥammad as much as the weight of all mountains and all rocks and bless our master Muḥammad and the family of master Muḥammad, on the number of dwellers of The Gardens and dwellers of The Fire and bless our master Muḥammad and the family of our master Muḥammad on the number of the righteous and on the number of corrupt ones and bless our master Muḥammad and the family of master Muḥammad as many times as the right has alternated with the day and make, O Allāh, our invoking blessings on him a shield from the punishment of The Fire ➢

وَسَبَباً لِإِبَاحَةِ دَارِ القَرَارِ إِنَّكَ أَنْتَ الْعَزِيزُ الْغَفَّارُ وَ صَلَّى اللهُ عَلَى سَيِّدِنَا مُحَمَّدٍ وَعَلَى آلِهِ الطَّيِّبِينَ وَذُرِّيَّتِهِ الْمُبَارَكِينَ وَصَحَابَتِهِ الْأَكْرَمِينَ وَأَزْوَاجِهِ أُمَّهَاتِ الْمُؤْمِنِينَ صَلَاةً مَوْصُولَةً تَتَرَدَّدُ إِلَى يَوْمِ الدِّينِ ❋

wa sababan li ibāḥati dāri 'l-qarāri innaka anta 'l-ʿAzīzu 'l-Ghaffār wa ṣalla 'Llāhu ʿalā Sayyīdinā Muḥammadin wa ʿalā ālihi 'ṭ-ṭayyibīna wa dhurrīyatihi 'l-mubārakīna wa ṣaḥābatihi 'l-akramīna wa azwājihi ummahāti 'l-mu'minīna ṣalātan mawṣūlatan tataraddadu ilā yawmi 'd-dīn •

and a means of us gaining permission to enter the abode of Permanence, for You are the Mighty, the forgiving and ﷺ our master Muḥammad and upon his virtuous family, his blessed descendants, his Honoured companions and his wives, Mother of the Believers, blessings which are continual and frequent until the Day of judgment! ❋

(٦) اللَّهُمَّ صَلِّ عَلَى سَيِّدِ الْأَبْرَارِ وَزَيْنِ الْمُرْسَلِينَ الْأَخْيَارِ وَأَكْرَمِ مَنْ أَظْلَمَ عَلَيْهِ اللَّيْلُ وَاشْرَقَ عَلَيْهِ النَّهَارُ(٣x) ❋

(6) Allāhumma ṣalli ʿalā Sayyidi 'l-abrāri wa zayni 'l-mursalīna 'l-akhyāri wa akrami man aẓlama ʿalayhi 'l-laylu wa ashraqa ʿalayhi 'n-nahār (3x) •

(6) O Allāh, bless the master of righteous, the adornment of the Messengers, the Choicest and Noblest ever to have been cloaked in the darkness of the night or bathed in the light of the day! (3x) ❋

(٧) اللَّهُمَّ يَا ذَا المَنِّ الَّذِي لَا يُكَافَى امْتِنَانُهُ وَالطَّوْلِ الَّذِي لَا يُجَازَى إِنْعَامُهُ وَإِحْسَانُهُ نَسْأَلُكَ بِكَ وَلَا نَسْأَلُكَ بِأَحَدٍ غَيْرِكَ أَنْ تُطْلِقَ أَلْسِنَتَنَا عِنْدَ السُّؤَالِ وَتُوَفِّقَنَا لِصَالِحِ الْأَعْمَالِ وَتَجْعَلَنَا مِنَ الآمِنِينَ يَوْمَ الرَّجْفِ وَالزِّلْزَالِ يَا ذَا العِزَّةِ وَالْجَلَالِ ❋

(7) Allāhumma yā dhā 'l-manni 'Lladhī lā yukāfa'u imtinānuhu wa 'ṭ-ṭawli 'Lladhī lā yujāza inʿāmuhu wa iḥsānuhu nas'aluka bika wa lā nas'aluka bi aḥadin ghayrika an tuṭliqa alsinatanā ʿinda 's-su'āli wa tuwaffiqanā li-ṣāliḥi 'l-āʿmāli wa tajʿalanā mina 'l-āminīna yawma 'r-rajfi wa 'z-zilzāli yā dha 'l-ʿizzati wa 'l-jalāl •

(7) O Allāh, Provider of Favor, Whose strength and might are unequalled, and Whose favour and virtue are beyond compare, we ask You and nobody else but You, to loosen our tongues in asking You, and grant us success in doing good works, and make us among the trustworthy ones on the Day of convulsions and earthquakes, O Allāh the Master of Might and Glory! ❋

(٨) أَسْأَلُكَ يَا نُورَ النُّورِ قَبْلَ الْأَزْمِنَةِ وَالدُّهُورِ أَنْتَ الْبَاقِي بِلَا زَوَالٍ الغَنِيُّ بِلَا مِثَالٍ

(8) As'aluka yā nūra 'n-nūri qabla 'l-azminati wa 'd-duhūr anta 'l-bāqīyu bi lā zawālin 'l-ghanīyyu bilā mithāl

(8) I ask You, The Light of the Light, which was before Time and Eternity!You are the abiding with no ending, the Rich with no equal, the Holy, the Pure, ➢

الْقُدُّوسُ الطَّاهِرُ الْعَلِيُّ الْقَاهِرُ الَّذِي لَا يُحِيطُ بِهِ مَكَانٌ وَلَا يَشْتَمِلُ عَلَيْهِ زَمَانٌ
أَسْأَلُكَ بِأَسْمَائِكَ الْحُسْنَى كُلِّهَا وَبِأَعْظَمِ أَسْمَائِكَ إِلَيْكَ وَ أَشْرَفِهَا عِنْدَكَ
مَنْزِلَةً وَأَجْزَلِهَا عِنْدَكَ ثَوَاباً وَأَسْرَعِهَا مِنْكَ إِجَابَةً وَبِإِسْمِكَ الْمَخْزُونِ الْمَكْنُونِ
الْجَلِيلِ الْأَجَلِّ الْكَبِيرِ الْأَكْبَرِ الْعَظِيمِ الْأَعْظَمِ الَّذِي تُحِبُّهُ وَتَرْضَى عَمَّنْ دَعَاكَ
بِهِ وَتَسْتَجِيبُ لَهُ دُعَاءَهُ

Al-quddūsu 'ṭ-ṭāhiru 'l-ʿalīyyu 'l-qāhiru 'Lladhī lā yuḥīṭu bihi makānun wa lā yashtamilu ʿalayhi zamānun as'aluka bi asmā'ika 'l-ḥusnā kullihā wa bi-āʿẓami asmā'ika ilayka wa ashrafihā ʿindaka manzilatan wa ajzalihā ʿindaka thawāban wa asraʿihā minka ijābatan wa bi ismika 'l-makhzūni 'l-maknūni 'l-jalīli 'l-ajalli 'l-kabīri 'l-akbari 'l-ʿaẓīmi 'l-aʿẓami 'Lladhī tuḥibbuhu wa tarḍa ʿamman daʿāka bihi wa tastajību lahu duʿā'ahu

the High, the Powerful, the One who is neither encompassed by space nor contained by time!I ask You in all of Your most beautiful names and in the Greatest of Your names, and for the sake of the rank most noble to You, and for the sake the reward most plentiful with You, and for the sake of the promptest response from You, and in Your protected and Hidden Name, The Most Exalted, the Exalted, the Greatest of the Great, the Most Magnificent of the Magnificent, the One who responds to and satisfies him who calls upon You in them and whose prayer is accepted! ➢

أَسْأَلُكَ اللَّهُمَّ بِلَا إِلَهَ إِلَّا أَنْتَ الْحَنَّانُ الْمَنَّانُ بَدِيعُ السَّمَاوَاتِ وَالْأَرْضِ ذُوْ الْجَلَالِ وَالْإِكْرَامِ عَالِمِ الْغَيبِ وَالشَّهَادَةِ الْكَبِيرِ الْمُتَعَالِ وَأَسْأَلُكَ بِإِسْمِكَ الْعَظِيمِ الْأَعْظَمِ الَّذِي إِذَا دُعِيتَ بِهِ أَجَبْتَ وَإِذَا سُئِلْتَ بِهِ أَعْطَيتَ وَأَسْأَلُكَ بِإِسْمِكَ الَّذِي يَذِلُّ لِعَظَمَتِهِ الْعُظَمَاءُ وَالْمُلُوكُ وَالسِّبَاعُ وَالْهَوَامُّ وَكُلُّ شَيْءٍ خَلَقْتَهُ يَا اللهُ **(قِفْ وَادْعُ بِمَا شِئْتَ فَهُنَا إِسْمُ اللهِ الْأَعْظَمُ بَيْنَ يَا اللهُ وَيَا رَبُّ)**

as'aluka 'Llāhumma bilā ilāha illā anta 'l-ḥannānu 'l-mannānu badīʿu 's-samāwāti wa 'l-arḍi dhu 'l-Jalāli wa 'l-Ikrāmi ʿAlimu 'l-ghaybi wa 'sh-shahādati 'l-Kabīru 'l-Mutaʿāl wa as'aluka bi ismika 'l-ʿaẓīmi 'l-āʿẓami 'Lladhī idhā duʿīta bihi ajabta wa idhā su'ilta bihi āʿṭayta wa as'aluka bi ismika 'Lladhī yadhillu li-ʿaẓamatihi 'l-ʿuẓamā'u wa 'l-mulūku wa 's-sibāʿu wa 'l-hawāmmu wa kullu shay'in khalaqtahu Yā Allāhu

I ask You there is no god but You, the compassionate the Benefactor, Creator of the Heavens and the Earth, Master of Glory and Honor, the knower of the Unseen and the Seen, the Great, the Exalted!I ask You in Your Greatest Name in which when we pray, our prayer is granted, and in which when we make a request, our request is granted, and I ask You by the Name in which we humble with its might the mighty ones the kings, the lions, the reptiles and everything You have created O Allāh, O Allāh the Lord, accept my prayer! **(Stop and supplicate with any supplication you like, because here is hidden Allāh's Greatest Name)** ➢

يَا رَبِّ اْسْتَجِبْ دَعْوَتِي يَا مَنْ لَهُ الْعِزَّةُ وَالْجَبَرُوتُ يَا ذَا الْمُلْكِ وَالْمَلَكُوتِ يَا مَنْ هُوَ حَيٌّ لَا يَمُوتُ سُبْحَانَكَ رَبِّي مَا أَعْظَمَ شَأْنَكَ وَأَرْفَعَ مَكَانَكَ أَنْتَ رَبِّي يَا مُتَقَدِّساً فِي جَبَرُوتِهِ إِلَيكَ أَرْغَبُ وَإِيَّاكَ أَرْهَبُ يَا عَظِيمُ يَا كَبِيرُ يَا جَبَّارُ يَا قَادِرُ يَا قَوِيُّ تَبَارَكْتَ يَا عَظِيمُ تَعَالَيتَ يَا عَلِيمُ سُبْحَانَكَ يَا عَظِيمُ سُبْحَانَكَ يَا جَلِيلُ

yā Rabbi 'stajib da'wati yā man lahu 'l-'izzatu wa 'l-jabarūtu yā dha 'l-Mulki wa 'l-Malakūti yā man huwa ḥayyun lā yamūtu subḥānaka rabbī mā ā'ẓama shānaka wa arfa'a makānaka anta rabbī yā mutaqaddisan fī jabarūtihi ilayka arghabu wa iyyāka arhabu yā 'Aẓīmu yā Kabīru yā Jabbāru yā Qādiru yā Qawwīyun tabārakta yā 'Aẓīmu ta'ālāyta yā 'Alīmu subḥānaka yā 'Aẓīmu subḥānaka yā Jalīlu

O Allāh You to whom is the majesty and omnipotence, O Allāh the Master of Sovereignty and Kingdoms, O Allāh You Who are the living Who never dies, glory to You, Lord. What is greater than Your Rank, higher than Your Position? You are my Lord! O Allāh The Holy One in His omnipotence, I beseech You and I fear You! O Allāh the Great, O Allāh, The Majestic, O Allāh, The Powerful, O Allāh The Almighty, O Allāh, The Strong, You have blessed Yourself! O Allāh the Great One, You have exalted Yourself! O Allāh the knowing One, glory to You the Great One, glory to You! O Allāh The Splendid, ➤

أَسْأَلُكَ بِإِسْمِكَ الْعَظِيمِ التَّامِّ الْكَبِيرِ أَنْ لَا تُسَلِّطَ عَلَيْنَا جَبَّاراً عَنِيداً وَلَا شَيْطَاناً مَرِيداً وَلَا إِنْسَاناً حَسُوداً وَلَا ضَعِيفاً مِنْ خَلْقِكَ وَلَا شَدِيداً وَلَا بَارّاً وَلَا فَاجِراً وَلَا عَبِيداً وَلَا عَنِيداً ❋

as'aluka bi-'ismika 'l-'aẓīmi 't-tāmmi 'l-kabīri an lā tusalliṭu 'alaynā jabbāran 'anīdan wa lā shayṭānan marīdan wa lā insānan ḥasūdan wa lā ḍa'īfan min khalqika wa lā shadīdan wa lā bārran wa lā fājiran wa lā 'abīdan wa lā 'anīdā •

I ask You in Your Great, Perfect and Majestic Name, not to give any stubborn tyrant dominion over me, nor any rebellious Satan, nor an envier nor a weak one among Your Creation, nor an oppressor, nor a ruinous one, nor a corrupt one, nor a slave, nor someone defiant. ❋

(٩) اللَّهُمَّ إِنِّي أَسْأَلُكَ فَإِنِّي أَشْهَدُ أَنَّكَ أَنْتَ اللهُ الَّذِي لَا إِلَهَ إِلَّا أَنْتَ الْوَاحِدُ الْأَحَدُ الصَّمَدُ الَّذِي لَمْ يَلِدْ وَلَمْ يُولَد وَلَمْ يَكُنْ لَهُ كُفُواً أَحَدٌ

(9) Allāhumma innī as'aluka fa innī ashhadu annaka anta 'Llāhu 'Lladhī lā ilāha illā anta al-Wāḥidu 'l-Aḥadu 'ṣ-Ṣamadu 'Lladhī lam yalid wa lam yūlad wa lam yakun lahu kufūwan aḥadun

(9) O Allāh, I ask You and I bear witness that You are Allāh, and there is no god but You, the One, the Only, the Eternal, the One who neither begets nor is begotten, and there is nothing like Him! ➢

يَا هُوَ يَا مَنْ لَا هُوَ إِلَّا هُوَ يَا مَنْ لَا إِلَّهَ إِلَّا هُو يَا أَزَلِيُّ يَا أَبَدِيُ يَا دَهْرِيُّ يَا دَيْمُومِيُّ يَا مَنْ هُوَ الْحَيُّ الَّذِي لَا يَمُوتُ يَا إِلَهَنَا وَإِلَهَ كُلِّ شَيْءٍ إِلَهاً وَاحِداً لَا إِلَهَ إِلَّا أَنْتَ ❋

yā Huwa yā man lā Huwa illā Huwa yā man lā ilāha illā Huwa yā azalīyyu yā abadīyyu yā dahrīyyu yā daymūmīyyu yā man Huwa'l-Ḥāyyu 'Lladhī lā yamūtu yā ilāhanā wa ilāha kulli shay'in ilāhan wāḥidan lā ilāha illā anta •

O He! O The One besides Whom there is no other He but Himself! O One besides Whom there is no god but He! My infinity, My Eternity, My Everlasting, The Living Who does not die, Our God and God of everything, God, Alone, there is no god but You! ❋

(١٠) اللَّهُمَّ فَاطِرَ السَّمَاوَاتِ وَالْأَرْضِ عَالِمَ الغَيب وَالشَّهَادَةِ الرَّحْمَنَ الرَّحِيمَ الْحَيَّ القَيُّومَ الدَّيَانَ الحَنَّانَ المَنَّانَ البَاعِثَ الوَارِثَ ذَا الجَلَالِ وَالْإِكْرَامِ

(10) Allāhumma fāṭira 's-samāwāti wa 'l-arḍi 'ālimā 'l-ghaybi wa 'sh-shāḥadati 'r-Raḥmāni 'r-Raḥīm 'l-Ḥayyu 'l-Qayyūma 'd-Dayāna 'l-Hannāna 'l-Mananu al-Bā'i-thu 'l-Wāritha Dhū 'l-Jalāli wa 'l-ikrām

(10) O Allāh, Creator of the Heavens and Earth, Knower of the unseen and the Seen, The Compassionate, The Merciful, The Living, The Everlasting, The Judge, The Benefactor, The Munificent, The Reviver, The Inheritor, The Master of Glory and Honor! ➢

قُلُوبُ الْخَلَائِقِ بِيَدِكَ نَوَاصِيهِم إِلَيْكَ فَأَنْتَ تَزْرَعُ الْخَيْرَ فِي قُلُوبِهِمْ وَتَمْحُو الشَّرَّ إِذَا شِئْتَ مِنْهُمْ فَأَسْأَلُكَ اللَّهُمَّ أَنْ تَمْحُوَ مِنْ قَلْبِي كُلَّ شَيْءٍ تَكْرَهُهُ وَأَنْ تَحْشُوَ قَلْبِي مِنْ خَشْيَتِكَ وَمَعْرِفَتِكَ وَرَهْبَتِكَ وَالرَّغْبَةِ فِيمَا عِنْدَكَ وَالْأَمْنِ وَالْعَافِيَةِ وَأَعْطِفْ عَلَيْنَا بِالرَّحْمَةِ وَالْبَرَكَةِ مِنْكَ وَأَلْهِمْنَا الصَّوَابَ وَالْحِكْمَةَ فَنَسْأَلُكَ اللَّهُمَّ عِلْمَ الْخَائِفِينَ وَإِنَابَةَ الْمُخْبِتِينَ وَإِخْلَاصَ الْمُوقِنِينَ

qulūbu 'l-khalā'iqi bi-yadika nawāṣīhim ilayka fa anta tazraʿu 'l-khayra fī qulūbihim wa tamḥu 'sh-sharra idhā shi'ta minhum fa as'aluka 'Llāhumma an tamḥu min qalbī kulla shay'in takrahuhu wa an taḥshūwa qalbī min khashīyatika wa māʿrifatika wa rahbatika wa 'r-raghbati fīmā ʿindaka wa 'l-amni wa 'l-ʿāfiyati wa 'aʿtif ʿalaynā bi 'r-raḥmati wa 'l-barakati minka wa al-himnā 'ṣ-ṣawāba wa 'l-ḥikmata fa nas'aluka 'Llāhumma ʿilma 'l-khā'ifīna wa inābata 'l-mukhbitīna wa ikhlāṣa 'l-mūqinīna

The hearts of all creatures are between Your hands, we entrust them to You, for You cause goodness to grow in their hearts and You erase the evil from them as You like! So I ask You that You erase from my heart everything that You hate and fill my heart with fear of You, knowledge of You, awe of You, longing for what is with You, and security and well-being, and have pity on us with mercy and blessings from You, and inspire in us that which is proper and wise. And I ask You, O Allāh, for the knowledge of those who fear, the repentance of the humble and the sincerity of the certain ➢

وَشُكْرَ الصَّابِرِينَ وَتَوْبَةَ الصِّدِّيقِينَ وَنَسْأَلُكَ اللَّهُمَّ بِنُورِ وَجْهِكَ الَّذِي مَلأَ أَرْكَانَ عَرْشِكَ أَنْ تَزْرَعَ فِي قَلْبِي مَعْرِفَتَكَ حَتَّى أَعْرِفَكَ حَقَّ مَعْرِفَتِكَ كَمَا يَنْبَغِي أَنْ تُعْرَفَ بِهِ وَ صَلَّى اللهُ عَلَى سَيِّدِنَا مُحَمَّدٍ خَاتَمِ النَّبِيِّينَ وَإِمَامِ الْمُرْسَلِينَ وَعَلَى آلِهِ وَصَحْبِهِ أَجْمَعِينَ وَسَلَامٌ عَلَى الْمُرْسَلِينَ وَالْحَمْدُ لله رَبِّ الْعَالَمِينَ ❋

wa shukra 'ṣ-ṣābirīna wa tawbaṭa 'ṣ-ṣiddīqīn wa nas'aluka 'Llāhumma bi nūri wajhika 'Lladhī malā' arkāna ʿarshika an tazraʿa fī qalbī maʿrifatika ḥattā aʿrifaka ḥaqqa māʿrifatika kamā yambaghī an tuʿrafa bihi wa ṣalla 'Llāhu ʿalā Sayyīdinā Muḥammadin khātami 'n-nabīyyīnā wa imāmi 'l-mursalīna wa ʿalā ālihi wa ṣaḥbihi ajmʿīna wa salāman ʿalā al-mursalīna wa 'l-ḥamdu lillāhi Rabbi 'l-ʿĀlamīn •

and the gratitude of the patient, and the penitence of all the truthful ones! ❋

And I ask You by the Light of Your Countenance which fills every corners of Your Throne, that You cause to grow in my heart knowledge of You until I know You, with true gnosis, in a what should be known about You, and the blessings and abundant peace of Allāh be upon our master Muḥammad, the Seal of the prophets and the leader of the messengers, and upon his family and companions, and praise be to Allāh, the Lord of the worlds! ➢

اللَّهُمَّ اغْفِرْ لِمُؤَلِّفِهِ وَارْحَمْهُ وَاجْعَلْهُ مِنَ الْمَحْشُورِينَ فِي زُمْرَةِ النَّبِيِّينَ وَالصِّدِّيقِينَ يَوْمَ الْقِيَامَةِ بِفَضْلِكَ يَا أَرْحَمَ الرَّاحِمِينَ ❋

Allāhumma ighfir li mu'allifihi wa 'rḥamhu wa 'j'alhu mina 'l-maḥshurīna fī zumrati 'n-nabīyyīn wa 'ṣ-ṣiddīqīna yawma 'l-qīyāmati bi-faḍlika yā arḥama 'r-rāḥimīn •

O Allāh forgive the author of this book, have mercy on him and keep him with the company of prophets and veracious ones on the Day of Resurrection through your favors O Most Merciful One. ❋

هَذَا الدُّعَاءُ يُقْرَأُ عَقِبَ خَتْمِ دَلَآئِلِ الخَيْرَاتِ

Read al-Fātihah for the author and the following supplication which is the completion of *The Index of Good Things*:

بِسْمِ اللهِ الرَّحْمَنِ الرَّحِيمِ

اللَّهُمَّ اشْرَحْ بِالصَّلاةِ عَلَيهِ صُدُورَنَا وَيَسِّرْ بِهَا أُمُورَنَا وَفرِّجْ بِهَا هُمُومَنَا وَاكْشِفْ بِهَا غُمُومَنَا وَاغفِرْ بِهَا ذُنُوبَنَا وَاقْضِ بِهَا دُيُونَنَا وَأَصْلِحْ بِهَا أَحْوَالَنَا وَبَلِّغْ بِهَا آمَالَنَا وَتَقَبَّل بِهَا تَوبَتَنَا وَاَغْسِلْ بِهَا حَوبَتَنَا

Bismillāhi 'r-Raḥmāni 'r-Raḥīm Allāhumma 'shraḥ bi 'ṣ-ṣalāti ʿalayhi ṣudūranā wa yassir bihā umūranā wa farrij bihā humūmanā wa 'kshif bihā ghumūmanā wa 'ghfir bihā dhunūbanā wa 'qḍi bihā duyūnanā wa 'ṣliḥ bihā aḥwālanā wa balligh bihā āmālanā wa taqabbal bihā tawbatanā wa 'aghsil bihā ḥawbatanā

In the name of Allāh all-Merciful, the Mercy giving. O Allāh, through our asking for blessings upon him expands our hearts and thereby ease our affairs and dispel our anxieties and remove our sorrow and thereby forgive our sins and relieve our debts and improve our states and thereby fulfill our hopes and accept our repentance and cleans ours misdeeds! ➤

وَأَنْصُرْ بِهَا حُجَّتَنَا وَطَهِّرْ بِهَا أَلْسِنَتَنَا وَآنِسْ بِهَا وَحْشَتَنَا وَأَرْحَمْ بِهَا غُرْبَتَنَا وَاجْعَلْهَا نُوراً بَيْنَ أَيْدِينَا وَمِنْ خَلْفِنَا وَعَنْ أَيْمَانِنَا وَعَنْ شَمَائِلِنَا وَمِنْ فَوقِنَا وَمِنْ تَحْتِنَا وَفِي حَيَاتِنَا وَمَوتِنَا وَقُبُورِنَا وَحَشْرِنَا وَنَشْرِنَا وَظِلاً يَوْمَ الْقِيَامَةِ عَلَى رُؤُوسِنَا وَثَقِّلْ بِهَا يَا رَبِّ مَوَازِينَ حَسَنَاتِنَا وَأَدِمْ بَرَكَاتِهَا عَلَيْنَا حَتَّى نَلْقَى نَبِيَّنَا وَ سَيِّدَنَا مُحَمَّداً ﷺ

wa 'nṣur bihā ḥujjatana wa ṭāhhir bihā alsinatanā wa ānis bihā waḥshatanā wa 'rḥam bihā ghurbatanā wa 'j'alhā nūran bayna 'aydīnā wa min khalfinā wa 'an aymāninā wa 'an shamā'ilinā wa min fawqinā wa min taḥtinā wa fī ḥayātinā wa mawtinā wa fī qubūrinā wa ḥashrinā wa nashrinā wa ẓillan fī 'l-qīyāmati 'alā ru'ūsinā wa thaqqil bihā yā Rabbi mawazīna ḥāsanātina wa adim barakātihā 'alaynā ḥattā nalqā nabīyyanā wa Sayyīdanā Muḥammadan ﷺ

And thereby help our pleas and purify our Tongues and end our loneliness and thereby relieve our separation and make it a light in front of us and behind us! To our right and to our left and about us and beneath us and in our lives and in our deaths and in our graves and in our gathering and in our resurrection and shade for us on the Day of Judgment over our heads and weight down the scales thereby with good actions and repeat its blessing on us until we meet with our Prophet our master Muḥammad ﷺ, ➤

وَنَحْنُ آمِنُونَ مُطْمَئِنُّونَ فَرِحُونَ مُسْتَبْشِرُونَ وَلَا تُفَرِّقْ بَيْنَنَا وَبَيْنَهُ
حَتَّى تُدْخِلْنَا مُدْخَلَهُ وَتَأْوِينَا إِلَى جِوَارِهِ الْكَرِيمِ مَعَ الَّذِينَ أَنْعَمْتَ
عَلَيْهِمْ مِنَ النَّبِيِّينَ وَالصِّدِّيقِينَ وَالشُّهَدَاءِ وَالصَّالِحِينَ وَحَسُنَ أُولَئِكَ
رَفِيقاً اللَّهُمَّ إِنَّا آمَنَّا بِهِ ﷺ وَلَمْ نَرَهُ فَمَتِّعْنَا اللَّهُمَّ فِي الدَّارَيْنِ بِرُؤْيَتِهِ

wa naḥnu āminūna muṭma'inūna fariḥūna mustabshirūna wa lā tufarriq baynanā wa baynahu ḥattā tudkhilanā madkhalahu wa ta'wīnā ilā jiwārihi 'l-karīmi maʿa 'Lladhīna anʿamta ʿalayhim mina 'n-Nabīyyīnā wa 'ṣ-ṣiddīqīnā wa 'sh-shuhadā'i wa 'ṣ-ṣāliḥina wa ḥasuna ūlā'ika rafiqa Allāhumma innā āmannā bihi ﷺ wa lam narahu famattiʿnā Allāhumma fī 'd-dārayni bi ru'yatihi

and his family and we believe, we are certain, we are overjoyed and we are the receivers of good news and do not separate us from him until you make us enter through his entrance hall accommodate us in his noble neighbourhood with those You have favoured among the Prophets, the Truthful Ones, the Martyrs and the Righteous Ones, and what a fine company they are! O Allāh, we have believed in him, the blessings and peace of Allāh ﷻ be upon him, without seeing him, so make us enjoy O Allāh, a vision of him in the two realms ➢

وَثَبِّتْ قُلُوبَنَا عَلَى مَحَبَّتِهِ وَأَسْتَعْمِلْنَا عَلَى سُنَّتِهِ وَتَوَفَّنَا عَلَى مِلَّتِهِ وَاحْشُرْنَا فِي زُمْرَتِهِ النَّاجِيَةِ وَحِزْبِهِ الْمُفْلِحِينَ وَانْفَعْنَا بِمَا انْطَوَت عَلَيهِ قُلوبَنَا مِنْ مَحَبَّتِهِ ﷺ يَوْمَ لَا جَدَّ وَلَا مَالَ وَلَا بَنِين وَأَوْرِدْنَا حَوْضَهُ الْأَصْفَى وَاسْقِنَا بِكَأسِهِ الْأَوْفَى وَيَسِّرْ عَلَينَا زِيَارَةَ حَرَمِكَ وَحَرَمِهِ مِنْ قَبْلِ أَنْ تُمِيتَنَا وَأَدِم عَلَينَا الْإِقَامَةَ بِحَرَمِكَ وَحَرَمِهِ ﷺ إِلَى أَنْ نُتَوَفَّى

wa thabbit qulūbanā ʿalā maḥabbatihi wa ʾstaʿmilnā ʿalā sunnatihi wa tawwaffanā ʿalā millatihi wa ʾḥshurnā fī zumratihi ʾn-nājiyati wa ḥizbihi ʾl-mufliḥīna wa ʾnfaʿna bimā ʾnṭawat ʿalayhi qulūbunā min maḥabbatihi ﷺ yawma lā jadda wa lā māla wa lā banīna wa awridnā ḥawḍahu ʾl-aṣfā wa ʾsqinā bi kāʾsihi ʾl-awfā wa yassir ʿalaynā ziyārata ḥaramika wa ḥaramihi min qabli an tumītanā wa adim ʿalaynā ʾl-iqāmata bi ḥaramika wa ḥaramihi ﷺ ilā an nutawaffa

and keep our hearts always in love with him and establish us upon his way and cause us to die following his religion and resurrect us in his secure company and among his Party of the Successful and avail us of that love of him ﷺ which is locked away in our hearts on the Day when no ancestors, no wealth and no sons avail and let us drink at his purest pools and to drink from his fullest chalice and make easy for us a visit to Your Sacred place (Mecca) and his Sacred Place (Medina) before our death, and let our stay at Your Sacred Place and His Sacred Place ﷺ last until we pass away! ➢

اللَّهُمَّ إِنَّا نَسْتَشْفِعُ بِهِ إِلَيْكَ إِذْ هُوَ أَوْجَهُ الشُّفعَاءِ إليك وَنُقسِمُ بِهِ عَلَيك إِذْ هُوَ أَعْظَمُ مَنْ أُقْسِم بِحَقِّهِ عَلَيْكَ وَنَتَوَسَّلُ بِهِ إِلَيْكَ إِذْ هُوَ أَقْرَبُ الوَسَائِلِ إِلَيْكَ نَشْكُو إِلَيْكَ يَا رَبِّ قَسْوَةَ قُلُوبِنَا وَكَثْرَةَ ذُنُوبِنَا وَطُولَ آمَالِنَا وَفَسَادَ أَعْمَالِنَا وَتَكَاسُلَنَا عَنْ الطَّاعَاتِ وَهُجُومَنَا عَلَى المُخَالَفَاتِ فَنِعْمَ المُشْتَكَى إِلَيْهِ أَنْتَ يَا رَبِّ بِكَ نَسْتَنْصِرُ عَلَى أَعْدَائِنَا وَأَنْفُسِنَا فَانْصُرْنَا

Allāhumma innā nastashfiʿu bihi ilayka idh Hūwa awjahu 'sh-shufaʿā'i ʿalayk wa nuqsimu bihi ʿalayka idh hūwa āʿẓamu man uqsima bi ḥaqqihi ʿalayka wa natawassalu bihi ilayka idh hūwa aqrabu 'l-wasā'ili ilayk nashkū ilayka yā rabbī qaswata qulūbinā wa kathrata dhunūbinā wa ṭūla āmālanā wa fasāda āʿmālinā wa takāsulanā ʿani 'ṭ-ṭāʿāt wa hujūmanā ʿalā 'l-mukhālafāt fa-niʿma 'l-mushtakā ilayhi anta yā rabbī bika nastanṣiru ʿalā āʿdā'inā wa anfusinā fa 'nṣurnā

O Allāh, we seek his intercession with You, for he is the most lauded intercessor with You and we entreat You through him for he is the greatest one to entreat through! We seek access to You through him for he is the closest access to You! We complain to You O Lord, of the hardness of our hearts and the abundance of our sins and the extent of our hopes, and the imperfection of our actions and our laziness to do good deeds and our haste to commit bad deeds. Bestow upon this plaintiff, O Lord, victory over our enemies and help our souls. ➢

وَعَلَى فَضْلِكَ نَتَوَكَّلُ فِي صَلاَحِنَا فَلاَ تَكِلْنَا إِلَى غَيرِكَ يَا رَبَّنَا وَإِلَى جَنَابِ رَسُولِكَ ﷺ نَنتَسِبُ فَلَا تُبعِدْنَا وَبِبَابِكَ نَقِفُ فَلَا تَطْرُدنَا وَإِيَّاكَ نَسْأَلُ فَلَا تُخَيِّبْنَا اللَّهُمَّ إِرْحَمْ تَضَرُّعَنَا وَآمِنْ خَوْفَنَا وَتَقَبَّلْ أَعْمَالَنَا وَأَصْلِحْ أَحْوَالَنَا وَاجْعَل بِطَاعَتِكَ اِشْتِغَالَنَا وَإِلَى الْخَيْرِ مَآلَنَا وَحَقِّقْ بِالزِّيَادَةِ آمَالَنَا وَاخْتِمْ بِالسَّعَادَةِ آجَالَنَا

wa ʿalā faḍlika natawakkalu fī ṣalāḥinā fa lā takilnā ilā ghayrika yā rabbanā Allāhumma wa ilā janābi rasūlika ﷺ nantasibu fa lā tubʿidnā wa bi bābika naqifu fa lā taṭrudnā wa iyyāka nas'alu fa lā tukhayyibnā. Allāhuma 'rḥam taḍarruʿanā wa āmin khawfanā wa taqabbal āʿmālanā wa aṣliḥ aḥwālanā wa 'jʿal bi ṭāʿatika ishtighālanā wa ilā 'l-khayri mālanā wa ḥaqqiq bi 'z-ziyādati āmālanā wa 'khtum bi 's-saʿādati ājālanā

And through Your Grace make us rely solely on Your good acts and not upon any thing else, O our Lord! O Allāh, we associate ourselves with the honour of Your Messenger ﷺ so do not distance us and we stop at Your Door so do not turn us away and we ask You alone so do not disappoint us! O Allāh, have mercy upon our imploring and allay our fears! Accept our actions and make us righteous! Make obedience to You our main occupation and make us use our wealth only for good and fulfill our hopes and more and seal our final destinations with happiness. ➢

هَذَا ذُلُّنَا ظَاهِرٌ بَيْنَ يَدَيْكَ وَحَالُنَا لَا يَخْفَى عَلَيْكَ أَمَرْتَنَا فَتَرَكْنَا وَنَهَيْتَنَا فَارْتَكَبْنَا وَلَا يَسَعُنَا إِلاَّ عَفْوُكَ فَاعْفُ عَنَّا يَا خَيْرَ مَأْمُولٍ وَأَكْرَمَ مَسْئُولٍ إِنَّكَ عَفُوٌّ كَرِيمٌ رَؤُوفٌ رَحِيمٌ يَا أَرْحَمَ الرَّاحِمِينَ وَ صَلَّى اللهُ عَلَى سَيِّدِنَا مُحَمَّدٍ وَعَلَى آلِهِ وَصَحْبِهِ وَسَلَّمَ تَسْلِيماً

وَالْحَمْدُ لله رَبِّ الْعَالَمِينَ وَهُوَ حَسْبُنَا وَنِعْمَ الْوَكِيلُ وَلَا حَوْلَ وَلَا قُوَّةَ إِلاَّ بِاللهِ الْعَلِيِّ الْعَظِيمِ ❋

hādhā dhullunā ẓāhiran bayna yadayk wa ḥālunā lā yakhfā ʿalayk amartanā fa taraknā wa nahaytanā fa 'rtakabnā wa lā yasaʿunā illā ʿafwuka faʿfuw ʿannā yā khayra mā'mūlin wa akrama mas'ūlin innaka ʿAfuwwun Karīmun Ra'ūfun Raḥīmun yā Arḥama 'r-Rāḥimīn wa ṣalla 'Llāhu ʿalā Sayyīdinā Muḥammadin wa ʿalā ālihi wa sallama taslīman wa 'l-ḥamdu li 'Llāhi Rabbi'l-ʿĀlamīn wa Hūwa ḥasbunā wa niʿma 'l-wakīlu wa lā ḥawla wa lā quwwata illā bi 'Llāhi 'l-ʿAlīyyi 'l-ʿAẓīm •

Thus is our loneliness made clear before You and our condition is not hidden from You! You have commanded us and we have been remiss! You have forbidden us and we have transgressed! Nothing is wider then Your clemency so pardon us Best Fulfiller of Hopes and Most Generous Requestee for You are The Pardoner, The Forgiver, The Merciful, Most Merciful of the Merciful and the blessings and peace of Allāh be upon our master Muḥammad and upon his family and companions and praise be to Allāh Lord of the worlds and there is no power and no might except with Allāh The Most High, The Tremendous. ❋

ثُمَّ تَقْرَأُ هَذِهِ الْكَلِمَاتِ الآتِيَةَ ١٤ مَرَّة :

Then read the following phrases 14 times each

اللَّهُمَّ صَلِّ عَلَى بَدرِ التَّمَامِ ❋ اللَّهُمَّ صَلِّ عَلَى نُورِ الظَّلَامِ ❋ اللَّهُمَّ صَلِّ عَلَى مِفْتَاحِ دَارِ السَّلَامِ ❋ اللَّهُمَّ صَلِّ عَلَى الشَّفِيعِ فِي جَمِيعِ الْأَنَامِ

Then you should recite these words 14 times:

Allāhumma ṣalli ʿalā badri 't-tamām Allāhumma ṣalli ʿalā nūri 'ẓ-ẓalām Allāhumma ṣalli ʿalā miftāḥi dāri 's-salām Allāhumma ṣalli ʿalā 'sh-shafīʿi fī jamīʿi 'l-anām •

O Allāh, bless the Perfect full Moon! O Allāh, bless the Light of the Darkness!O Allāh, bless the Key to the Abode of Peace! O Allāh, bless the intercessor of all creation! ❋

ثُمَّ تَقْرَأُ هَذِهِ الْأَبْيَاتِ الْمَنْسُوبَةَ لِلْمُؤَلِّفِ وَهِيَ:

Then read the following verses ascribed to the author:

يَا رَحْمَةَ اللهِ إِنِّي خَائِفٌ وَجِلٌ يَا نِعْمَةَ اللهِ إِنِّي مُفْلِسٌ عَانِي

Yā raḥmatallāhi innī khā'ifun wajilun Yā niʿmata 'Llāhi innī muflisun ʿāni

O Mercy of Allāh! I am afraid, filled with dread. O Grace of Allāh I am ruined ➢

وَلَيسَ لِي عَمَـلٌ أَلْقَى الْعَلِيمَ بِهِ سِوَى مَحَبَّتَكَ العُظْمَـى وَإِيمَانِي

فَكُـنْ أَمَانِي مِنْ شَرِّ الْحَيَاةِ وَمِنْ شَرِّ المَمَاتِ وَمِنْ إِحْـرَاقِ جُثْمَانِي

وَكُـنْ غِنَايَ الَّذِي مَا بَعْدَهُ فَلَسٌ وَكُنْ فَكَاكِي مِنْ أَغْلَالِ عِصْيَانِي

تَحِيَّةُ الصَّمَـدِ المَـوْلَى وَرَحْمَتُـهُ مَا غَنَّتِ الوُرْقُ فِي أَورَاقِ أَغْصَانِي

wa laysa lī ʿamalun alqā 'l-ʿAlīma bihi siwā maḥabbatika 'l-ʿuẓmā wa īmānī

fa-kun amānī min sharri 'l-ḥayāti wa min shārri 'l-mamāti wa min iḥrāqi juthmānī

wa kun ghināya 'Lladhī mā baʿdahu falasun wa kun fakākiya min aghlāli ʿiṣyānī

taḥīyyatu 'ṣ-Ṣamadi 'l-Mawlā wa raḥmatuhu mā ghannati 'l-wurqu fī awrāqi aghṣānī

help me and I have no goods acts with which to present The All-Knowing except great love for you and my faith!

Be my protection from the evil of life and from The evil of death and from the burning of my mortal frame,

and fulfill my every need saving me from ruin, and be my release from the fetters of disobedience!

As abundant as the leaves in the leafiness of the boughs, upon You, ➢

عَلَيكَ يَا عُرْوَتِي الْوُثْقَى وَيَا سَنَدِي الْأَوْفَى وَمَنْ مَدْحُهُ رَوحِي وَرَيْحَانِي *

ʿalayka yā ʿurwatiya ʾl-wuthqā wa yā sanadī ʾl-awfā wa man mad-ḥuhu rawḥī wa rayḥānī •

O Trusty Handhold, O My support, the Faithful One and whoever praises him is my spirit and my fragrance! *

Additional *Ṣalawāt*:

صَلَوَاتُ الشِّفَا

Ṣalawāt of Healing:

اللّٰهُمَّ صَلِّ عَلَى سَيِّدِنَا مُحَمَّدٍ طِبِّ الْقُلُوبِ وَدَوَائِهَا وَعَافِيَةِ الْأَبْدَانِ وَشِفَائِهَا

وَنُورِ الْأَبْصَارِ وَضِيائِهَا وَعَلَى آلِهِ وَصَحْبِهِ وَسَلِّمْ ❁

Allāhumma ṣalli ʿalā Sayyīdinā Muḥammadin ṭibbi 'l-qulūbi wa dawā'ihā wa ʿāfiyati 'l-abdāni wa shifā'ihā wa nūri 'l-abṣāri wa ḍiyā'ihā wa ʿalā ālihi wa ṣaḥbihi wa sallim •

O Allāh send blessings upon our master Muḥammad the medicine of hearts and its healing, and the good health of the bodies and its recovery, and the light of vision and it seeing; and upon his family and companions.

صَلَوَاتُ الذَّاتِ

Ṣalawātu 'dh-Dhāt
Praise of the Essence (Equal to 100,000 *Ṣalawāt*):

اللّٰهُمَّ صَلِّ عَلَى سَيِّدِنَا مُحَمَّدٍ نُورِ الذَّاتِ وَالسِّرِّ السَّارِي فِي جَمِيعِ الْأَسْمَاءِ

وَالصِّفَاتِ ﷺ ❁

Allāhumma ṣalli ʿalā Sayyīdinā Muḥammadin Nūri 'dh-Dhāti wa 's-sirri 's-sāri fī jamīʿi 'l-asmā'i wa 'ṣ-ṣifāti ﷺ •

O Allāh exalt our master Muḥammad, the Light of the Essence, and the Secret which is running through all the Names and Attributes; Allāh's blessings and greetings upon him. ❁

Dedication

رَبَّنَا اغْفِرْ لِي وَلِوَالِدَيَّ وَلِلْمُؤْمِنِينَ يَوْمَ يَقُومُ الْحِسَابُ

Rabbanā 'ghfir lī wa li-walidayya wa li 'l-muminīna yawma yaqūmu 'l-ḥisāb

O our Lord! cover (us) with Thy Forgiveness - me, my parents, and (all) Believers, on the Day that the Reckoning will be established![30]

ISCA wishes to thank manyof its constant ardent members for their unremitting support, and for their making the publication of this priceless jewel of a book possible. Some individuals who assisted asked us to dedicate the rewards of recitation from this book for the benefit of their loved ones. Others made this dedication secretly through their intentions, while yet others did not want us to mention their names. ISCA, its chairman, staff and members are grateful to each and every one of them.

Please dedicate your recitation to the souls of the ancestors of the people mentioned here and for the souls of the whole Nation of Sayyidina Muhammad ﷺ

The names of the donors:

Hajjah Naziha Kabbani and Family
Dr Jamal Akbar and Family
Dr Anwar Waheed and Family
Dr Wassim El-Harake and Family and Parents
Dr Asad Cheema and Family
Abul Hossain and Family
Marwa Azizi and Family
Bouzid Boubakr and Family

---

[30] Surah Ibrāhīm, 14:41.

Nisar and Sarah Sandu and Family
Ahmad Fuad and Family
Diomande Vakoua and Family
Yasir Shaykh and Family
Pappa Ibrahim and Family
Farid Elsayed and Family
Waheed and Raana Akhbar
Senad Kalajdzic and Family
Ali Diallo and Family
Adam Bamba and Family
Jamal Abdul Wahid Muhammad and Family
Zaim Ahmed and Family
Zul Fiqar Ahmed and Family
Dr Rahimuddin Nazeer and Family
Zeeshan Ali and Family
Abdul Haqq Muhammad and Family
Hani Nimr and Family
Mohammad Bilal and Family
Ali Reza Astani and Family
Rizwan Qadri and Family
Oulimata and Family
Soda Faty and Family
Uzma for her parents Mumtaz Khanum and Ihsan ul Haq Khan
Sarah Sanders
Hafeez Khan and Family
Fatema Akthar and Family
Wissam Ndir and Family
Asim Hashmi and Family
Saadat Baig and Family
Amadou Arona Sy. and Family
Dr. Tasnim Shameem and Family
Amira Kerrar and family
Adam Shamash and Family
Syed Shahzaman and Family

Hichem Ouardani and Family
Ramampy Iminja and Family
Rosmin Robertson and Family
Hassan Arif Syed Zaidi and Family
Abdullah Sayed and Family
Rabia Zaman and Family
Dr. Karim Tourk and Family
Bahauddin Kylberg and Family
Dr. Munir Sperling and Family

Notes

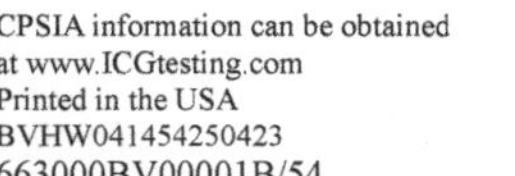

CPSIA information can be obtained
at www.ICGtesting.com
Printed in the USA
BVHW041454250423
663000BV00001B/54

9 781930 409965